I Luv Halloween vol. 1
written by Keith Giffen
illustrated by Benjamin Roman

Lettering - James Dashiell
Cover Colorist - Mike Garcia
Cover Design - Gary Shum

Editor - Rob Valois
Digital Imaging Manager - Chris Buford
Production Managers - Jennifer Miller and Mutsumi Miyazaki
Managing Editor - Lindsey Johnston
Editorial Director - Jeremy Ross
VP of Production - Ron Klamert
Publisher and E.I.C. - Mike Kiley
President and C.O.O. - John Parker
C.E.O. - Stuart Levy

A ⬤ TOKYOPOP. Manga

TOKYOPOP Inc.
5900 Wilshire Blvd. Suite 2000
Los Angeles, CA 90036

E-mail: info@TOKYOPOP.com
Come visit us online at www.TOKYOPOP.com

ISBN: 1-59532-831-9

First TOKYOPOP printing: October 2005
10 9 8 7 6 5
Printed in the USA

I Luv Halloween

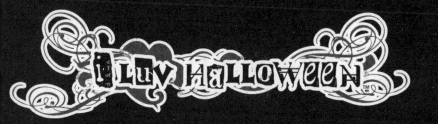

Volume One

Art by: **Benjamin Roman**
Story by: **Keith Giffen**

TOKYOPOP®

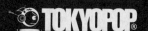

HAMBURG // LONDON // LOS ANGELES // TOKYO

I LUV HALLOWEEN™

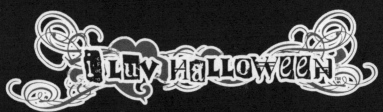

CHAPTER ONE:
FINCH

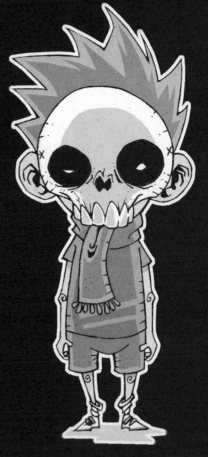

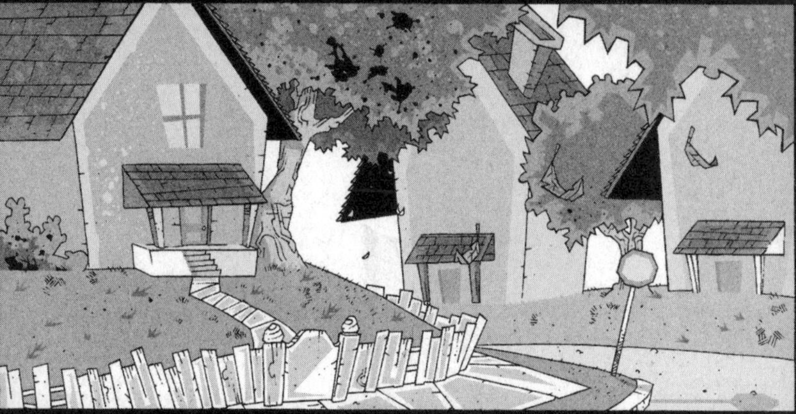

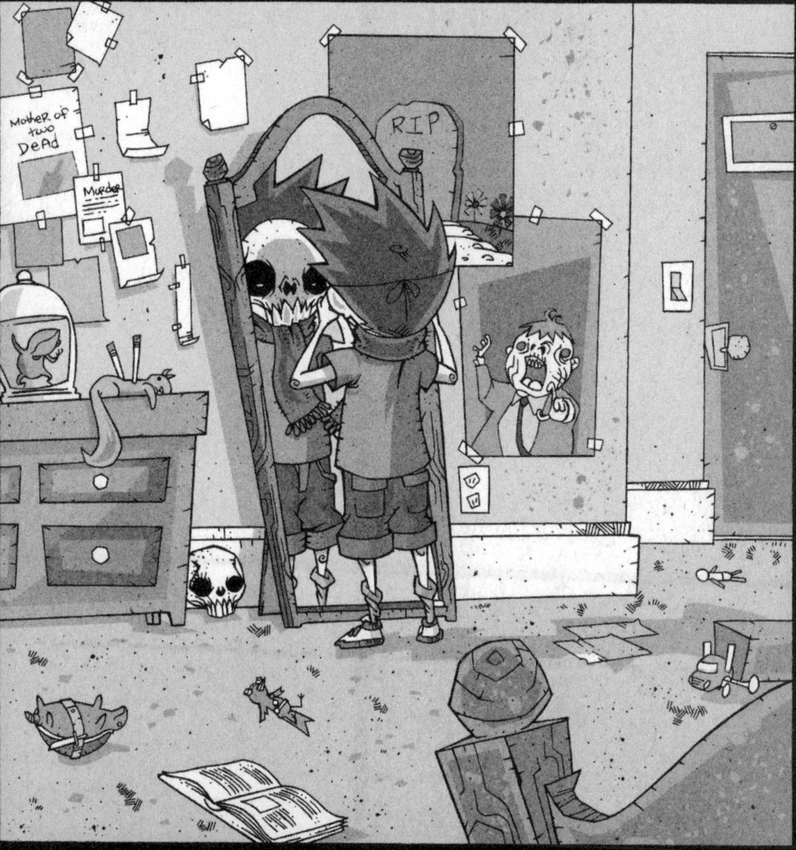
Mother of two Dead
Murder
RIP

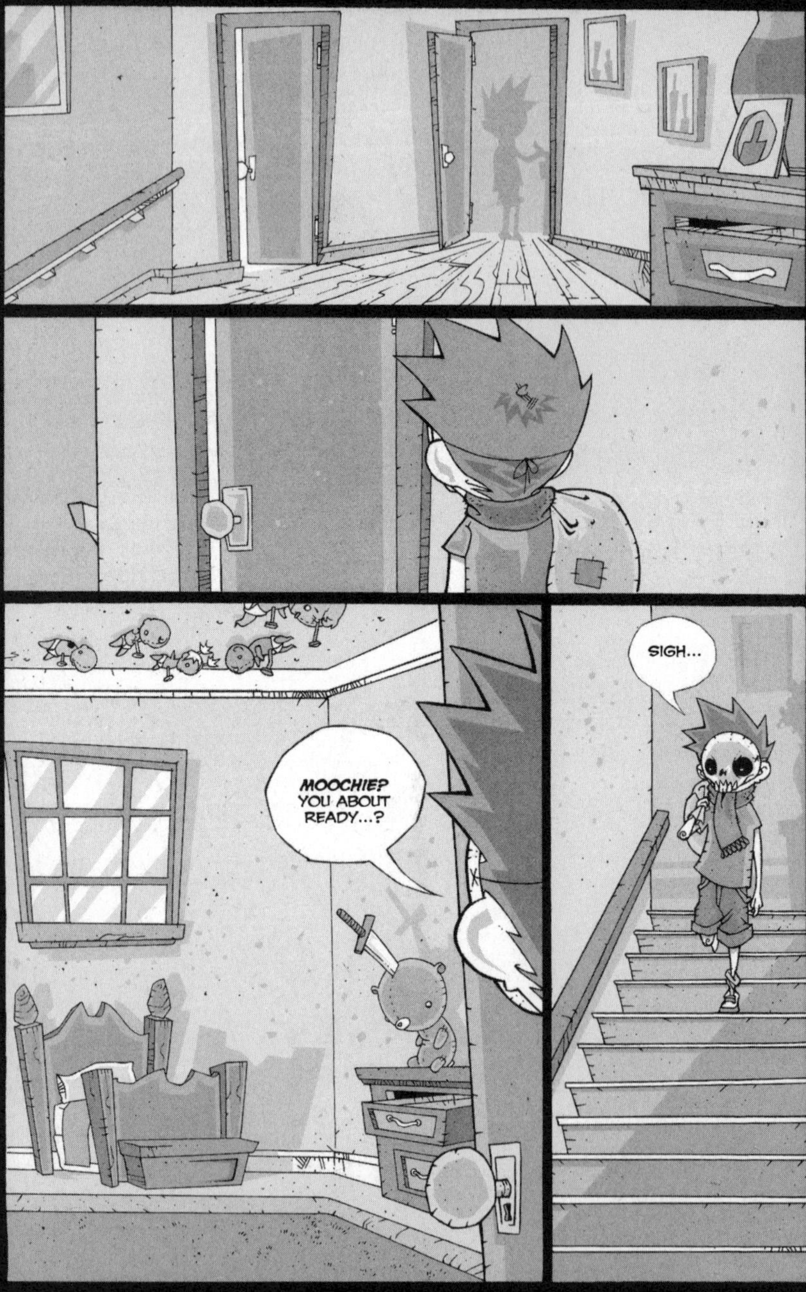
MOOCHIE? YOU ABOUT READY...?
SIGH...

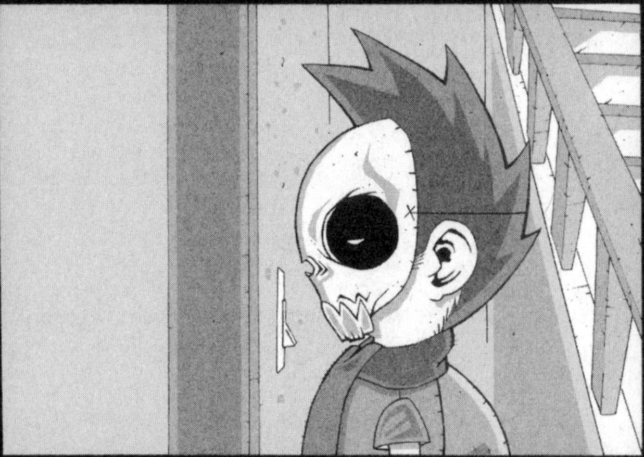

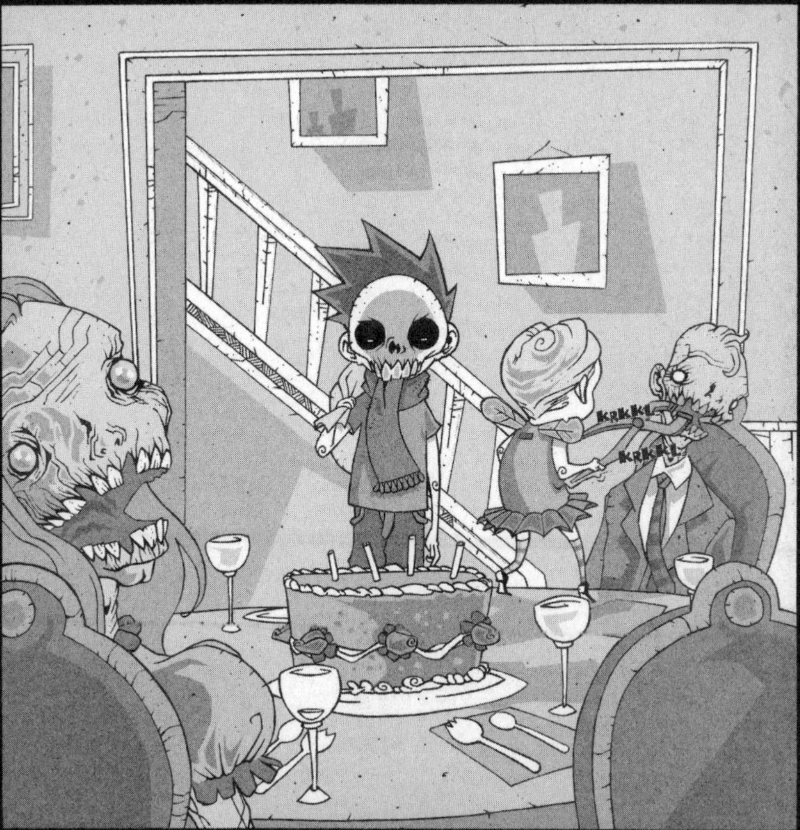
KRKKL
KRKKL

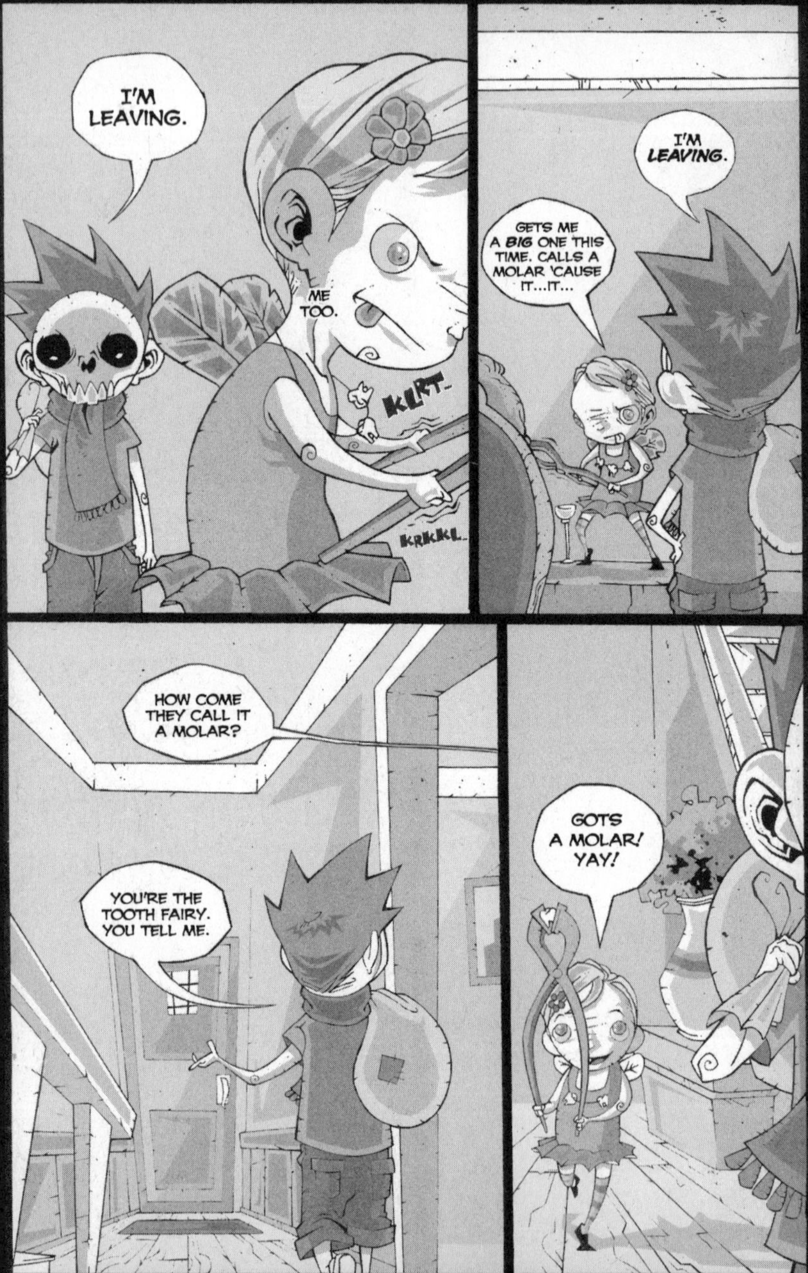
I'M LEAVING.
ME TOO.
KLRT
KRKKL
I'M *LEAVING*.
GETS ME A *BIG* ONE THIS TIME. CALLS A MOLAR 'CAUSE IT...IT...
HOW COME THEY CALL IT A MOLAR?
YOU'RE THE TOOTH FAIRY. YOU TELL ME.
GOTS A MOLAR! YAY!

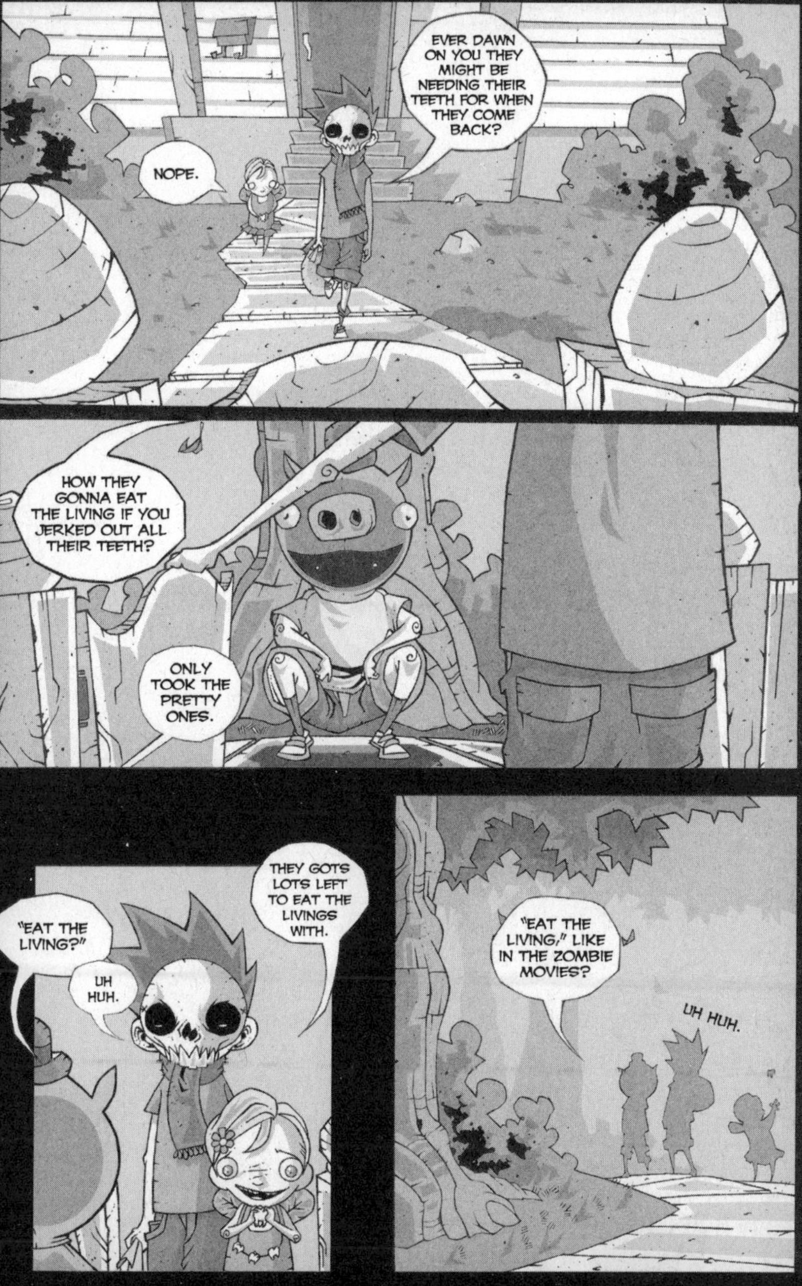
EVER DAWN ON YOU THEY MIGHT BE NEEDING THEIR TEETH FOR WHEN THEY COME BACK?
NOPE.
HOW THEY GONNA EAT THE LIVING IF YOU JERKED OUT ALL THEIR TEETH?
ONLY TOOK THE PRETTY ONES.
THEY GOTS LOTS LEFT TO EAT THE LIVINGS WITH.
"EAT THE LIVING?"
UH HUH.
"EAT THE LIVING," LIKE IN THE ZOMBIE MOVIES?
UH HUH.

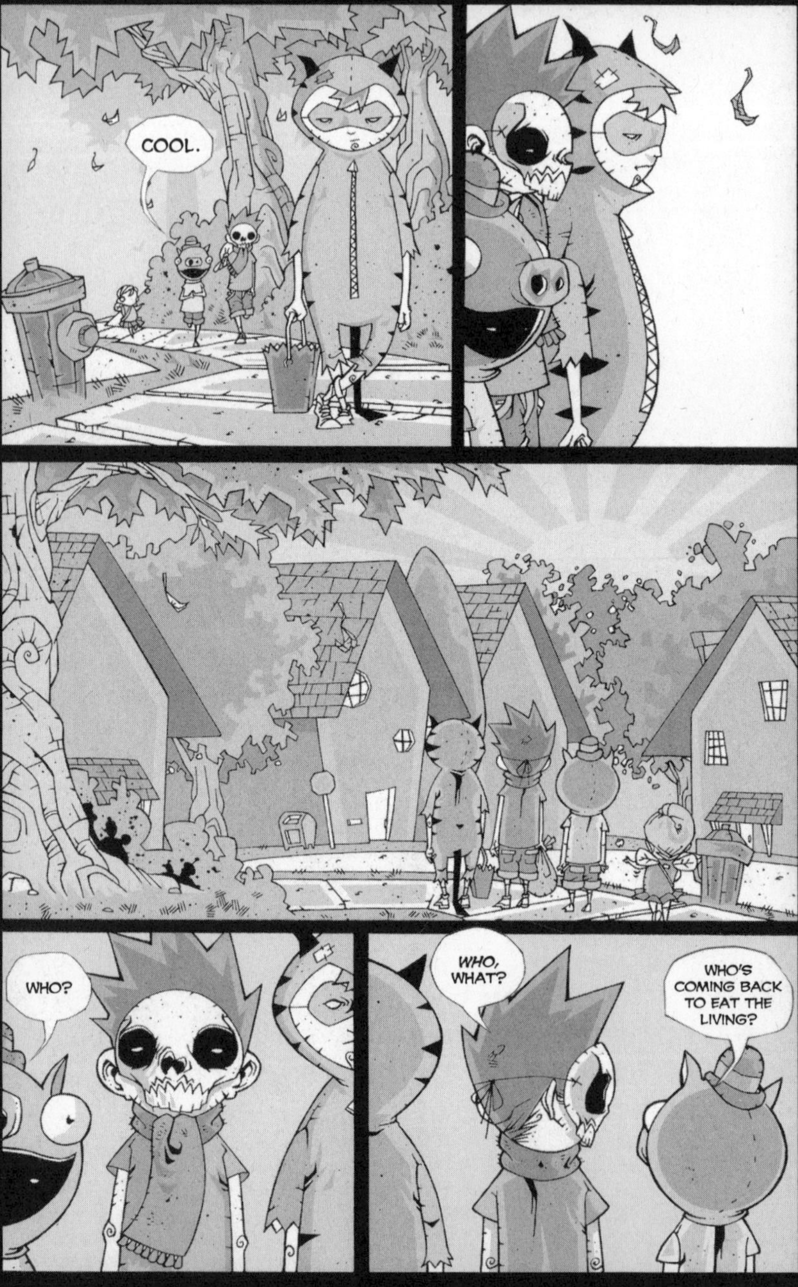
COOL.
WHO?
WHO, WHAT?
WHO'S COMING BACK TO EAT THE LIVING?

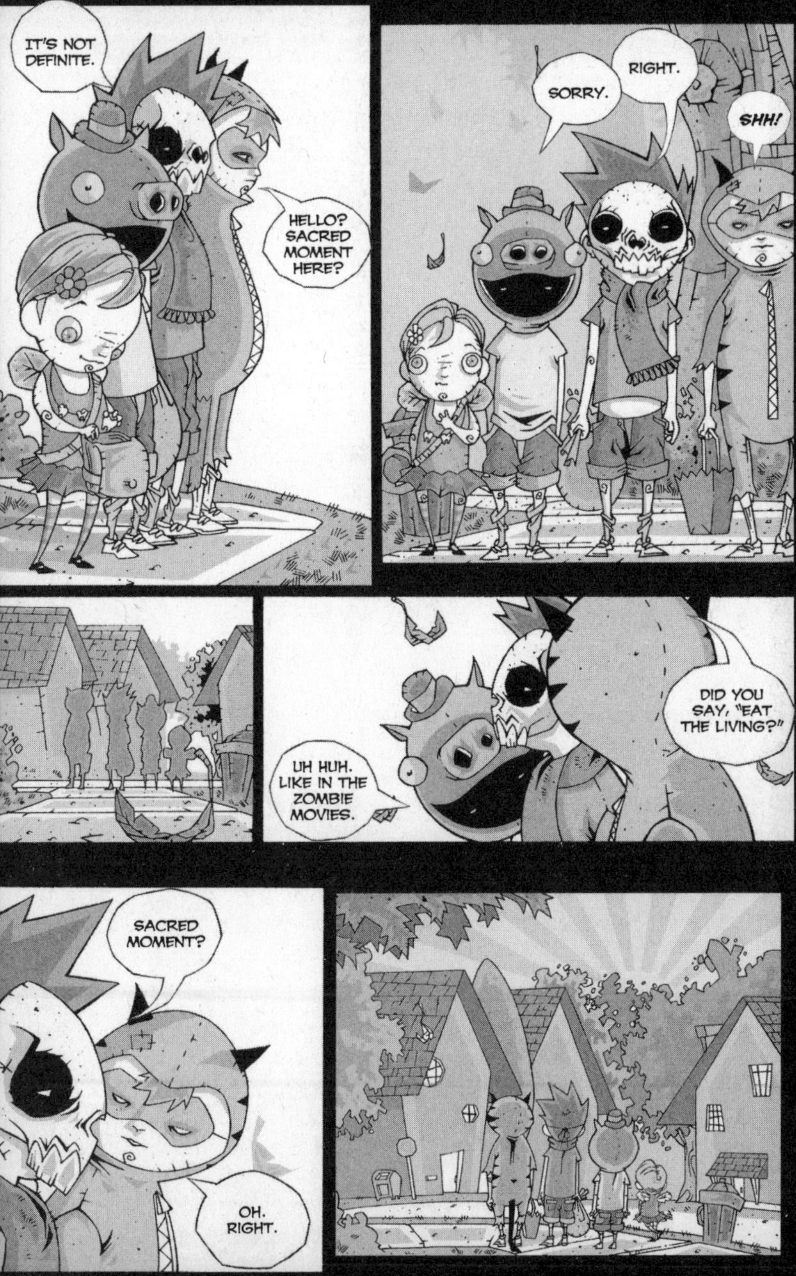
IT'S NOT DEFINITE.
HELLO? SACRED MOMENT HERE?
SORRY.
RIGHT.
SHH!
DID YOU SAY, "EAT THE LIVING?"
UH HUH. LIKE IN THE ZOMBIE MOVIES.
SACRED MOMENT?
OH. RIGHT.

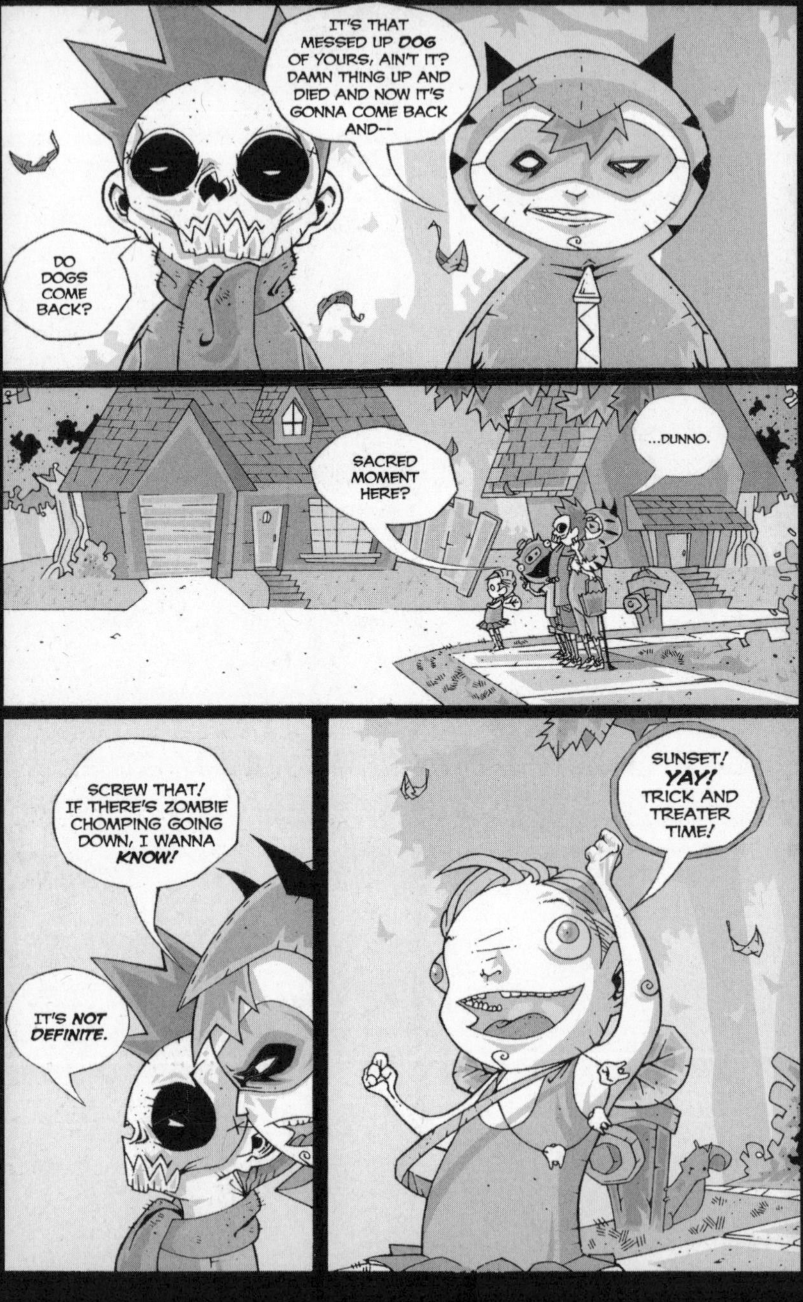
IT'S THAT MESSED UP DOG OF YOURS, AIN'T IT? DAMN THING UP AND DIED AND NOW IT'S GONNA COME BACK AND--
DO DOGS COME BACK?
SACRED MOMENT HERE?
...DUNNO.
SCREW THAT! IF THERE'S ZOMBIE CHOMPING GOING DOWN, I WANNA KNOW!
IT'S NOT DEFINITE.
SUNSET! YAY! TRICK AND TREATER TIME!

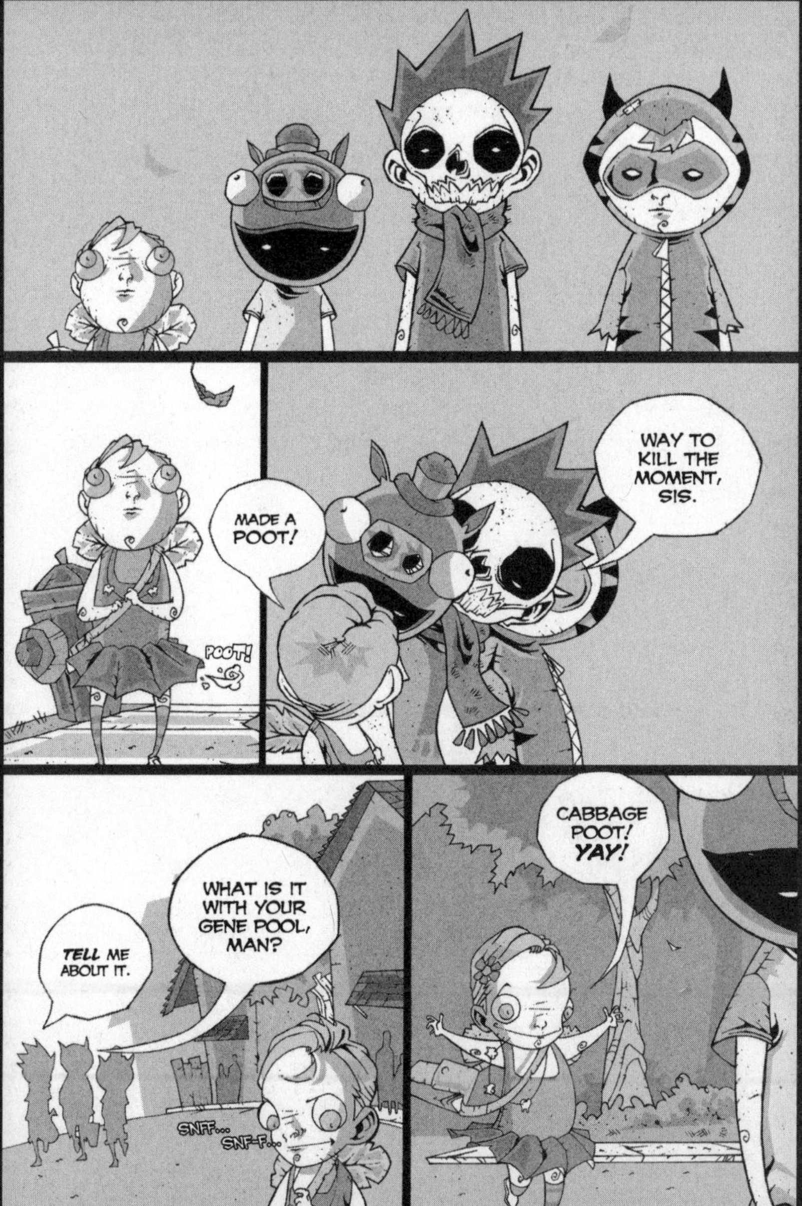
POOT!
MADE A POOT!
WAY TO KILL THE MOMENT, SIS.
WHAT IS IT WITH YOUR GENE POOL, MAN?
TELL ME ABOUT IT.
SNFF... SNF-F...
CABBAGE POOT! YAY!

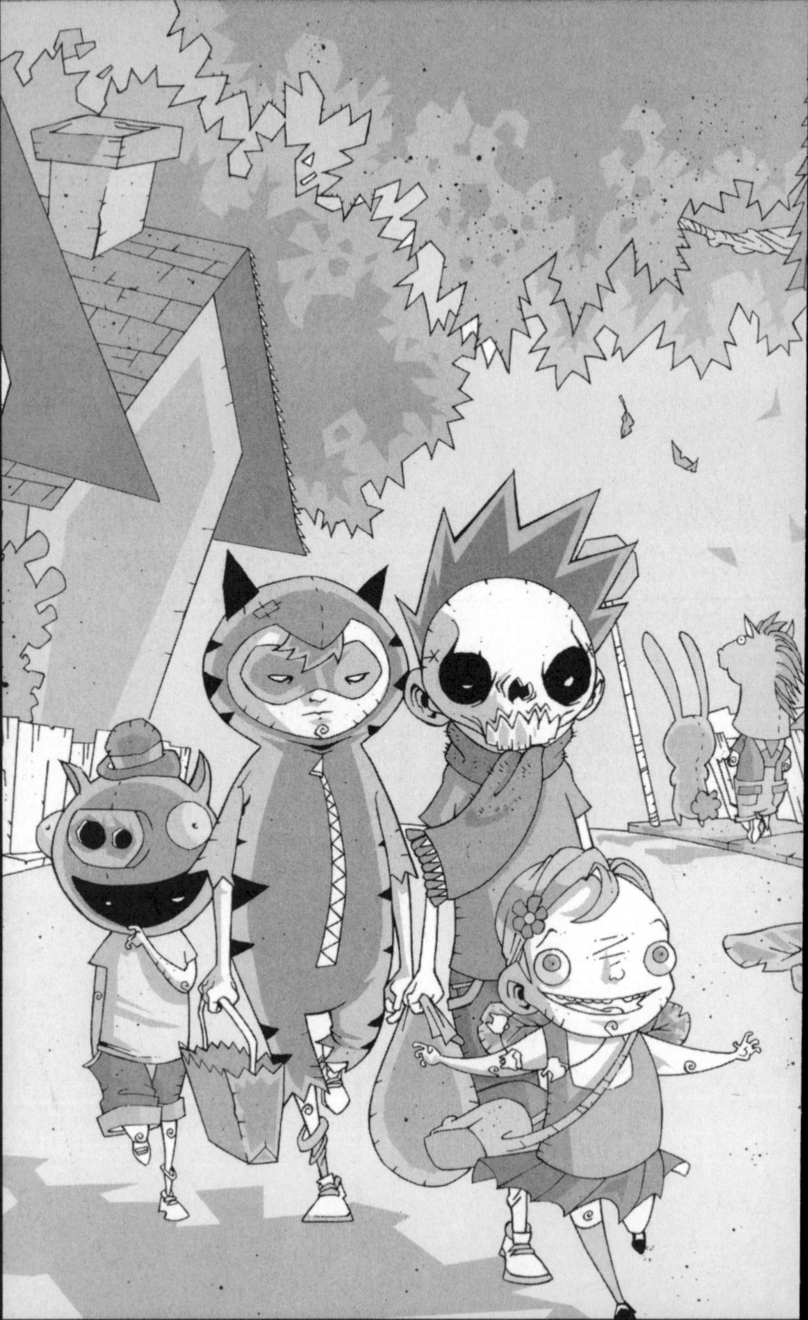

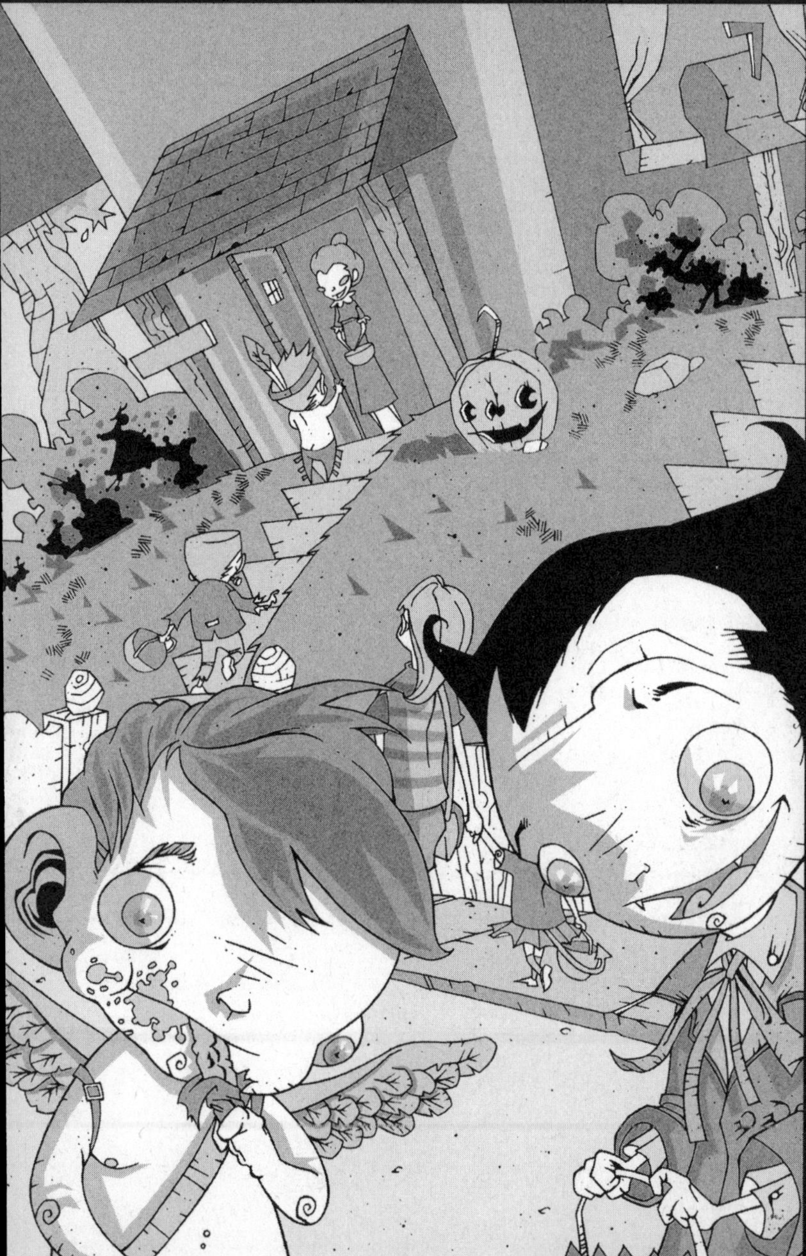

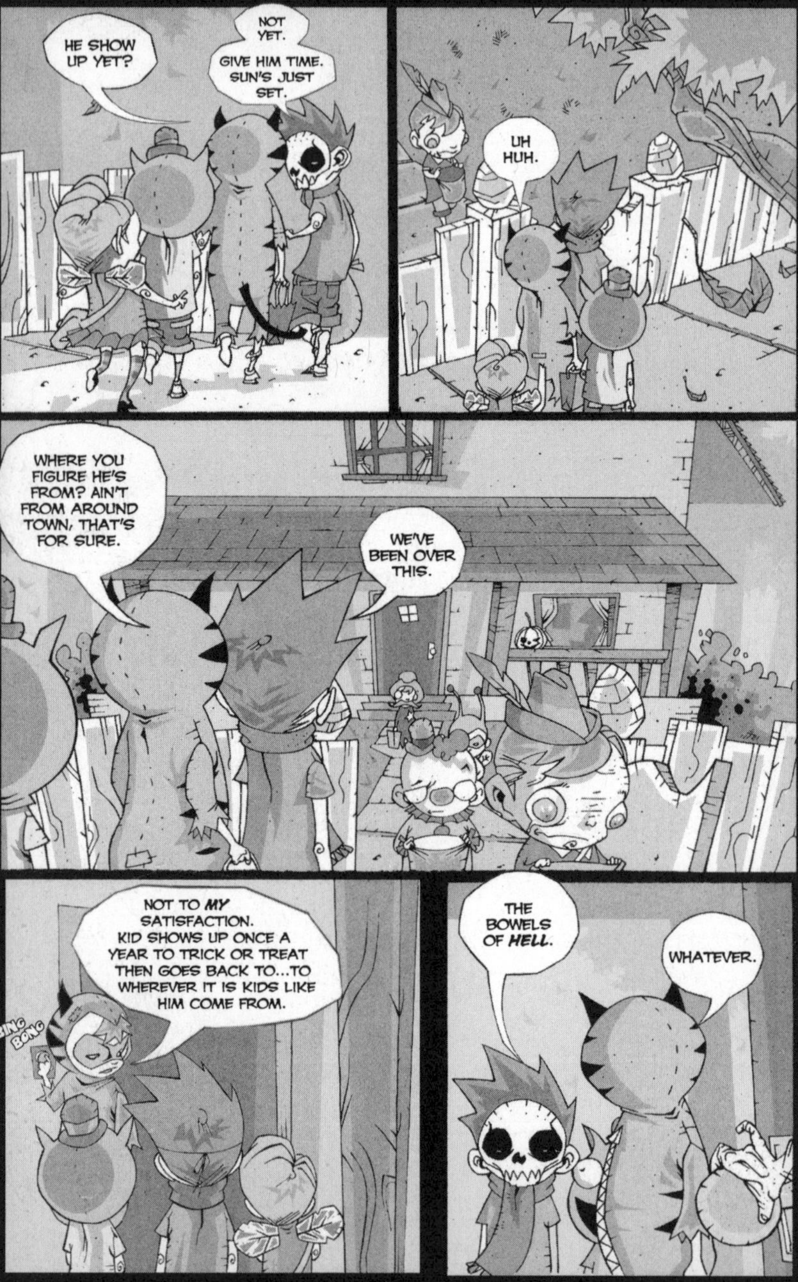
HE SHOW UP YET?
NOT YET.
GIVE HIM TIME. SUN'S JUST SET.
UH HUH.
WHERE YOU FIGURE HE'S FROM? AIN'T FROM AROUND TOWN, THAT'S FOR SURE.
WE'VE BEEN OVER THIS.
NOT TO *MY* SATISFACTION.
KID SHOWS UP ONCE A YEAR TO TRICK OR TREAT THEN GOES BACK TO...TO WHEREVER IT IS KIDS LIKE HIM COME FROM.
BING BONG
THE BOWELS OF ***HELL***.
WHATEVER.

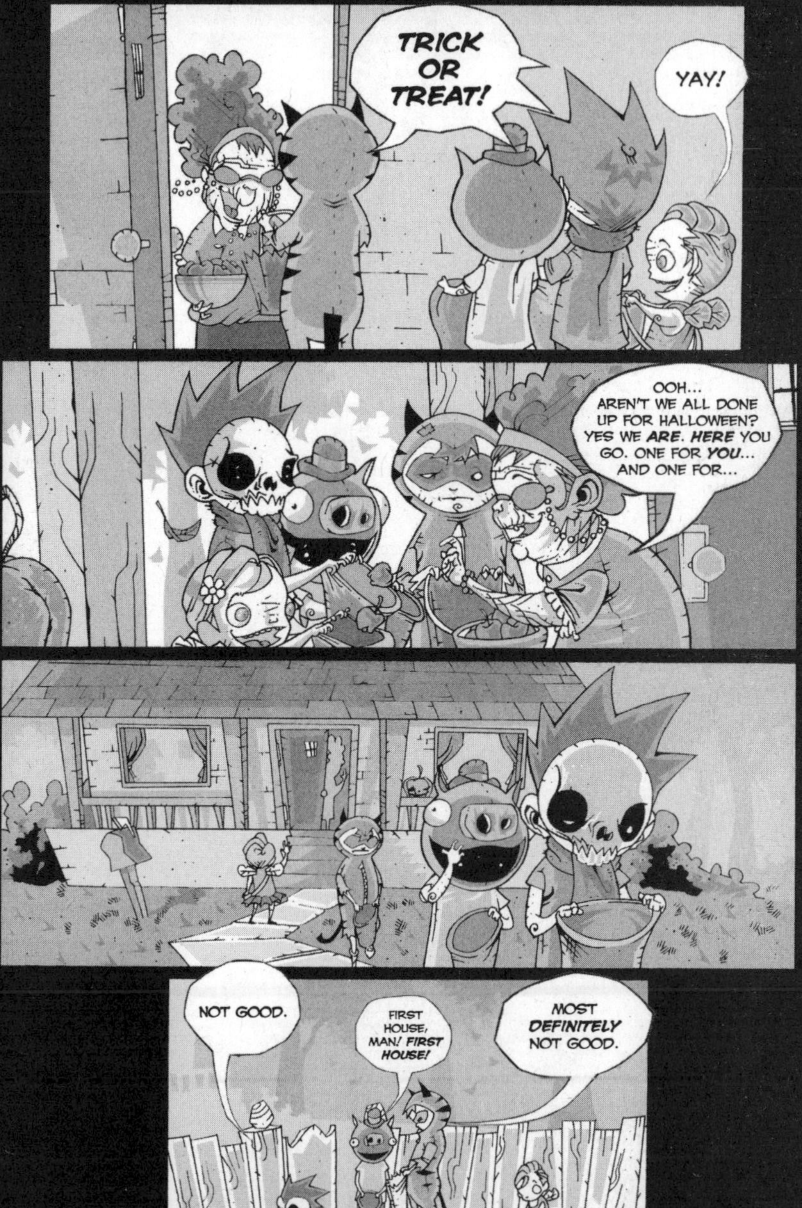
TRICK OR TREAT!
YAY!
OOH... AREN'T WE ALL DONE UP FOR HALLOWEEN? YES WE *ARE*. *HERE* YOU GO. ONE FOR *YOU*... AND ONE FOR...
NOT GOOD.
FIRST HOUSE, MAN! *FIRST HOUSE!*
MOST *DEFINITELY* NOT GOOD.

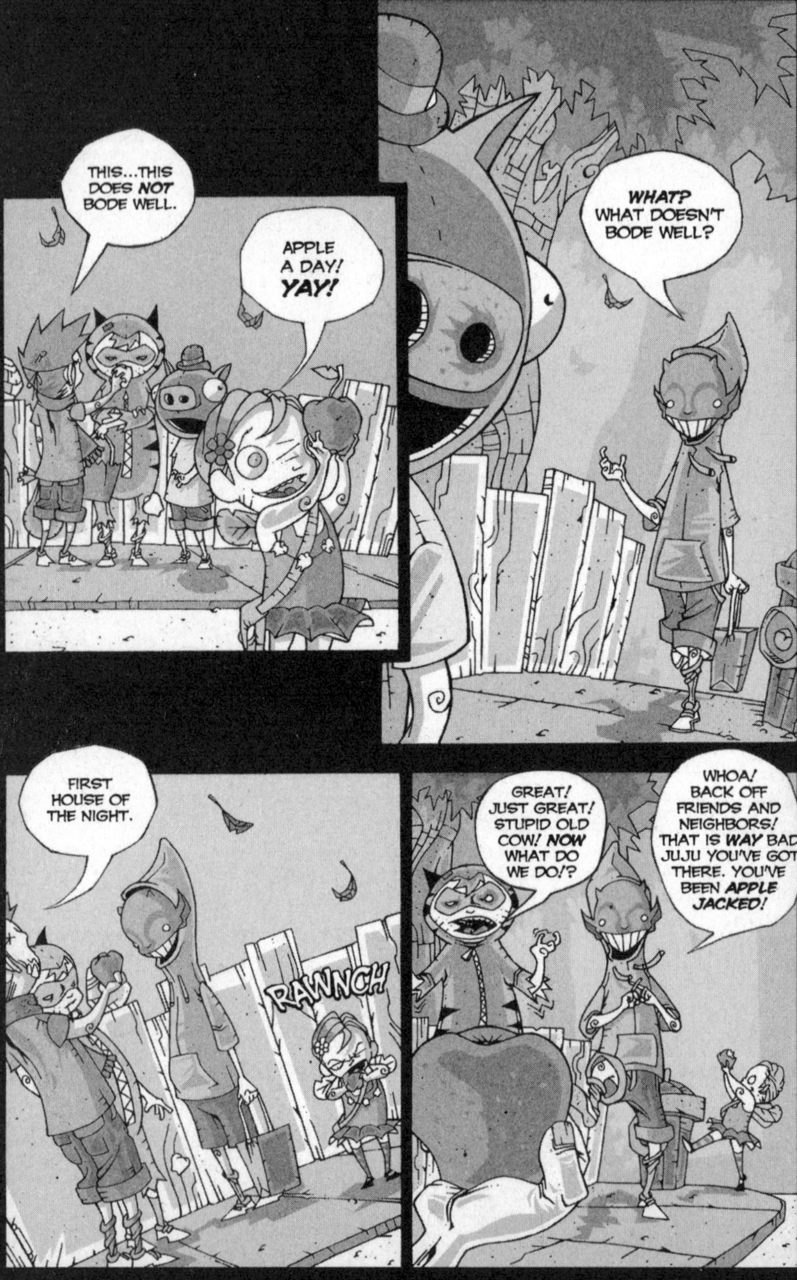
THIS...THIS DOES **NOT** BODE WELL.
APPLE A DAY! **YAY!**
WHAT? WHAT DOESN'T BODE WELL?
FIRST HOUSE OF THE NIGHT.
RAWNCH
GREAT! JUST GREAT! STUPID OLD COW! **NOW** WHAT DO WE DO!?
WHOA! BACK OFF FRIENDS AND NEIGHBORS! THAT IS **WAY** BAD JUJU YOU'VE GOT THERE. YOU'VE BEEN **APPLE JACKED!**

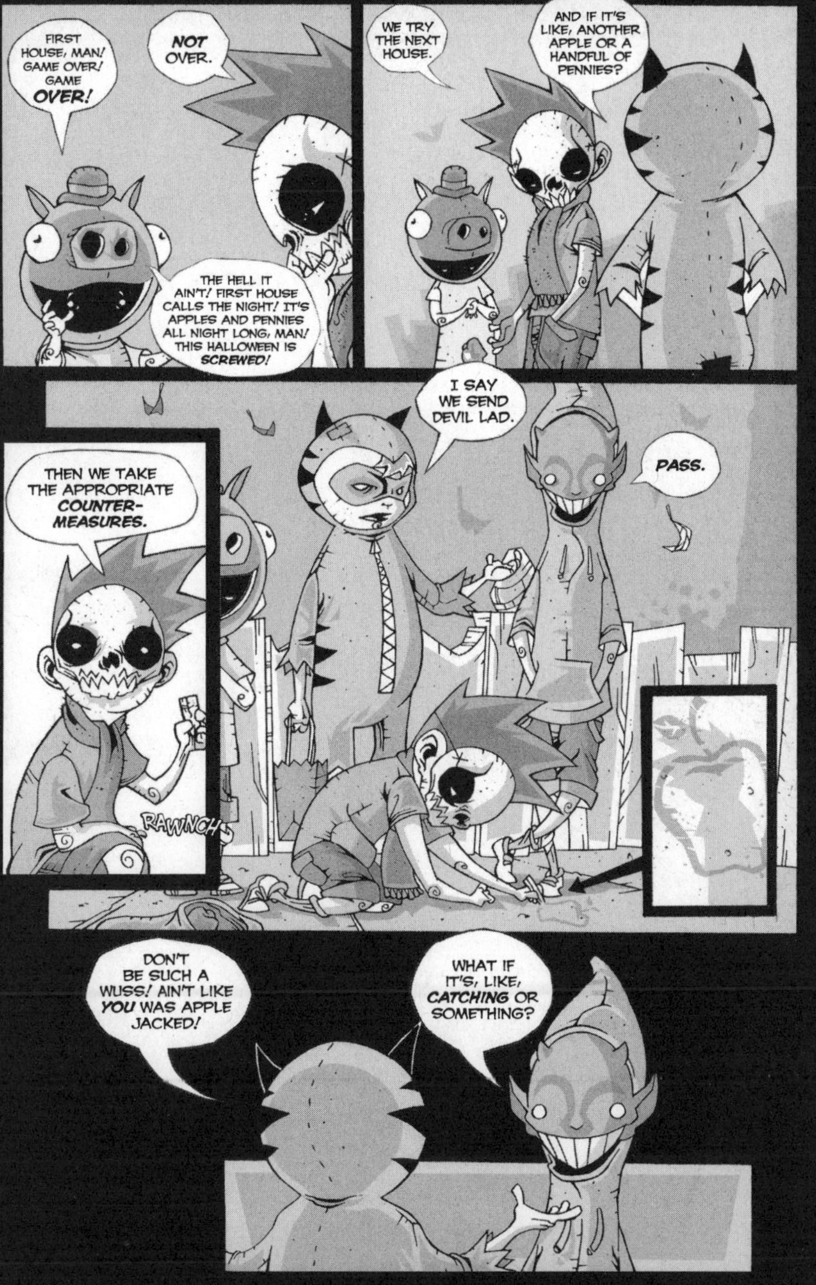
FIRST HOUSE, MAN! GAME OVER! GAME OVER!
NOT OVER.
THE HELL IT AIN'T! FIRST HOUSE CALLS THE NIGHT! IT'S APPLES AND PENNIES ALL NIGHT LONG, MAN! THIS HALLOWEEN IS SCREWED!
WE TRY THE NEXT HOUSE.
AND IF IT'S LIKE, ANOTHER APPLE OR A HANDFUL OF PENNIES?
THEN WE TAKE THE APPROPRIATE COUNTER-MEASURES.
RAWNCH
I SAY WE SEND DEVIL LAD.
PASS.
DON'T BE SUCH A WUSS! AIN'T LIKE YOU WAS APPLE JACKED!
WHAT IF IT'S, LIKE, CATCHING OR SOMETHING?

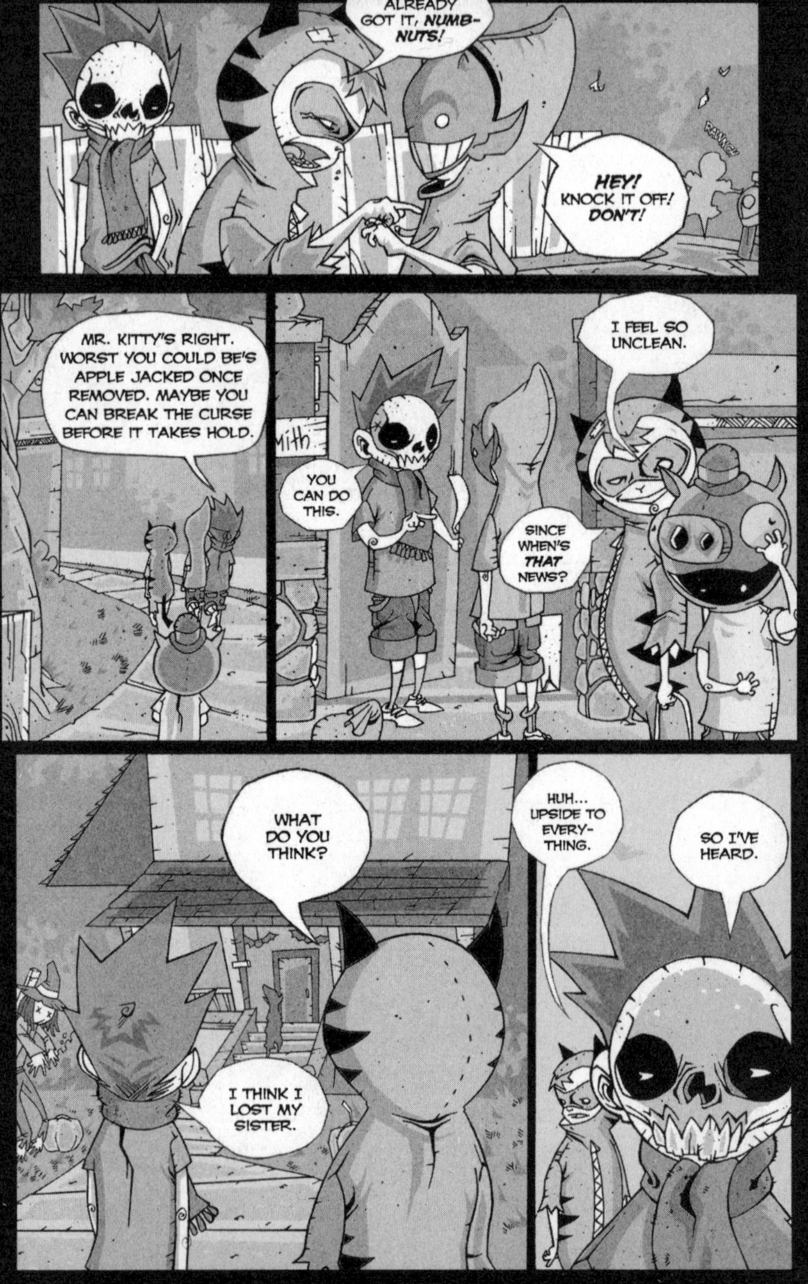
THEN YOU ALREADY GOT IT, NUMB-NUTS!
HEY! KNOCK IT OFF! DON'T!
MR. KITTY'S RIGHT. WORST YOU COULD BE'S APPLE JACKED ONCE REMOVED. MAYBE YOU CAN BREAK THE CURSE BEFORE IT TAKES HOLD.
I FEEL SO UNCLEAN.
YOU CAN DO THIS.
SINCE WHEN'S THAT NEWS?
WHAT DO YOU THINK?
I THINK I LOST MY SISTER.
HUH... UPSIDE TO EVERY-THING.
SO I'VE HEARD.

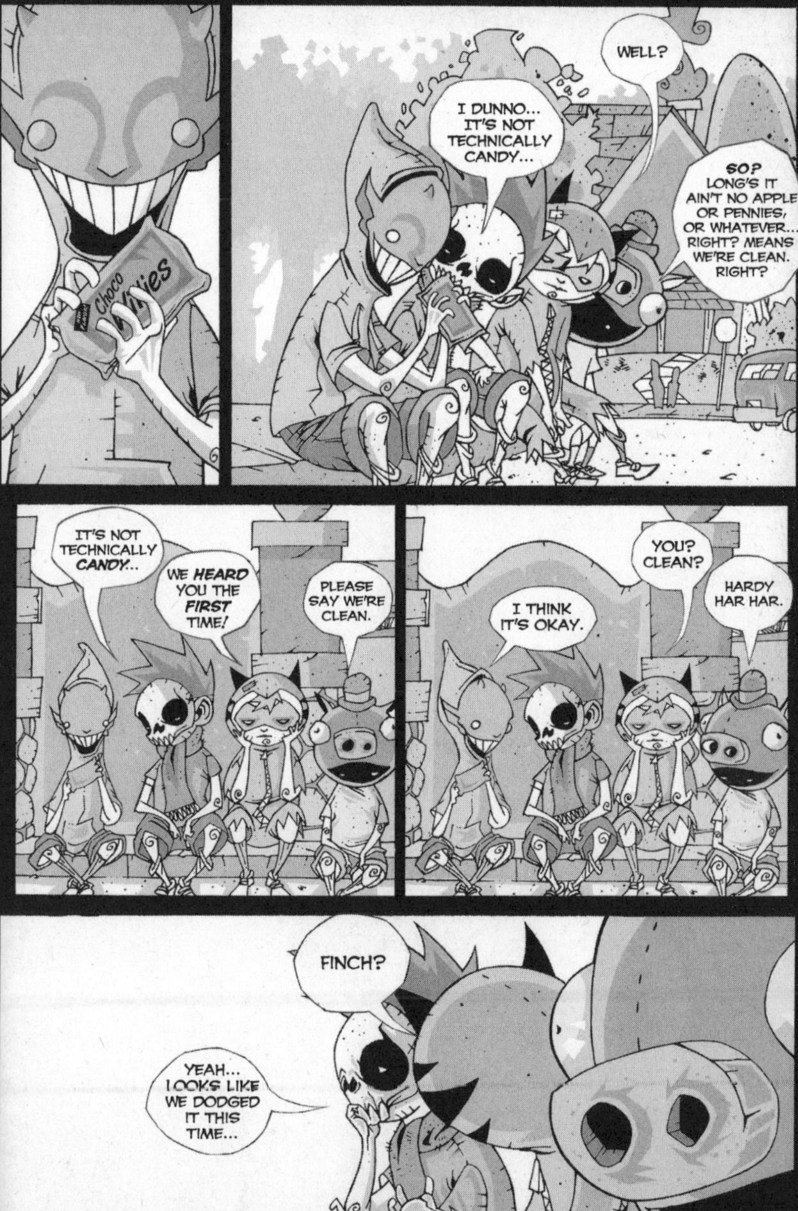
Choco
WELL?
I DUNNO... IT'S NOT TECHNICALLY CANDY...
SO? LONG'S IT AIN'T NO APPLE OR PENNIES, OR WHATEVER... RIGHT? MEANS WE'RE CLEAN. RIGHT?
IT'S NOT TECHNICALLY CANDY...
WE HEARD YOU THE FIRST TIME!
PLEASE SAY WE'RE CLEAN.
I THINK IT'S OKAY.
YOU? CLEAN?
HARDY HAR HAR.
FINCH?
YEAH... LOOKS LIKE WE DODGED IT THIS TIME...

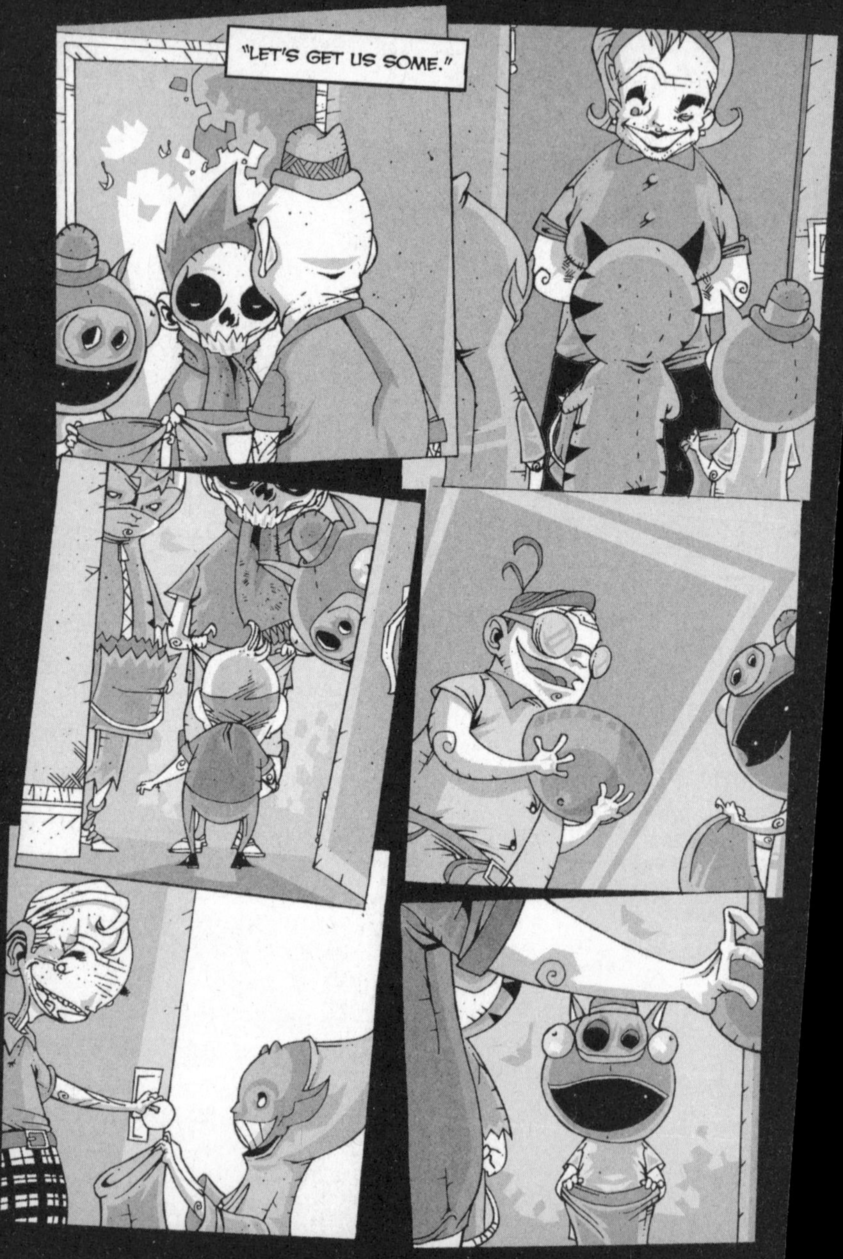
"LET'S GET US SOME."

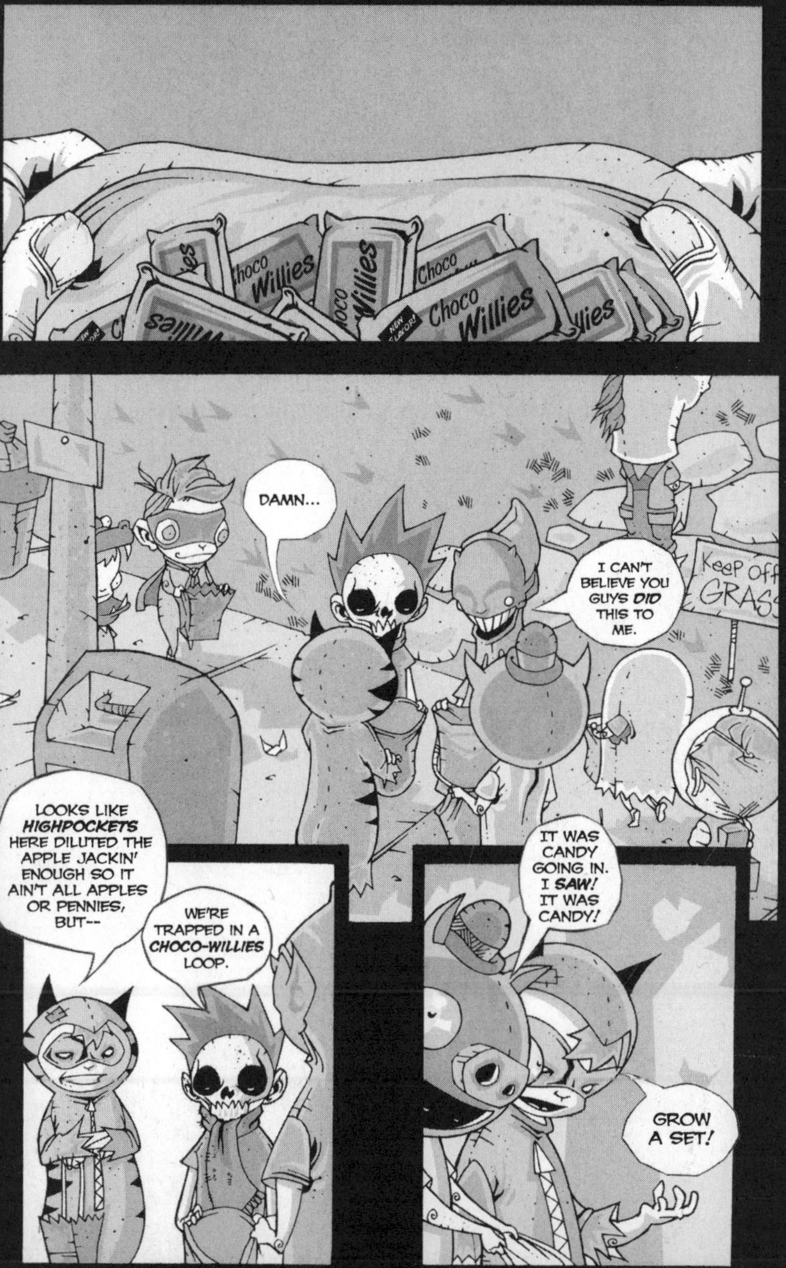
Choco Willies
NEW FLAVOR!
DAMN...
I CAN'T BELIEVE YOU GUYS *DID* THIS TO ME.
Keep off GRASS
LOOKS LIKE ***HIGHPOCKETS*** HERE DILUTED THE APPLE JACKIN' ENOUGH SO IT AIN'T ALL APPLES OR PENNIES, BUT--
WE'RE TRAPPED IN A ***CHOCO-WILLIES*** LOOP.
IT WAS CANDY GOING IN. I ***SAW!*** IT WAS CANDY*!*
GROW A SET*!*

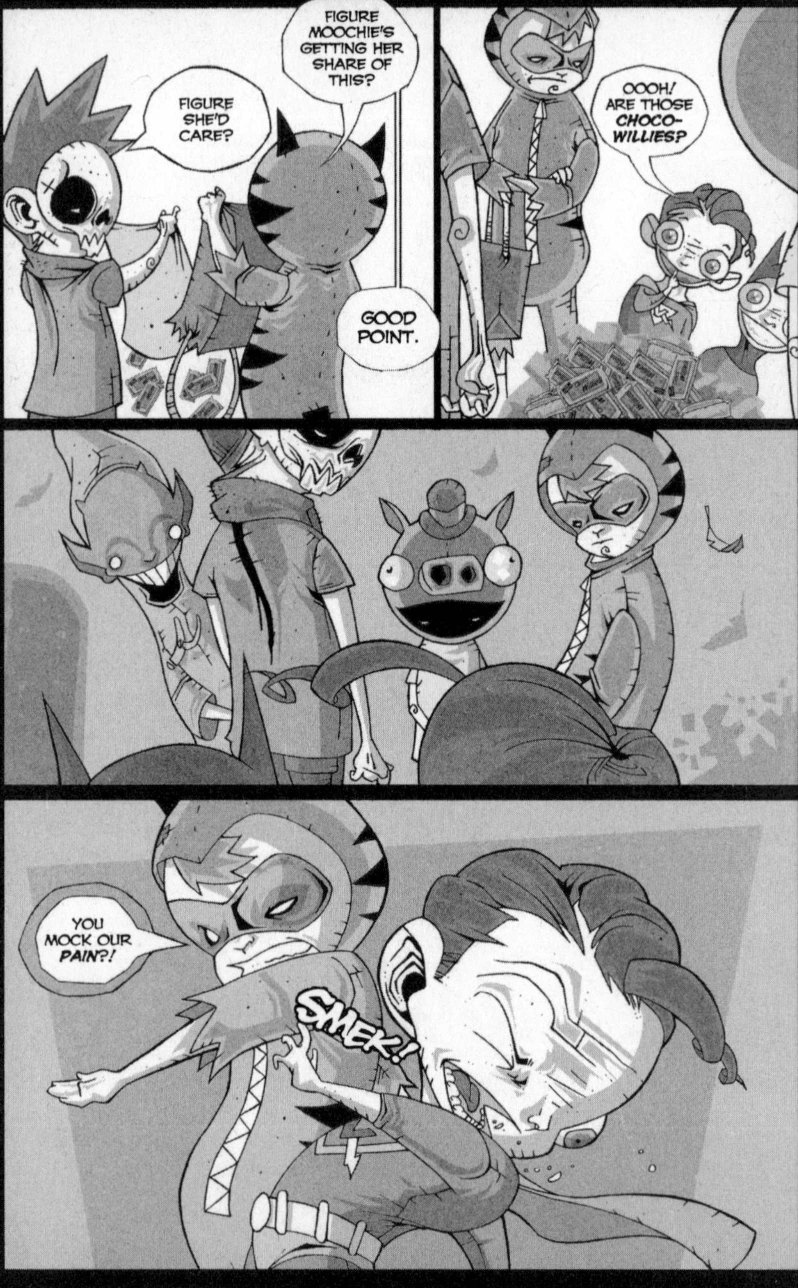
FIGURE MOOCHIE'S GETTING HER SHARE OF THIS?
FIGURE SHE'D CARE?
GOOD POINT.
OOOH! ARE THOSE *CHOCO-WILLIES?*
YOU MOCK OUR *PAIN?!*
SMEK!

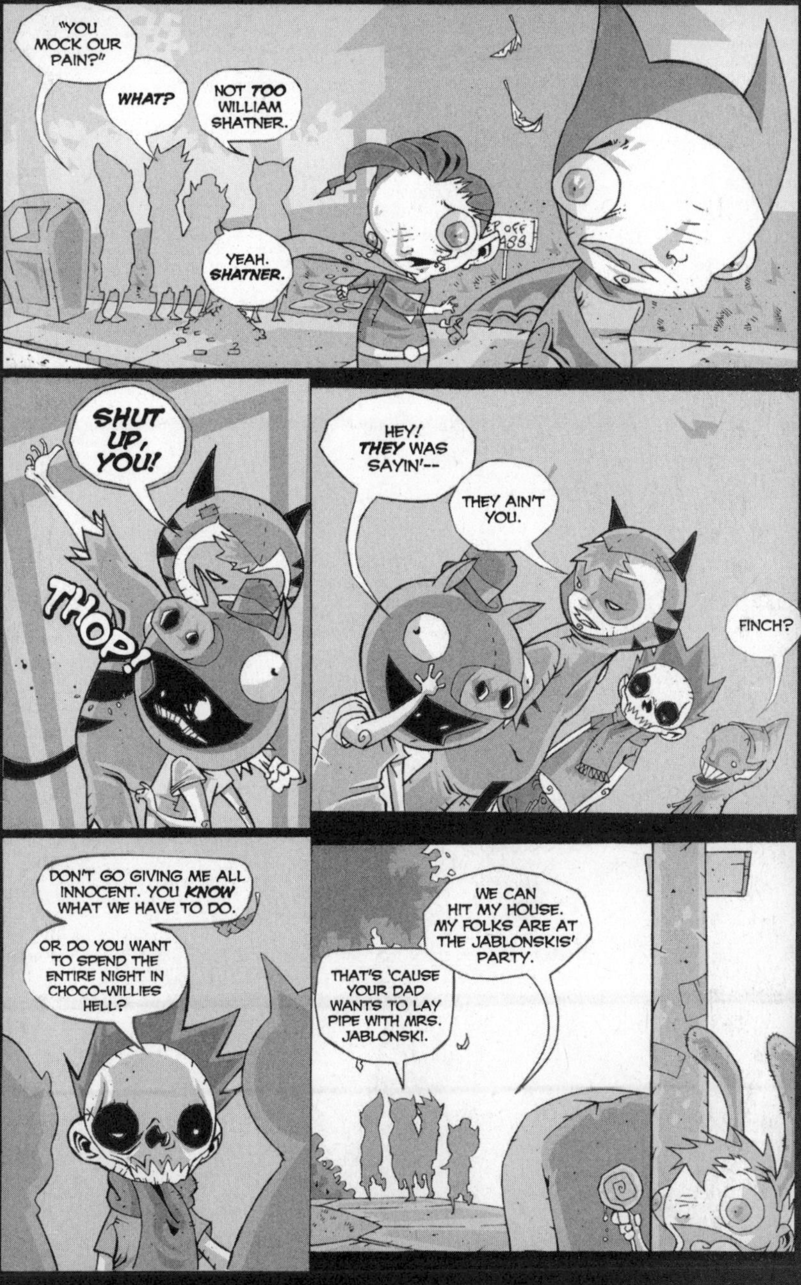
"YOU MOCK OUR PAIN?"
WHAT?
NOT TOO WILLIAM SHATNER.
YEAH. SHATNER.
SHUT UP, YOU!
THOP!
HEY! THEY WAS SAYIN'--
THEY AIN'T YOU.
FINCH?
DON'T GO GIVING ME ALL INNOCENT. YOU KNOW WHAT WE HAVE TO DO.
OR DO YOU WANT TO SPEND THE ENTIRE NIGHT IN CHOCO-WILLIES HELL?
WE CAN HIT MY HOUSE. MY FOLKS ARE AT THE JABLONSKIS' PARTY.
THAT'S 'CAUSE YOUR DAD WANTS TO LAY PIPE WITH MRS. JABLONSKI.

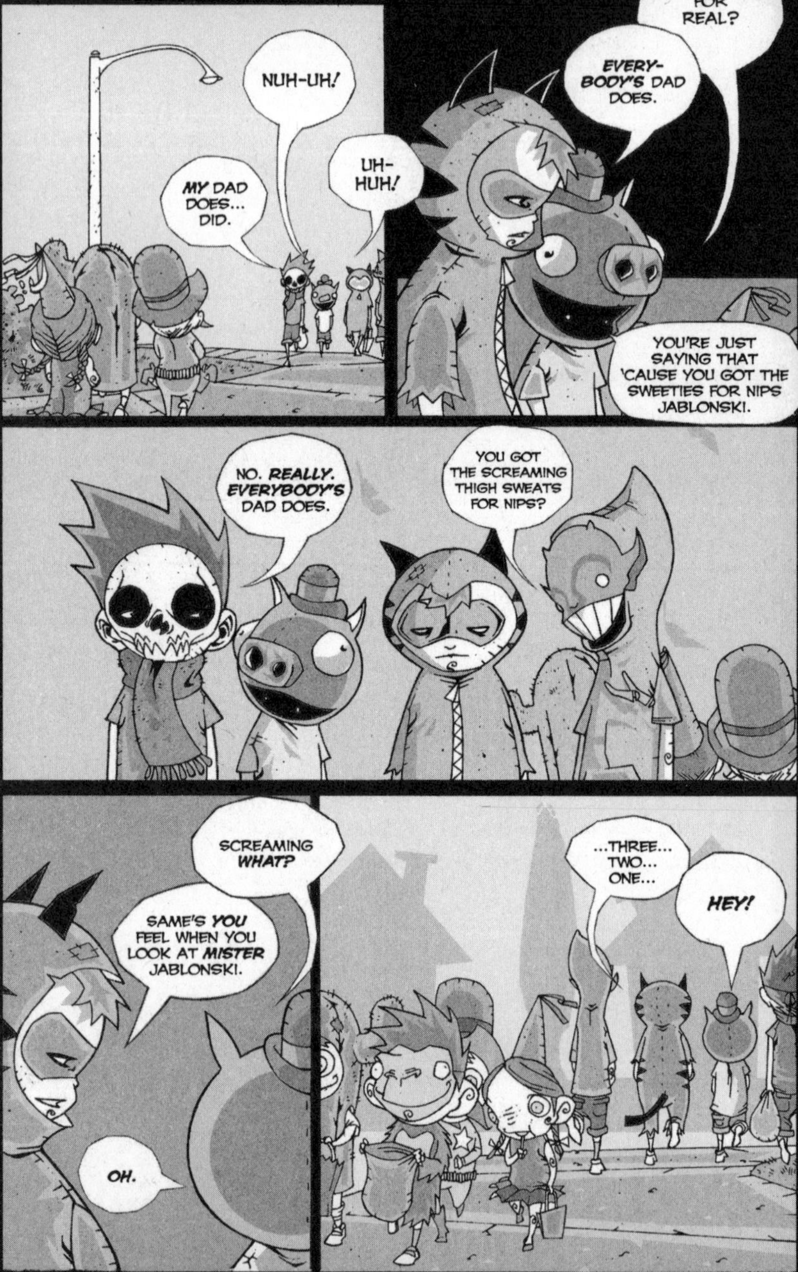
MY DAD DOES... DID.
NUH-UH!
UH-HUH!
FOR REAL?
EVERYBODY'S DAD DOES.
YOU'RE JUST SAYING THAT 'CAUSE YOU GOT THE SWEETIES FOR NIPS JABLONSKI.
NO. REALLY. EVERYBODY'S DAD DOES.
YOU GOT THE SCREAMING THIGH SWEATS FOR NIPS?
SCREAMING WHAT?
SAME'S YOU FEEL WHEN YOU LOOK AT MISTER JABLONSKI.
OH.
...THREE... TWO... ONE...
HEY!

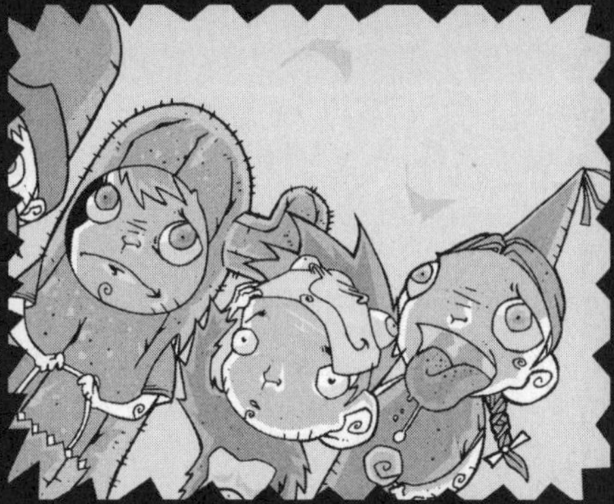

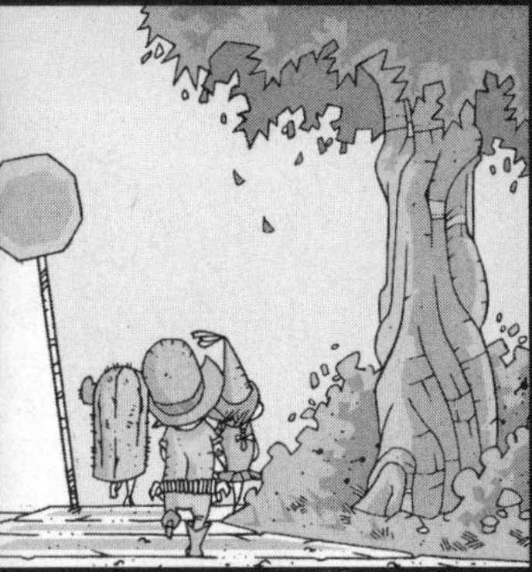

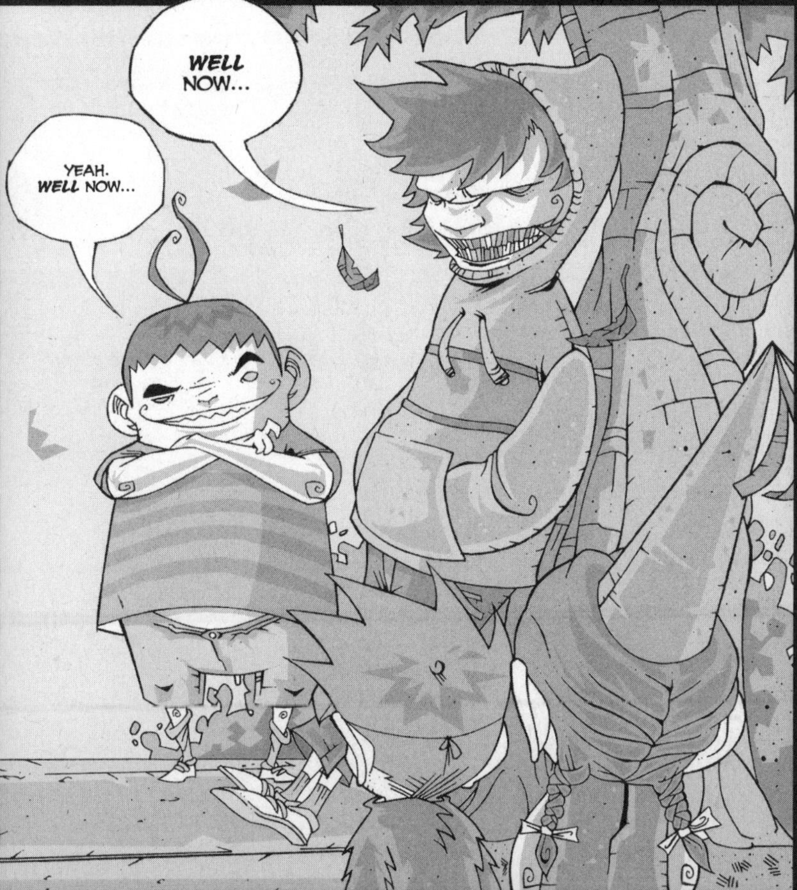
WELL NOW...
YEAH. WELL NOW...

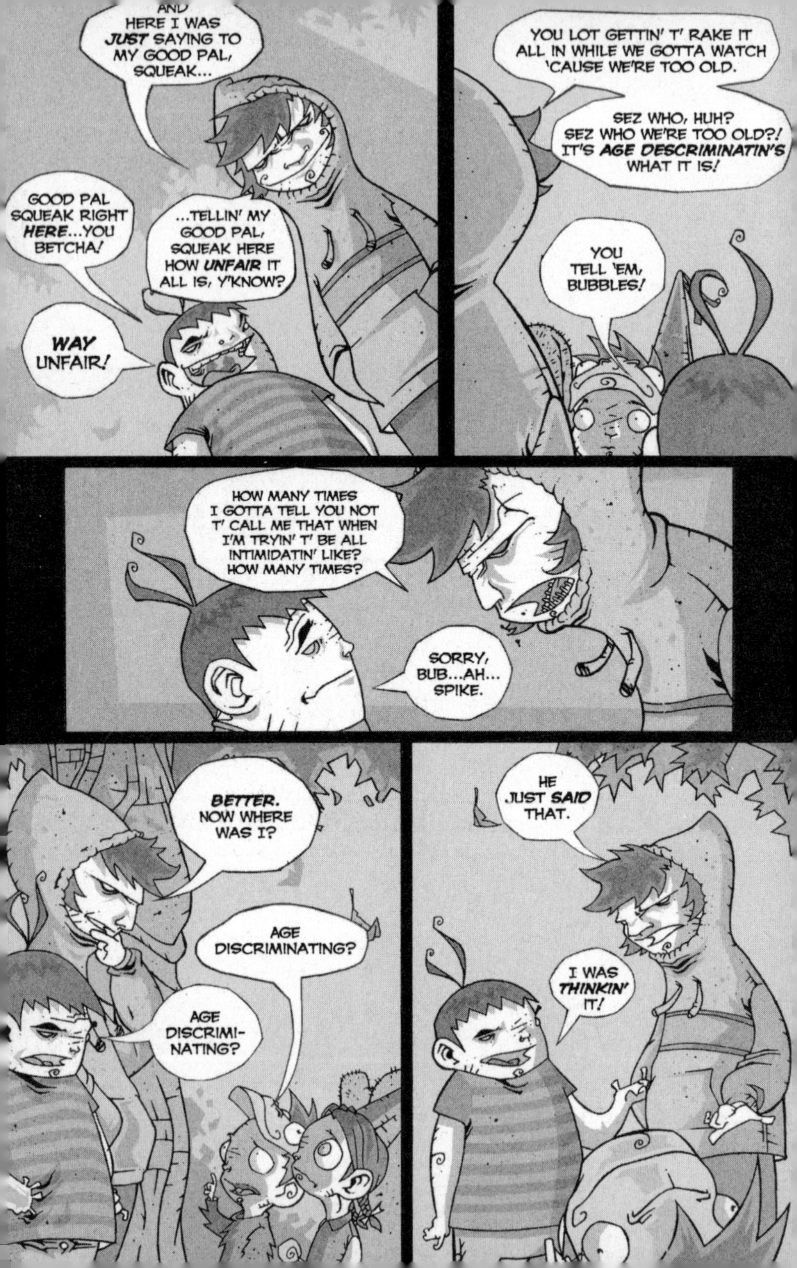
AND HERE I WAS JUST SAYING TO MY GOOD PAL, SQUEAK...
...TELLIN' MY GOOD PAL, SQUEAK HERE HOW UNFAIR IT ALL IS, Y'KNOW?
GOOD PAL SQUEAK RIGHT HERE...YOU BETCHA!
WAY UNFAIR!
YOU LOT GETTIN' T' RAKE IT ALL IN WHILE WE GOTTA WATCH 'CAUSE WE'RE TOO OLD.
SEZ WHO, HUH? SEZ WHO WE'RE TOO OLD?! IT'S AGE DESCRIMINATIN'S WHAT IT IS!
YOU TELL 'EM, BUBBLES!
HOW MANY TIMES I GOTTA TELL YOU NOT T' CALL ME THAT WHEN I'M TRYIN' T' BE ALL INTIMIDATIN' LIKE? HOW MANY TIMES?
SORRY, BUB...AH... SPIKE.
BETTER. NOW WHERE WAS I?
AGE DISCRIMINATING?
AGE DISCRIMI-NATING?
HE JUST SAID THAT.
I WAS THINKIN' IT!

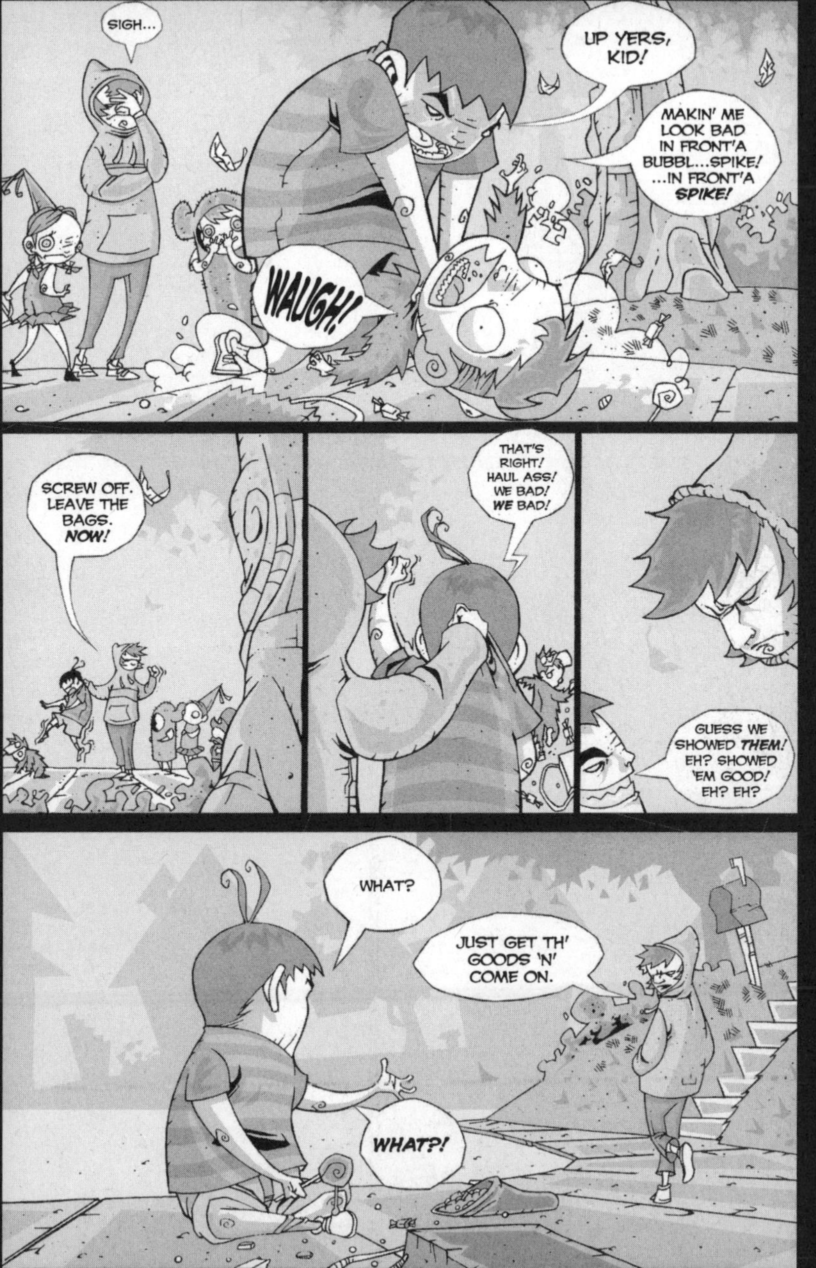
SIGH...
UP YERS, KID!
MAKIN' ME LOOK BAD IN FRONT'A BUBBL...SPIKE! ...IN FRONT'A SPIKE!
WAUGH!
SCREW OFF. LEAVE THE BAGS. NOW!
THAT'S RIGHT! HAUL ASS! WE BAD! WE BAD!
GUESS WE SHOWED THEM! EH? SHOWED 'EM GOOD! EH? EH?
WHAT?
JUST GET TH' GOODS 'N' COME ON.
WHAT?!

I Luv Halloween

CHAPTER TWO:
PIG PIG

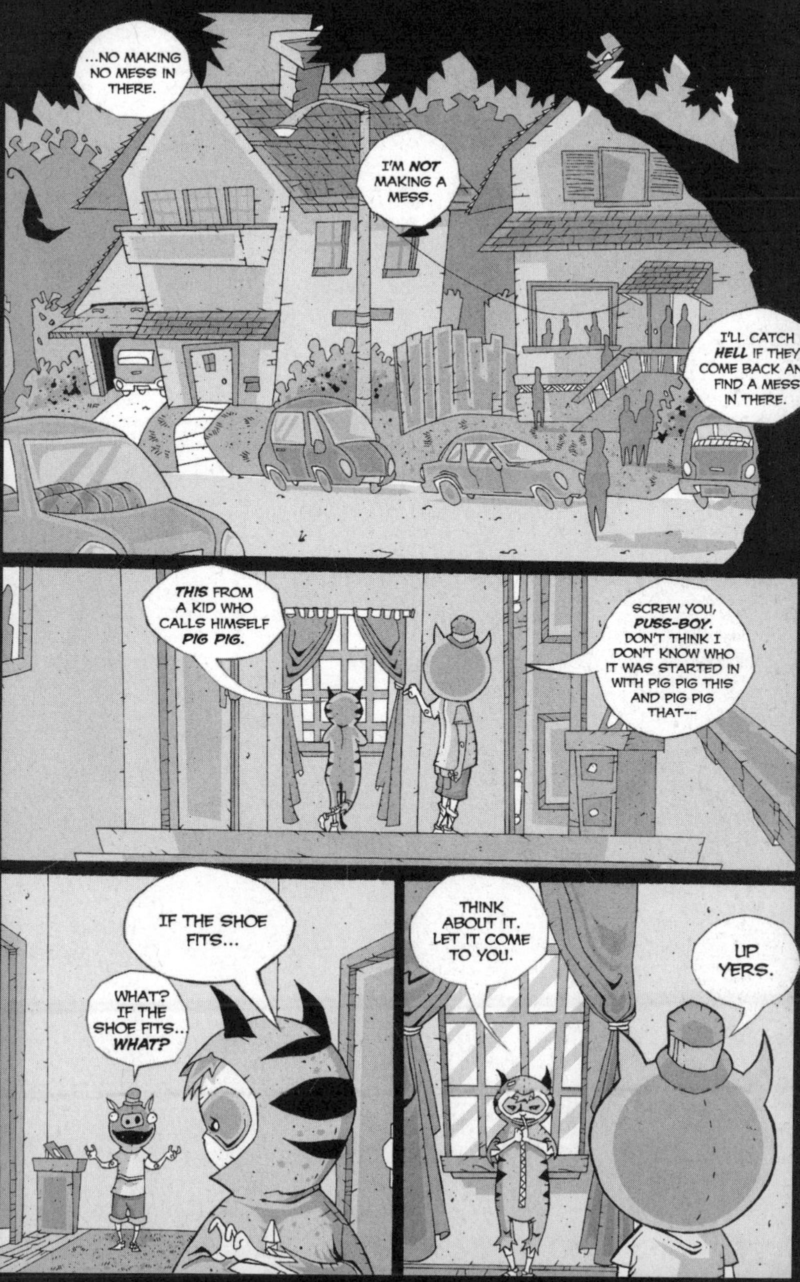
...NO MAKING NO MESS IN THERE.
I'M **NOT** MAKING A MESS.
I'LL CATCH **HELL** IF THEY COME BACK AND FIND A MESS IN THERE.
THIS FROM A KID WHO CALLS HIMSELF **PIG PIG.**
SCREW YOU, **PUSS-BOY.** DON'T THINK I DON'T KNOW WHO IT WAS STARTED IN WITH PIG PIG THIS AND PIG PIG THAT--
IF THE SHOE FITS...
WHAT? IF THE SHOE FITS... **WHAT?**
THINK ABOUT IT. LET IT COME TO YOU.
UP YERS.

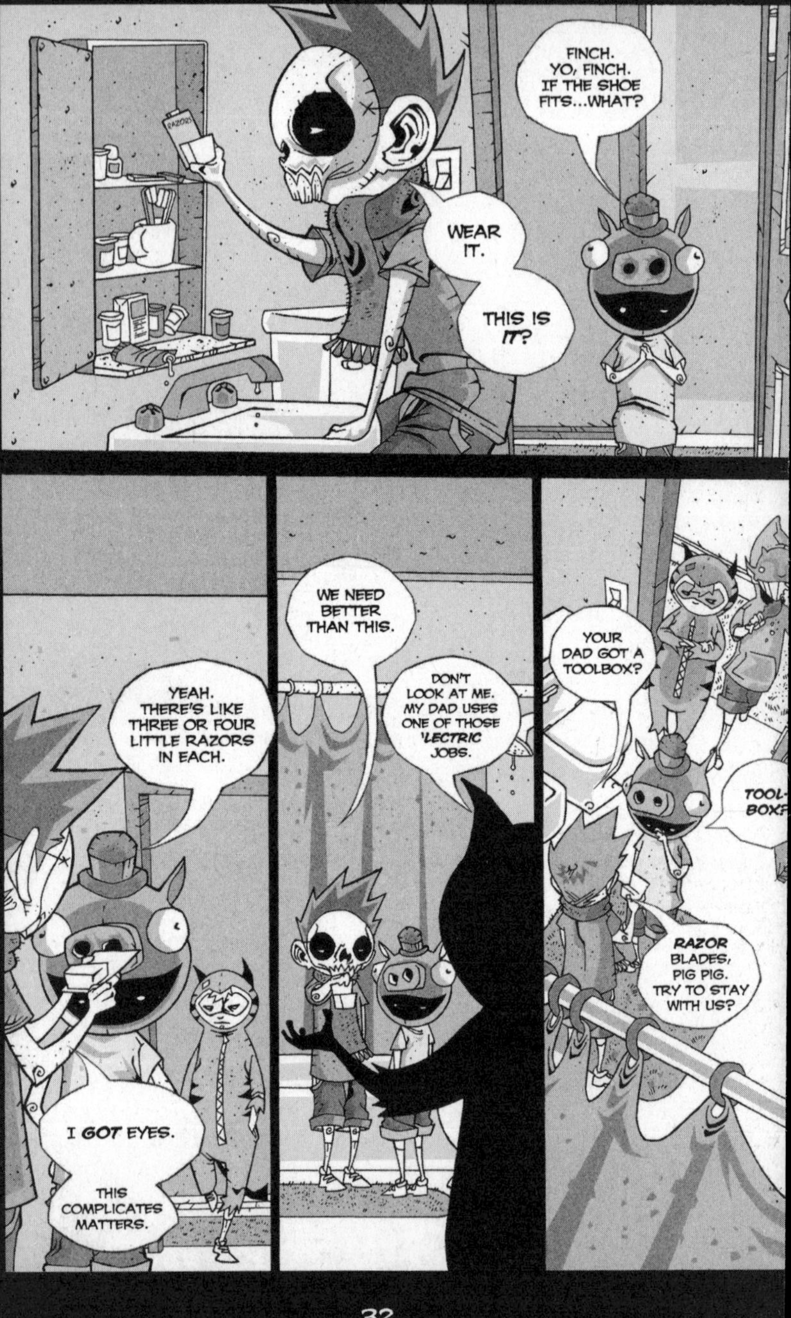
FINCH. YO, FINCH. IF THE SHOE FITS...WHAT?
WEAR IT.
THIS IS *IT*?
YEAH. THERE'S LIKE THREE OR FOUR LITTLE RAZORS IN EACH.
I ***GOT*** EYES.
THIS COMPLICATES MATTERS.
WE NEED BETTER THAN THIS.
DON'T LOOK AT ME. MY DAD USES ONE OF THOSE *'LECTRIC* JOBS.
YOUR DAD GOT A TOOLBOX?
TOOL-BOX?
RAZOR BLADES, PIG PIG. TRY TO STAY WITH US?

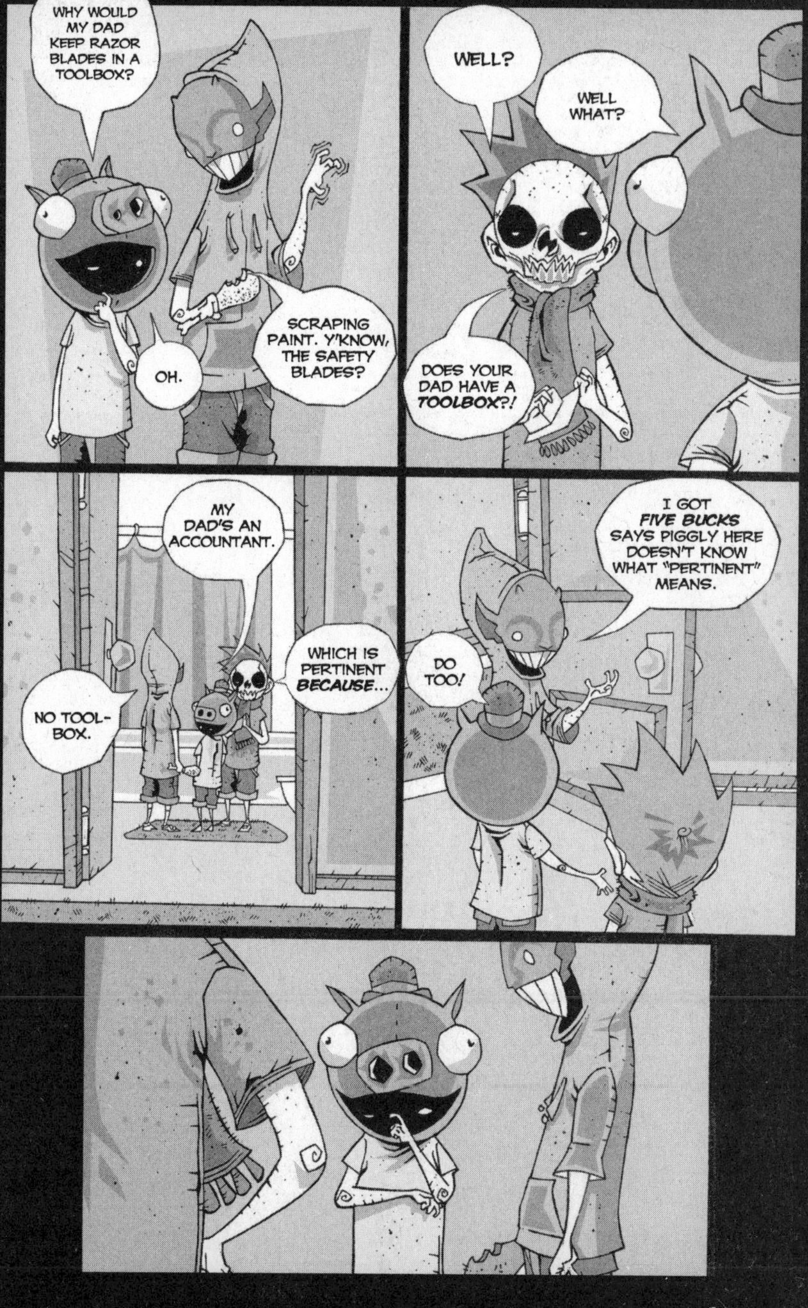
WHY WOULD MY DAD KEEP RAZOR BLADES IN A TOOLBOX?
SCRAPING PAINT. Y'KNOW, THE SAFETY BLADES?
OH.
WELL?
WELL WHAT?
DOES YOUR DAD HAVE A *TOOLBOX*?!
MY DAD'S AN ACCOUNTANT.
NO TOOL-BOX.
WHICH IS PERTINENT *BECAUSE*...
I GOT *FIVE BUCKS* SAYS PIGGLY HERE DOESN'T KNOW WHAT "PERTINENT" MEANS.
DO TOO!

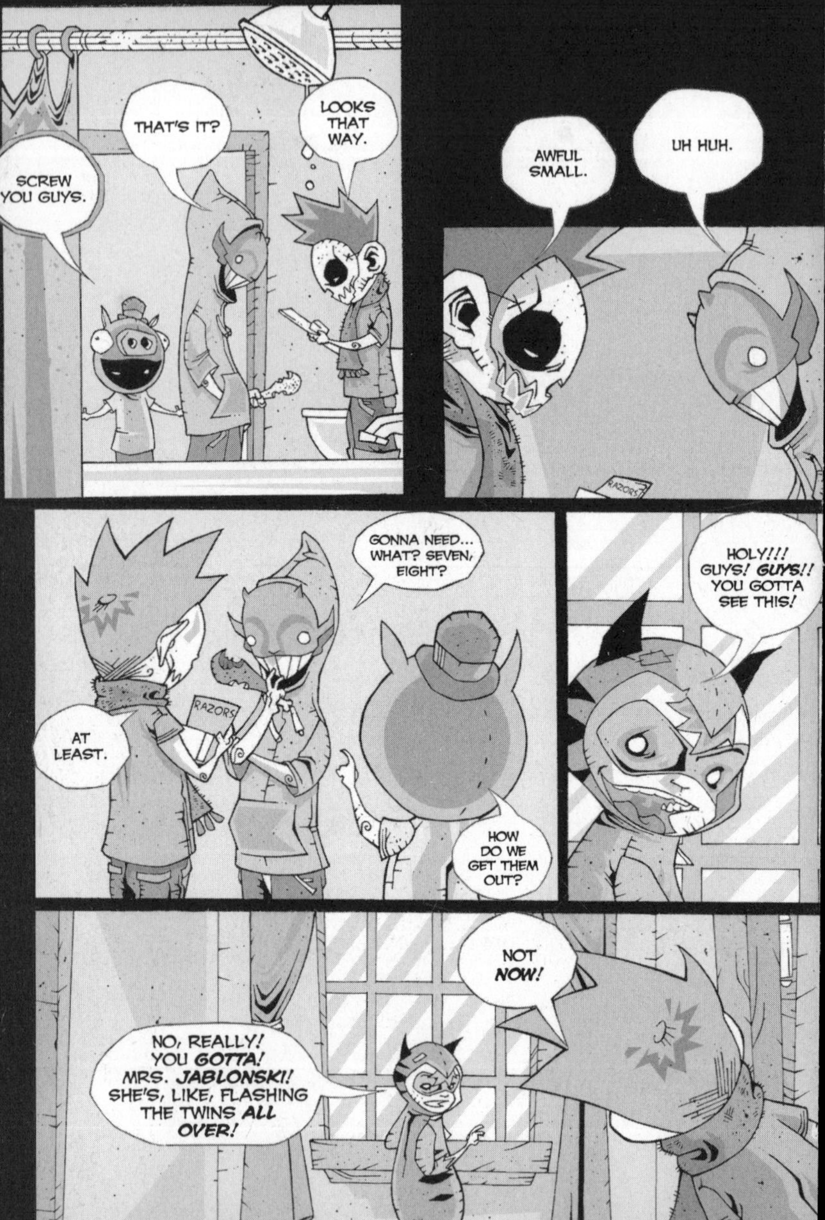
THAT'S IT?
LOOKS THAT WAY.
SCREW YOU GUYS.
AWFUL SMALL.
UH HUH.
GONNA NEED... WHAT? SEVEN, EIGHT?
AT LEAST.
HOW DO WE GET THEM OUT?
HOLY!!! GUYS! GUYS!! YOU GOTTA SEE THIS!
NOT NOW!
NO, REALLY! YOU GOTTA! MRS. JABLONSKI! SHE'S, LIKE, FLASHING THE TWINS ALL OVER!
RAZORS

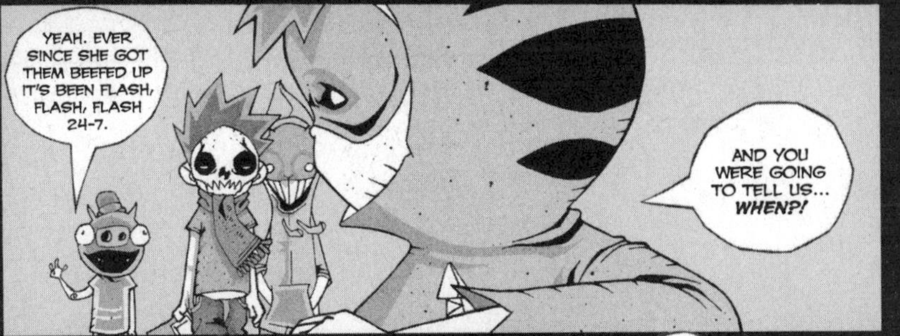
YEAH. EVER SINCE SHE GOT THEM BEEFED UP IT'S BEEN FLASH, FLASH, FLASH 24-7.
AND YOU WERE GOING TO TELL US... *WHEN?!*

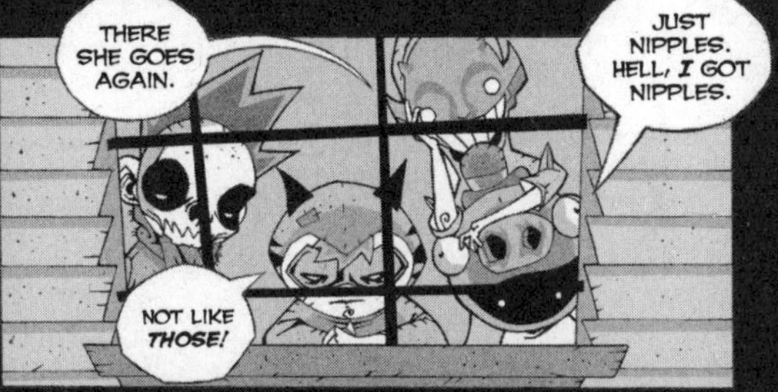
THERE SHE GOES AGAIN.
JUST NIPPLES. HELL, *I* GOT NIPPLES.
NOT LIKE *THOSE!*

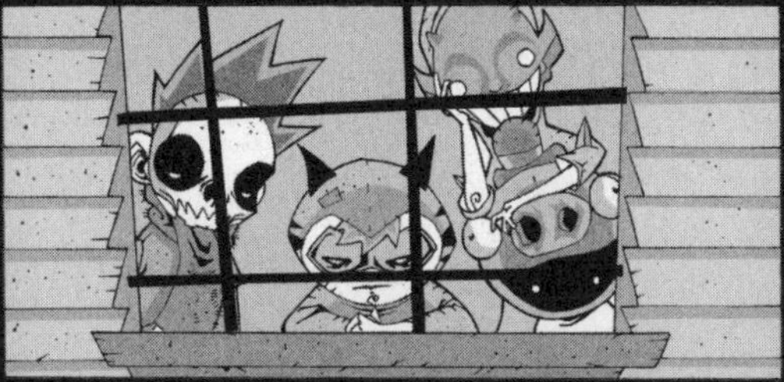

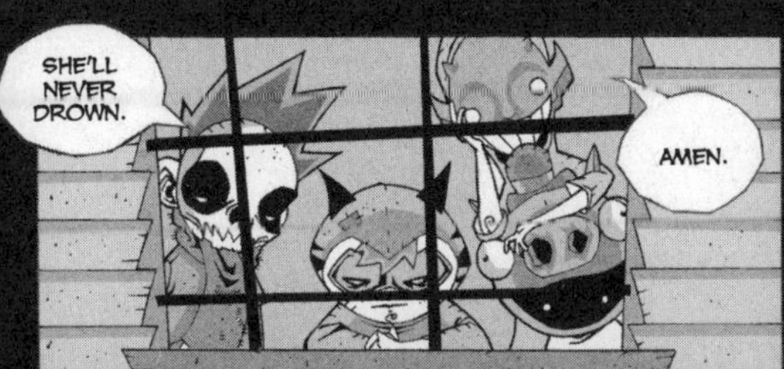
SHE'LL NEVER DROWN.
AMEN.

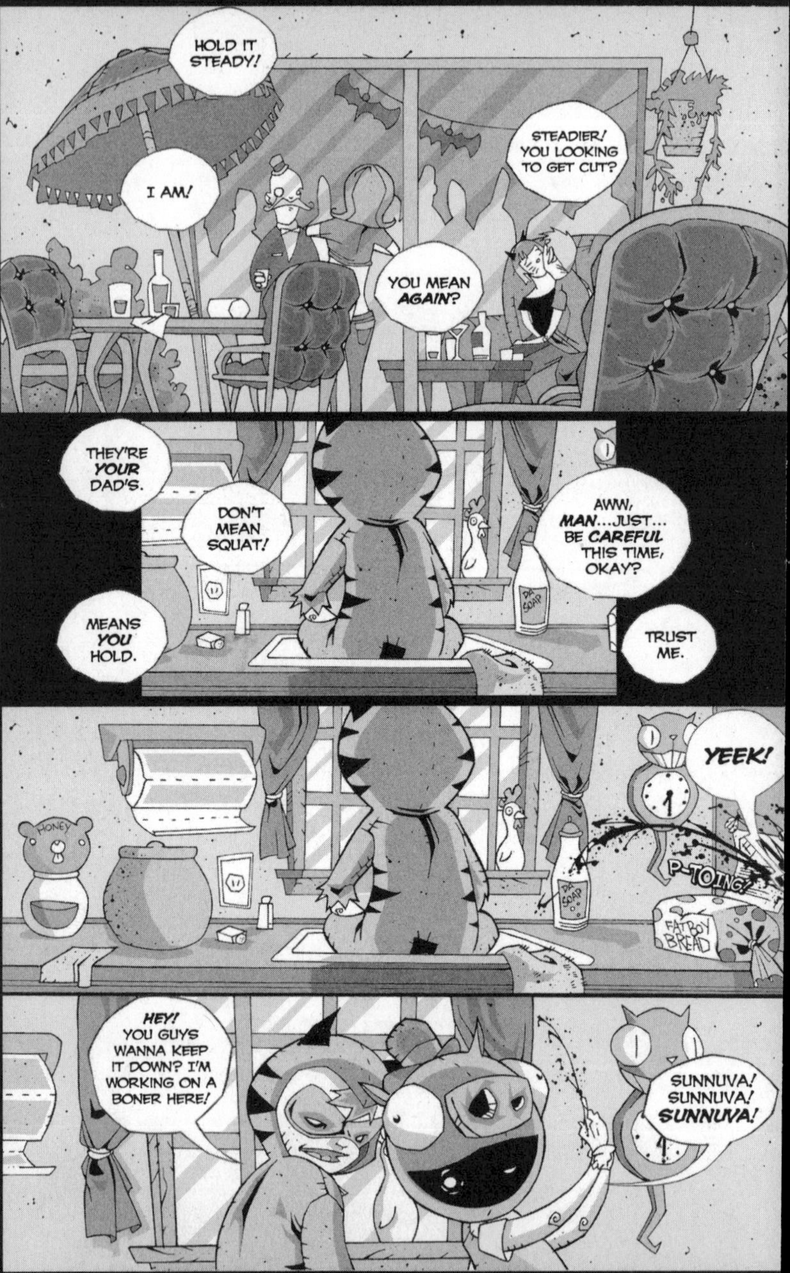
HOLD IT STEADY!
I AM!
STEADIER! YOU LOOKING TO GET CUT?
YOU MEAN *AGAIN*?
THEY'RE *YOUR* DAD'S.
DON'T MEAN SQUAT!
MEANS *YOU* HOLD.
AWW, *MAN*...JUST... BE *CAREFUL* THIS TIME, OKAY?
TRUST ME.
DA SOAP
HONEY
DA SOAP
P-TOING!
YEEK!
FATBOY BREAD
HEY! YOU GUYS WANNA KEEP IT DOWN? I'M WORKING ON A BONER HERE!
SUNNUVA! SUNNUVA! *SUNNUVA!*

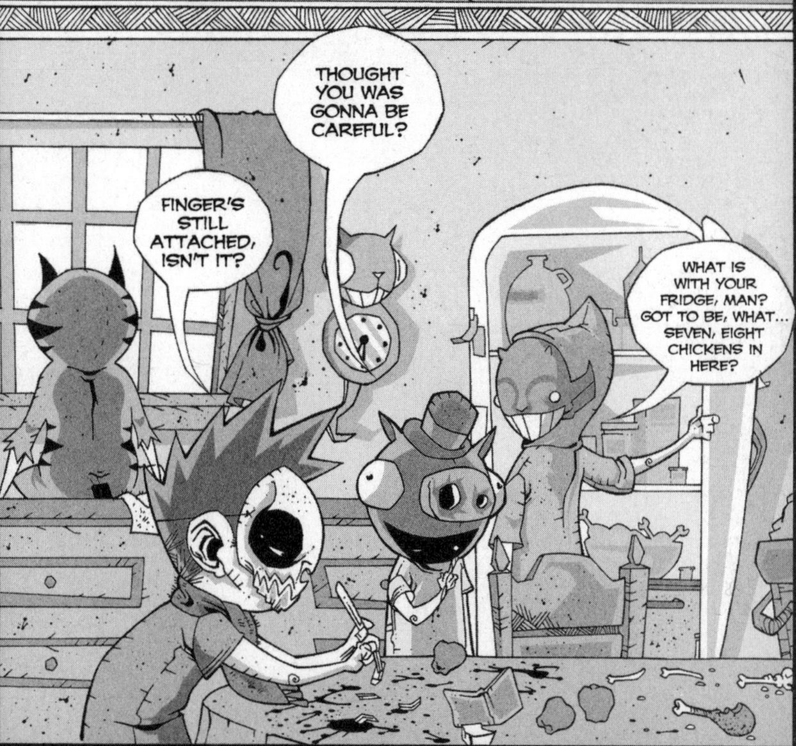
THOUGHT YOU WAS GONNA BE CAREFUL?
FINGER'S STILL ATTACHED, ISN'T IT?
WHAT IS WITH YOUR FRIDGE, MAN? GOT TO BE, WHAT... SEVEN, EIGHT CHICKENS IN HERE?

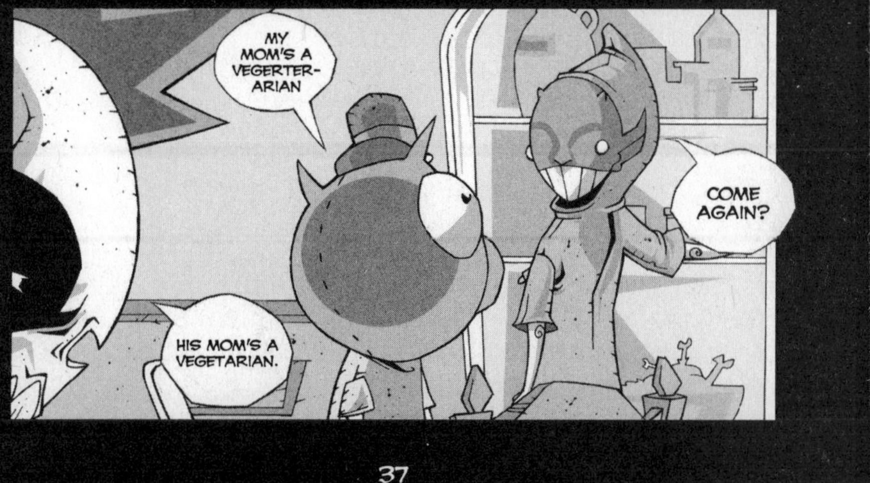
MY MOM'S A VEGERTER-ARIAN
COME AGAIN?
HIS MOM'S A VEGETARIAN.

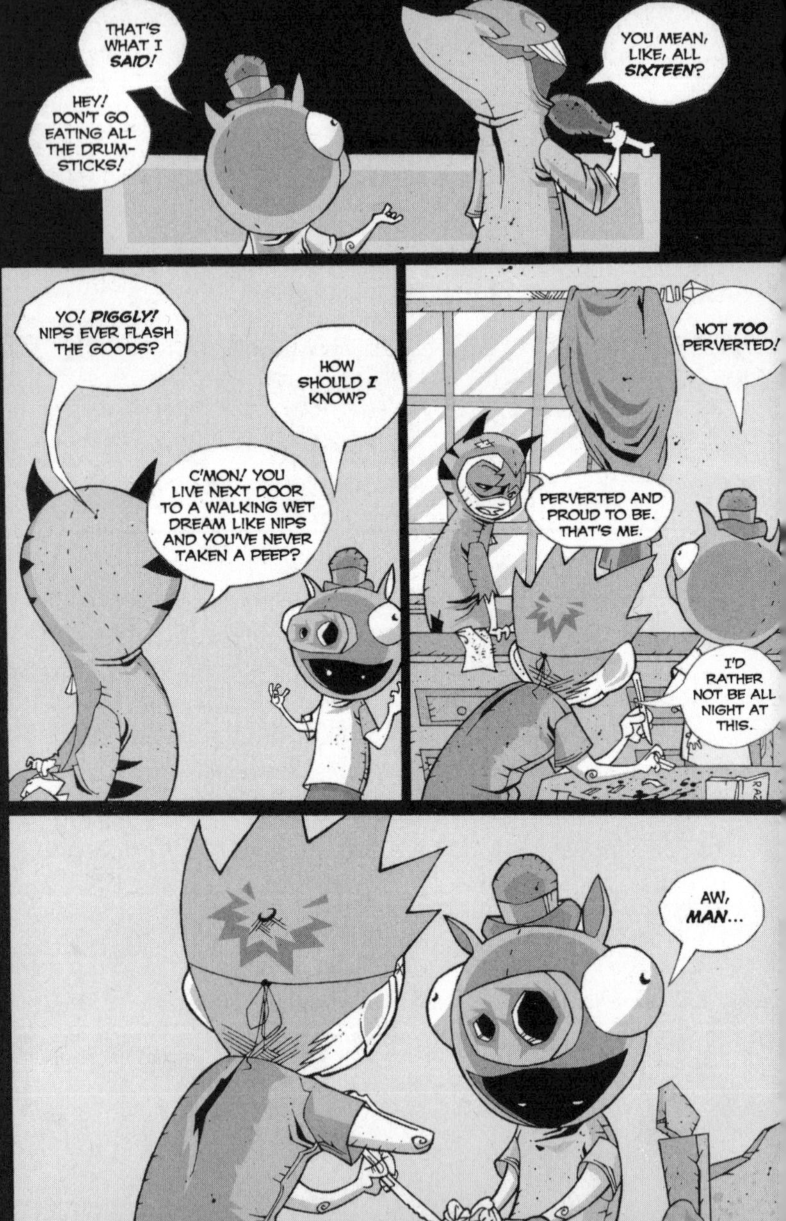
THAT'S WHAT I *SAID!*
HEY! DON'T GO EATING ALL THE DRUM-STICKS!
YOU MEAN, LIKE, ALL *SIXTEEN?*
YO! *PIGGLY!* NIPS EVER FLASH THE GOODS?
HOW SHOULD *I* KNOW?
C'MON! YOU LIVE NEXT DOOR TO A WALKING WET DREAM LIKE NIPS AND YOU'VE NEVER TAKEN A PEEP?
NOT *TOO* PERVERTED!
PERVERTED AND PROUD TO BE. THAT'S ME.
I'D RATHER NOT BE ALL NIGHT AT THIS.
AW, *MAN*...

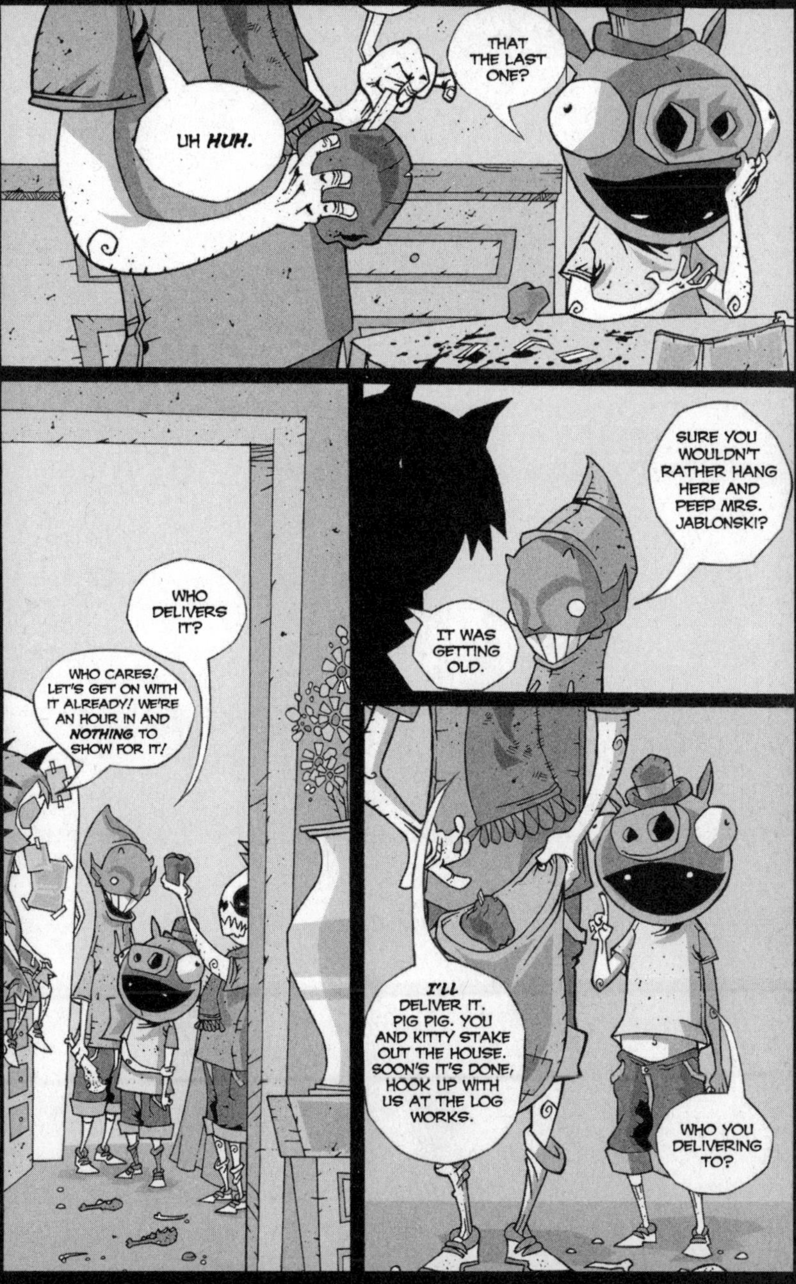
THAT THE LAST ONE?
UH HUH.
WHO DELIVERS IT?
WHO CARES! LET'S GET ON WITH IT ALREADY! WE'RE AN HOUR IN AND NOTHING TO SHOW FOR IT!
SURE YOU WOULDN'T RATHER HANG HERE AND PEEP MRS. JABLONSKI?
IT WAS GETTING OLD.
I'LL DELIVER IT. PIG PIG. YOU AND KITTY STAKE OUT THE HOUSE. SOON'S IT'S DONE, HOOK UP WITH US AT THE LOG WORKS.
WHO YOU DELIVERING TO?

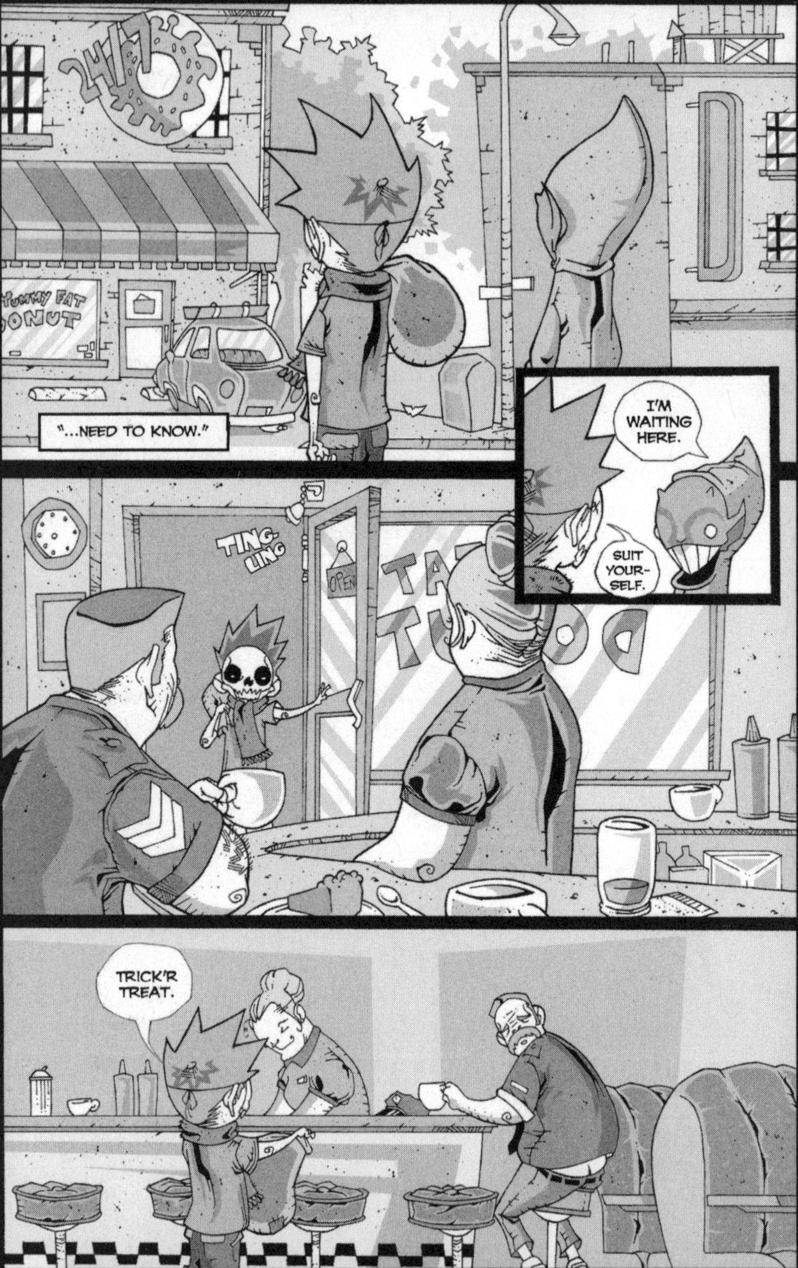
"...NEED TO KNOW."
I'M WAITING HERE.
SUIT YOURSELF.
TING-LING
OPEN
TATTOO
TRICK'R TREAT.

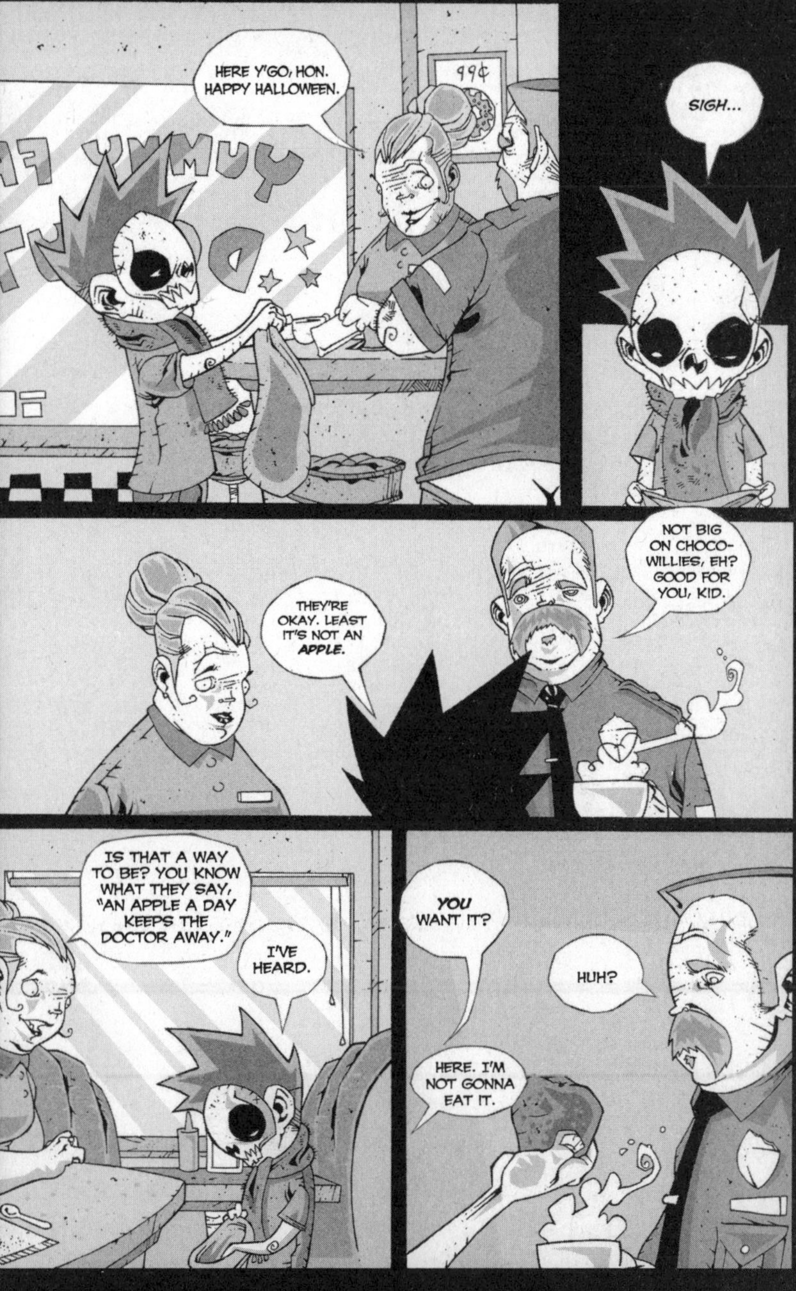
99¢
HERE Y'GO, HON. HAPPY HALLOWEEN.
SIGH...
NOT BIG ON CHOCO-WILLIES, EH? GOOD FOR YOU, KID.
THEY'RE OKAY. LEAST IT'S NOT AN *APPLE.*
IS THAT A WAY TO BE? YOU KNOW WHAT THEY SAY, "AN APPLE A DAY KEEPS THE DOCTOR AWAY."
I'VE HEARD.
YOU WANT IT?
HUH?
HERE. I'M NOT GONNA EAT IT.

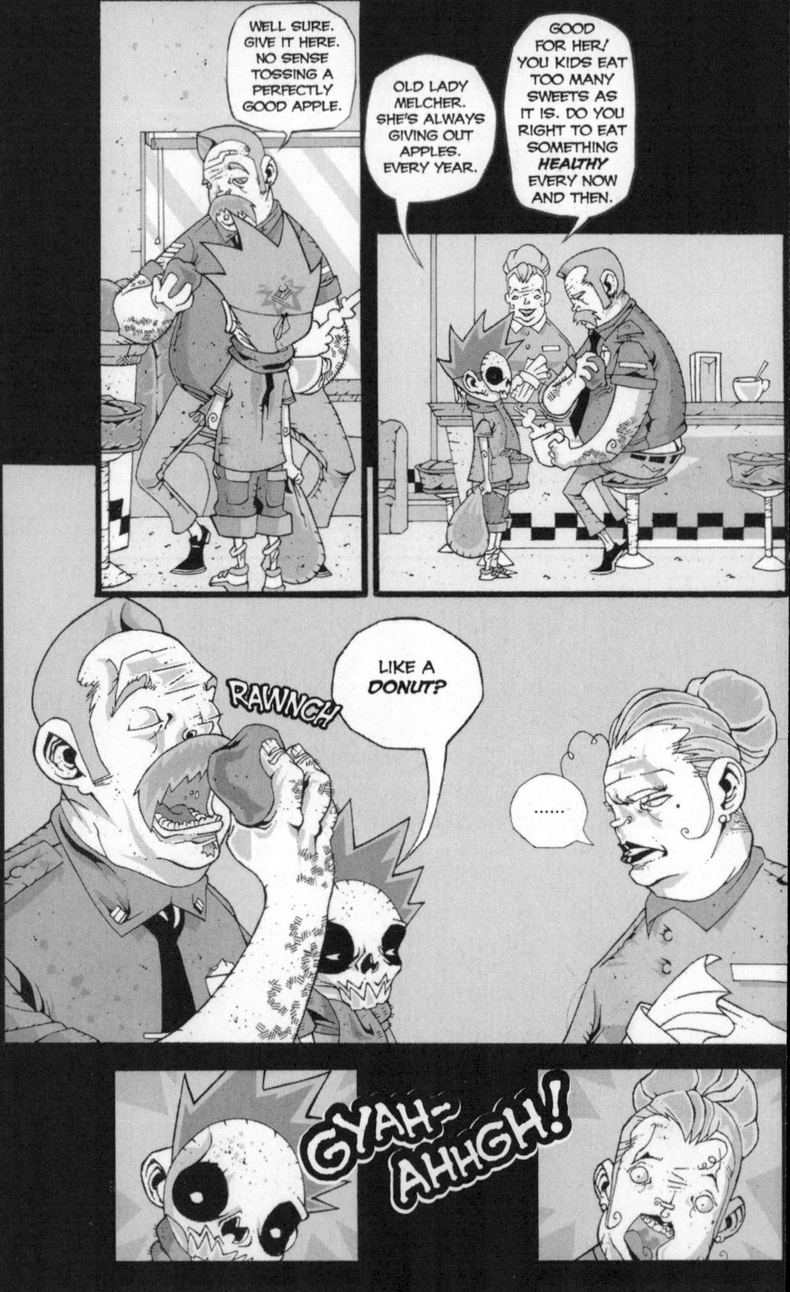

WELL SURE. GIVE IT HERE. NO SENSE TOSSING A PERFECTLY GOOD APPLE.
OLD LADY MELCHER. SHE'S ALWAYS GIVING OUT APPLES. EVERY YEAR.
GOOD FOR HER! YOU KIDS EAT TOO MANY SWEETS AS IT IS. DO YOU RIGHT TO EAT SOMETHING ***HEALTHY*** EVERY NOW AND THEN.
RAWNCH
LIKE A ***DONUT?***
......
GYAH-AHHGH!

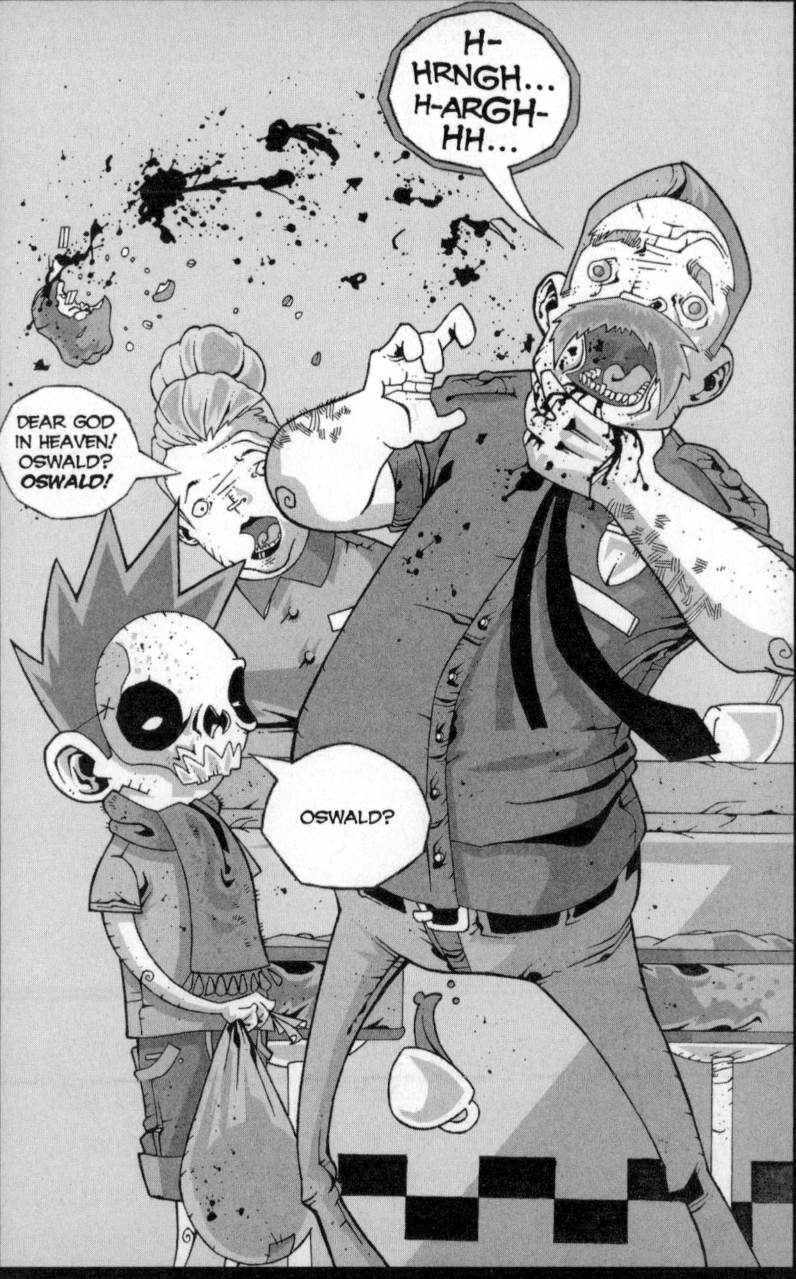
H-
HRNGH...
H-ARGH-
HH...
DEAR GOD
IN HEAVEN!
OSWALD?
OSWALD!
OSWALD?

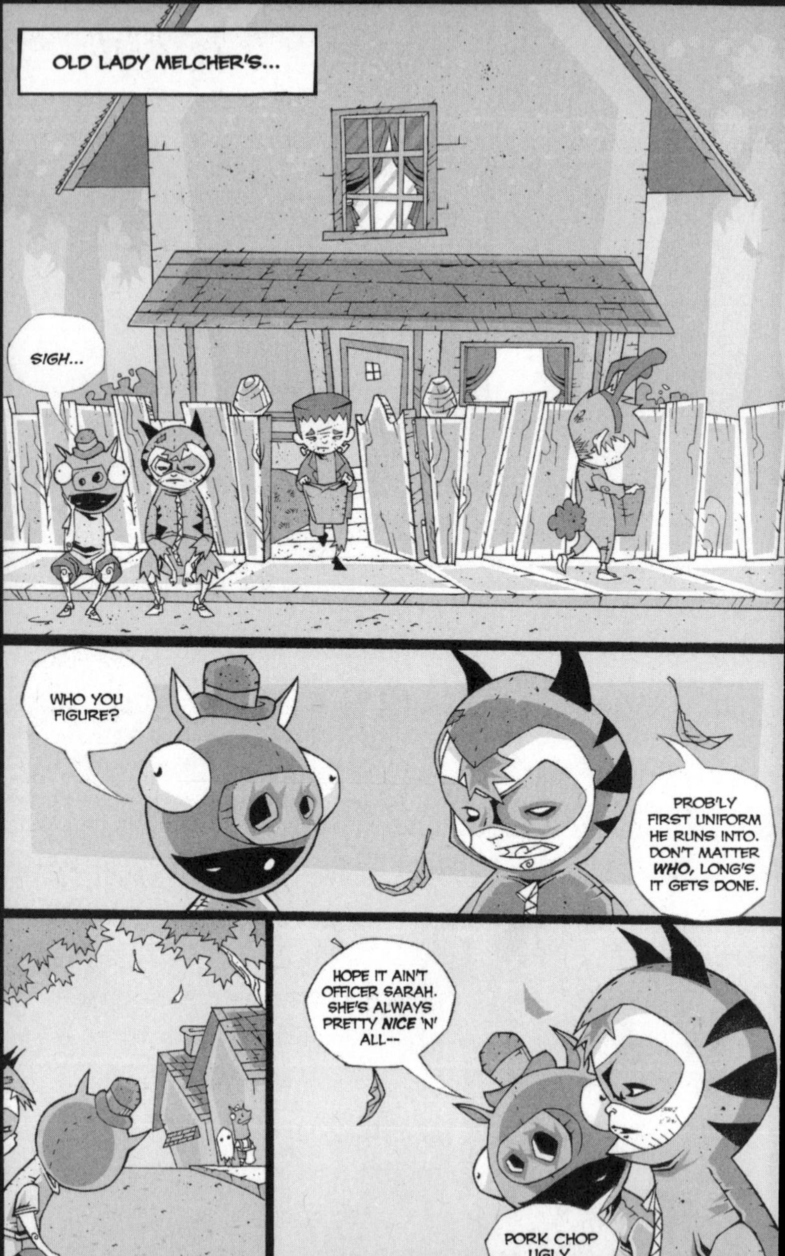
OLD LADY MELCHER'S...
SIGH...
WHO YOU FIGURE?
PROB'LY FIRST UNIFORM HE RUNS INTO. DON'T MATTER *WHO,* LONG'S IT GETS DONE.
HOPE IT AIN'T OFFICER SARAH. SHE'S ALWAYS PRETTY *NICE* 'N' ALL--
PORK CHOP UGLY.

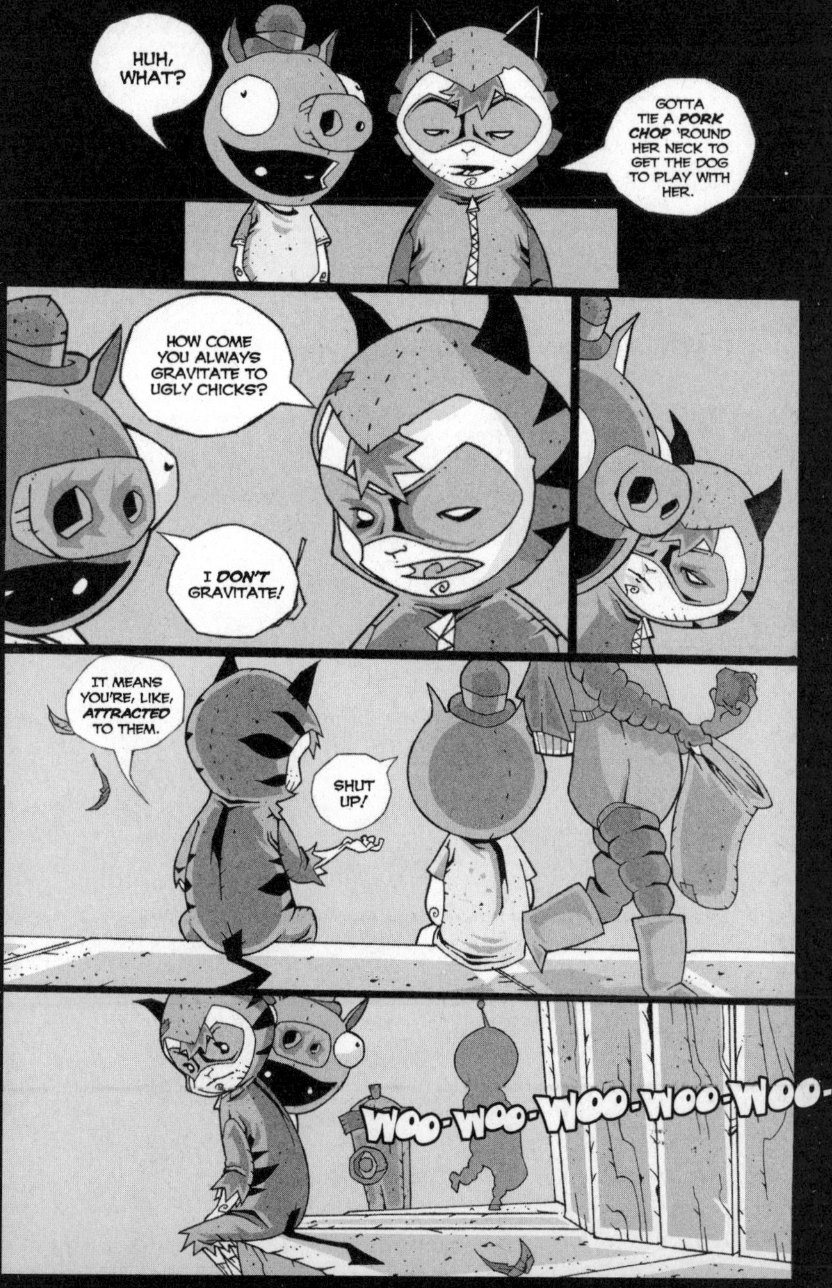

HUH, WHAT?
GOTTA TIE A ***PORK CHOP*** 'ROUND HER NECK TO GET THE DOG TO PLAY WITH HER.
HOW COME YOU ALWAYS GRAVITATE TO UGLY CHICKS?
I ***DON'T*** GRAVITATE!
IT MEANS YOU'RE, LIKE, ***ATTRACTED*** TO THEM.
SHUT UP!
WOO-WOO-WOO-WOO-WOO-

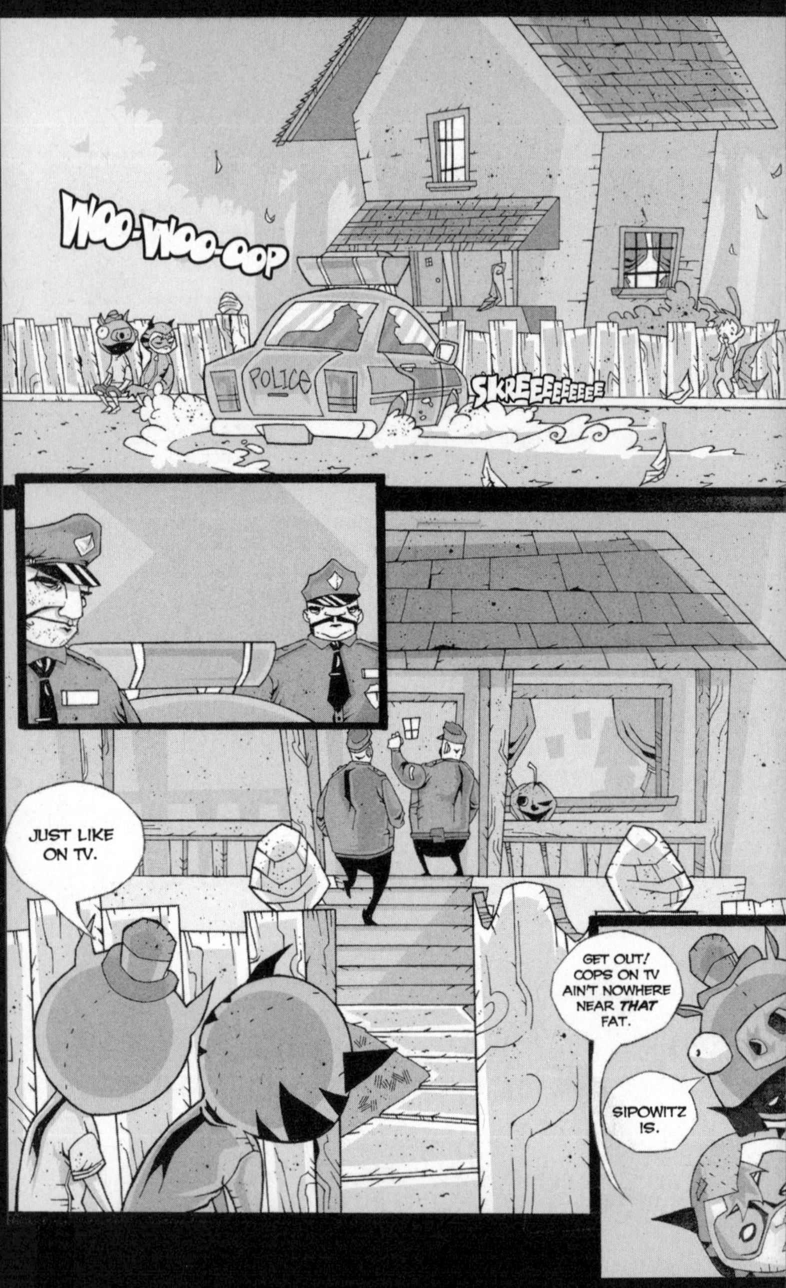
WOO-WOO-OOP
POLICE
SKREEEEEEEEE
JUST LIKE ON TV.
GET OUT! COPS ON TV AIN'T NOWHERE NEAR *THAT* FAT.
SIPOWITZ IS.

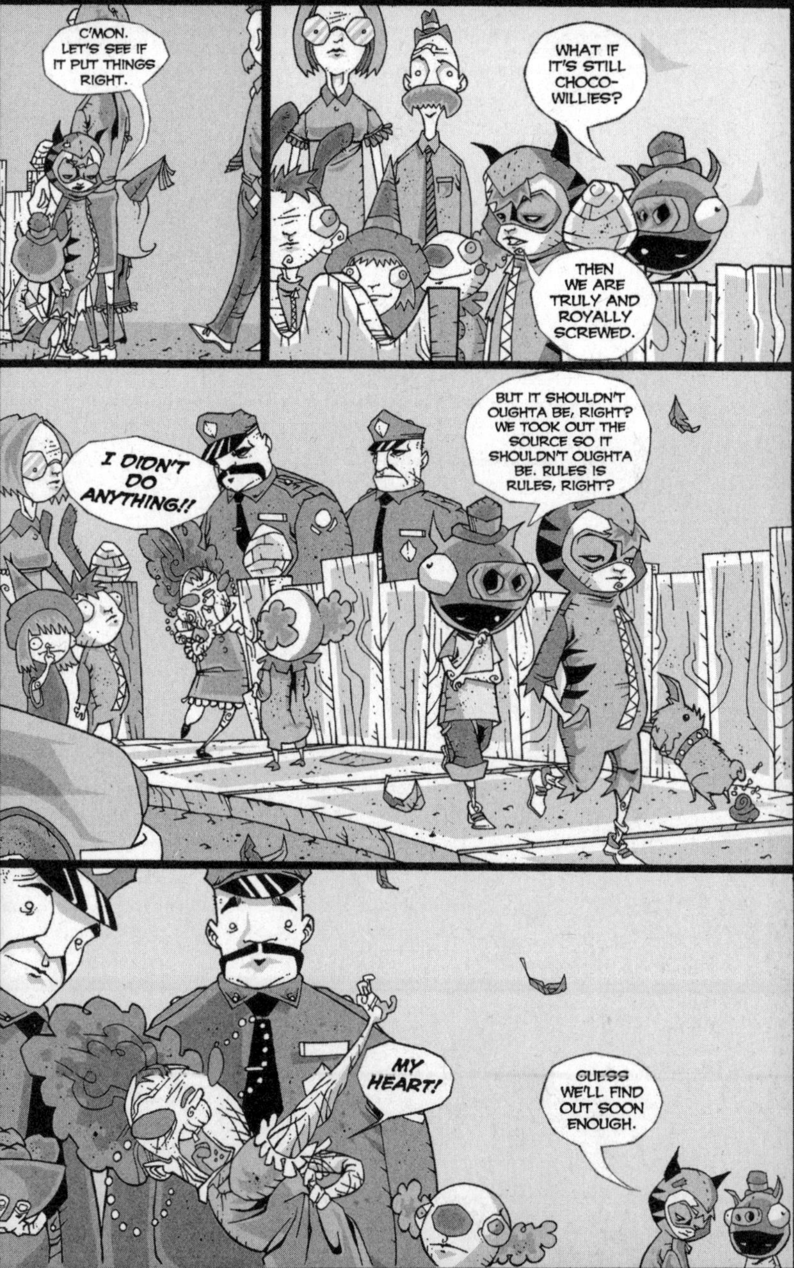
C'MON. LET'S SEE IF IT PUT THINGS RIGHT.
WHAT IF IT'S STILL CHOCO-WILLIES?
THEN WE ARE TRULY AND ROYALLY SCREWED.
I DIDN'T DO ANYTHING!!
BUT IT SHOULDN'T OUGHTA BE, RIGHT? WE TOOK OUT THE SOURCE SO IT SHOULDN'T OUGHTA BE. RULES IS RULES, RIGHT?
MY HEART!
GUESS WE'LL FIND OUT SOON ENOUGH.

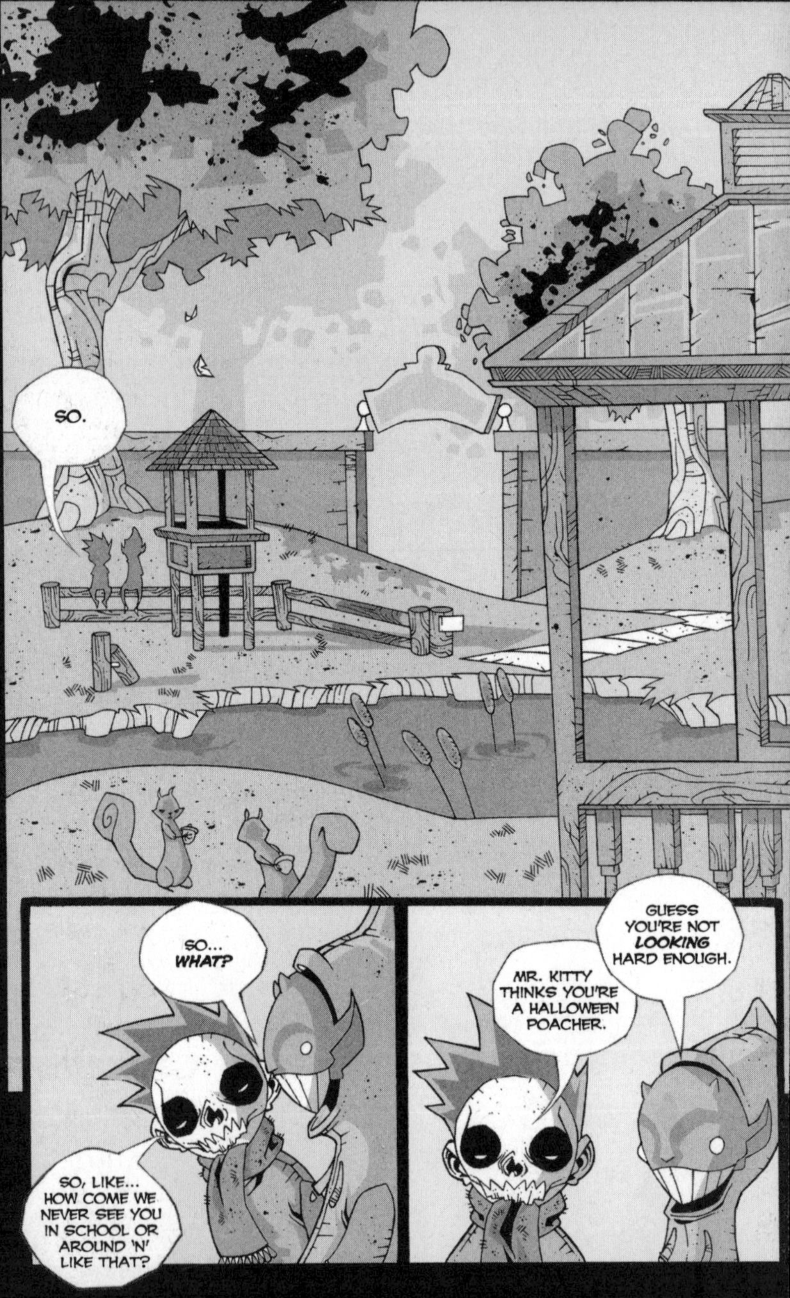
SO.
SO... *WHAT?*
SO, LIKE... HOW COME WE NEVER SEE YOU IN SCHOOL OR AROUND 'N' LIKE THAT?
GUESS YOU'RE NOT *LOOKING* HARD ENOUGH.
MR. KITTY THINKS YOU'RE A HALLOWEEN POACHER.

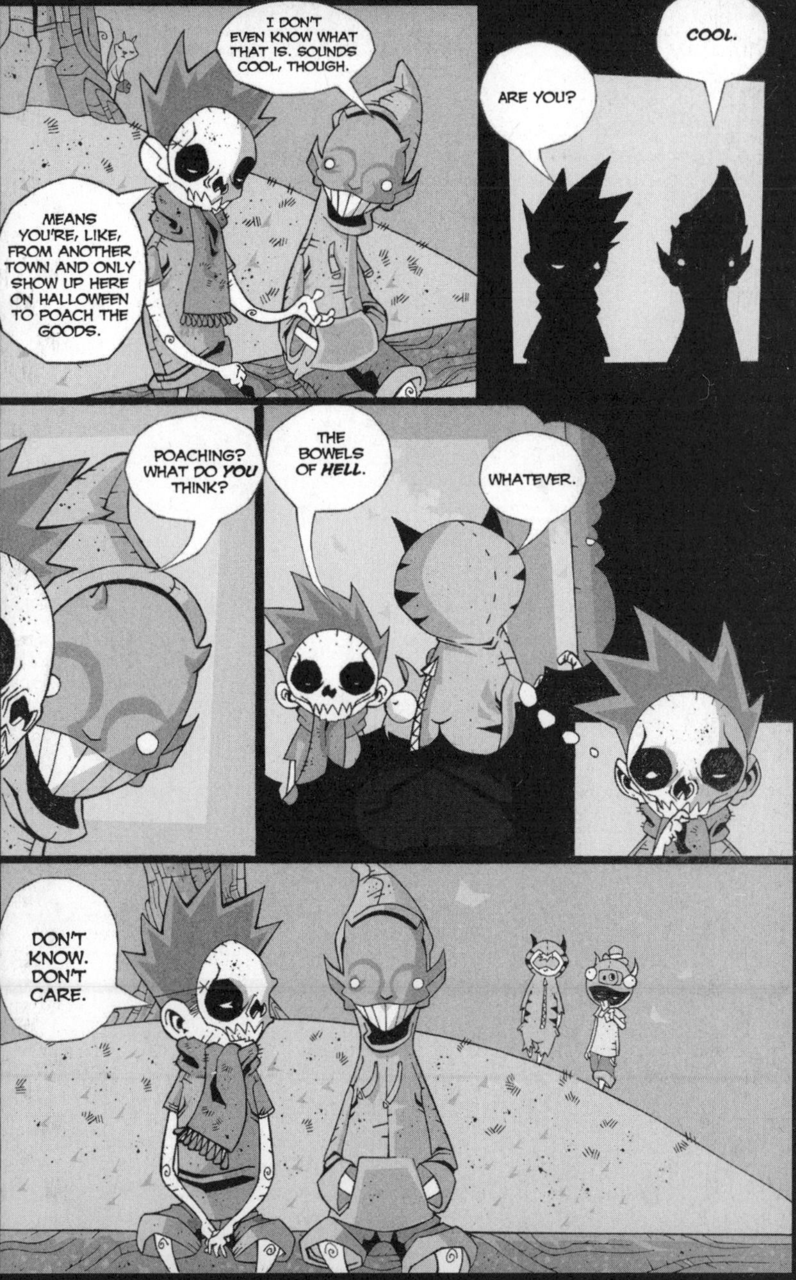
I DON'T EVEN KNOW WHAT THAT IS. SOUNDS COOL, THOUGH.
MEANS YOU'RE, LIKE, FROM ANOTHER TOWN AND ONLY SHOW UP HERE ON HALLOWEEN TO POACH THE GOODS.
ARE YOU?
COOL.
POACHING? WHAT DO *YOU* THINK?
THE BOWELS OF ***HELL***.
WHATEVER.
DON'T KNOW. DON'T CARE.

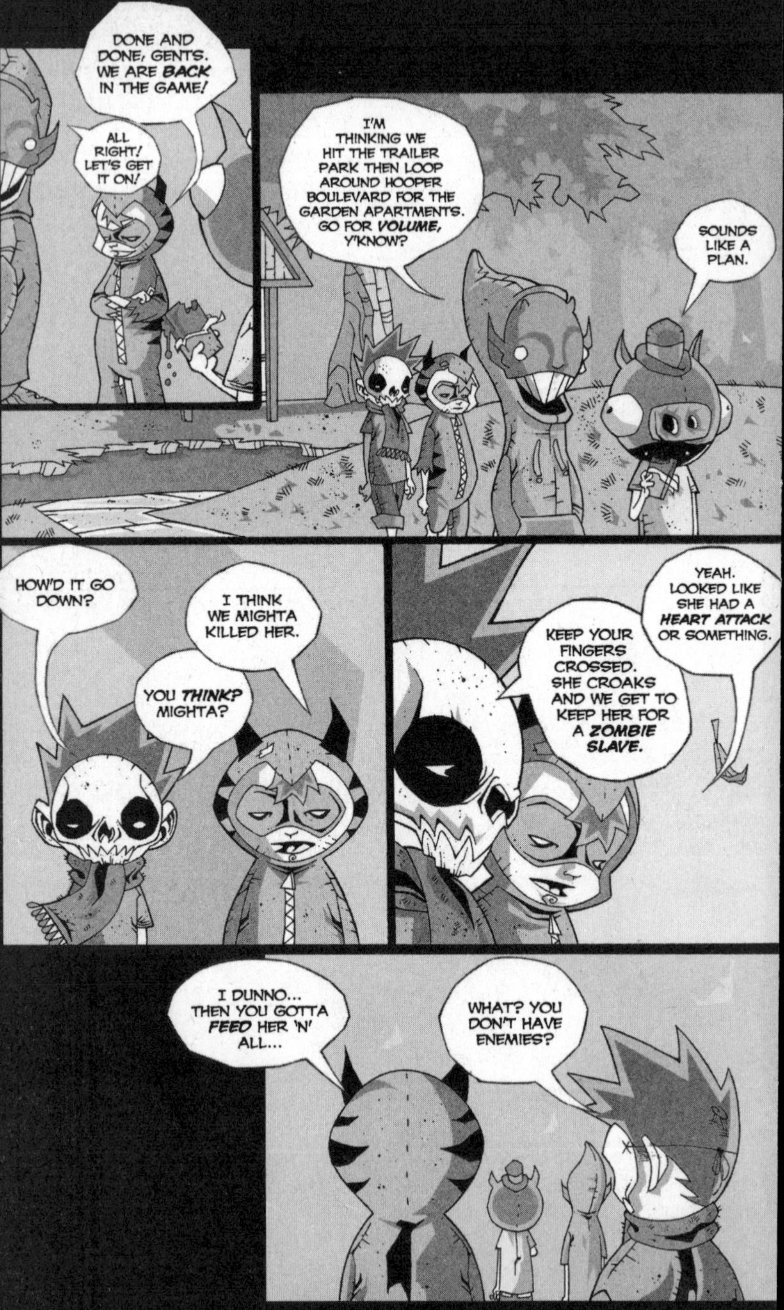
DONE AND DONE, GENTS. WE ARE **BACK** IN THE GAME!
ALL RIGHT! LET'S GET IT ON!
I'M THINKING WE HIT THE TRAILER PARK THEN LOOP AROUND HOOPER BOULEVARD FOR THE GARDEN APARTMENTS. GO FOR **VOLUME,** Y'KNOW?
SOUNDS LIKE A PLAN.
HOW'D IT GO DOWN?
I THINK WE MIGHTA KILLED HER.
YOU **THINK?** MIGHTA?
YEAH. LOOKED LIKE SHE HAD A **HEART ATTACK** OR SOMETHING.
KEEP YOUR FINGERS CROSSED. SHE CROAKS AND WE GET TO KEEP HER FOR A **ZOMBIE SLAVE.**
I DUNNO... THEN YOU GOTTA **FEED** HER 'N' ALL...
WHAT? YOU DON'T HAVE ENEMIES?

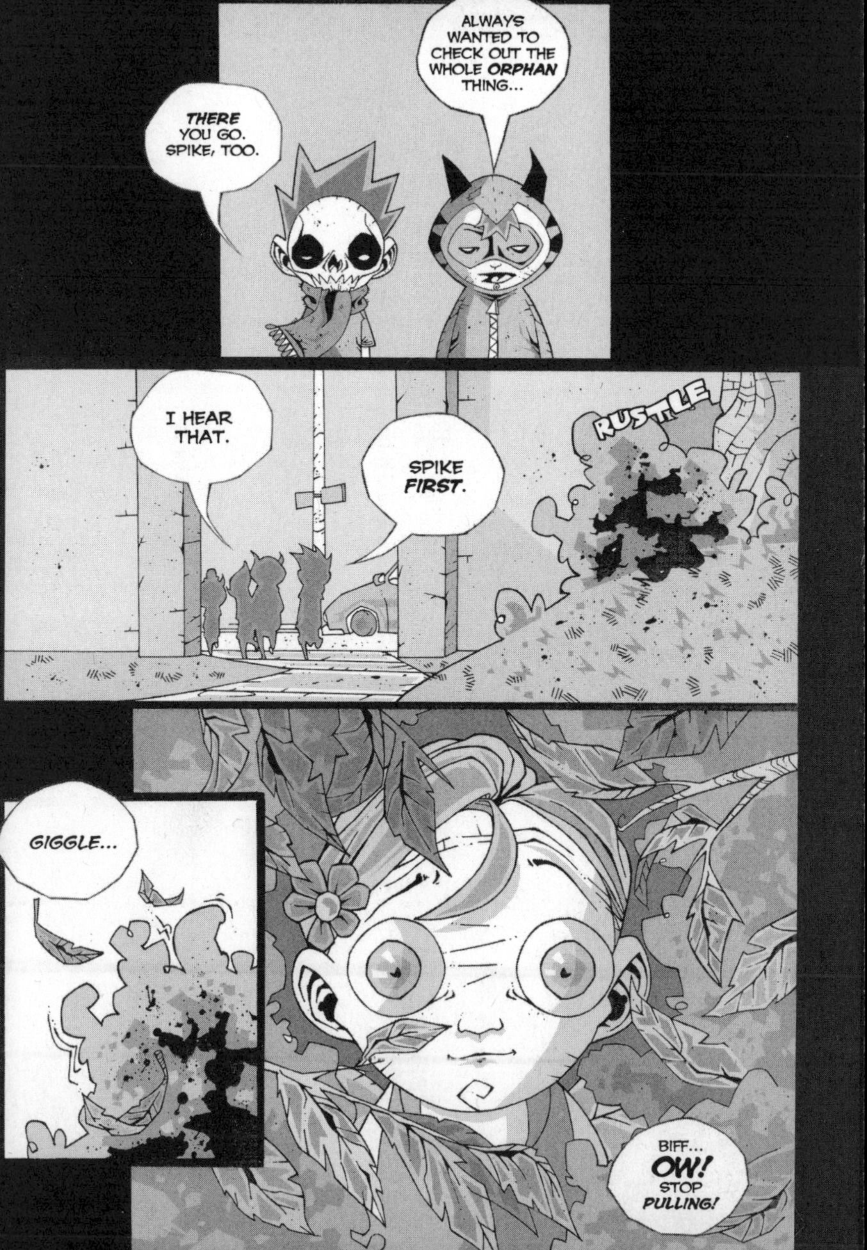
ALWAYS WANTED TO CHECK OUT THE WHOLE ORPHAN THING...
THERE YOU GO. SPIKE, TOO.
RUSTLE
SPIKE FIRST.
I HEAR THAT.
BIFF... OW! STOP PULLING!
GIGGLE...

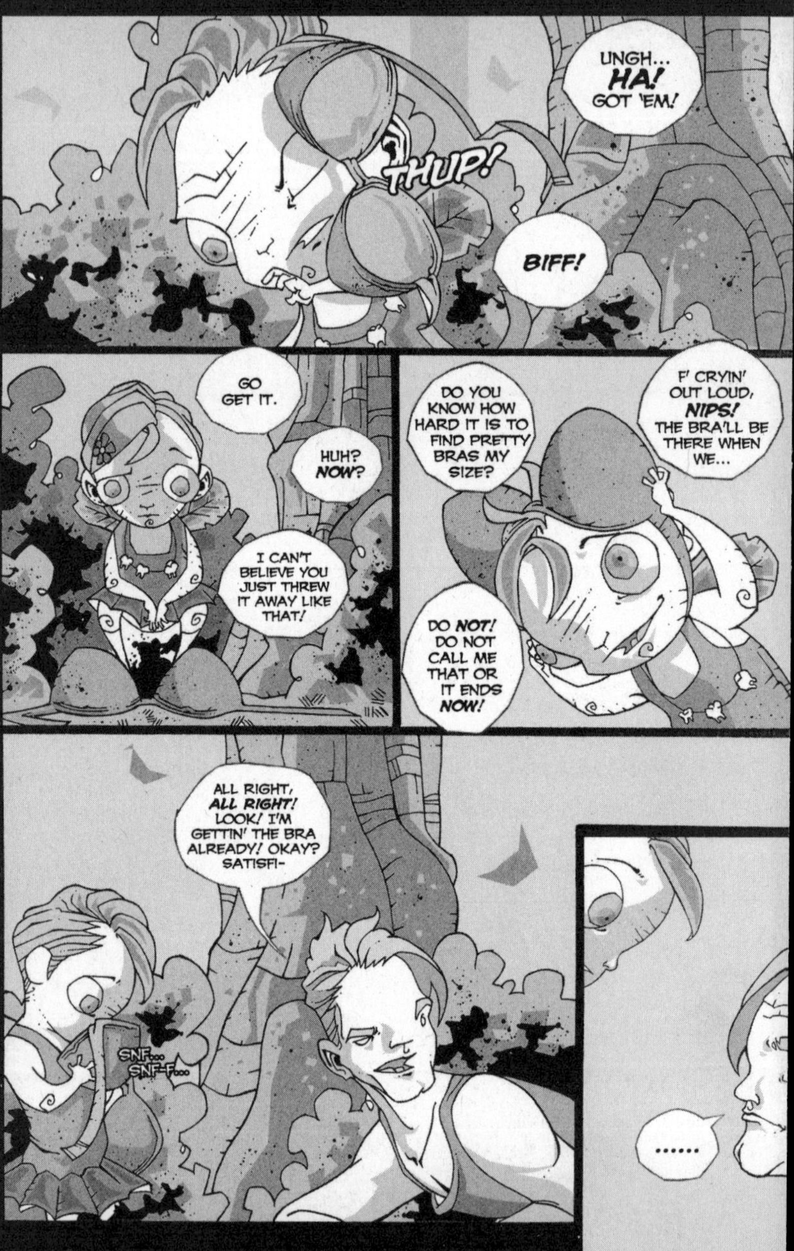
UNGH... **HA!** GOT 'EM!
THUP!
BIFF!
GO GET IT.
HUH? **NOW**?
I CAN'T BELIEVE YOU JUST THREW IT AWAY LIKE THAT!
DO YOU KNOW HOW HARD IT IS TO FIND PRETTY BRAS MY SIZE?
F' CRYIN' OUT LOUD, **NIPS!** THE BRA'LL BE THERE WHEN WE...
DO **NOT!** DO NOT CALL ME THAT OR IT ENDS **NOW!**
ALL RIGHT, **ALL RIGHT!** LOOK! I'M GETTIN' THE BRA ALREADY! OKAY? SATISFI-
SNF... SNF-F...
......

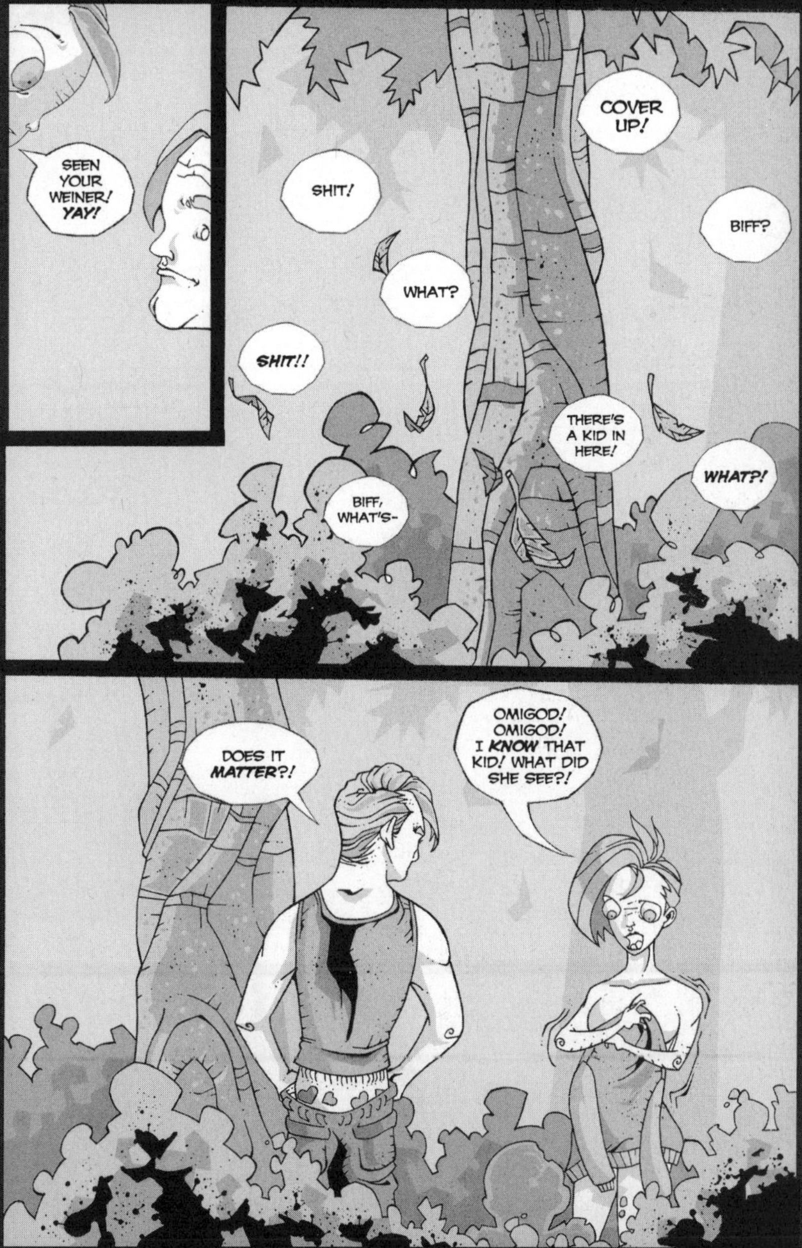
SEEN YOUR WEINER! YAY!
COVER UP!
SHIT!
BIFF?
WHAT?
SHIT!!
THERE'S A KID IN HERE!
WHAT?!
BIFF, WHAT'S-
DOES IT MATTER?!
OMIGOD! OMIGOD! I KNOW THAT KID! WHAT DID SHE SEE?!

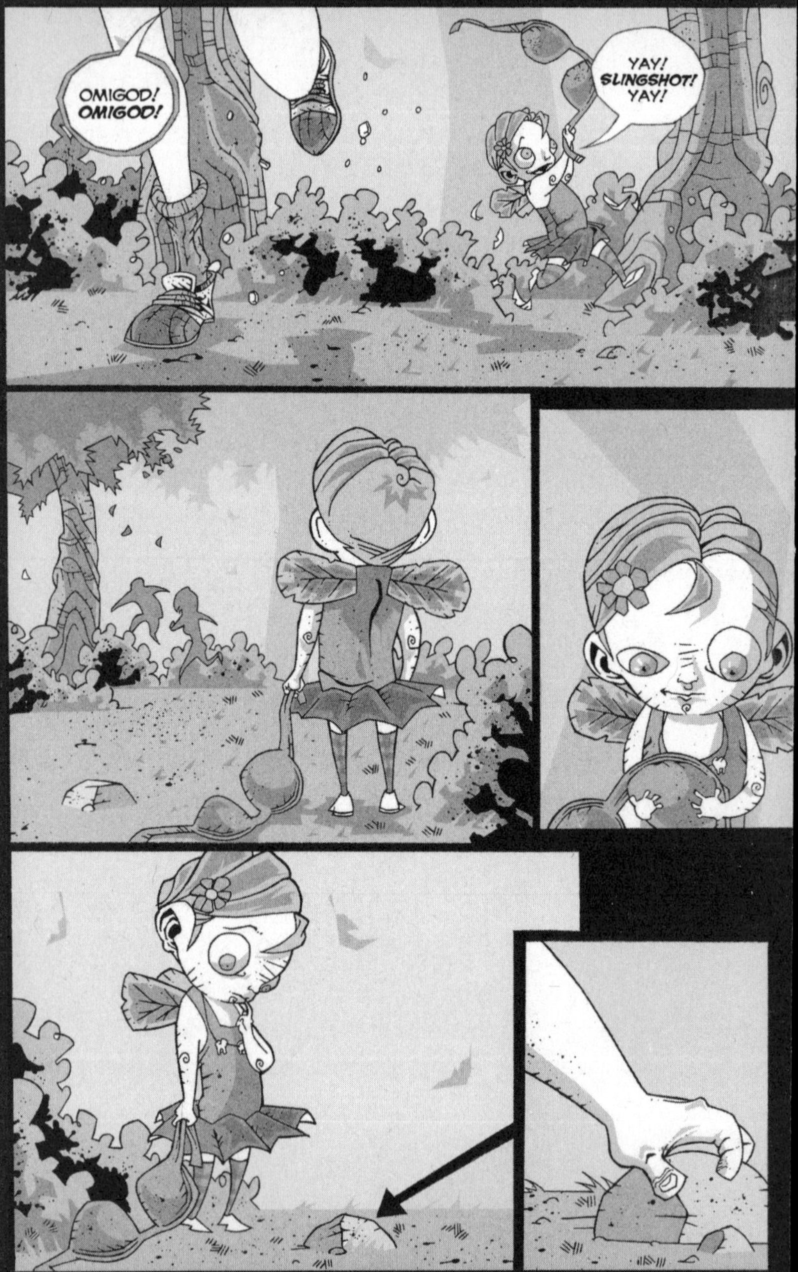
OMIGOD! OMIGOD!
YAY! SLINGSHOT! YAY!

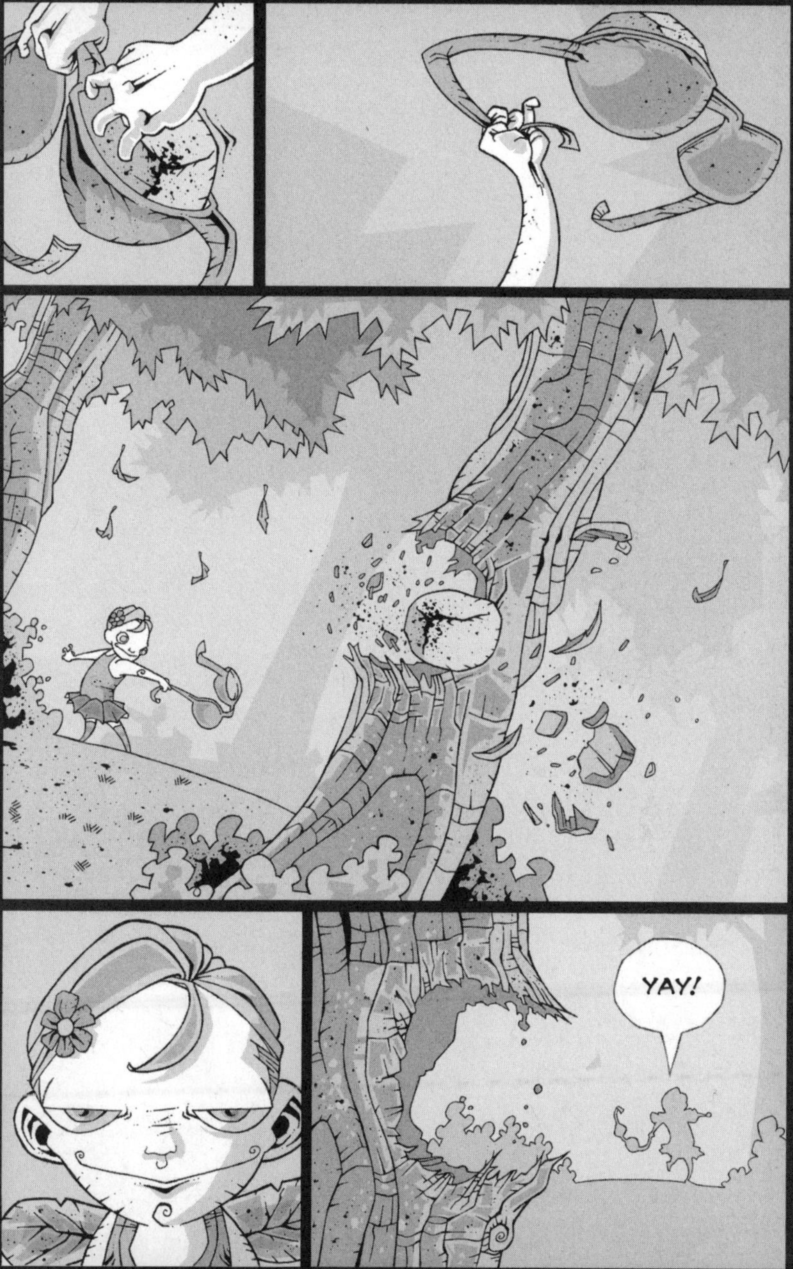
YAY!

i Luv Halloween™

Chapter three:
Bubbles and Squeak

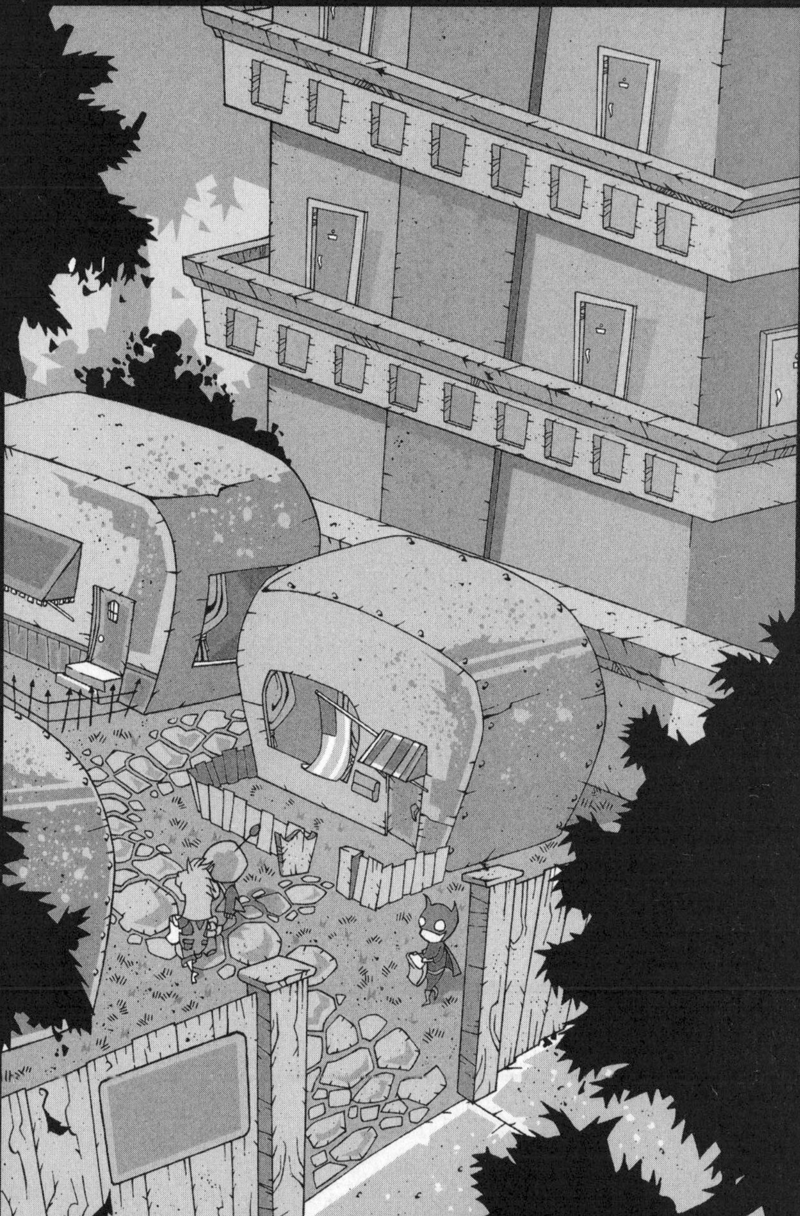

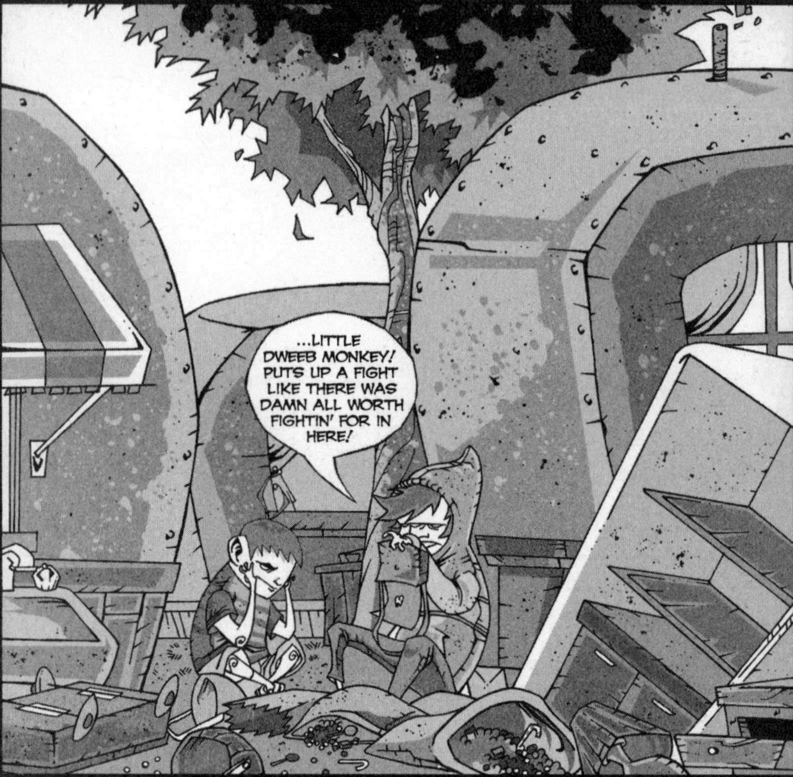
...LITTLE DWEEB MONKEY! PUTS UP A FIGHT LIKE THERE WAS DAMN ALL WORTH FIGHTIN' FOR IN HERE!

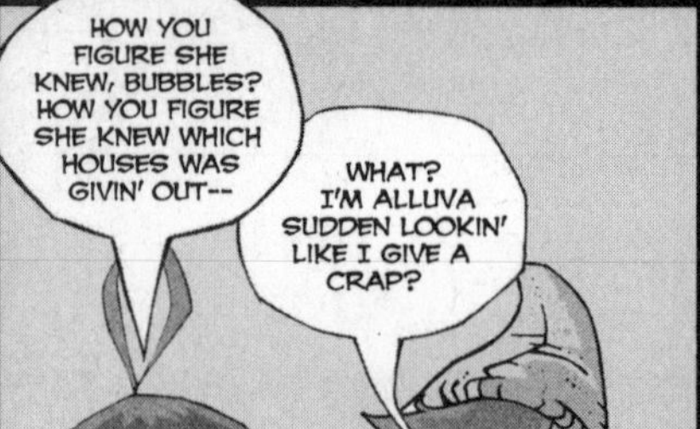
HOW YOU FIGURE SHE KNEW, BUBBLES? HOW YOU FIGURE SHE KNEW WHICH HOUSES WAS GIVIN' OUT--
WHAT? I'M ALLUVA SUDDEN LOOKIN' LIKE I GIVE A CRAP?

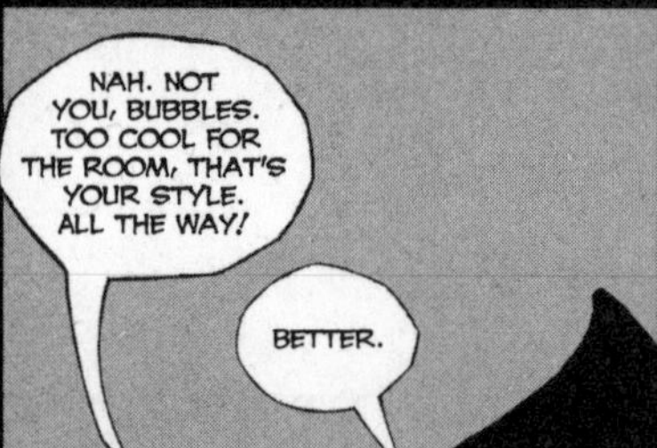
NAH. NOT YOU, BUBBLES. TOO COOL FOR THE ROOM, THAT'S YOUR STYLE. ALL THE WAY!
BETTER.

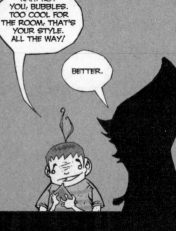

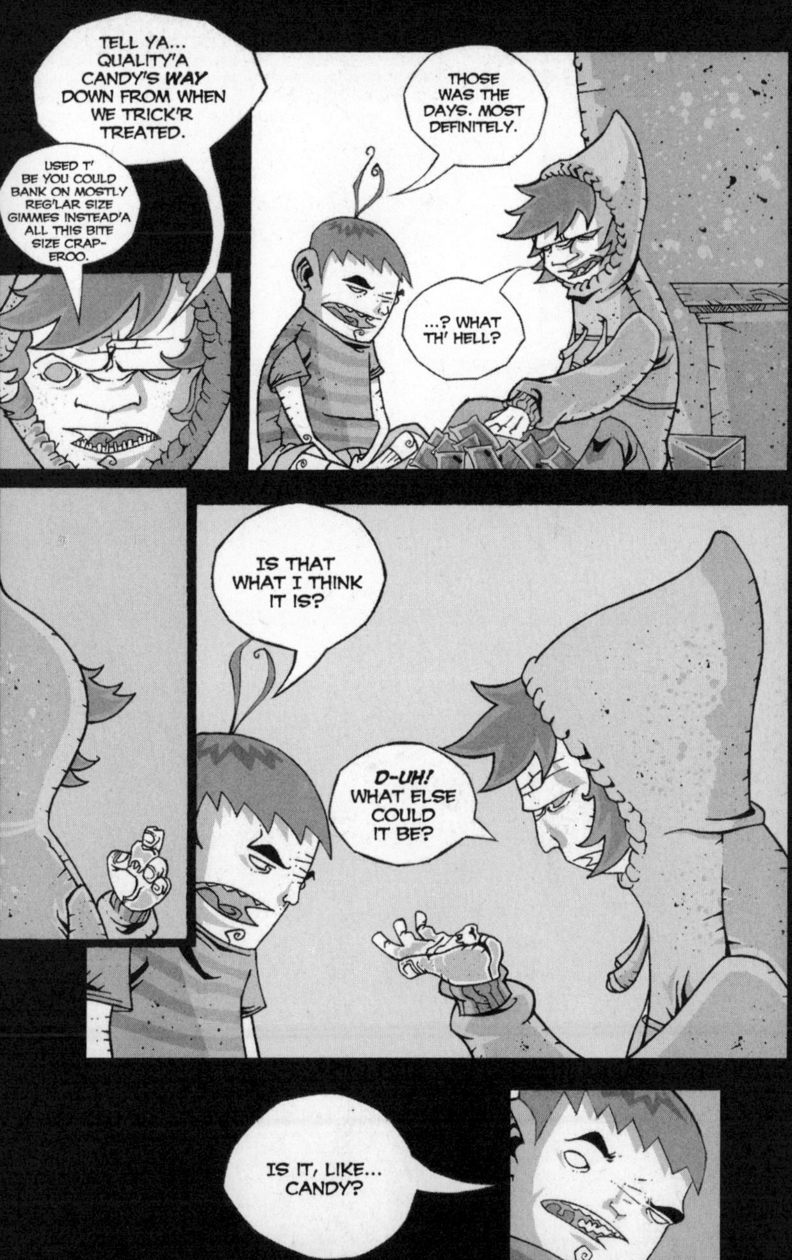
TELL YA... QUALITY'A CANDY'S **WAY** DOWN FROM WHEN WE TRICK'R TREATED.
USED T' BE YOU COULD BANK ON MOSTLY REG'LAR SIZE GIMMES INSTEAD'A ALL THIS BITE SIZE CRAP-EROO.
THOSE WAS THE DAYS. MOST DEFINITELY.
...? WHAT TH' HELL?
IS THAT WHAT I THINK IT IS?
D-UH! WHAT ELSE COULD IT BE?
IS IT, LIKE... CANDY?

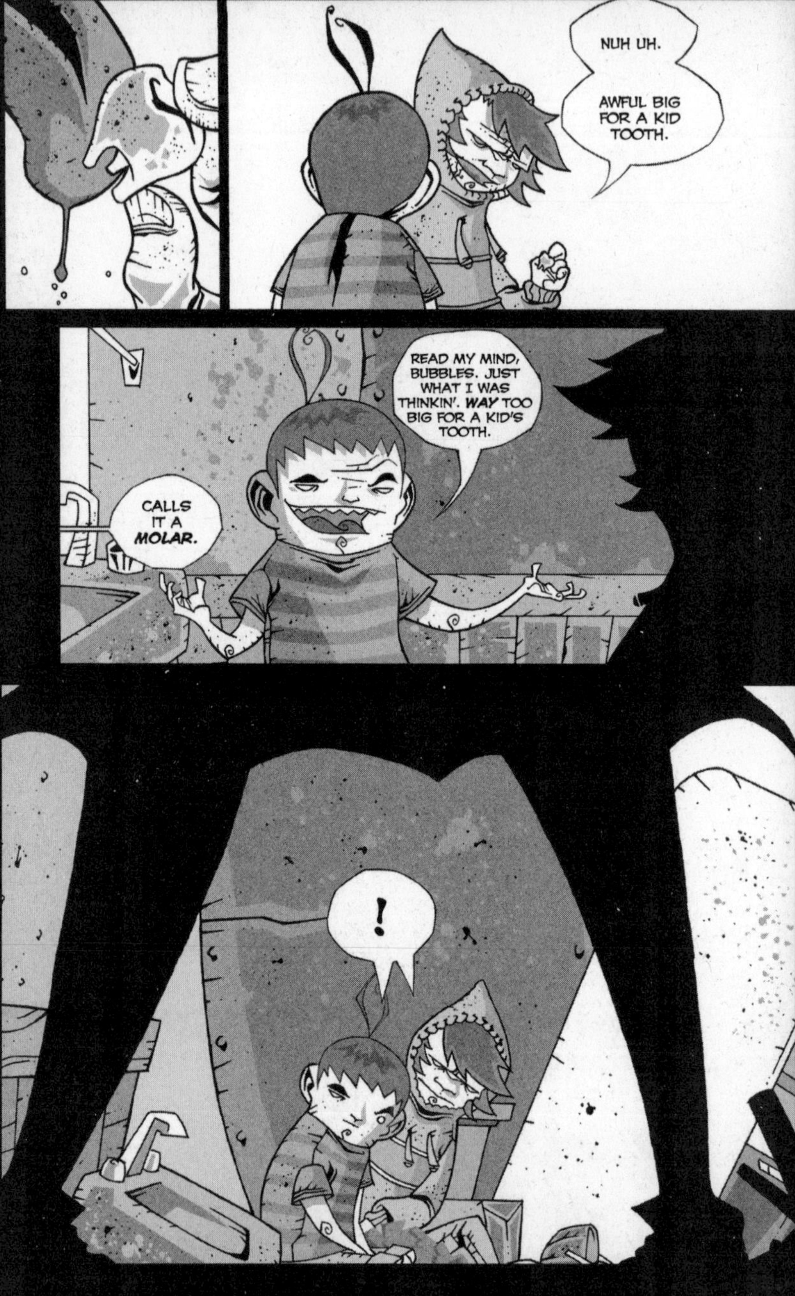
NUH UH.
AWFUL BIG FOR A KID TOOTH.
READ MY MIND, BUBBLES. JUST WHAT I WAS THINKIN'. WAY TOO BIG FOR A KID'S TOOTH.
CALLS IT A MOLAR.
!

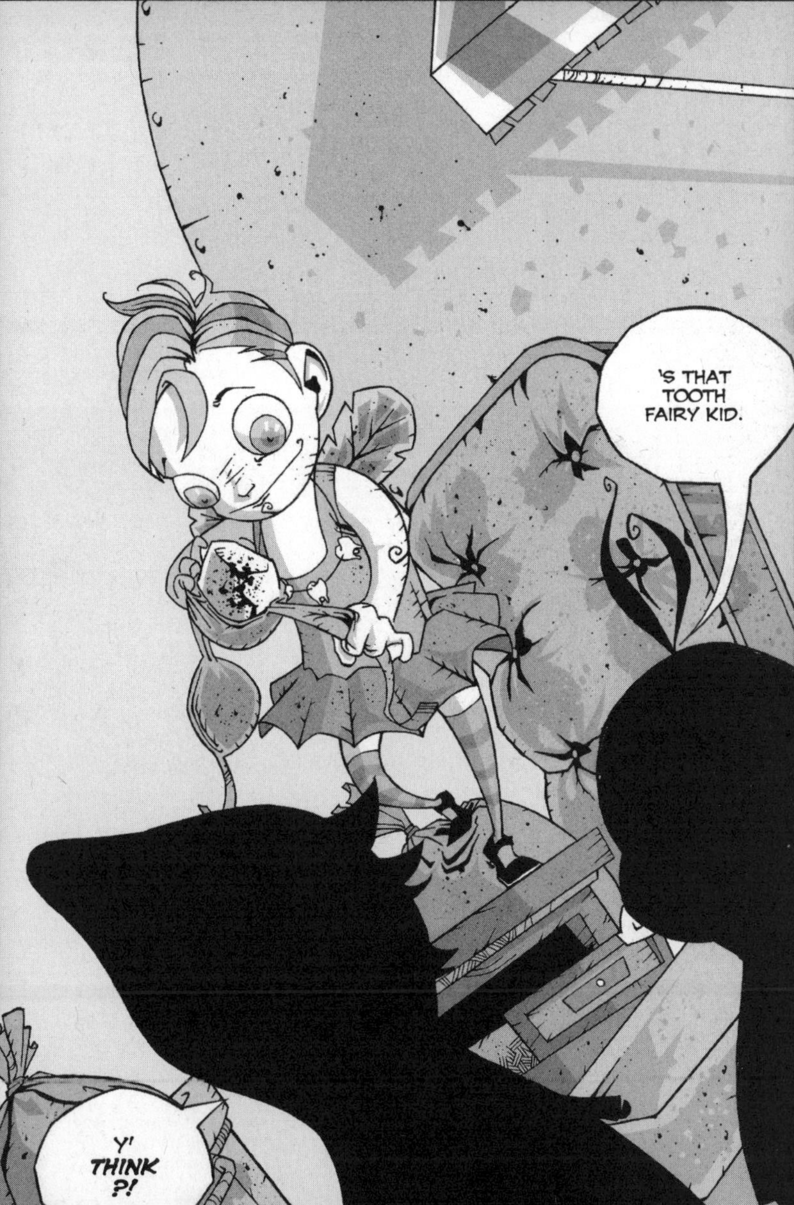
'S THAT TOOTH FAIRY KID.
Y' THINK ?!

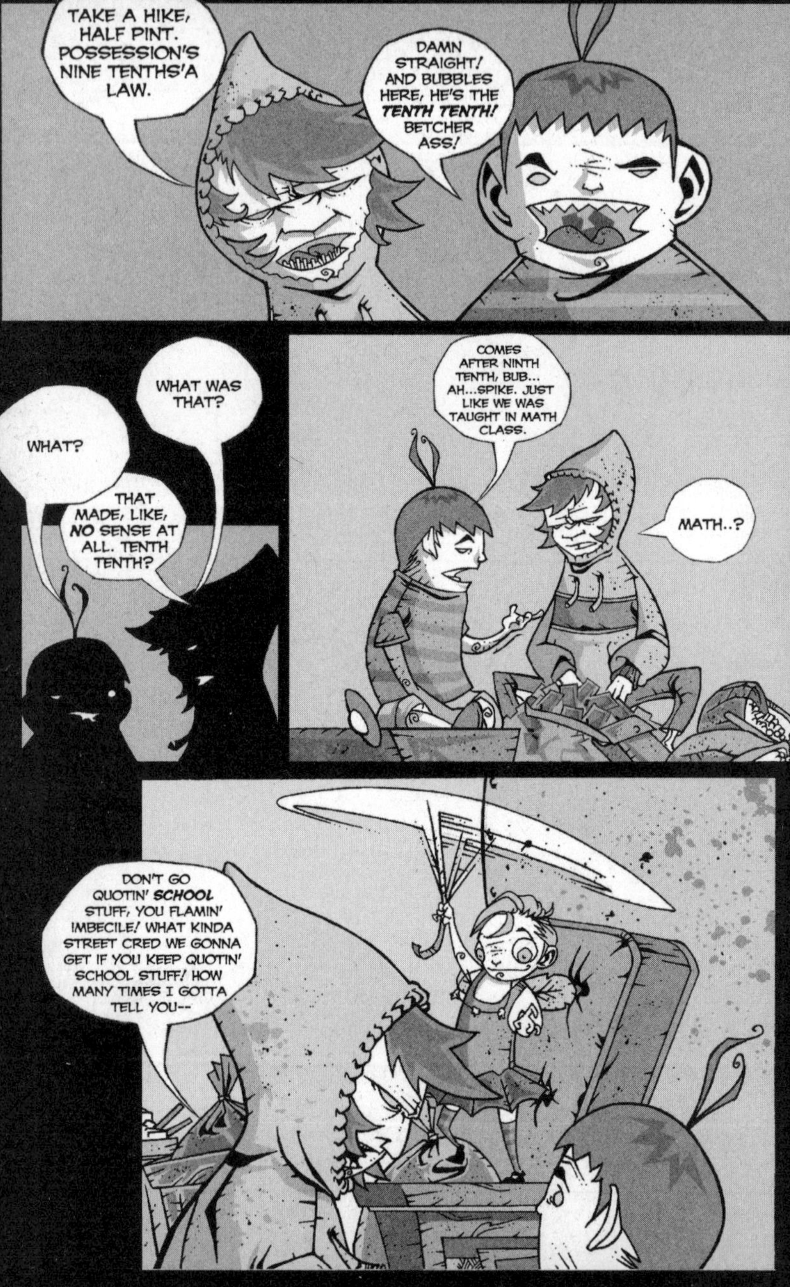
TAKE A HIKE, HALF PINT. POSSESSION'S NINE TENTHS'A LAW.
DAMN STRAIGHT! AND BUBBLES HERE, HE'S THE *TENTH TENTH!* BETCHER ASS!
WHAT WAS THAT?
WHAT?
THAT MADE, LIKE, **NO** SENSE AT ALL. TENTH TENTH?
COMES AFTER NINTH TENTH, BUB... AH...SPIKE. JUST LIKE WE WAS TAUGHT IN MATH CLASS.
MATH..?
DON'T GO QUOTIN' **SCHOOL** STUFF, YOU FLAMIN' IMBECILE! WHAT KINDA STREET CRED WE GONNA GET IF YOU KEEP QUOTIN' SCHOOL STUFF! HOW MANY TIMES I GOTTA TELL YOU--

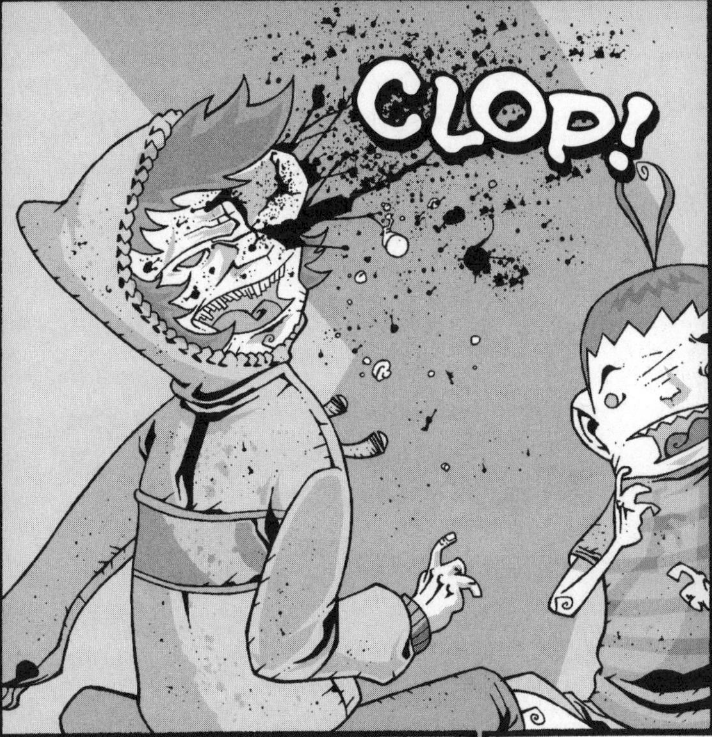
CLOP!
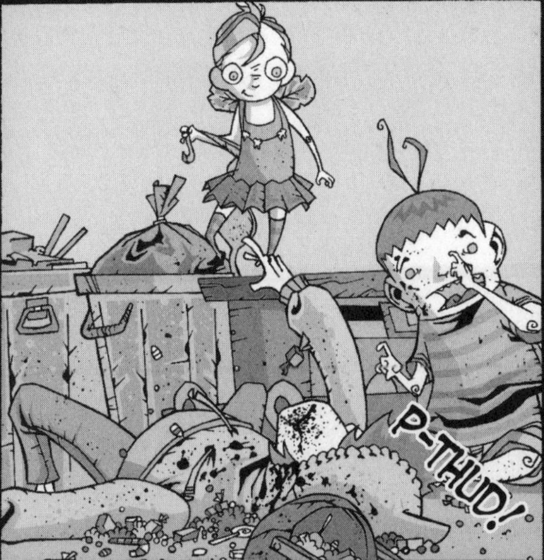
P-THUD!
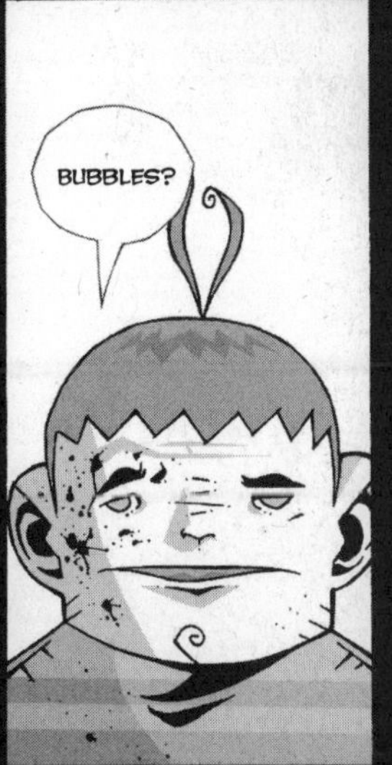
BUBBLES?

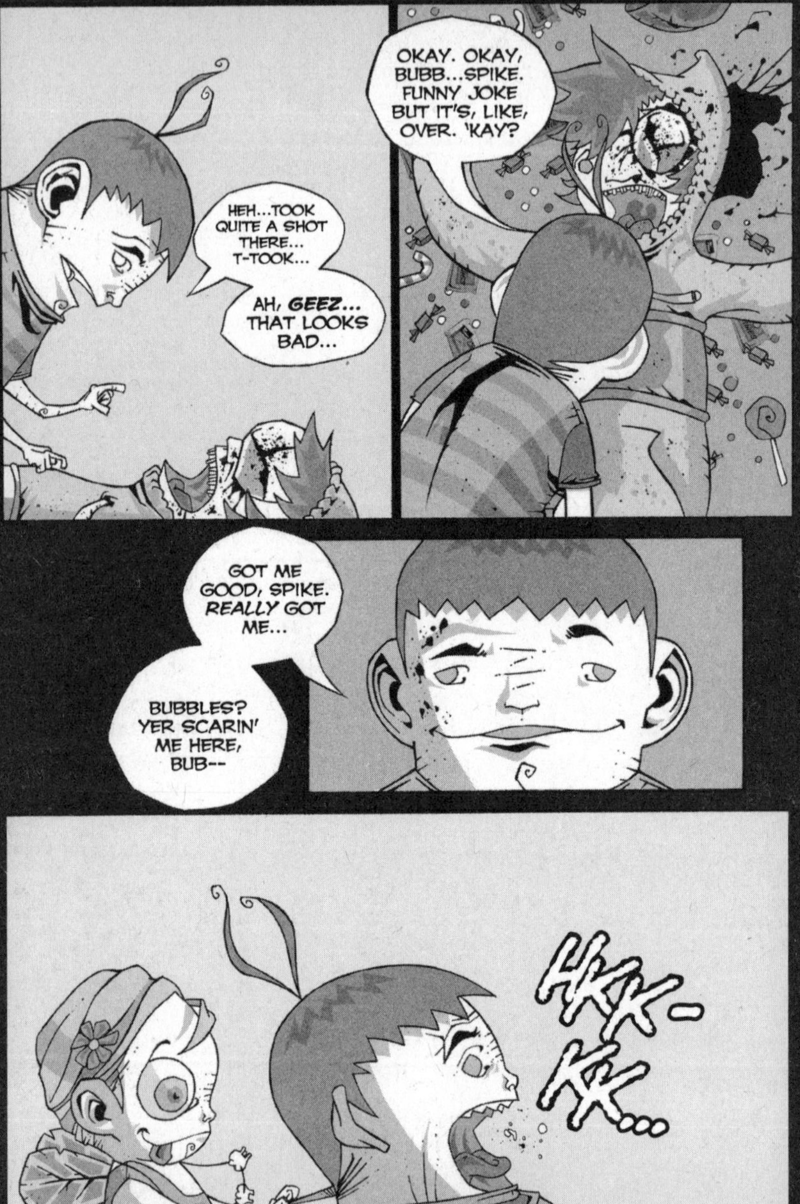
HEH...TOOK QUITE A SHOT THERE... T-TOOK...
AH, **GEEZ...** THAT LOOKS BAD...
OKAY. OKAY, BUBB...SPIKE. FUNNY JOKE BUT IT'S, LIKE, OVER. 'KAY?
GOT ME GOOD, SPIKE. *REALLY* GOT ME...
BUBBLES? YER SCARIN' ME HERE, BUB--
HKK-KK...

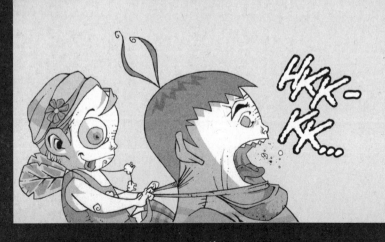

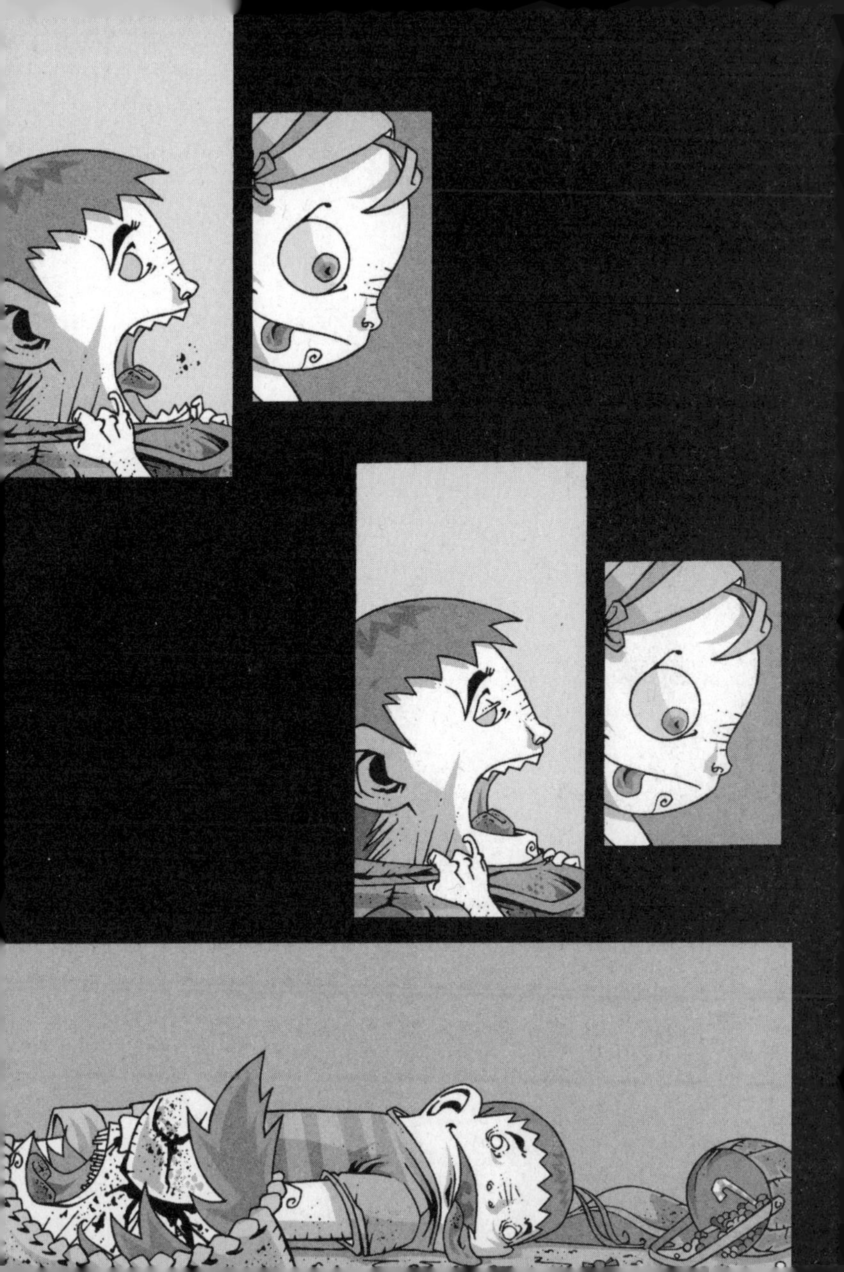

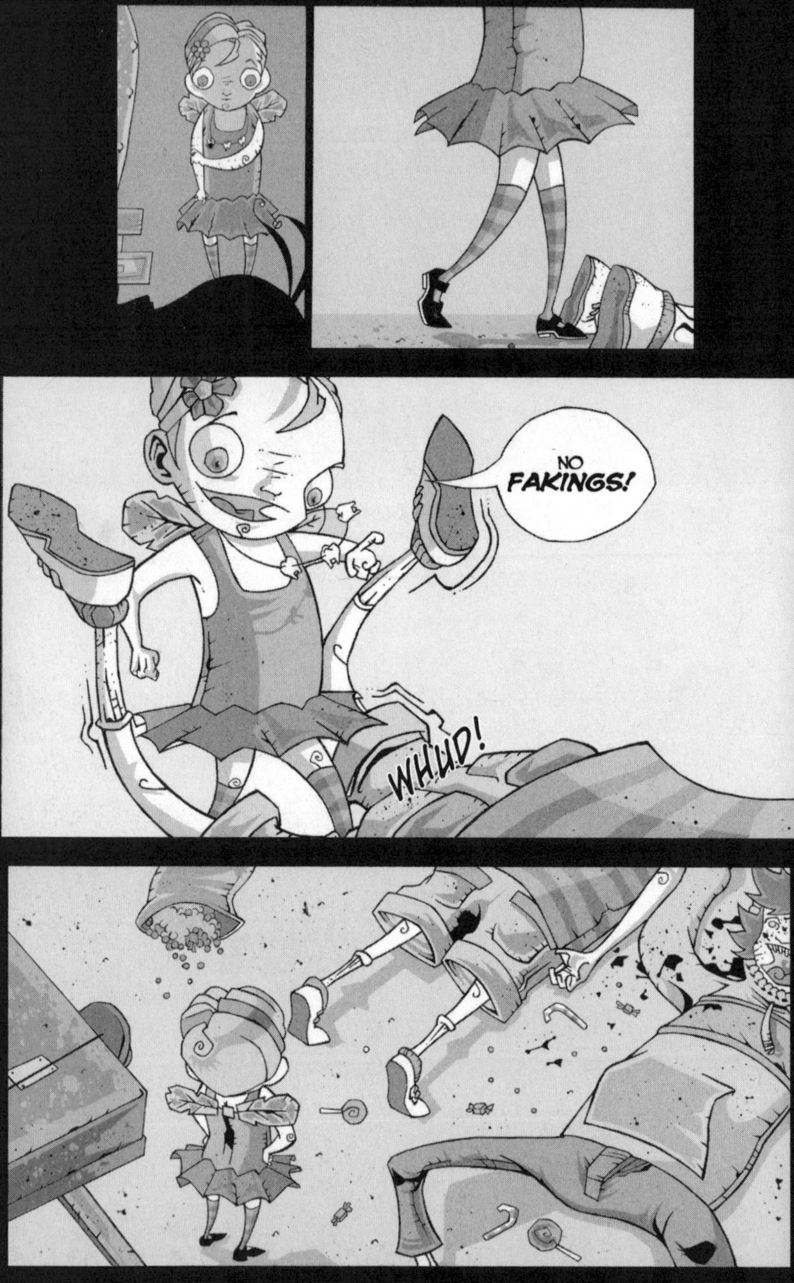
NO FAKINGS!
WHUD!

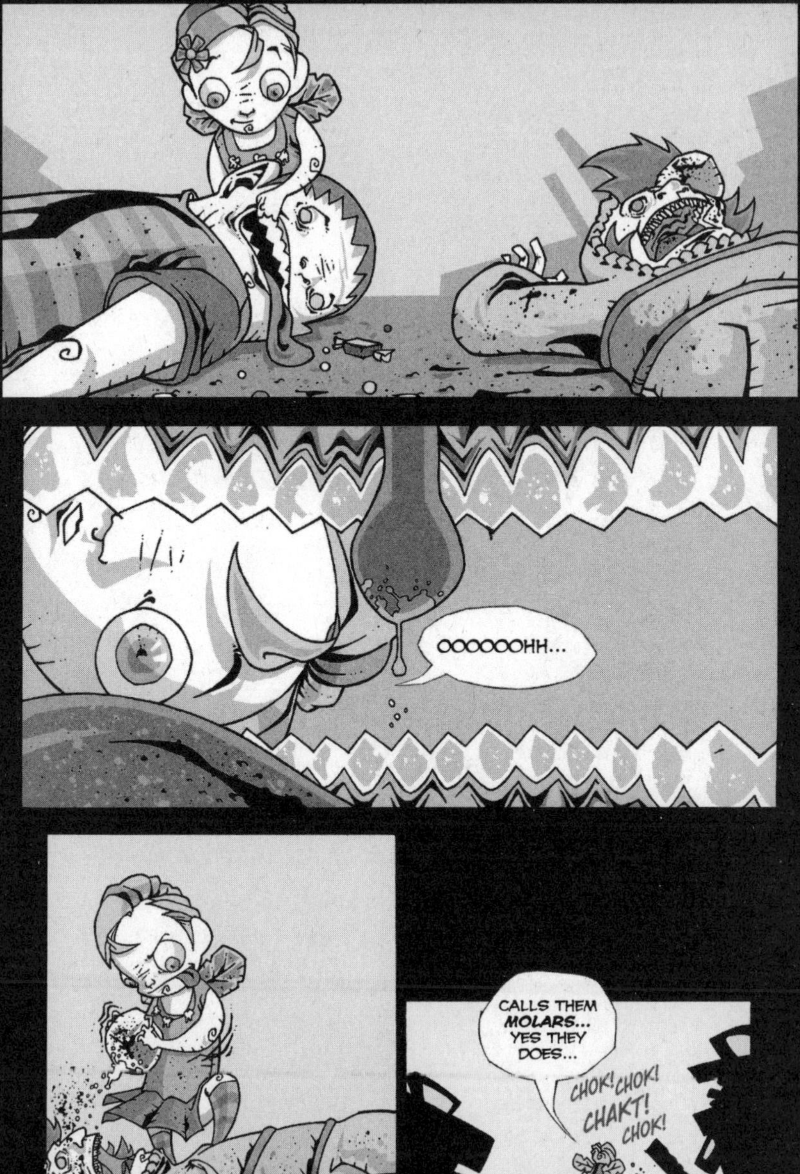
OOOOOOHH...
CALLS THEM MOLARS... YES THEY DOES...
CHOK! CHOK!
CHAKT!
CHOK!

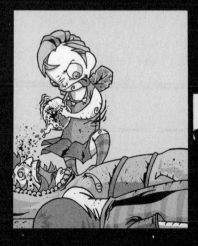

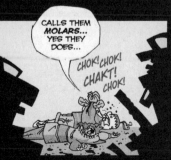

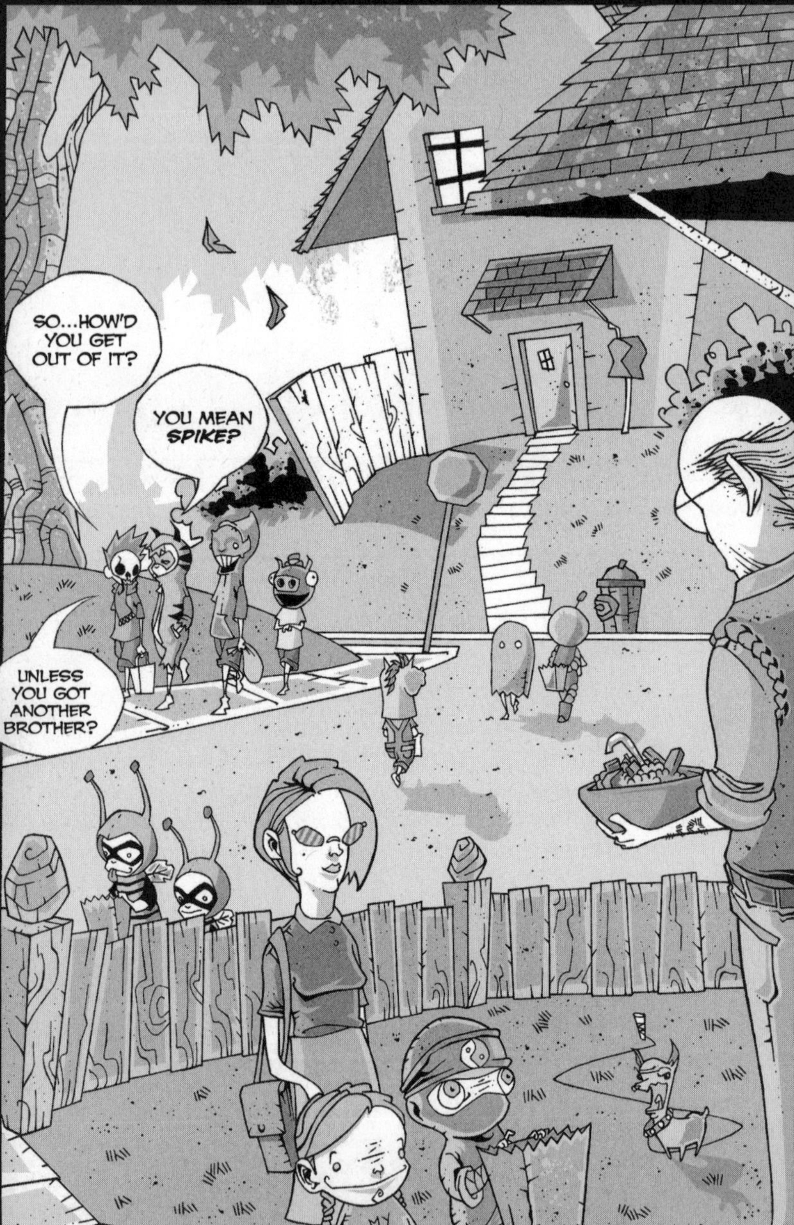
SO...HOW'D YOU GET OUT OF IT?
YOU MEAN *SPIKE?*
UNLESS YOU GOT ANOTHER BROTHER?
MY COSTUME SUX!

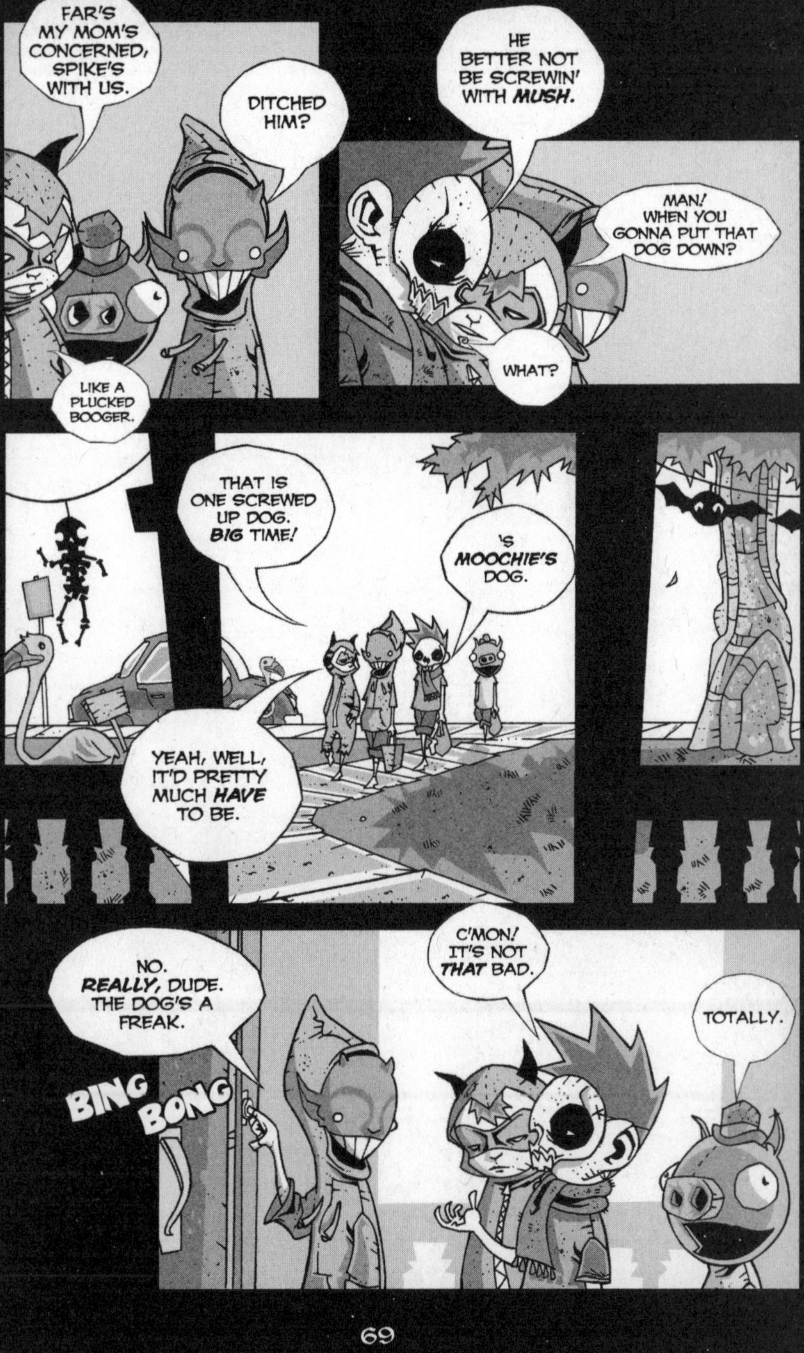
FAR'S MY MOM'S CONCERNED, SPIKE'S WITH US.
DITCHED HIM?
LIKE A PLUCKED BOOGER.
HE BETTER NOT BE SCREWIN' WITH *MUSH*.
MAN! WHEN YOU GONNA PUT THAT DOG DOWN?
WHAT?
THAT IS ONE SCREWED UP DOG. *BIG* TIME!
'S *MOOCHIE'S* DOG.
YEAH, WELL, IT'D PRETTY MUCH *HAVE* TO BE.
BING BONG
NO. *REALLY,* DUDE. THE DOG'S A FREAK.
C'MON! IT'S NOT *THAT* BAD.
TOTALLY.

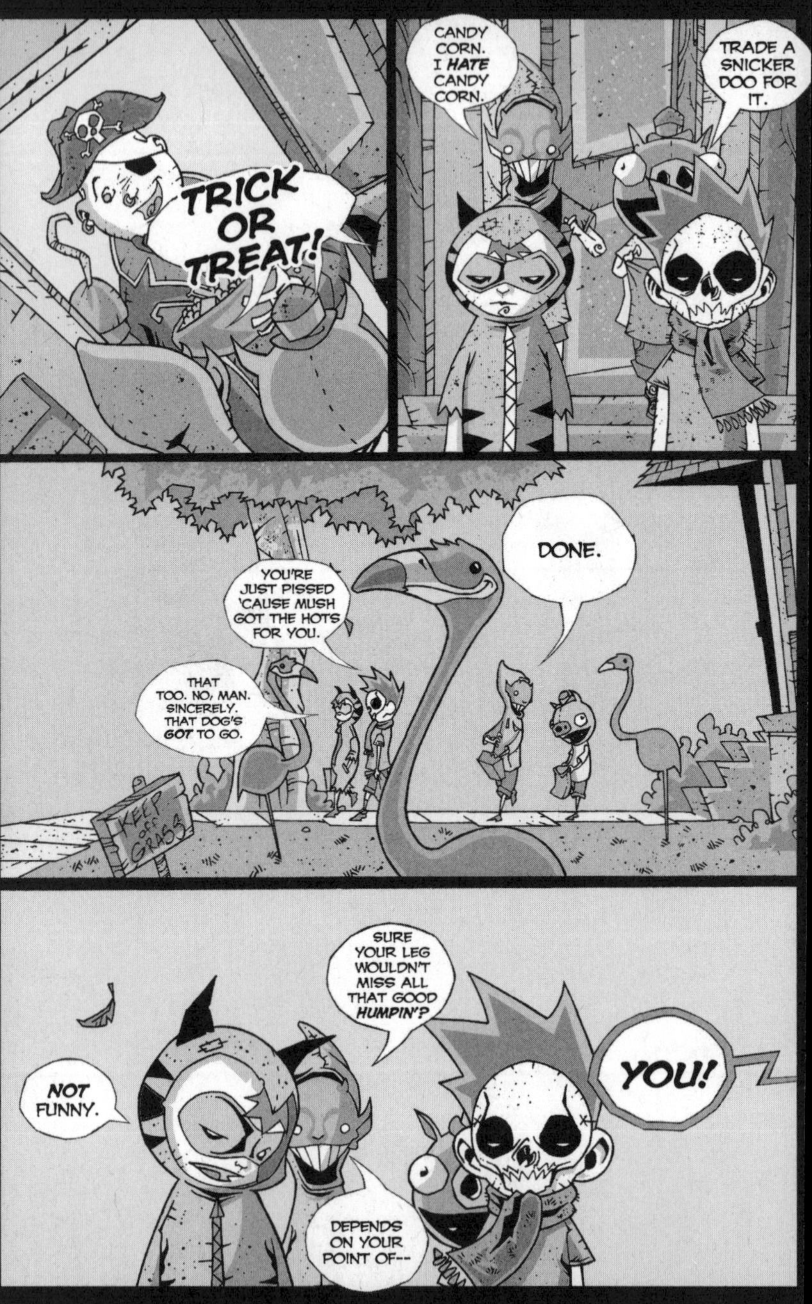
TRICK OR TREAT!
CANDY CORN. I *HATE* CANDY CORN.
TRADE A SNICKER DOO FOR IT.
DONE.
YOU'RE JUST PISSED 'CAUSE MUSH GOT THE HOT'S FOR YOU.
THAT TOO. NO, MAN. SINCERELY. THAT DOG'S *GOT* TO GO.
KEEP off GRASS
SURE YOUR LEG WOULDN'T MISS ALL THAT GOOD *HUMPIN'*?
NOT FUNNY.
DEPENDS ON YOUR POINT OF--
YOU!

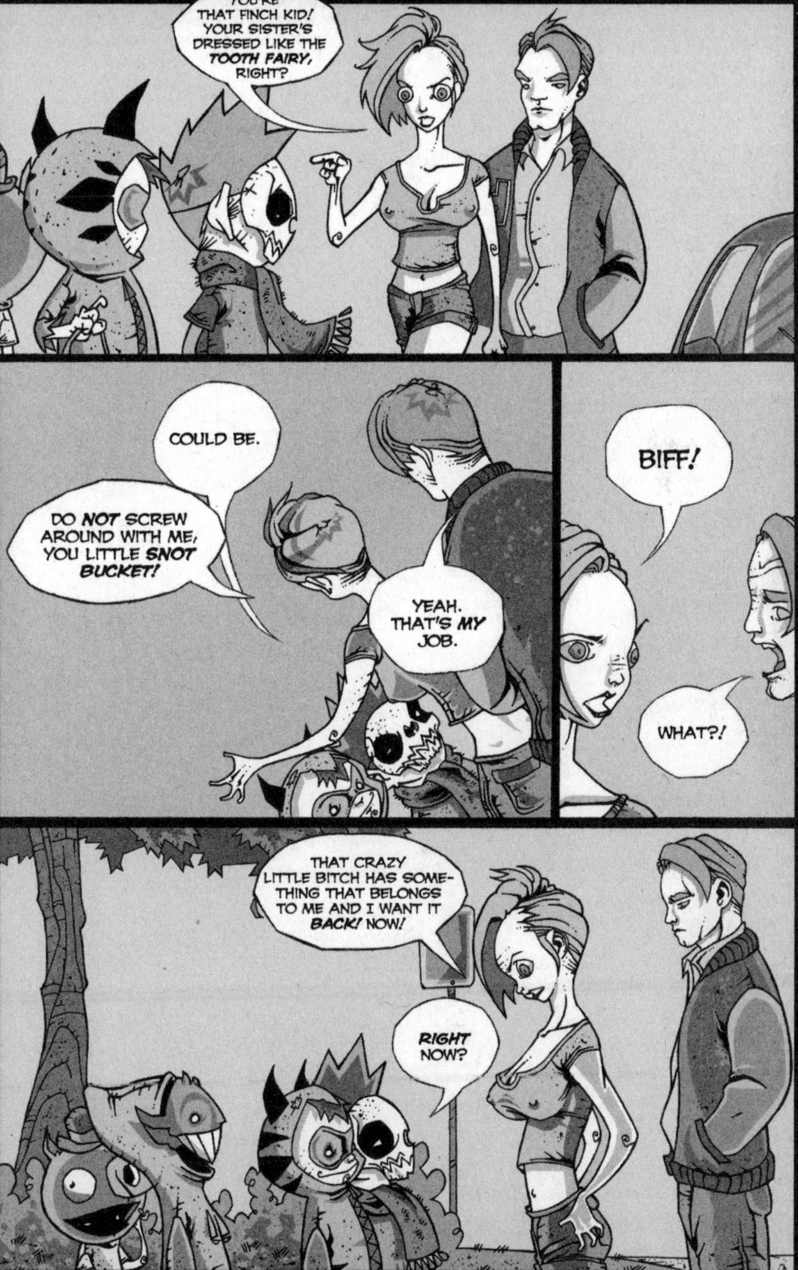
YOU'RE THAT FINCH KID! YOUR SISTER'S DRESSED LIKE THE *TOOTH FAIRY,* RIGHT?
COULD BE.
DO *NOT* SCREW AROUND WITH ME, YOU LITTLE *SNOT BUCKET!*
YEAH. THAT'S *MY* JOB.
BIFF!
WHAT?!
THAT CRAZY LITTLE BITCH HAS SOME-THING THAT BELONGS TO ME AND I WANT IT *BACK!* NOW!
RIGHT NOW?

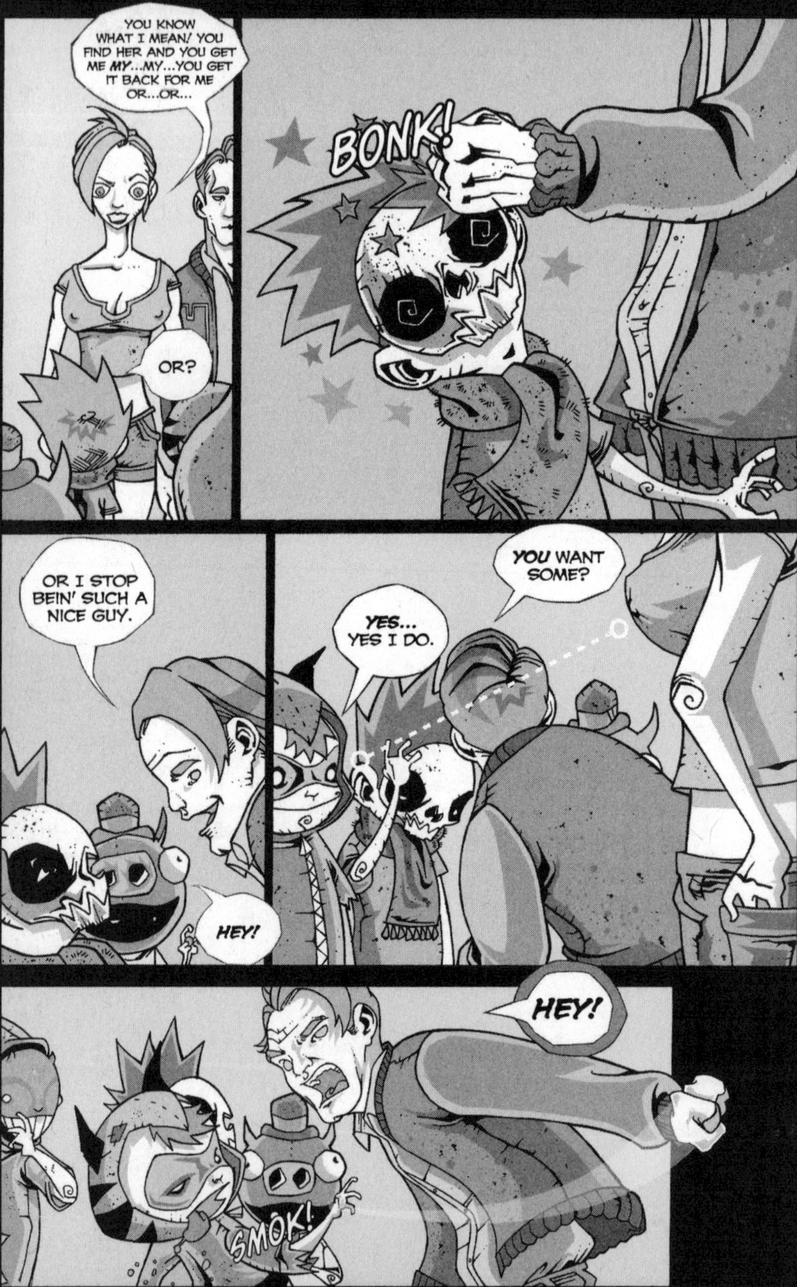
YOU KNOW WHAT I MEAN! YOU FIND HER AND YOU GET ME *MY*...MY...YOU GET IT BACK FOR ME OR...OR...
OR?
BONK!
OR I STOP BEIN' SUCH A NICE GUY.
HEY!
YOU WANT SOME?
YES... YES I DO.
HEY!
SMOK!

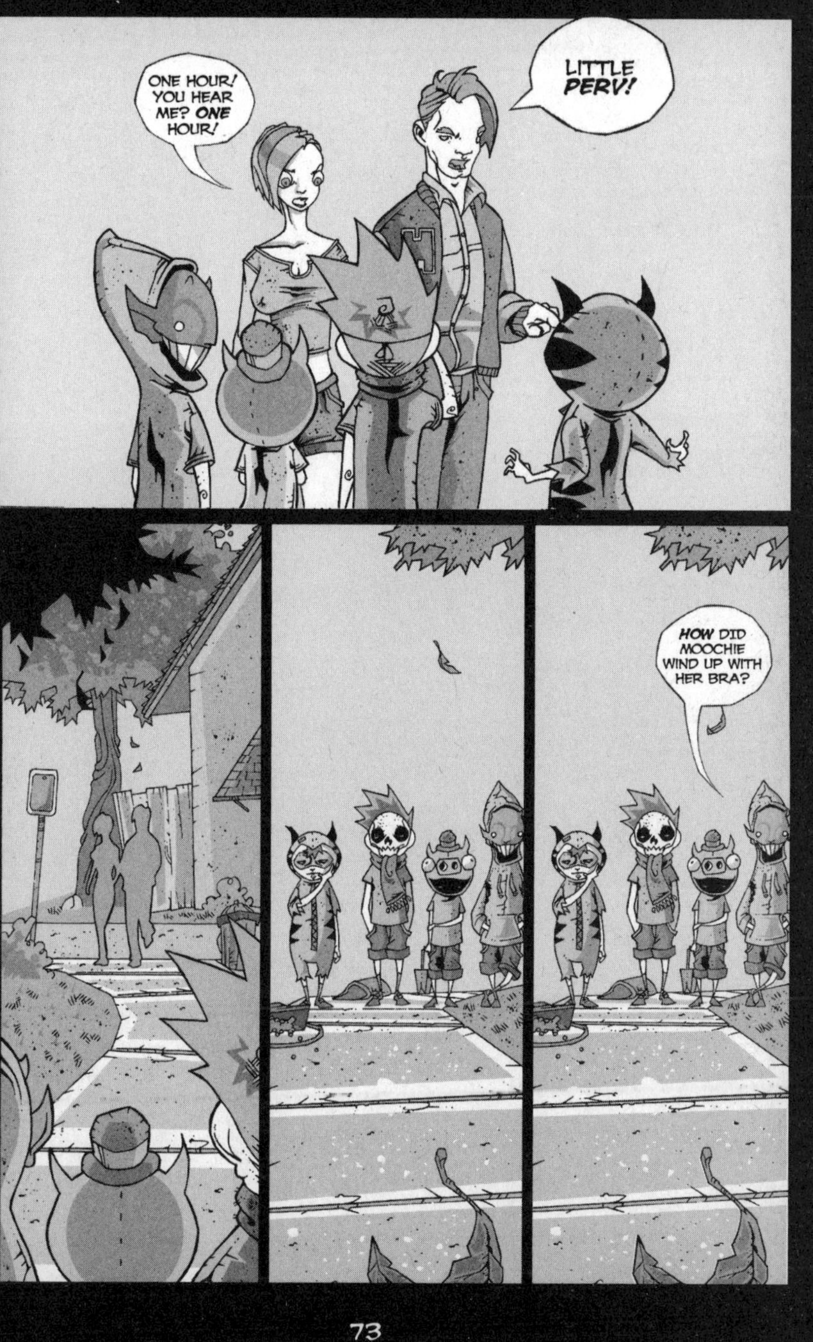
LITTLE PERV!
ONE HOUR! YOU HEAR ME? ONE HOUR!
HOW DID MOOCHIE WIND UP WITH HER BRA?

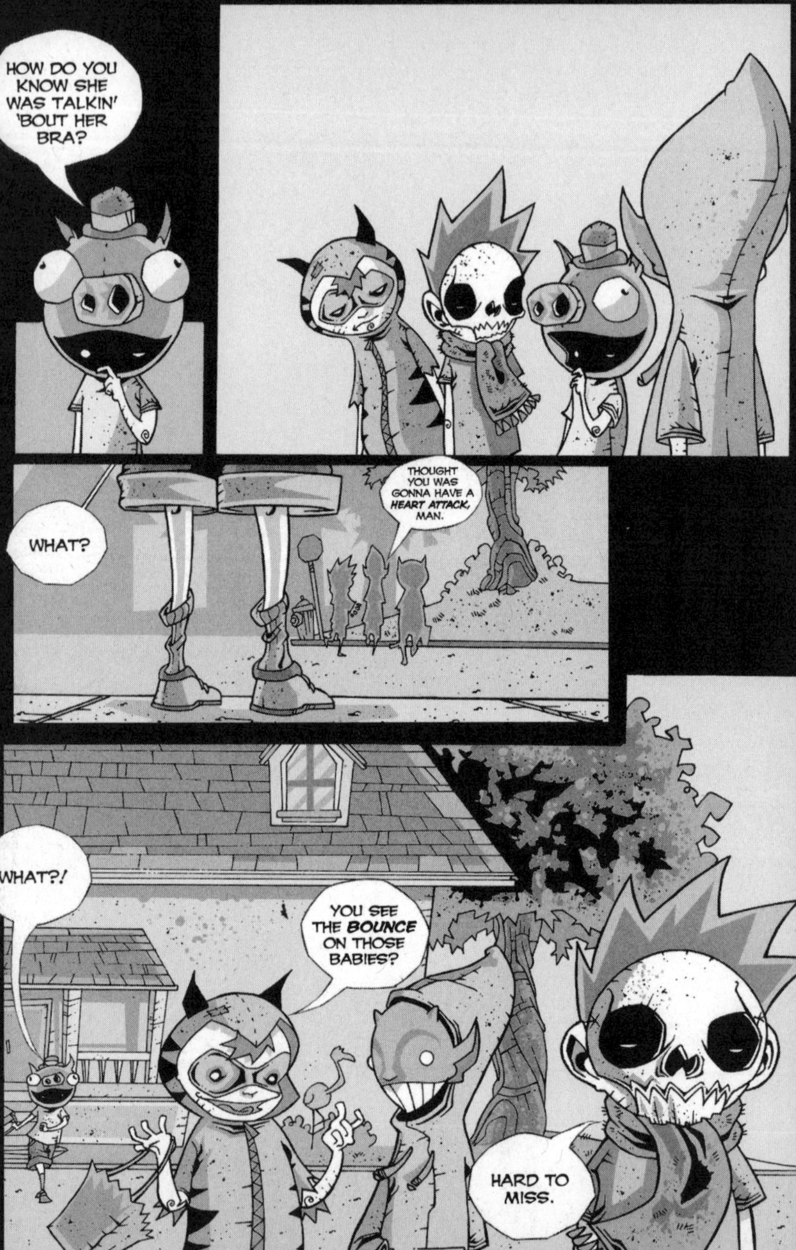
HOW DO YOU KNOW SHE WAS TALKIN' 'BOUT HER BRA?
WHAT?
THOUGHT YOU WAS GONNA HAVE A HEART ATTACK, MAN.
WHAT?!
YOU SEE THE BOUNCE ON THOSE BABIES?
HARD TO MISS.

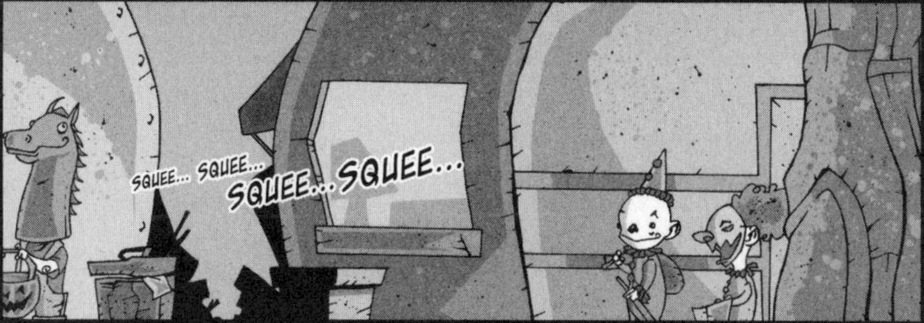
SQUEE... SQUEE...
SQUEE... SQUEE...
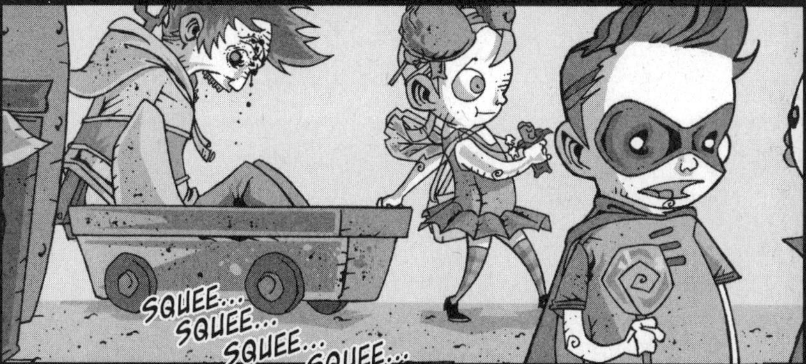
SQUEE...
SQUEE...
SQUEE...
SQUEE...
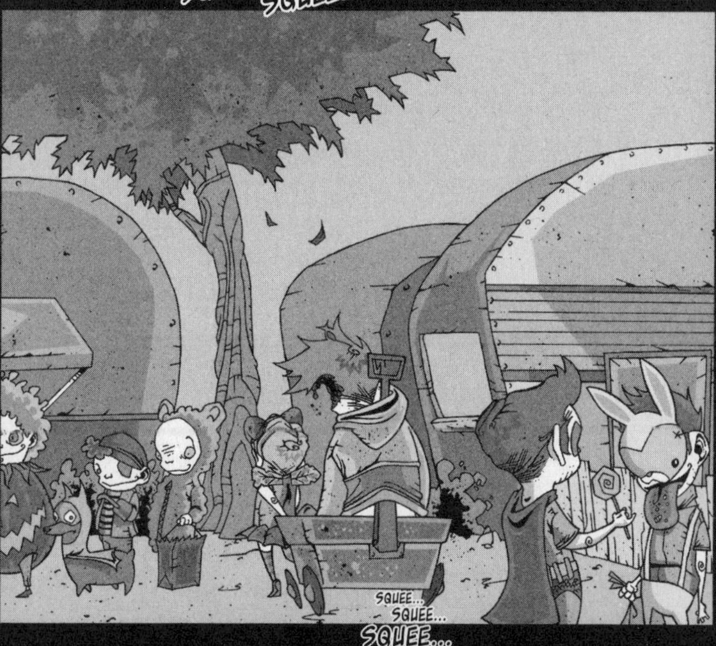
SQUEE...
SQUEE...
SQUEE...
SQUEE...

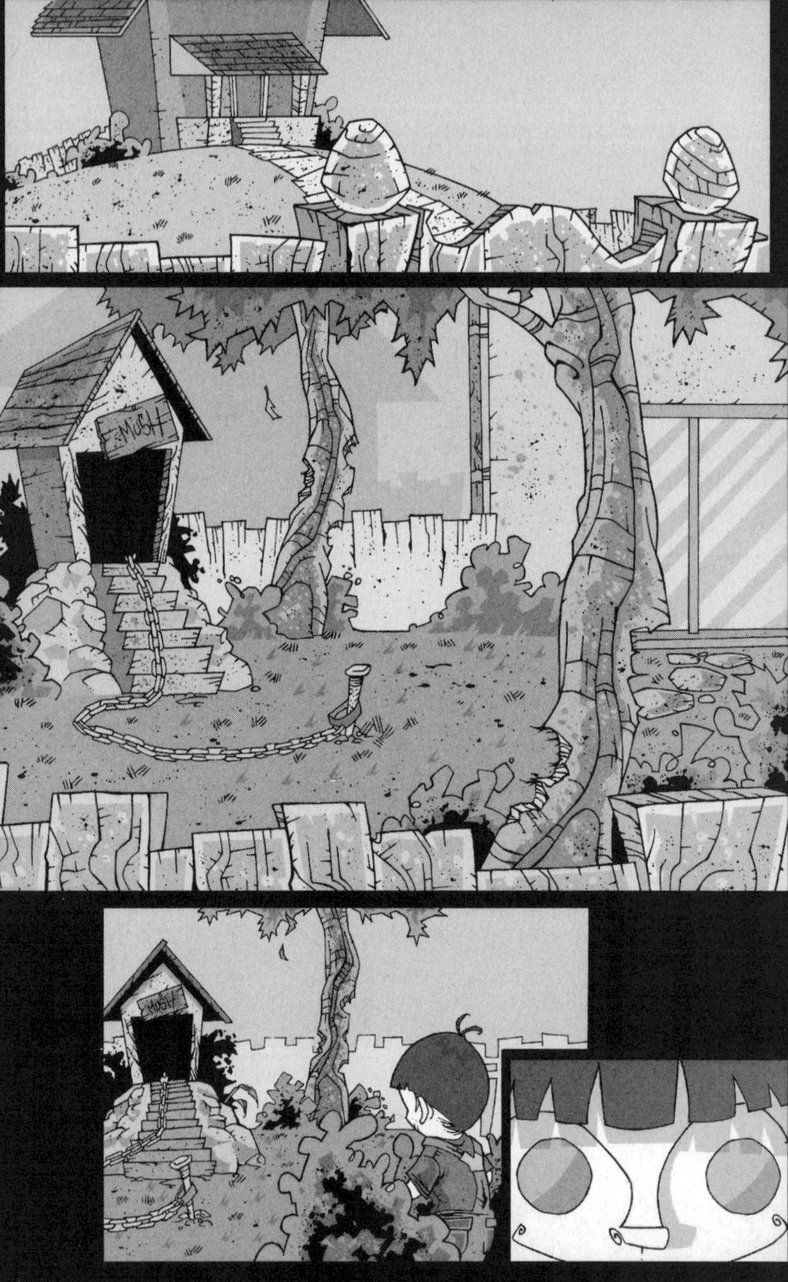
MUSH

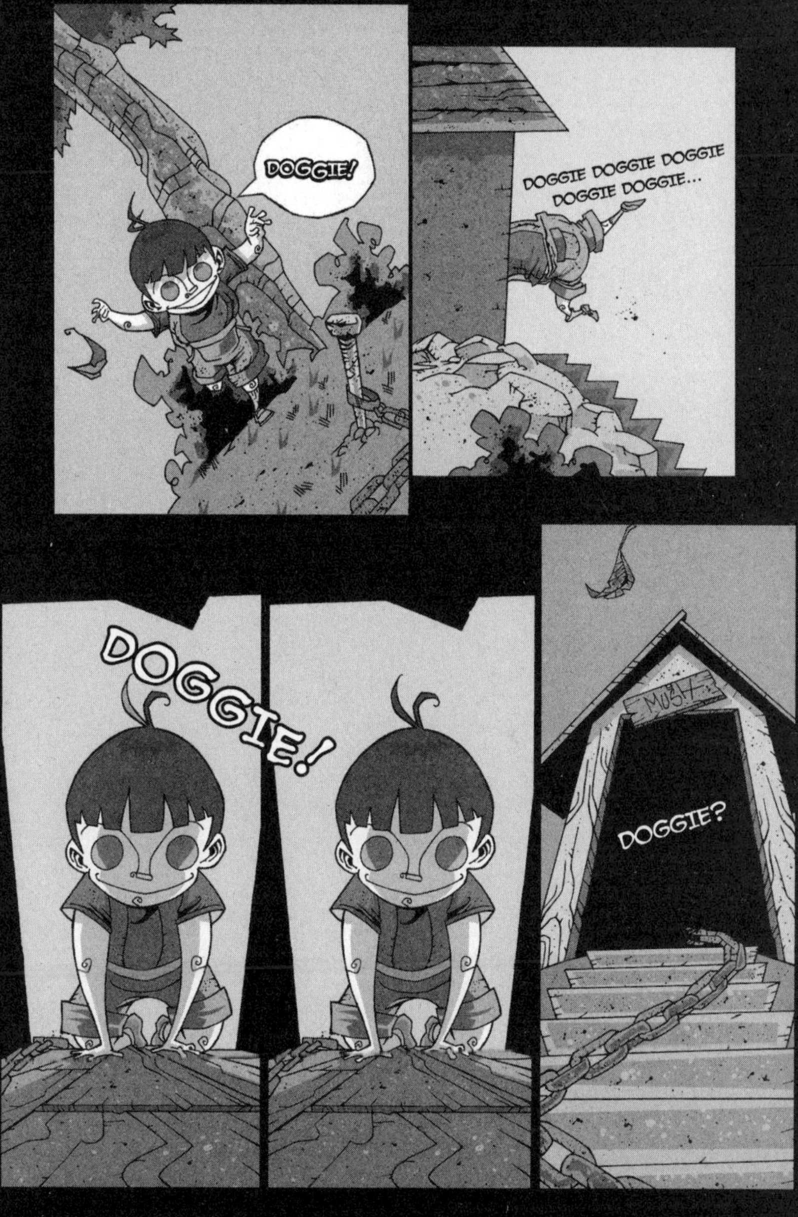
DOGGIE!
DOGGIE DOGGIE DOGGIE DOGGIE DOGGIE...
DOGGIE!
MUSH
DOGGIE?

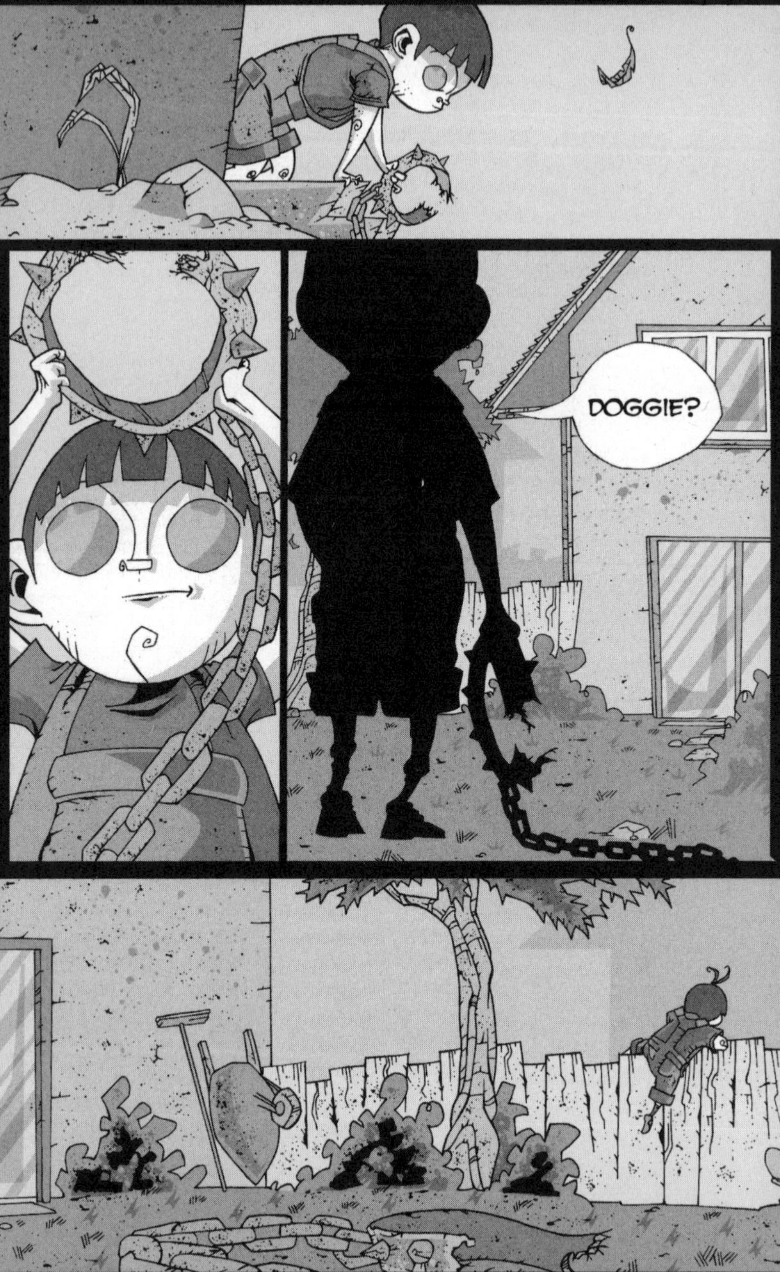
DOGGIE?

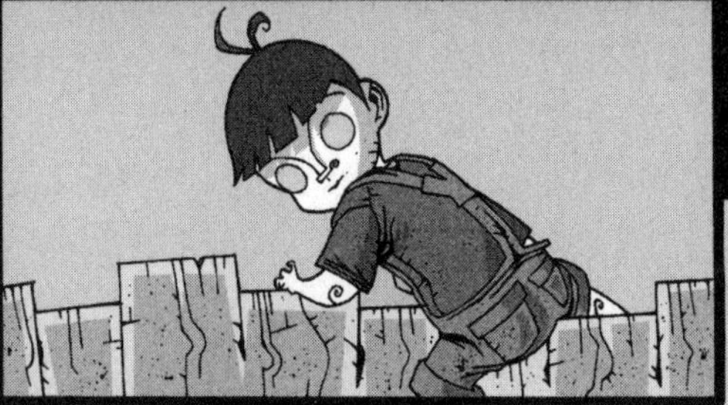
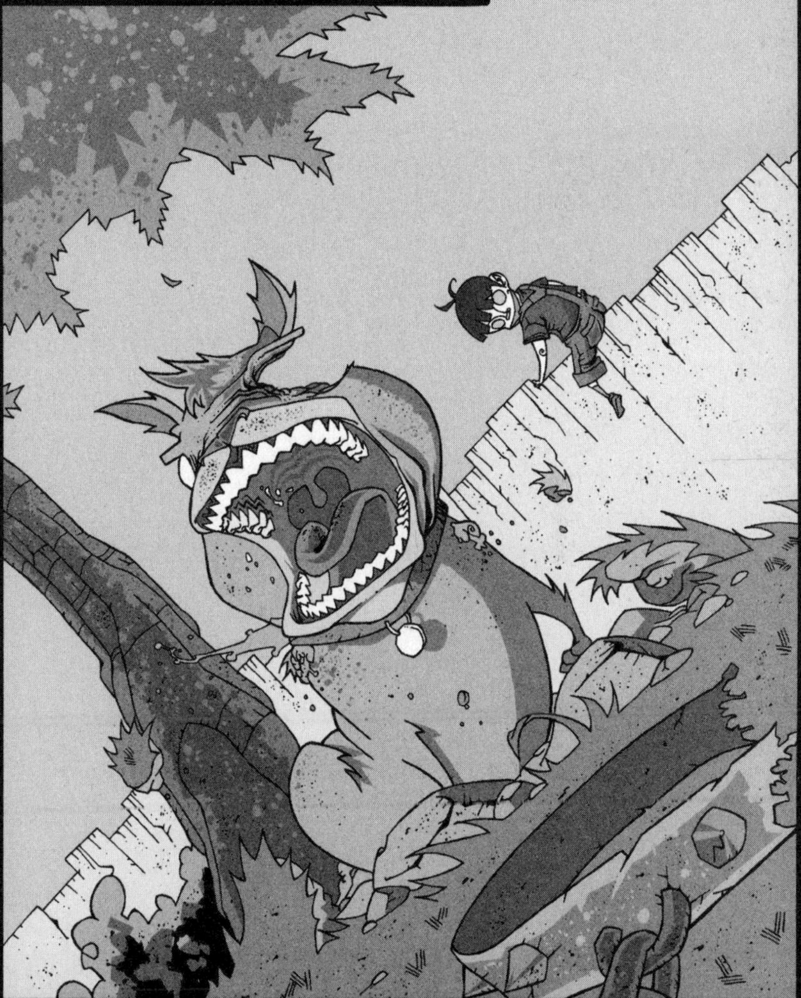

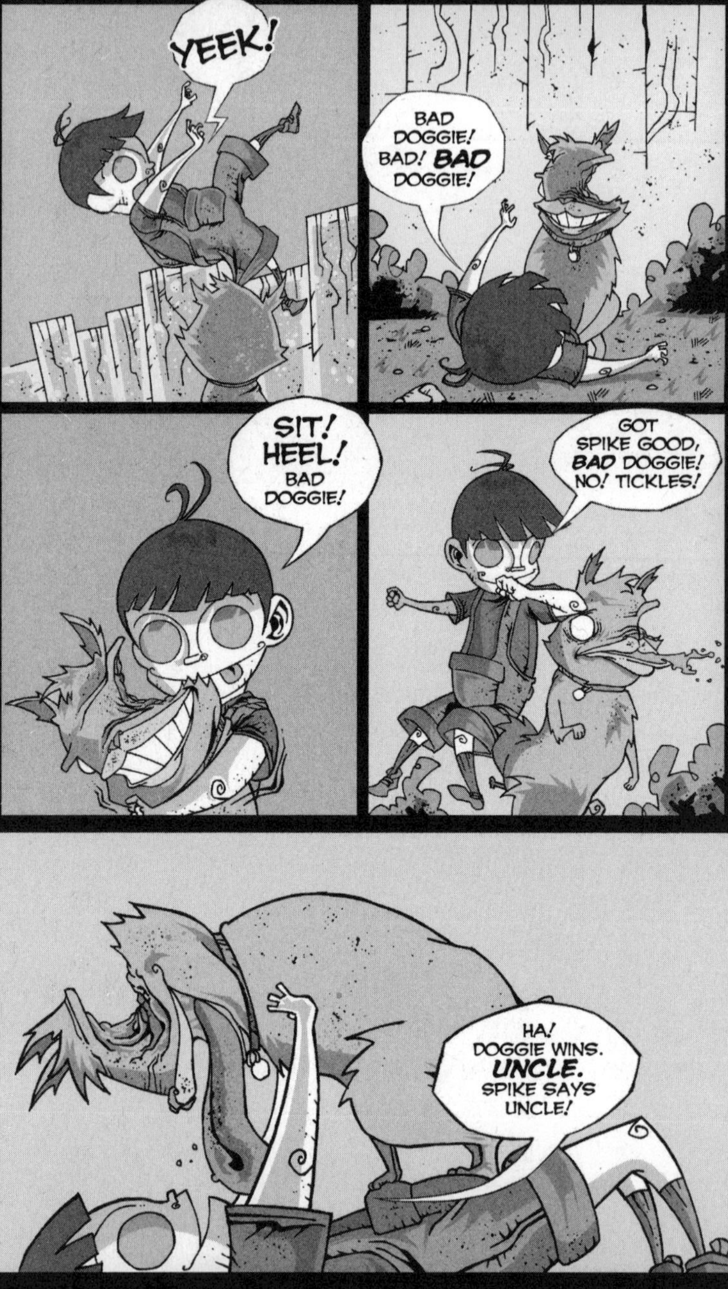
YEEK!
BAD DOGGIE! BAD! BAD DOGGIE!
SIT! HEEL! BAD DOGGIE!
GOT SPIKE GOOD, BAD DOGGIE! NO! TICKLES!
HA! DOGGIE WINS. UNCLE. SPIKE SAYS UNCLE!

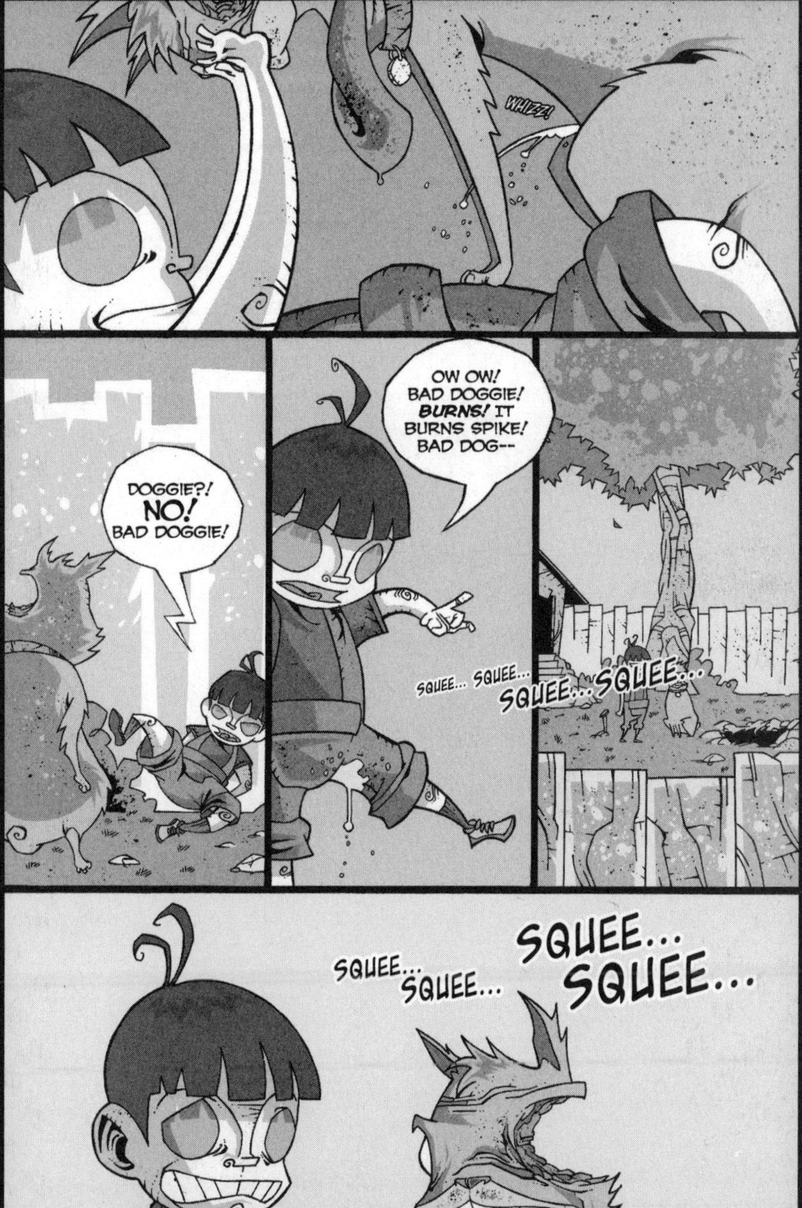
WHIZZ!
DOGGIE?! NO! BAD DOGGIE!
OW OW! BAD DOGGIE! BURNS! IT BURNS SPIKE! BAD DOG--
SQUEE... SQUEE... SQUEE... SQUEE...
SQUEE... SQUEE... SQUEE... SQUEE...

I LUV HALLOWEEN

CHAPTER FOUR:
LI'L BITH

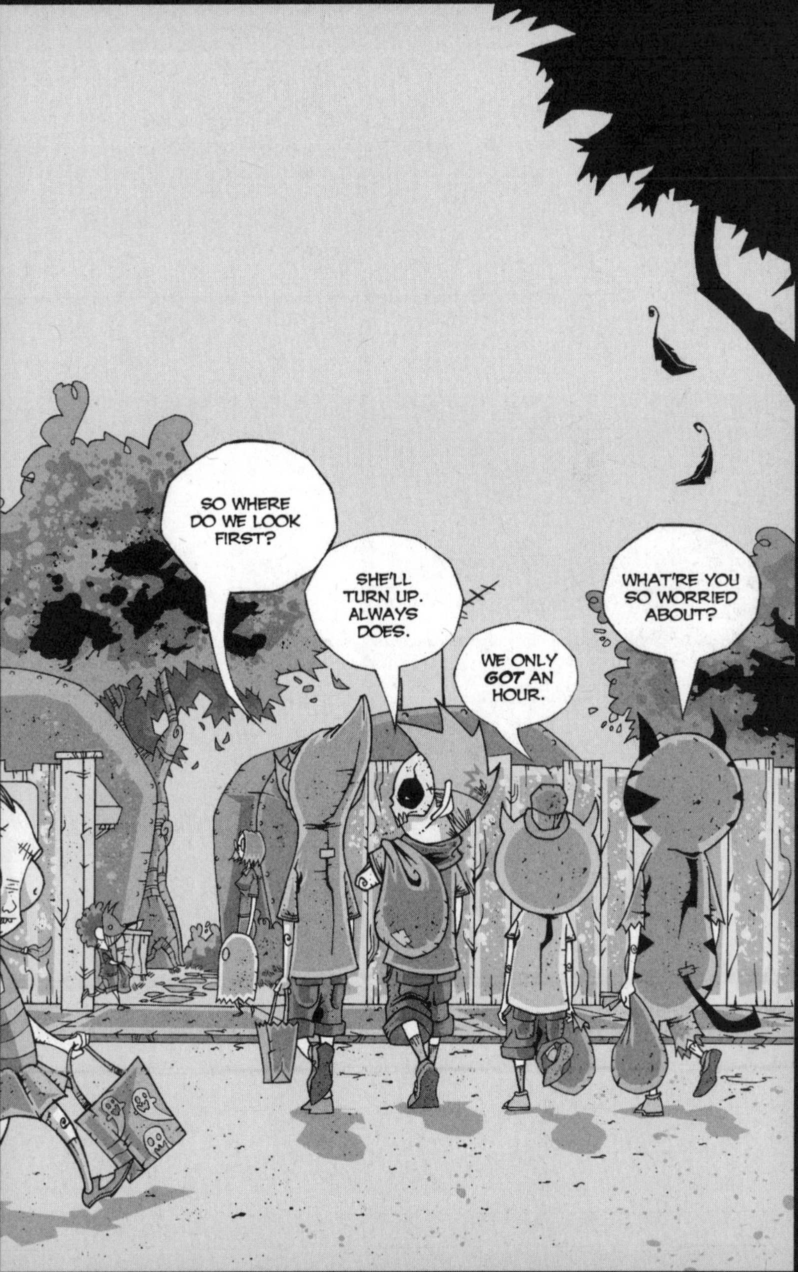
SO WHERE DO WE LOOK FIRST?
SHE'LL TURN UP. ALWAYS DOES.
WE ONLY **GOT** AN HOUR.
WHAT'RE YOU SO WORRIED ABOUT?

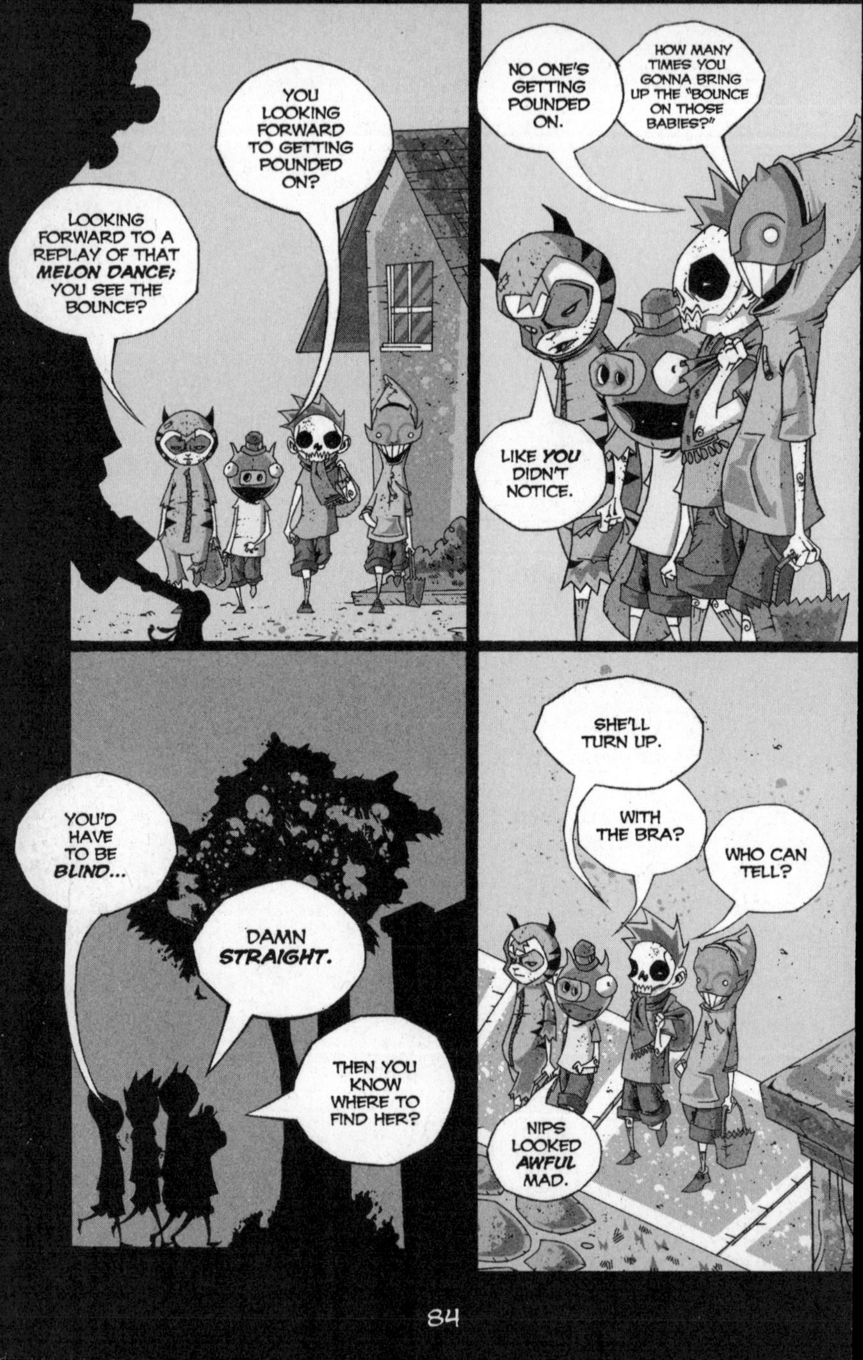
LOOKING FORWARD TO A REPLAY OF THAT *MELON DANCE;* YOU SEE THE BOUNCE?
YOU LOOKING FORWARD TO GETTING POUNDED ON?
NO ONE'S GETTING POUNDED ON.
HOW MANY TIMES YOU GONNA BRING UP THE "BOUNCE ON THOSE BABIES?"
LIKE *YOU* DIDN'T NOTICE.
YOU'D HAVE TO BE *BLIND...*
DAMN *STRAIGHT.*
THEN YOU KNOW WHERE TO FIND HER?
SHE'LL TURN UP.
WITH THE BRA?
WHO CAN TELL?
NIPS LOOKED *AWFUL* MAD.

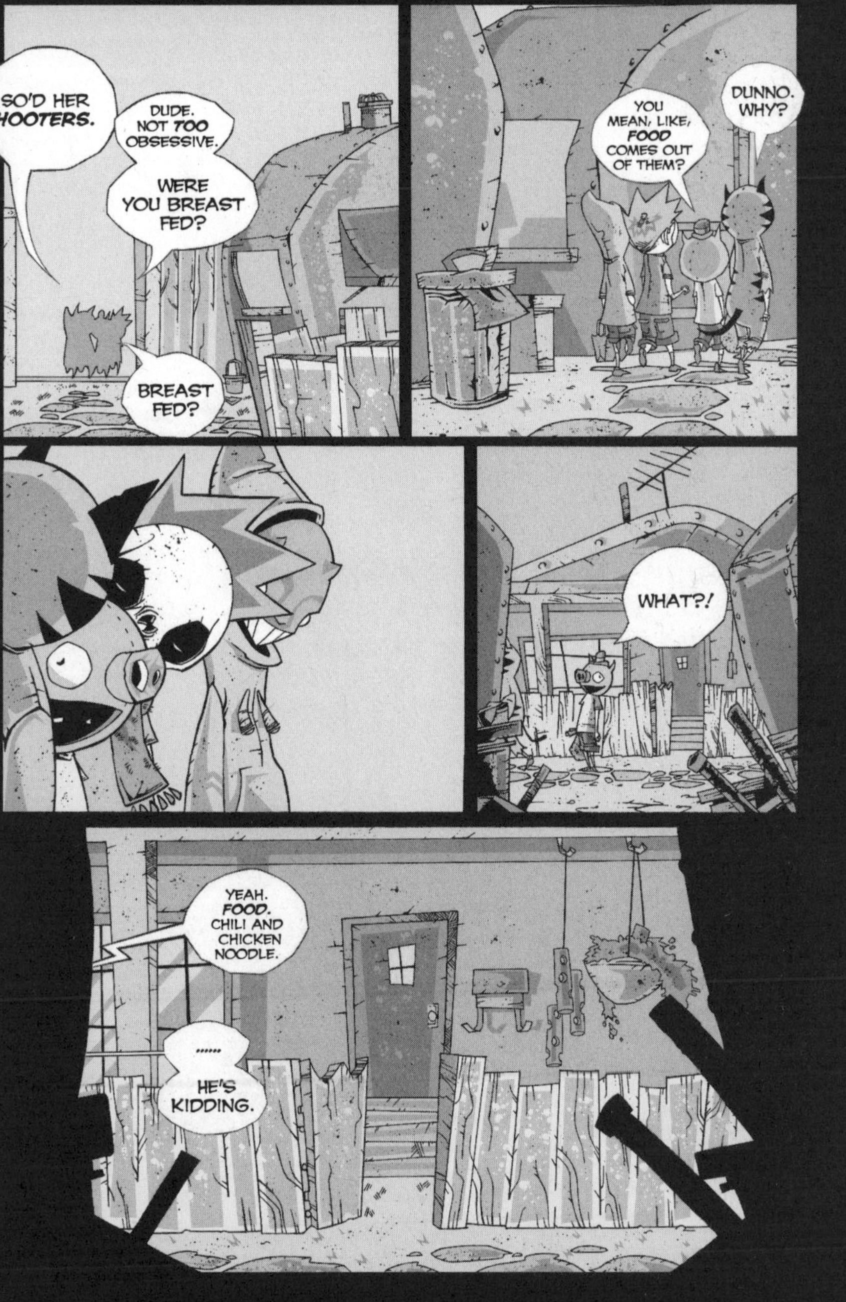
SO'D HER ***HOOTERS.***
DUDE. NOT ***TOO*** OBSESSIVE.
WERE YOU BREAST FED?
BREAST FED?
YOU MEAN, LIKE, ***FOOD*** COMES OUT OF THEM?
DUNNO. WHY?
WHAT?!
YEAH. ***FOOD.*** CHILI AND CHICKEN NOODLE.
......
HE'S KIDDING.

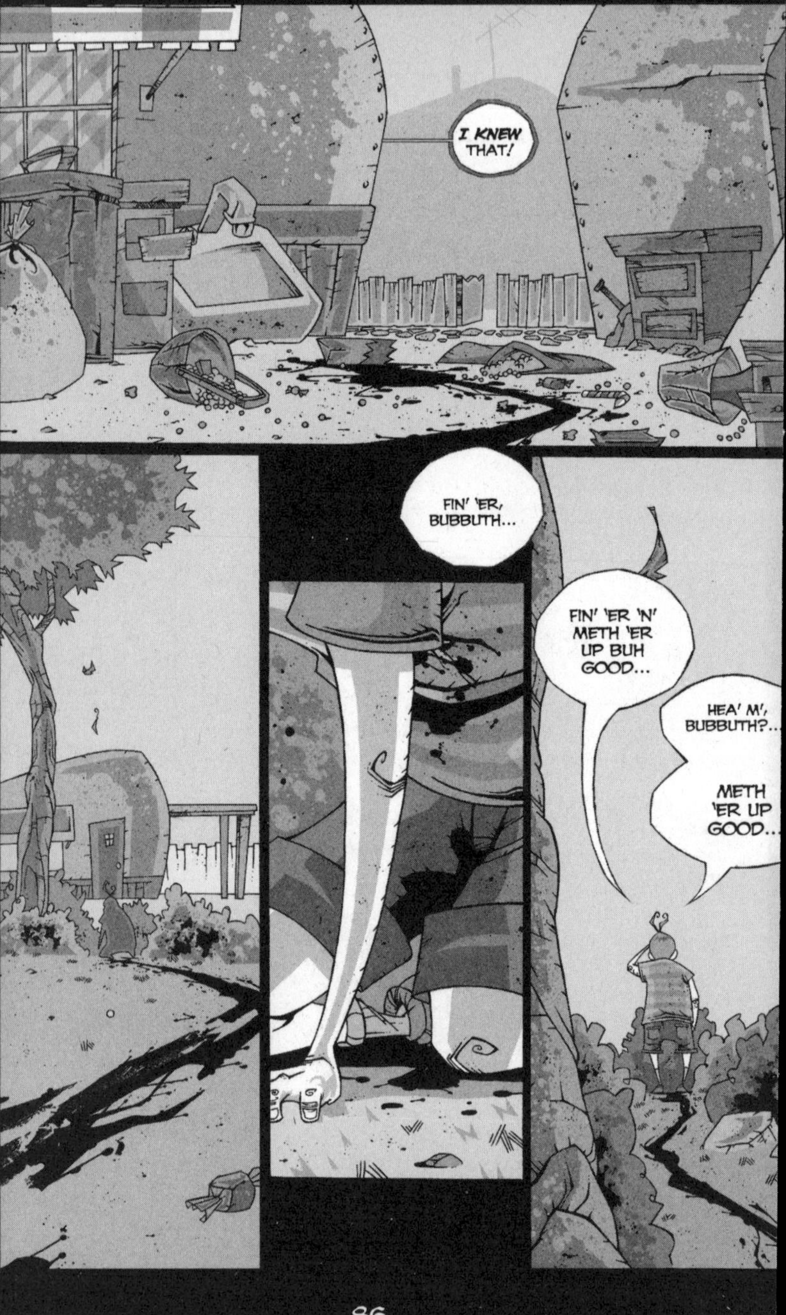
I KNEW THAT!
FIN' 'ER, BUBBUTH...
FIN' 'ER 'N' METH 'ER UP BUH GOOD...
HEA' M', BUBBUTH?...
METH 'ER UP GOOD...

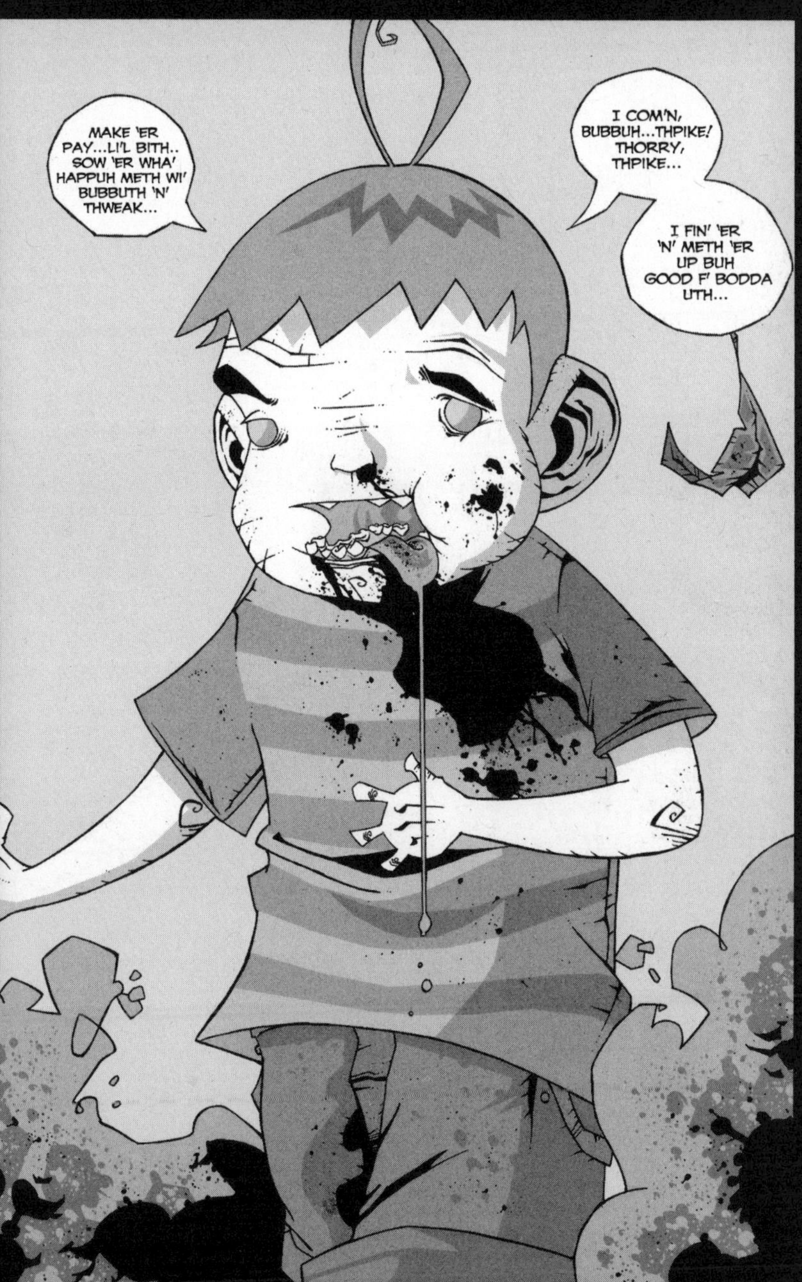
MAKE 'ER PAY...LI'L BITH.. SOW 'ER WHA' HAPPUH METH WI' BUBBUTH 'N' THWEAK...
I COM'N, BUBBUH...THPIKE! THORRY, THPIKE...
I FIN' 'ER 'N' METH 'ER UP BUH GOOD F' BODDA UTH...

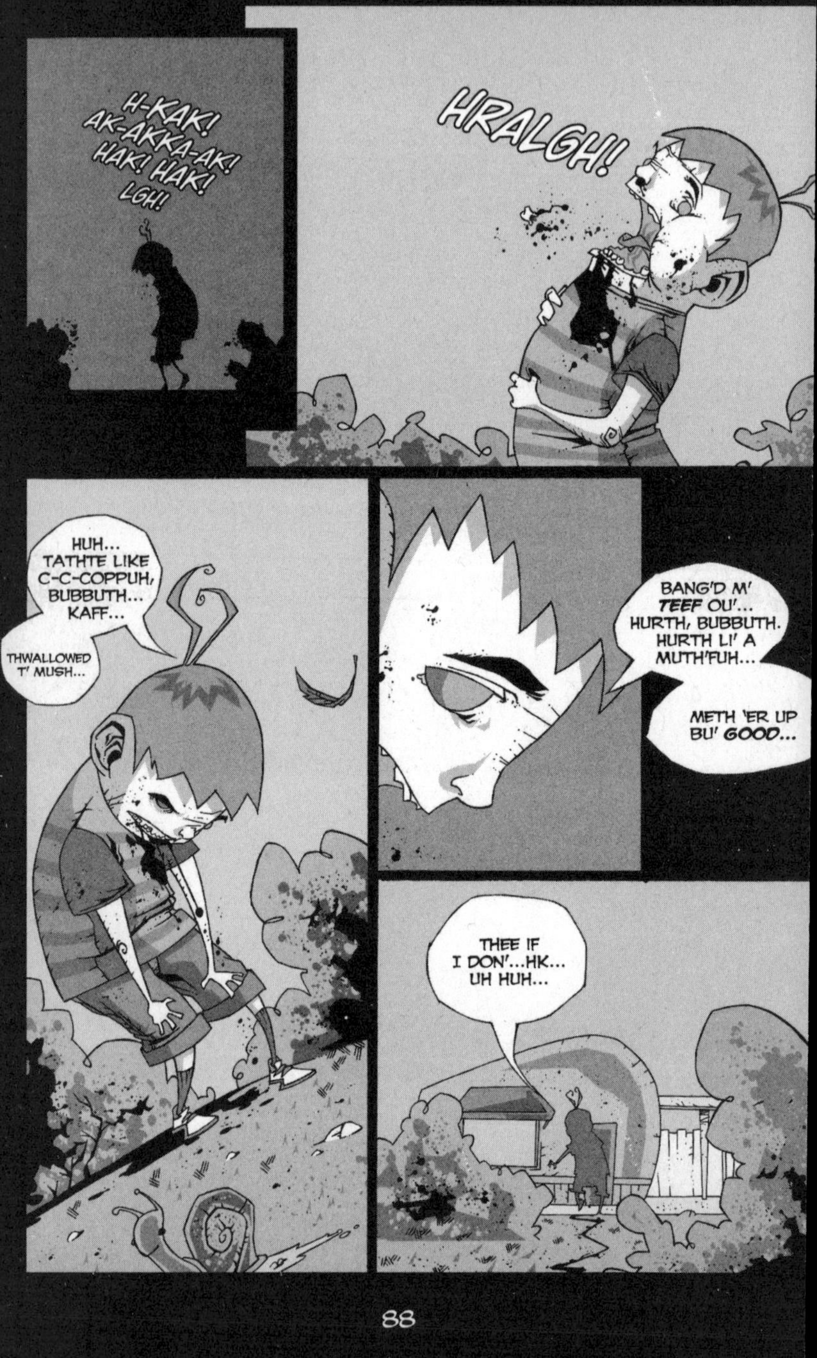
H-KAK! AK-AKKA-AK! HAK! HAK! LGH!
HRALGH!
HUH... TATHTE LIKE C-C-COPPUH, BUBBUTH... KAFF...
THWALLOWED T' MUSH...
BANG'D M' *TEEF* OU'... HURTH, BUBBUTH. HURTH LI' A MUTH'FUH...
METH 'ER UP BU' **GOOD...**
THEE IF I DON'...HK... UH HUH...

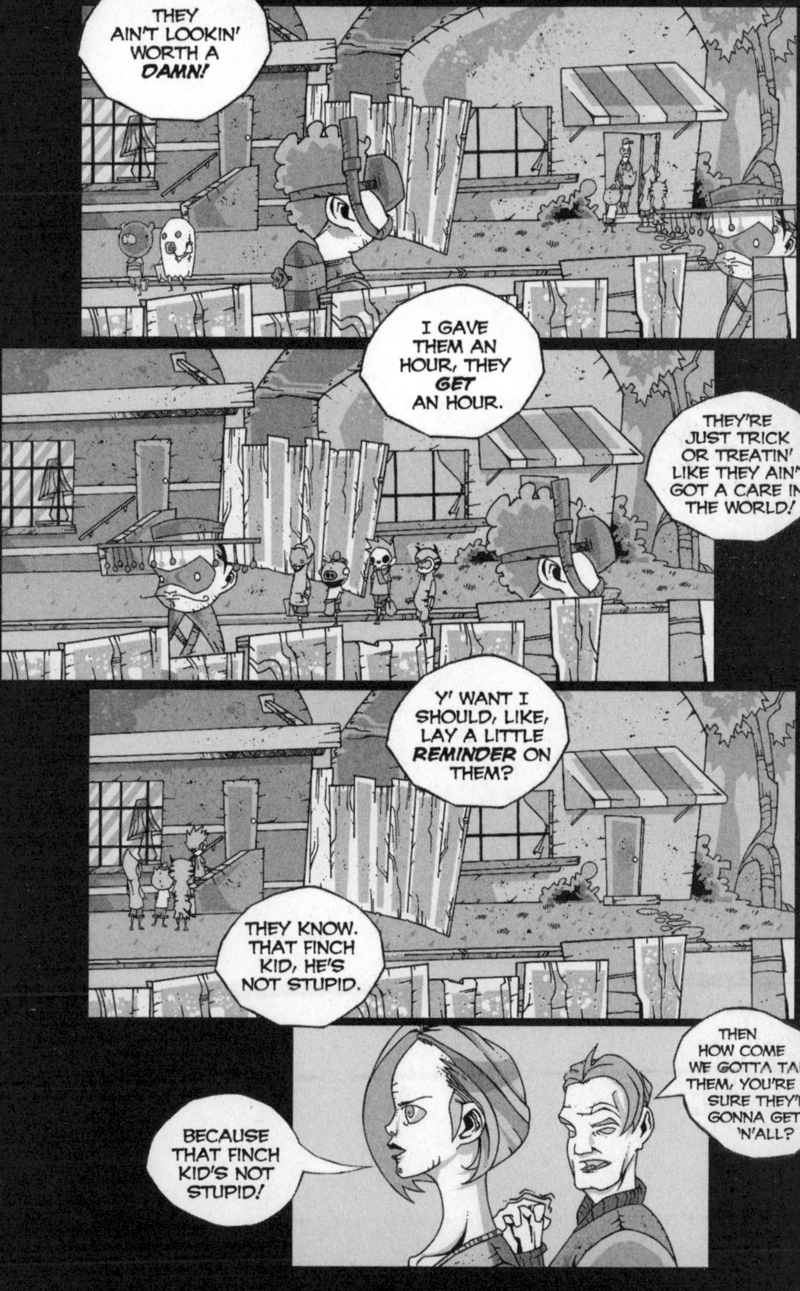
THEY AIN'T LOOKIN' WORTH A *DAMN!*
THEY'RE JUST TRICK OR TREATIN' LIKE THEY AIN'T GOT A CARE IN THE WORLD!
I GAVE THEM AN HOUR, THEY *GET* AN HOUR.
Y' WANT I SHOULD, LIKE, LAY A LITTLE *REMINDER* ON THEM?
THEY KNOW. THAT FINCH KID, HE'S NOT STUPID.
THEN HOW COME WE GOTTA TAIL THEM, YOU'RE SO SURE THEY'RE GONNA GET IT 'N'ALL?
BECAUSE THAT FINCH KID'S NOT STUPID!

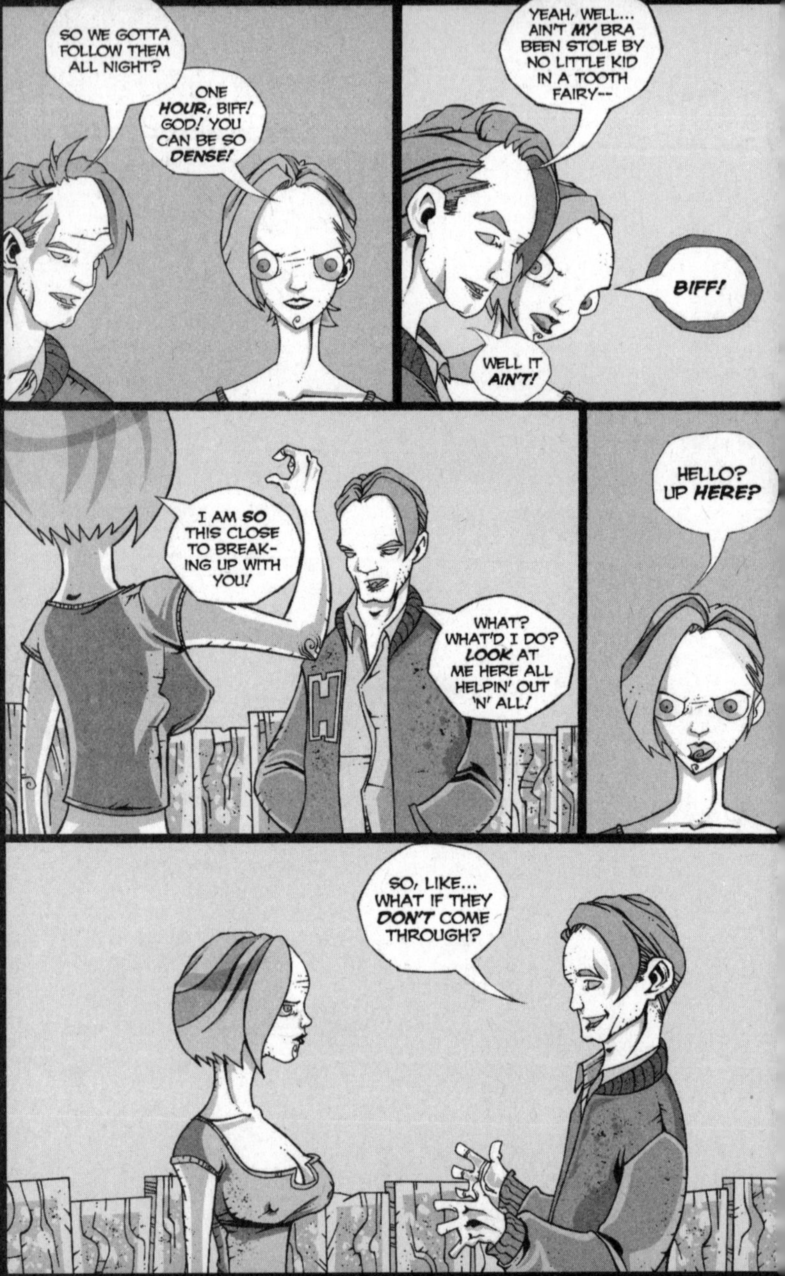
SO WE GOTTA FOLLOW THEM ALL NIGHT?
ONE **HOUR**, BIFF! GOD! YOU CAN BE SO **DENSE!**
YEAH, WELL... AIN'T **MY** BRA BEEN STOLE BY NO LITTLE KID IN A TOOTH FAIRY--
BIFF!
WELL IT **AIN'T!**
I AM **SO** THIS CLOSE TO BREAKING UP WITH YOU!
WHAT? WHAT'D I DO? **LOOK** AT ME HERE ALL HELPIN' OUT 'N' ALL!
HELLO? UP **HERE?**
SO, LIKE... WHAT IF THEY **DON'T** COME THROUGH?

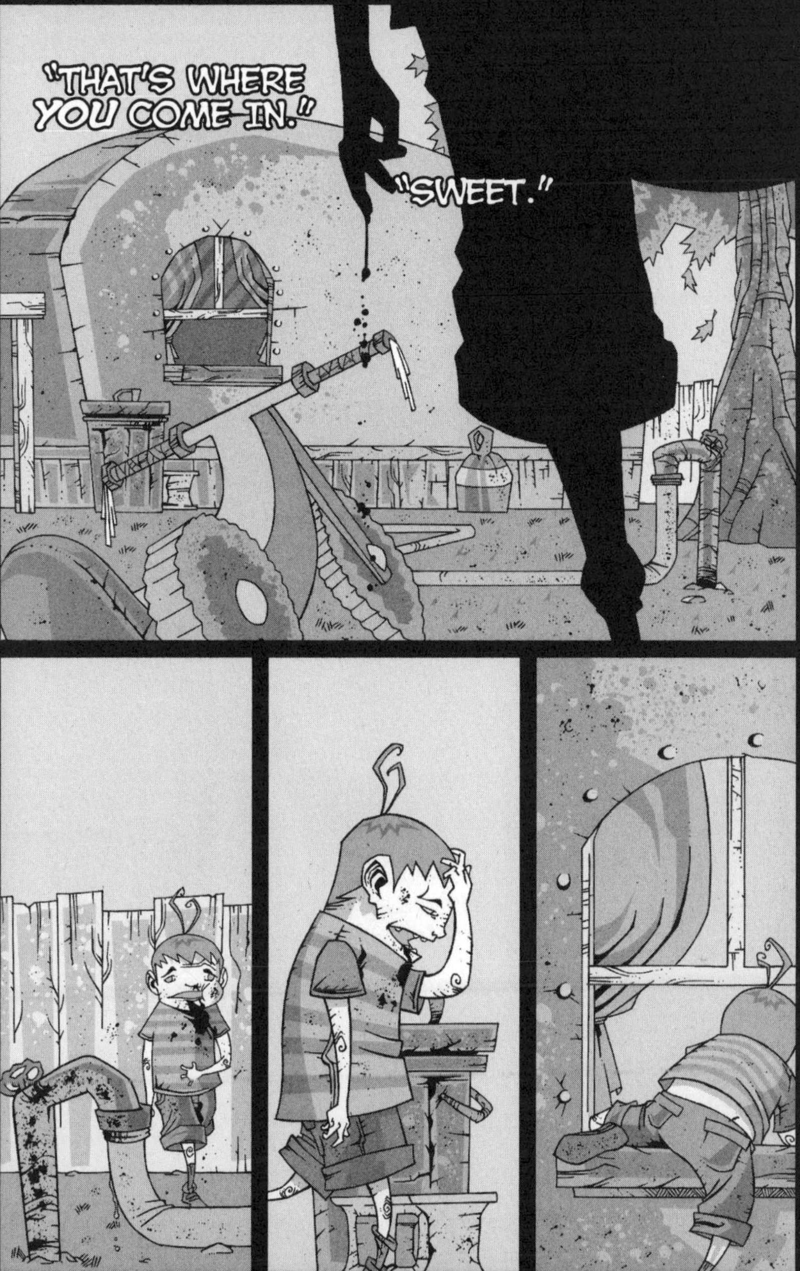
"THAT'S WHERE YOU COME IN."
"SWEET."

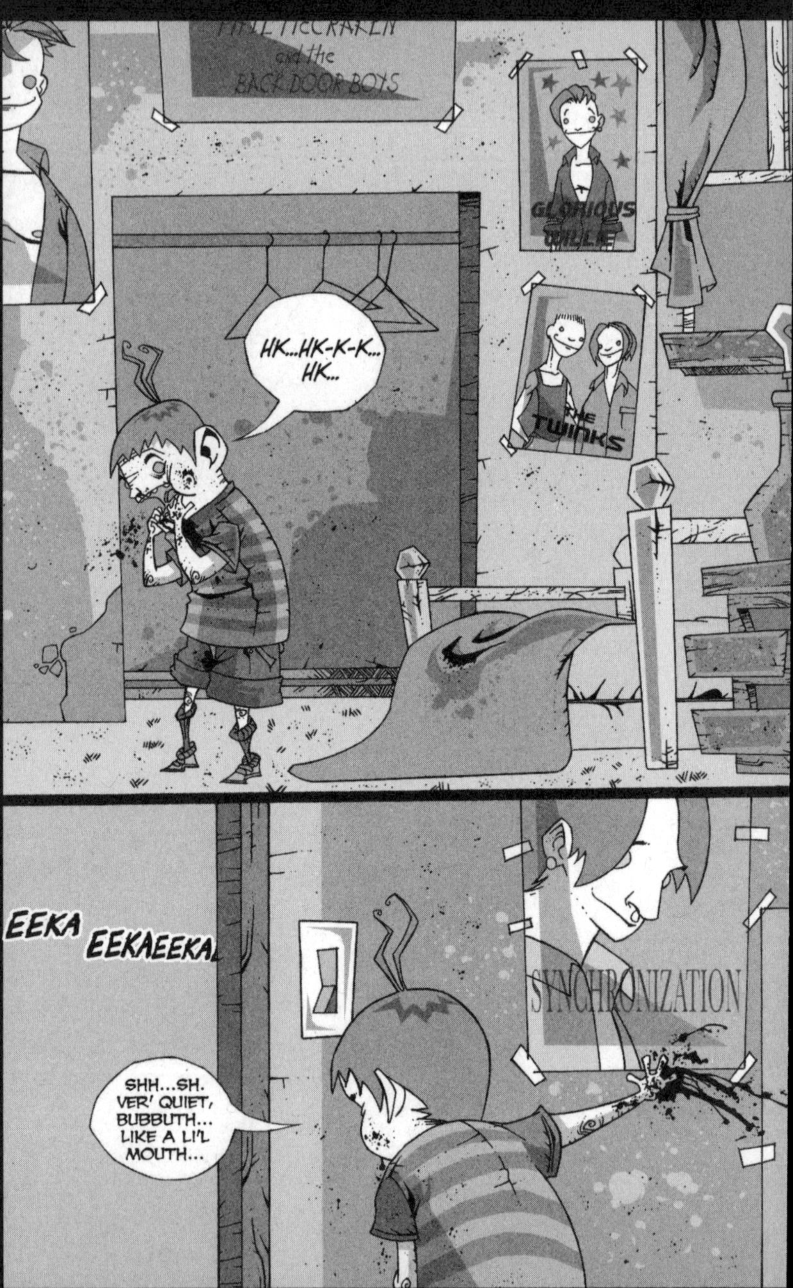
and the
BACK DOOR BOYS
GLORIOUS WILLIE
THE TWINKS
HK...HK-K-K... HK...
EEKA
EEKAEEKA
SYNCHRONIZATION
SHH...SH. VER' QUIET, BUBBUTH... LIKE A LI'L MOUTH...

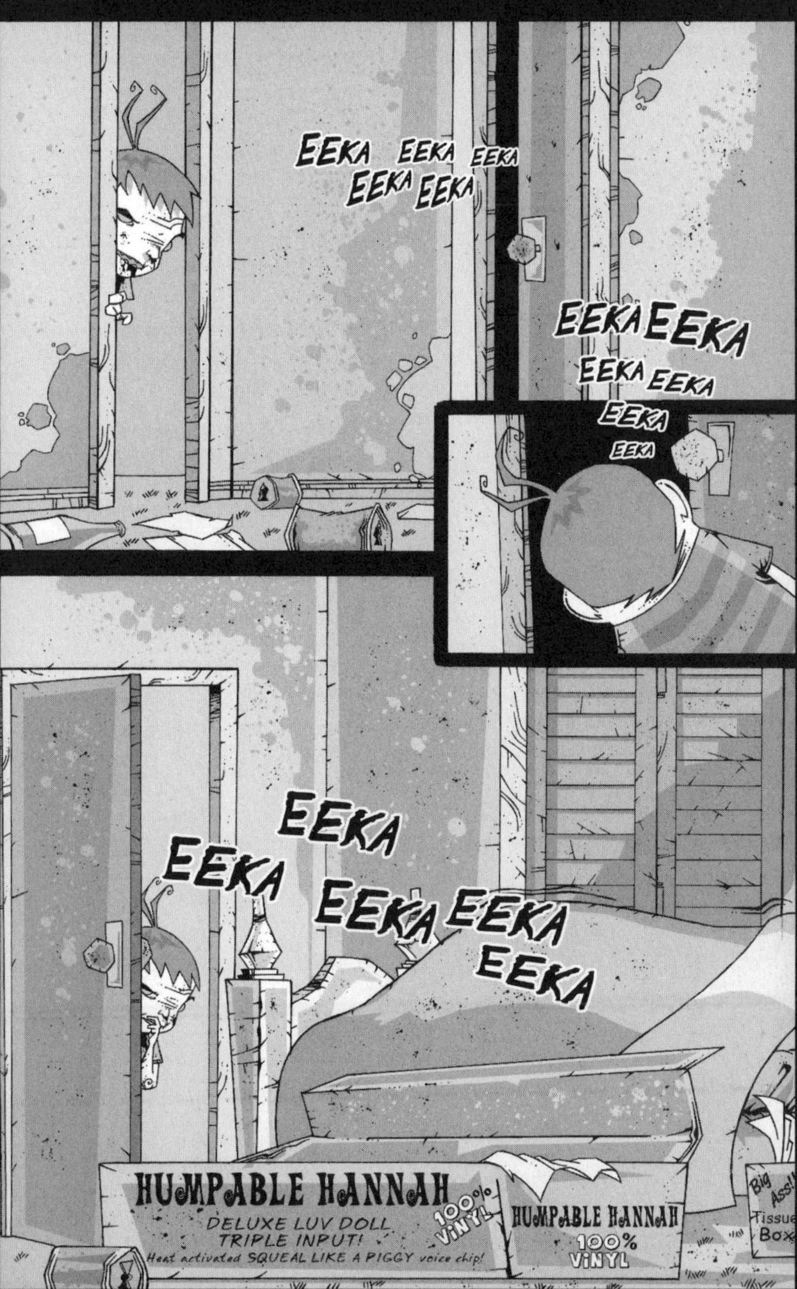

EEKA EEKA EEKA
EEKA EEKA
EEKA EEKA
EEKA EEKA
EEKA
EEKA
EEKA
EEKA
EEKA EEKA
EEKA
HUMPABLE HANNAH
DELUXE LUV DOLL
TRIPLE INPUT!
Heat activated SQUEAL LIKE A PIGGY voice chip!
100% VINYL
HUMPABLE HANNAH
100% VINYL
Big Ass!
Tissue Box

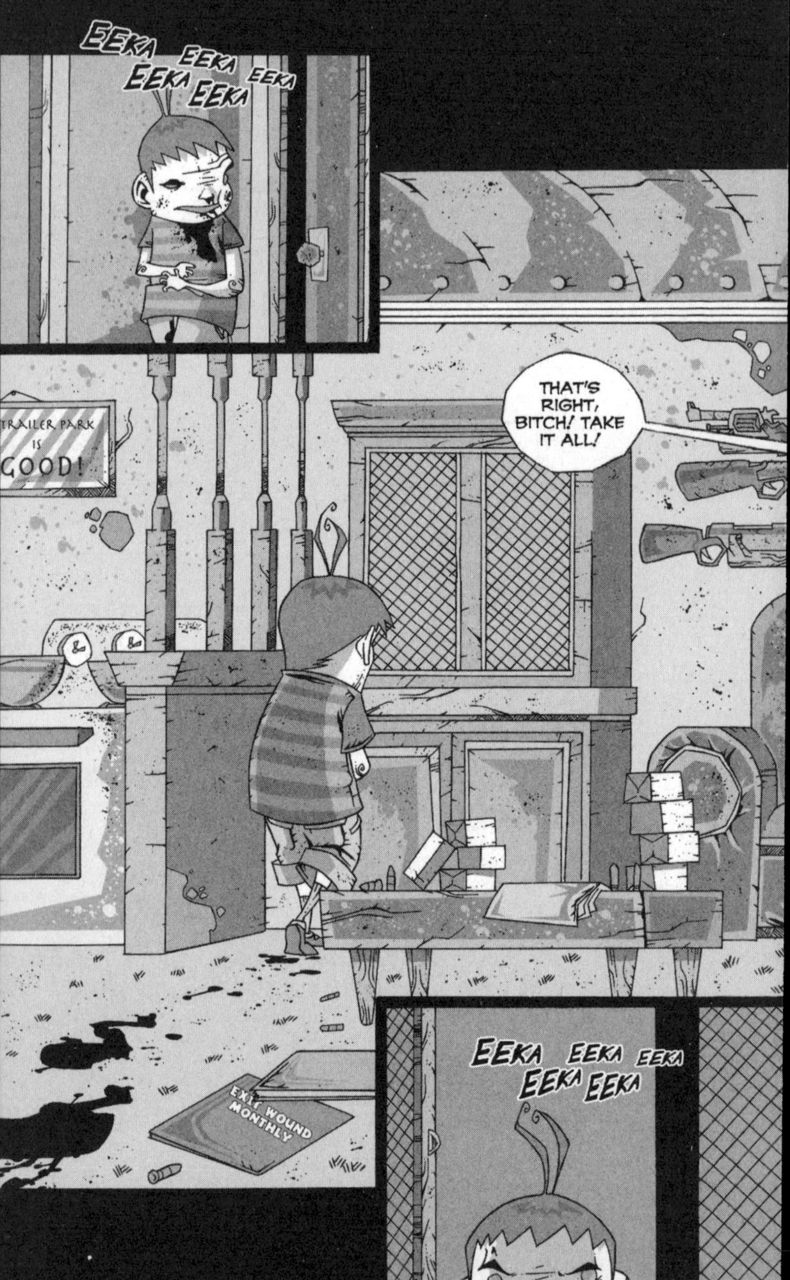
EEKA EEKA EEKA EEKA EEKA
TRAILER PARK IS GOOD!
THAT'S RIGHT, BITCH! TAKE IT ALL!
EXIT WOUND MONTHLY
EEKA EEKA EEKA EEKA EEKA

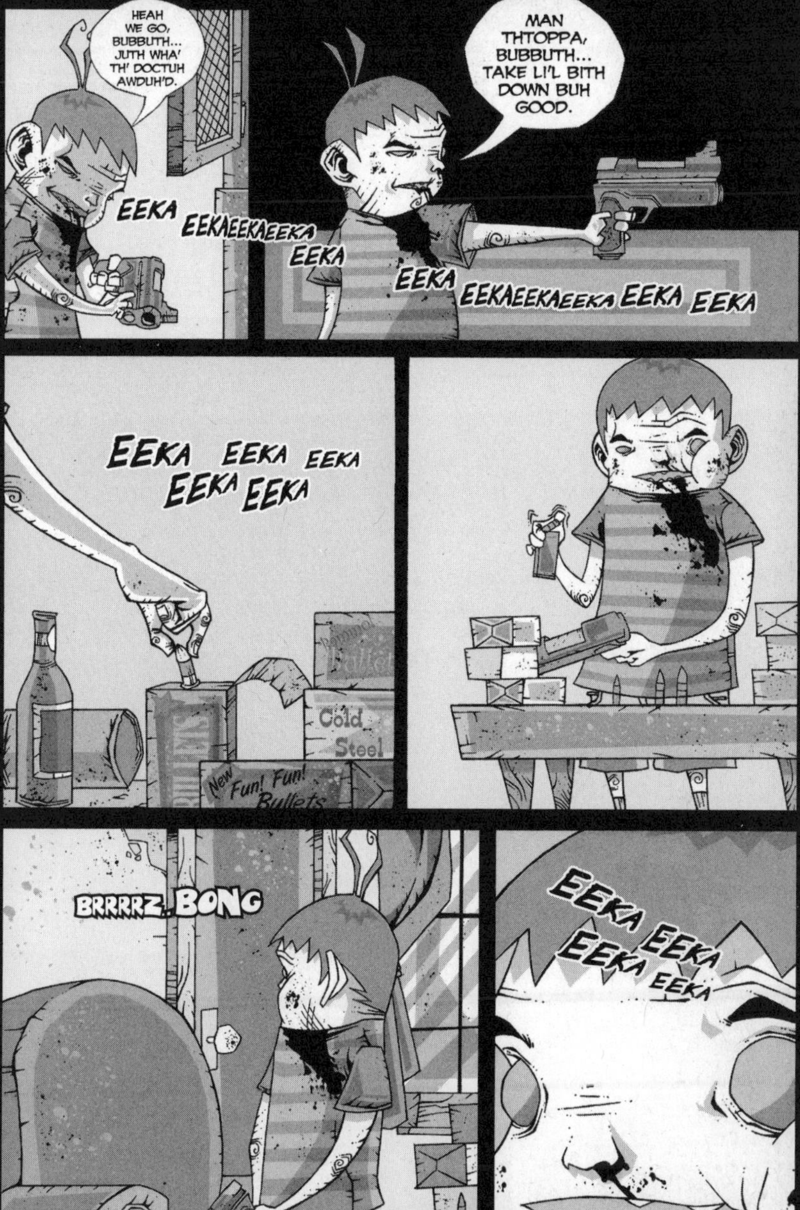
HEAH WE GO, BUBBUTH... JUTH WHA' TH' DOCTUH AWDUH'D.
MAN THTOPPA, BUBBUTH... TAKE LI'L BITH DOWN BUH GOOD.
EEKA EEKAEEKAEEKA EEKA EEKA EEKAEEKAEEKA EEKA EEKA
EEKA EEKA EEKA EEKA EEKA
Cold Steel
New Fun! Fun! Bullets
BRRRRZ..BONG
EEKA EEKA EEKA EEKA

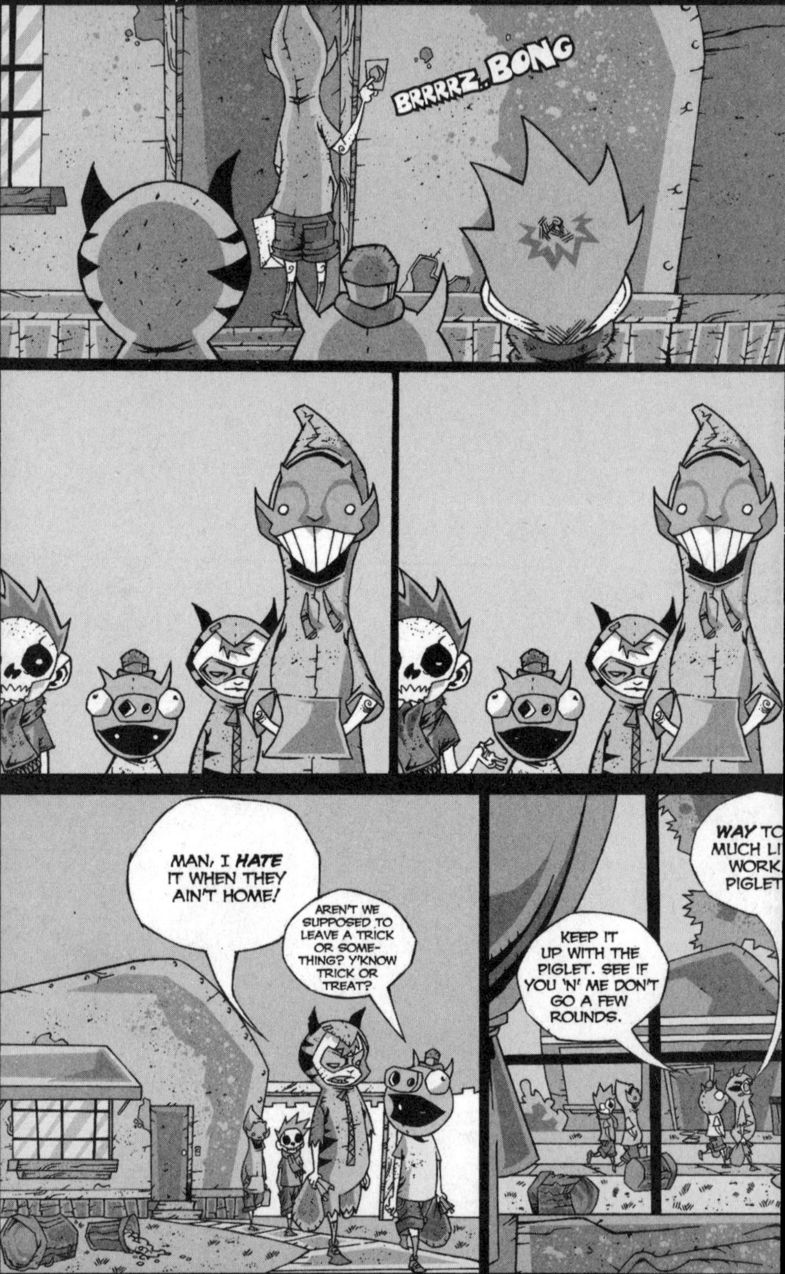
BRRRRZ..BONG
MAN, I HATE IT WHEN THEY AIN'T HOME!
AREN'T WE SUPPOSED TO LEAVE A TRICK OR SOME-THING? Y'KNOW TRICK OR TREAT?
WAY TO MUCH LI WORK, PIGLET
KEEP IT UP WITH THE PIGLET. SEE IF YOU 'N' ME DON'T GO A FEW ROUNDS.

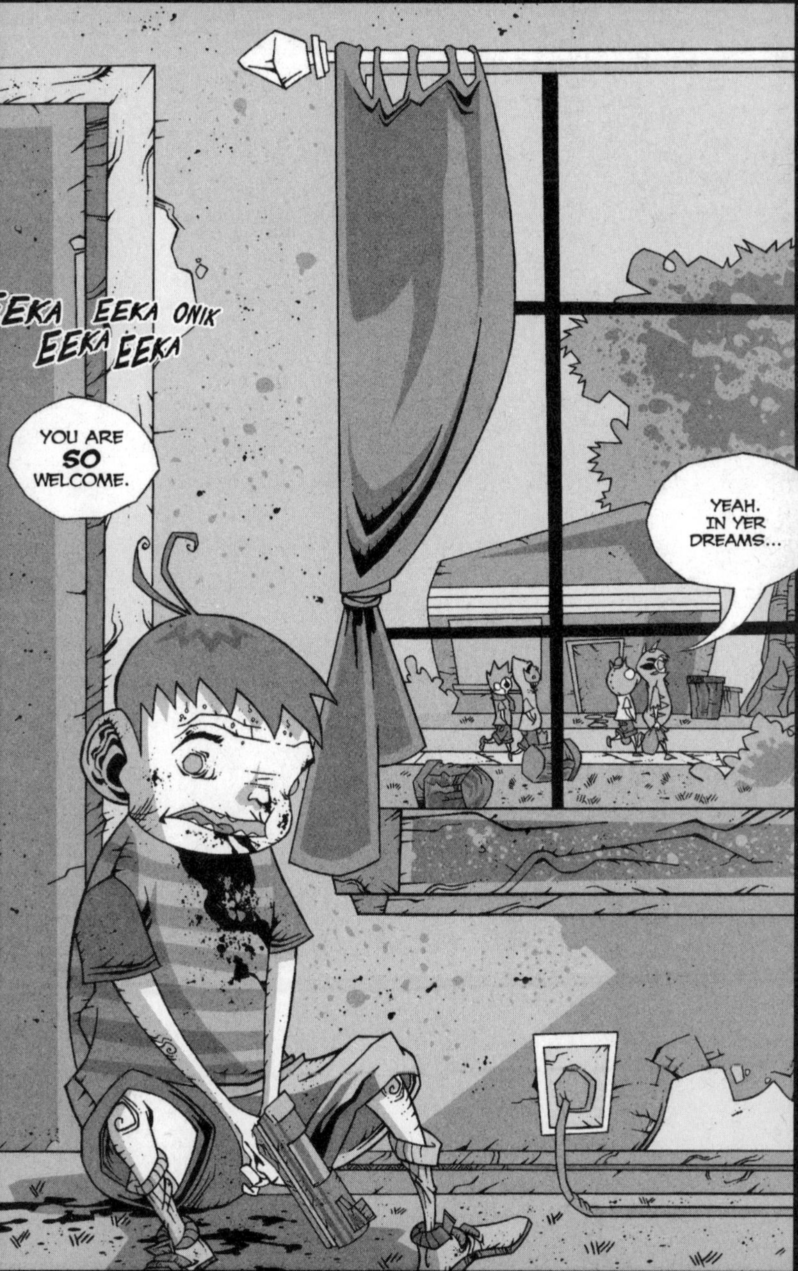
EKA EEKA ONIK
EEKA EEKA
YOU ARE SO WELCOME.
YEAH. IN YER DREAMS...

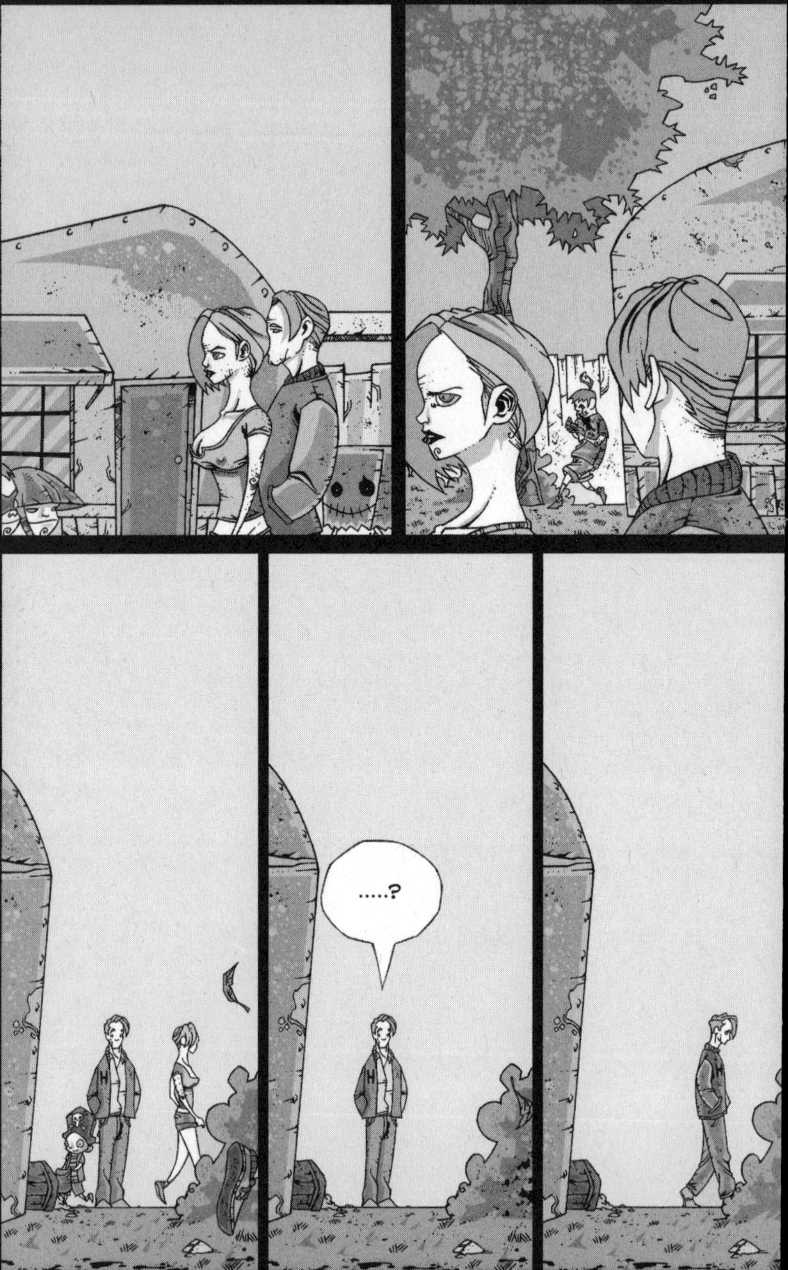
.....?

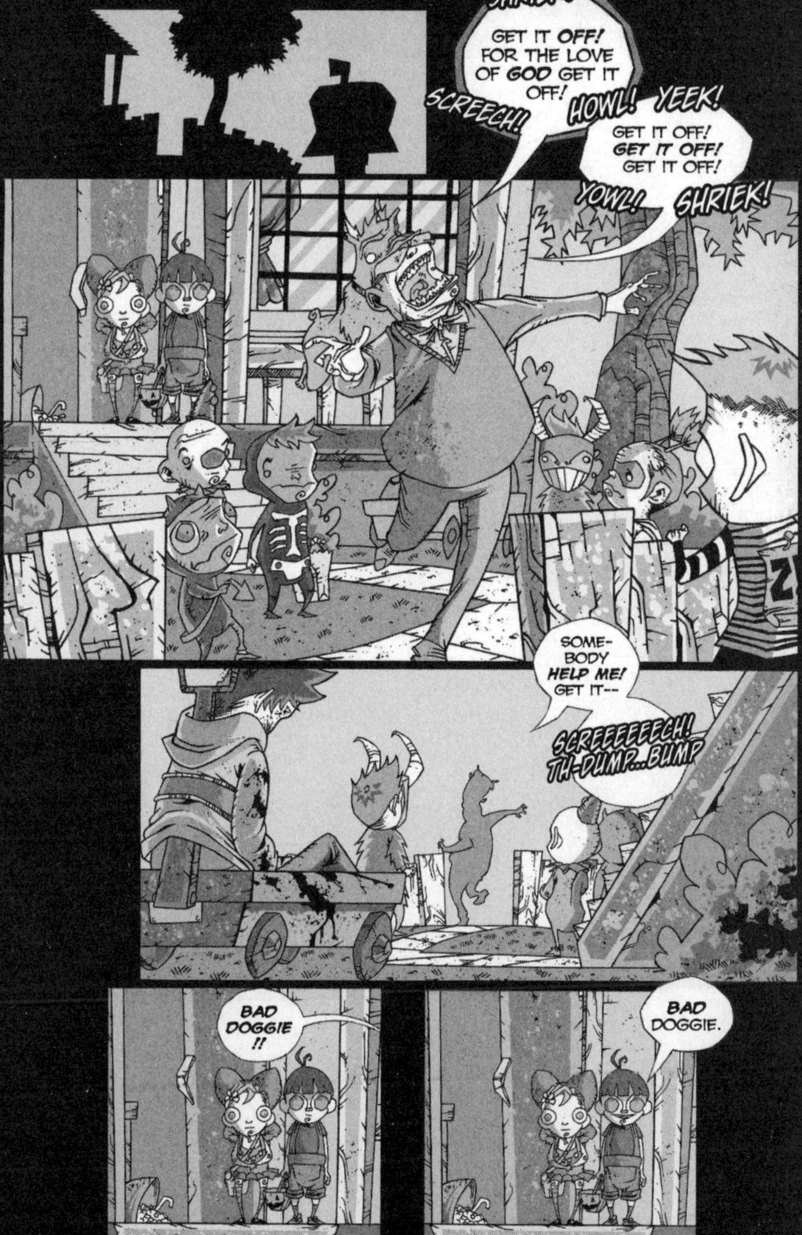
SHRIEK!
GET IT OFF! FOR THE LOVE OF GOD GET IT OFF!
SCREECH!
HOWL!
YEEK!
GET IT OFF! GET IT OFF! GET IT OFF!
YOWL!
SHRIEK!
SOME-BODY HELP ME! GET IT--
SCREEEEEEECH! TH-DUMP...BUMP
BAD DOGGIE !!
BAD DOGGIE.

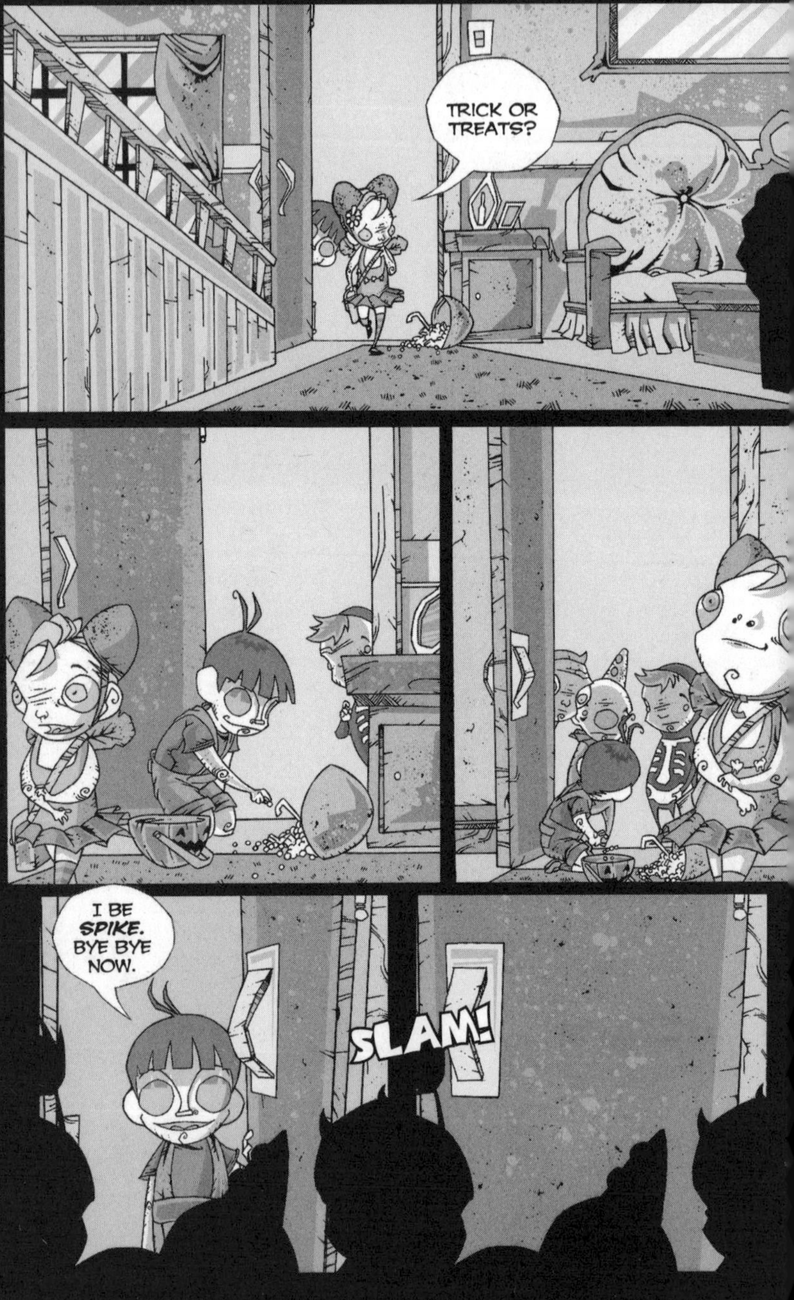
TRICK OR TREATS?
I BE SPIKE. BYE BYE NOW.
SLAM!

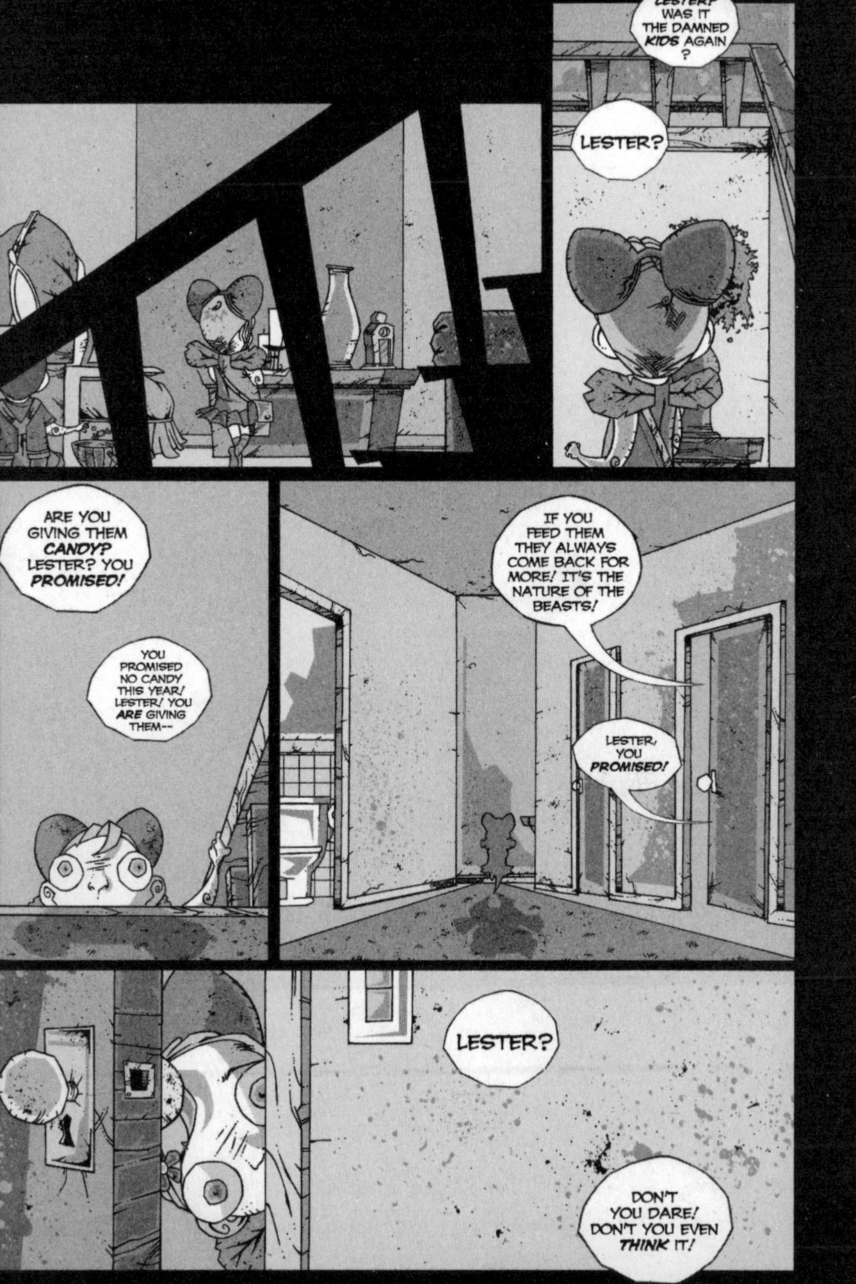

LESTER? WAS IT THE DAMNED KIDS AGAIN ?
LESTER?
ARE YOU GIVING THEM CANDY? LESTER? YOU PROMISED!
YOU PROMISED NO CANDY THIS YEAR! LESTER! YOU ARE GIVING THEM--
IF YOU FEED THEM THEY ALWAYS COME BACK FOR MORE! IT'S THE NATURE OF THE BEASTS!
LESTER, YOU PROMISED!
LESTER?
DON'T YOU DARE! DON'T YOU EVEN THINK IT!

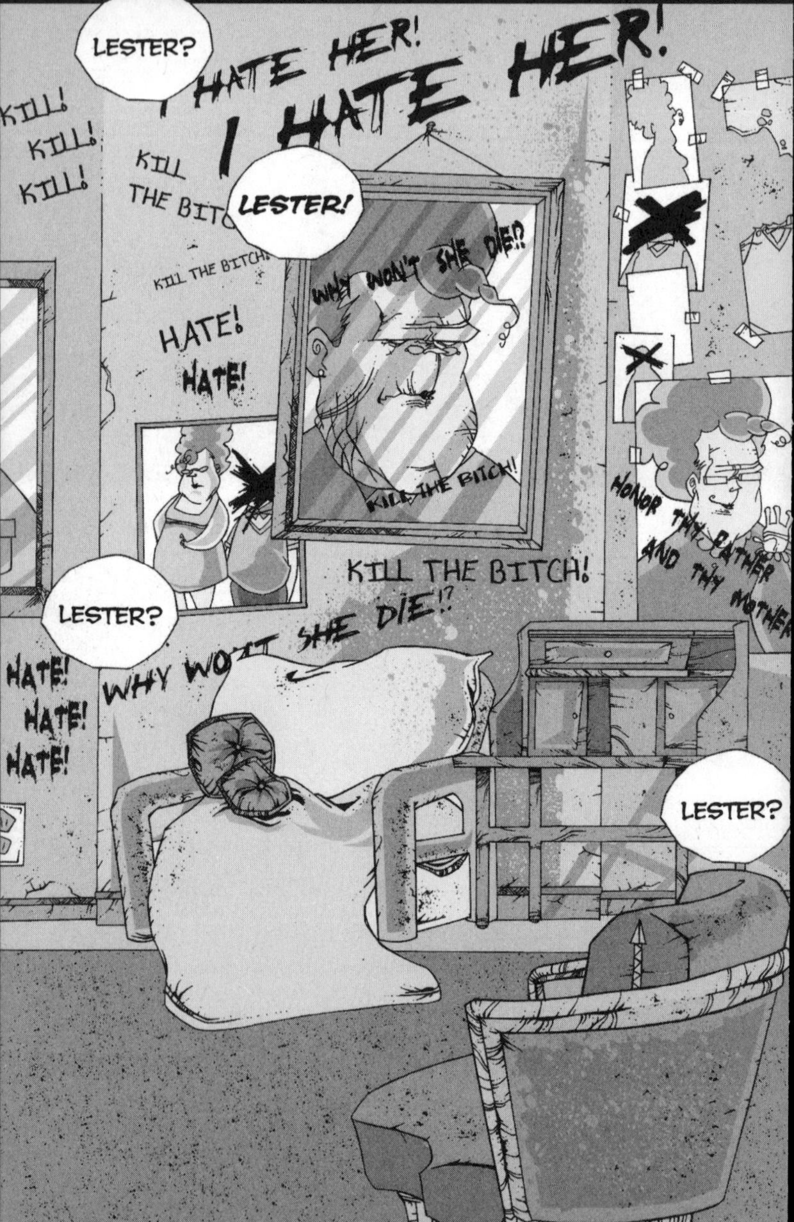
LESTER?
I HATE HER!
I HATE HER!
KILL!
KILL!
KILL!
KILL THE BITCH!
LESTER!
KILL THE BITCH!
WHY WON'T SHE DIE!?
HATE!
HATE!
KILL THE BITCH!
HONOR THY FATHER AND THY MOTHER
KILL THE BITCH!
LESTER?
WHY WON'T SHE DIE!?
HATE!
HATE!
HATE!
LESTER?

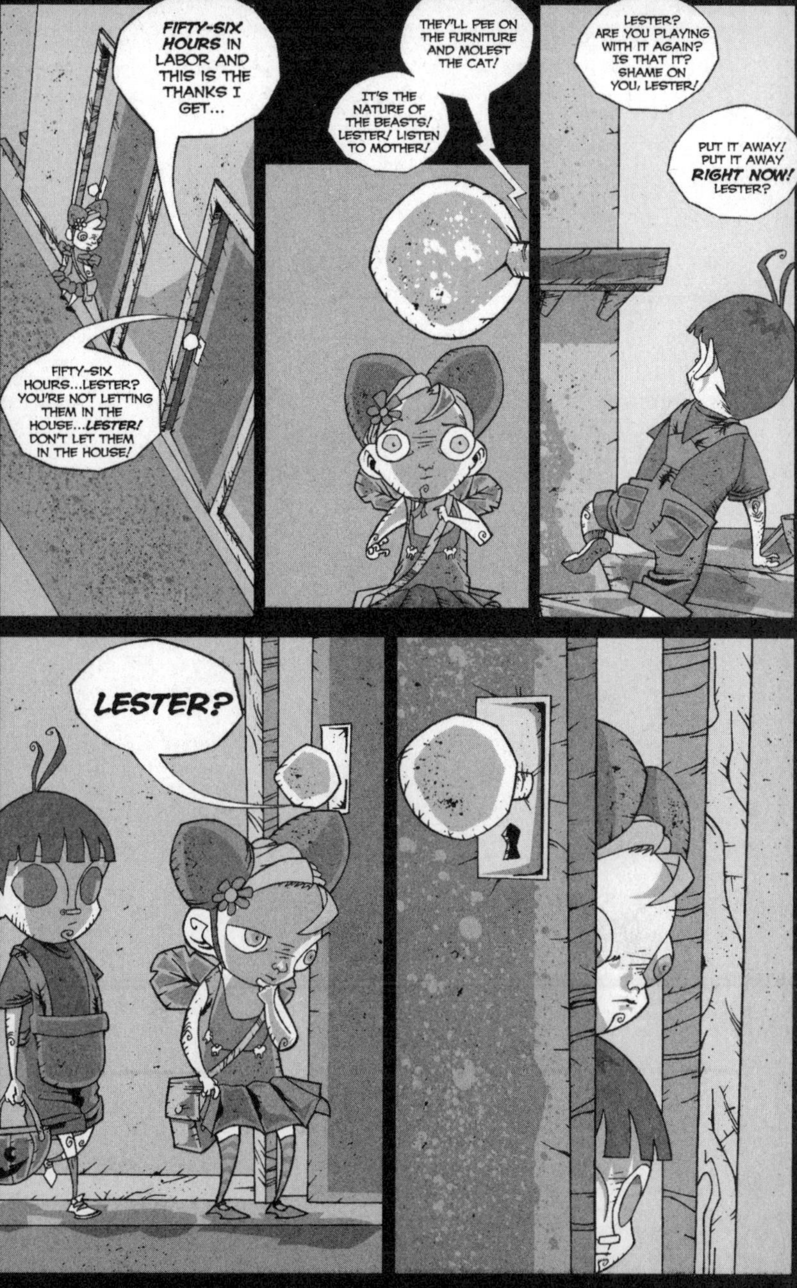
FIFTY-SIX HOURS IN LABOR AND THIS IS THE THANKS I GET...
FIFTY-SIX HOURS...LESTER? YOU'RE NOT LETTING THEM IN THE HOUSE...LESTER! DON'T LET THEM IN THE HOUSE!
IT'S THE NATURE OF THE BEASTS! LESTER! LISTEN TO MOTHER!
THEY'LL PEE ON THE FURNITURE AND MOLEST THE CAT!
LESTER? ARE YOU PLAYING WITH IT AGAIN? IS THAT IT? SHAME ON YOU, LESTER!
PUT IT AWAY! PUT IT AWAY RIGHT NOW! LESTER?
LESTER?

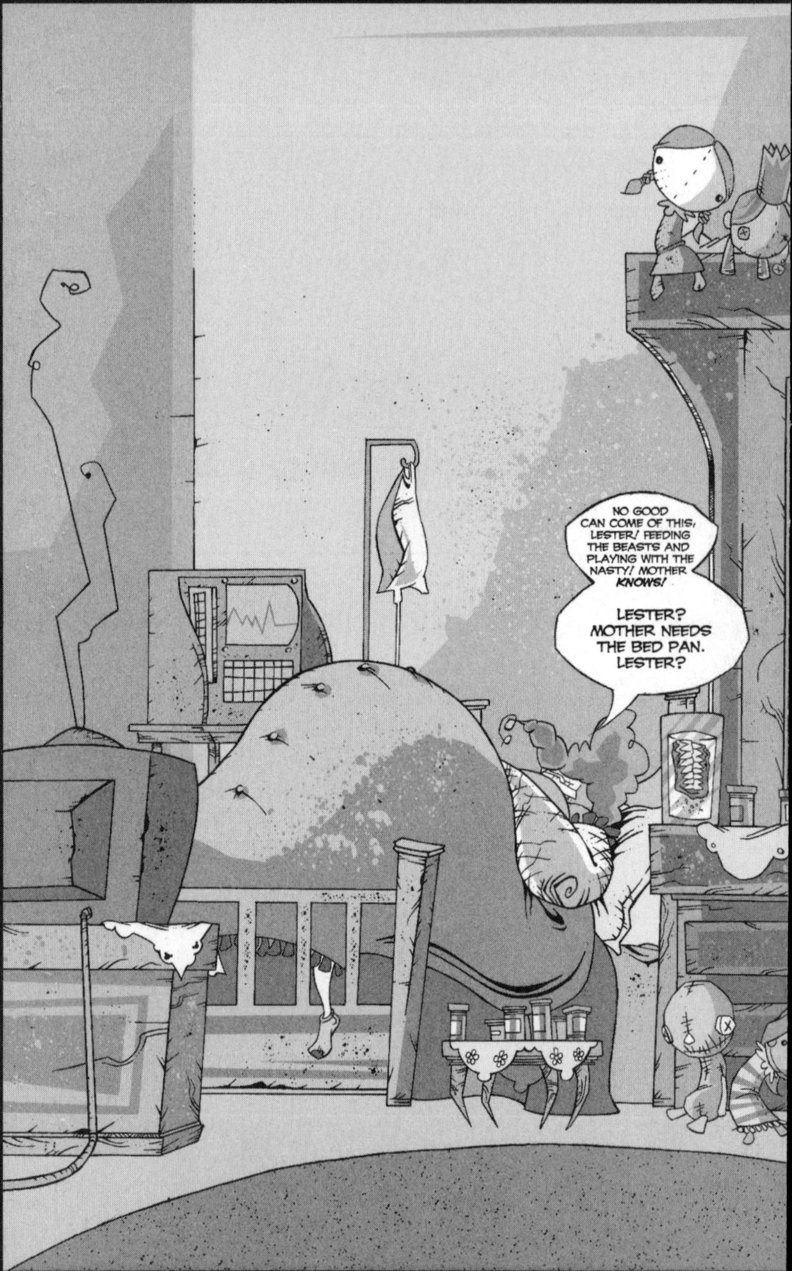
NO GOOD CAN COME OF THIS, LESTER! FEEDING THE BEASTS AND PLAYING WITH THE NASTY! MOTHER *KNOWS!*
LESTER? MOTHER NEEDS THE BED PAN. LESTER?

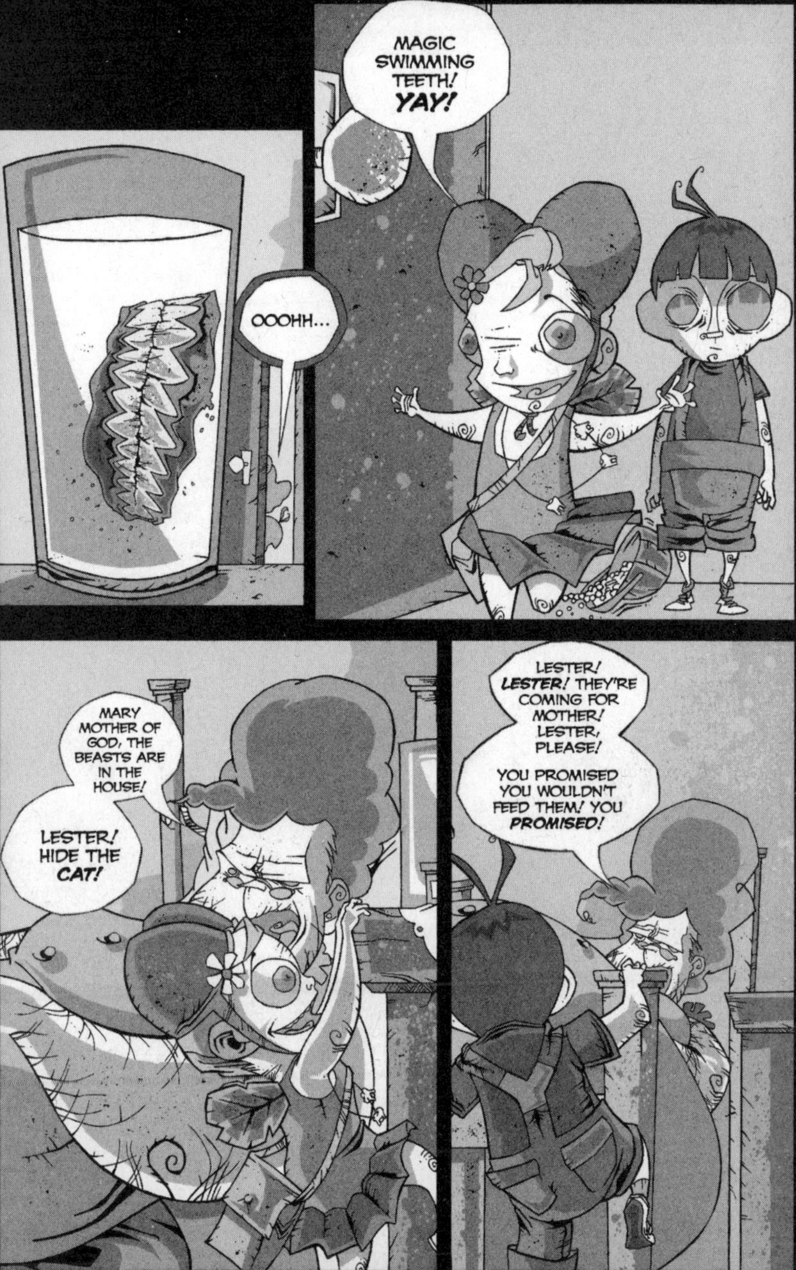
OOOHH...
MAGIC SWIMMING TEETH! *YAY!*
MARY MOTHER OF GOD, THE BEASTS ARE IN THE HOUSE!
LESTER! HIDE THE *CAT!*
LESTER! *LESTER!* THEY'RE COMING FOR MOTHER! LESTER, PLEASE!
YOU PROMISED YOU WOULDN'T FEED THEM! YOU *PROMISED!*

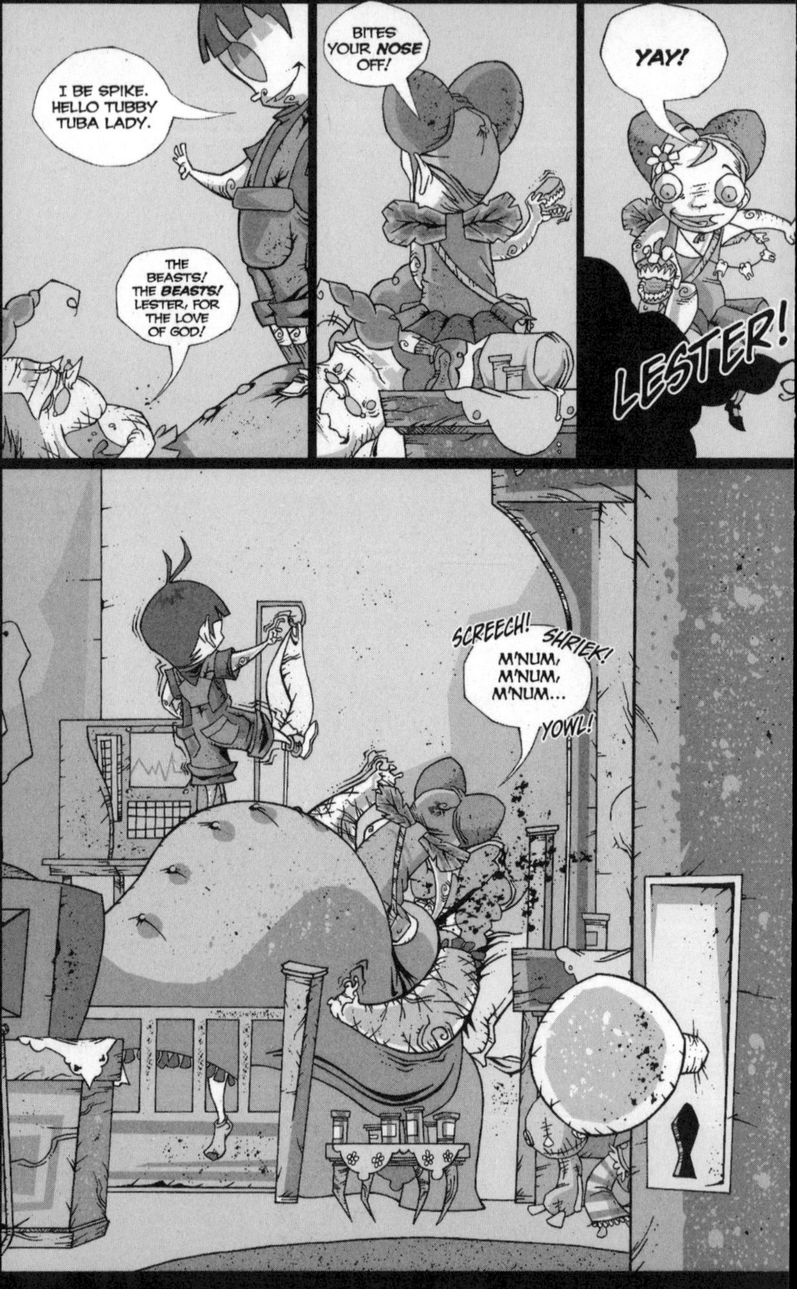
I BE SPIKE. HELLO TUBBY TUBA LADY.
THE BEASTS! THE BEASTS! LESTER, FOR THE LOVE OF GOD!
BITES YOUR NOSE OFF!
YAY!
LESTER!
SCREECH!
SHRIEK!
M'NUM, M'NUM, M'NUM...
YOWL!

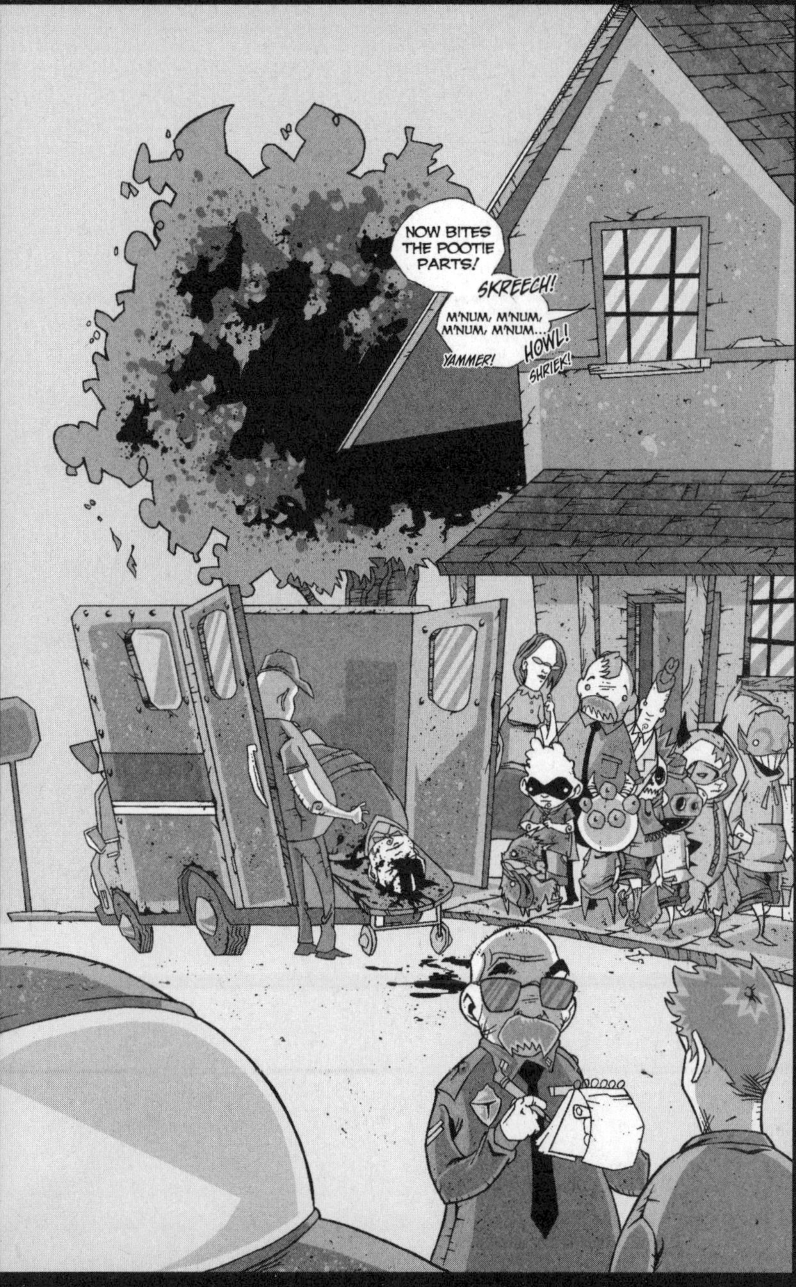
NOW BITES THE POOTIE PARTS!
SKREECH!
M'NUM, M'NUM, M'NUM, M'NUM...
HOWL!
YAMMER!
SHRIEK!

i Luv Halloween

Chapter Five:
MUSH

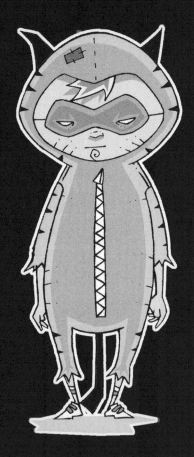

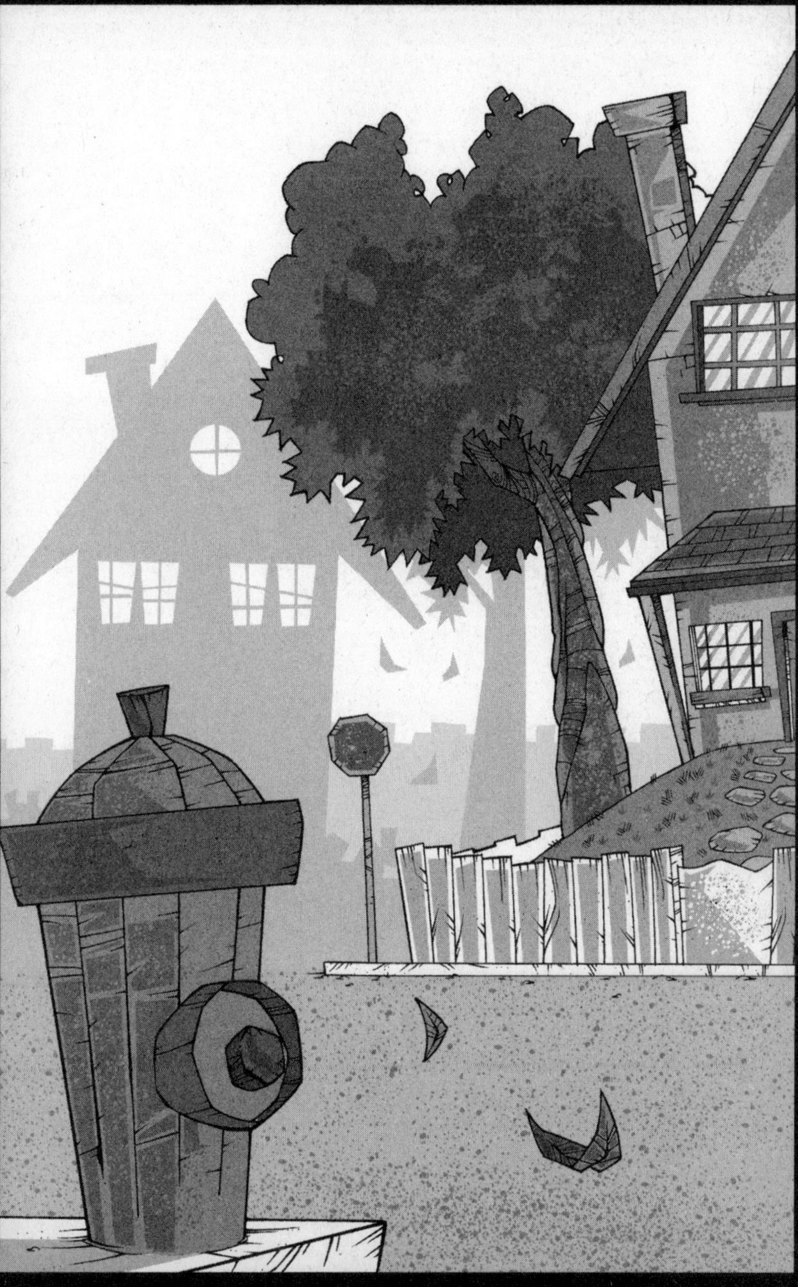

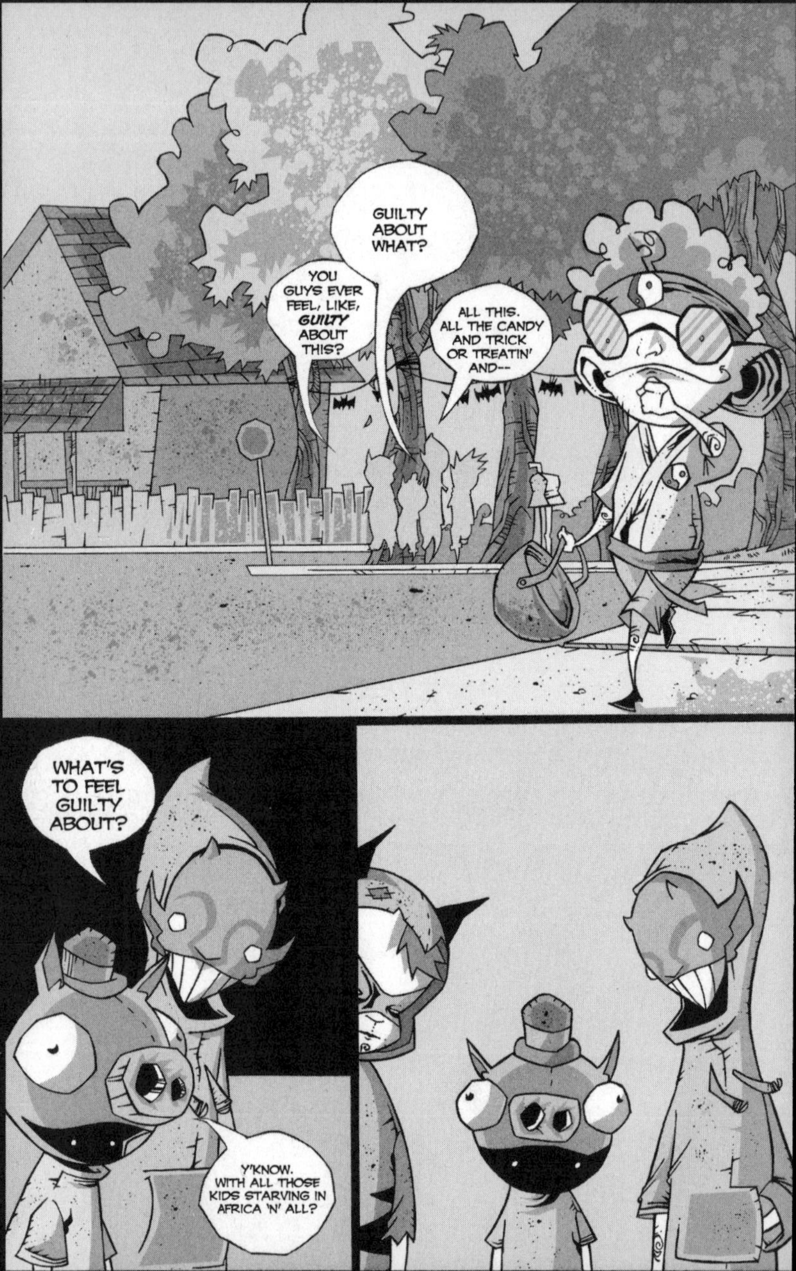
YOU GUYS EVER FEEL, LIKE, *GUILTY* ABOUT THIS?
GUILTY ABOUT WHAT?
ALL THIS. ALL THE CANDY AND TRICK OR TREATIN' AND--
WHAT'S TO FEEL GUILTY ABOUT?
Y'KNOW. WITH ALL THOSE KIDS STARVING IN AFRICA 'N' ALL?

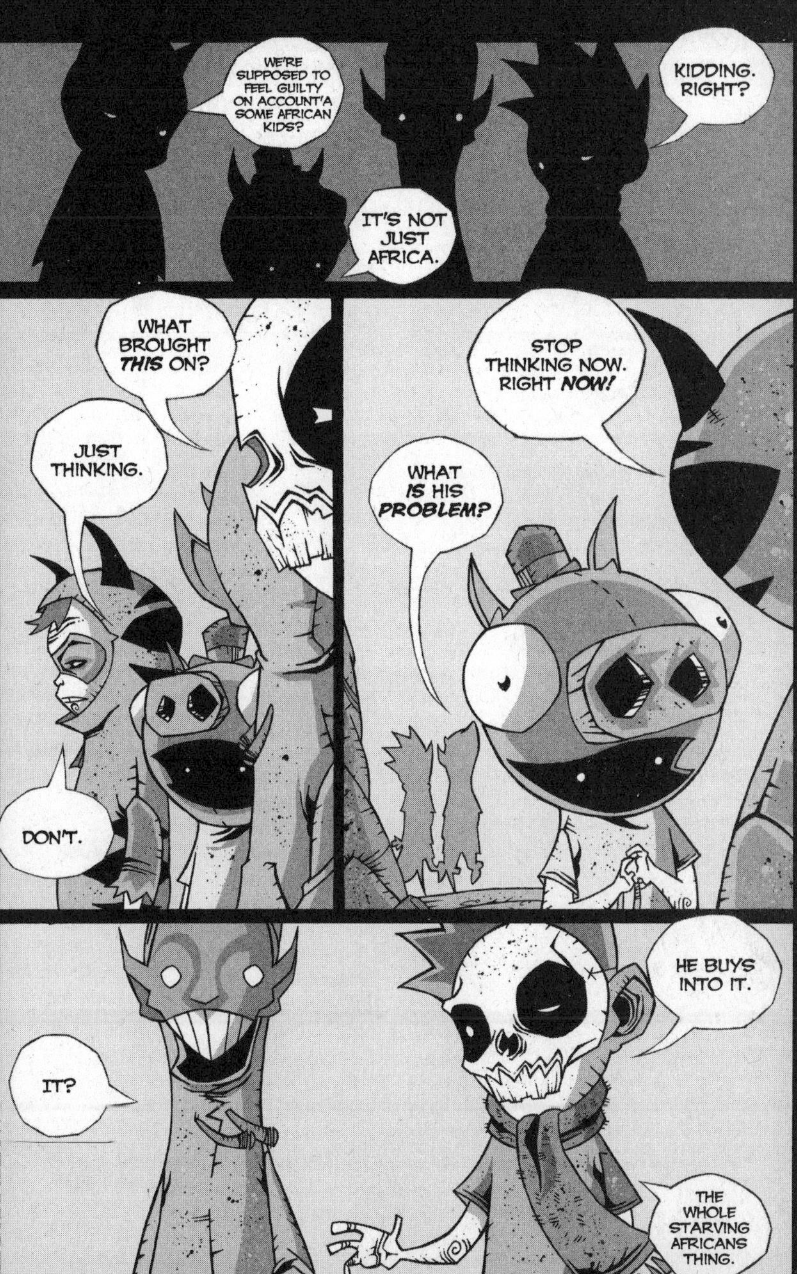
WE'RE SUPPOSED TO FEEL GUILTY ON ACCOUNT'A SOME AFRICAN KIDS?
KIDDING. RIGHT?
IT'S NOT JUST AFRICA.
WHAT BROUGHT *THIS* ON?
JUST THINKING.
DON'T.
STOP THINKING NOW. RIGHT *NOW!*
WHAT *IS* HIS *PROBLEM?*
HE BUYS INTO IT.
IT?
THE WHOLE STARVING AFRICANS THING.

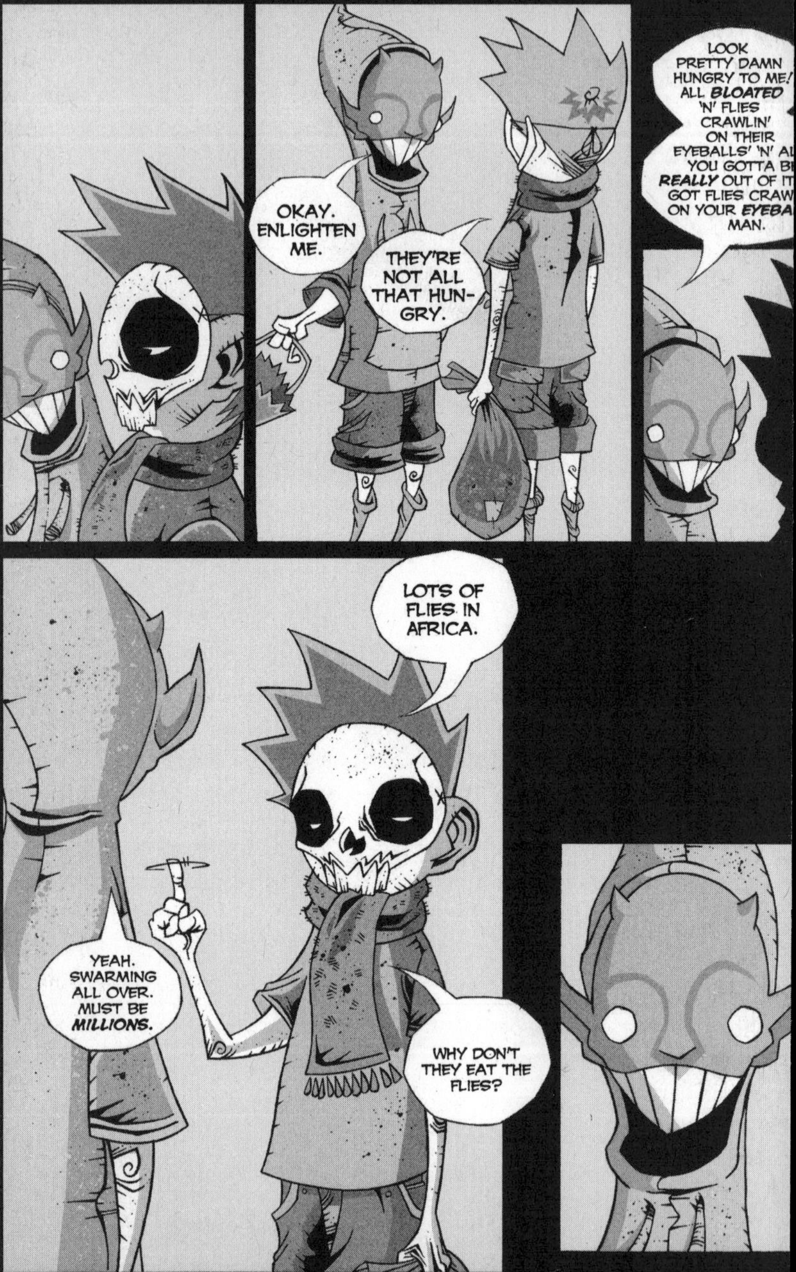
OKAY. ENLIGHTEN ME.
THEY'RE NOT ALL THAT HUN-GRY.
LOOK PRETTY DAMN HUNGRY TO ME! ALL ***BLOATED*** 'N' FLIES CRAWLIN' ON THEIR EYEBALLS' 'N' AL YOU GOTTA B ***REALLY*** OUT OF IT GOT FLIES CRAW ON YOUR ***EYEBA*** MAN.
LOTS OF FLIES IN AFRICA.
YEAH. SWARMING ALL OVER. MUST BE ***MILLIONS.***
WHY DON'T THEY EAT THE FLIES?

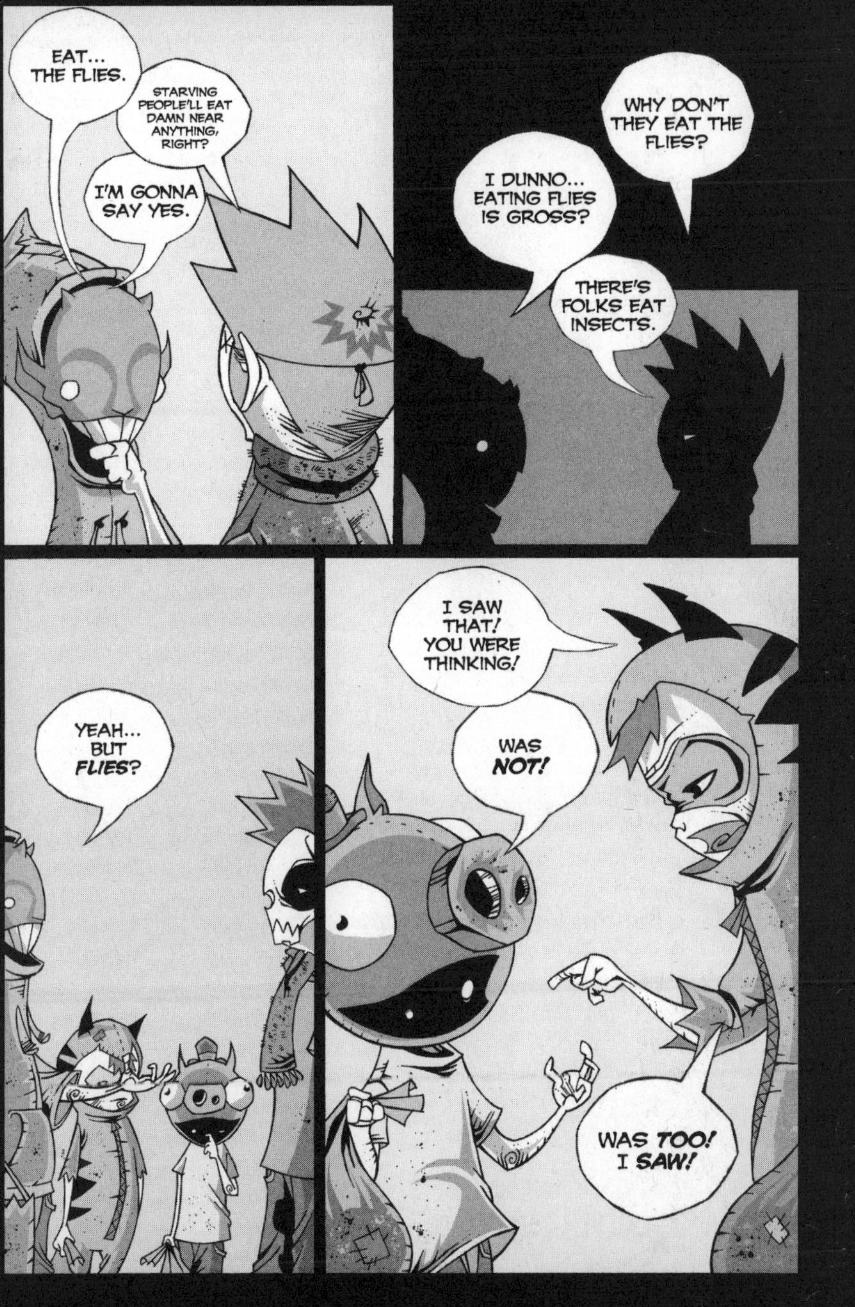
EAT... THE FLIES.
STARVING PEOPLE'LL EAT DAMN NEAR ANYTHING, RIGHT?
I'M GONNA SAY YES.
WHY DON'T THEY EAT THE FLIES?
I DUNNO... EATING FLIES IS GROSS?
THERE'S FOLKS EAT INSECTS.
YEAH... BUT *FLIES*?
I SAW THAT! YOU WERE THINKING!
WAS *NOT!*
WAS *TOO!* I *SAW!*

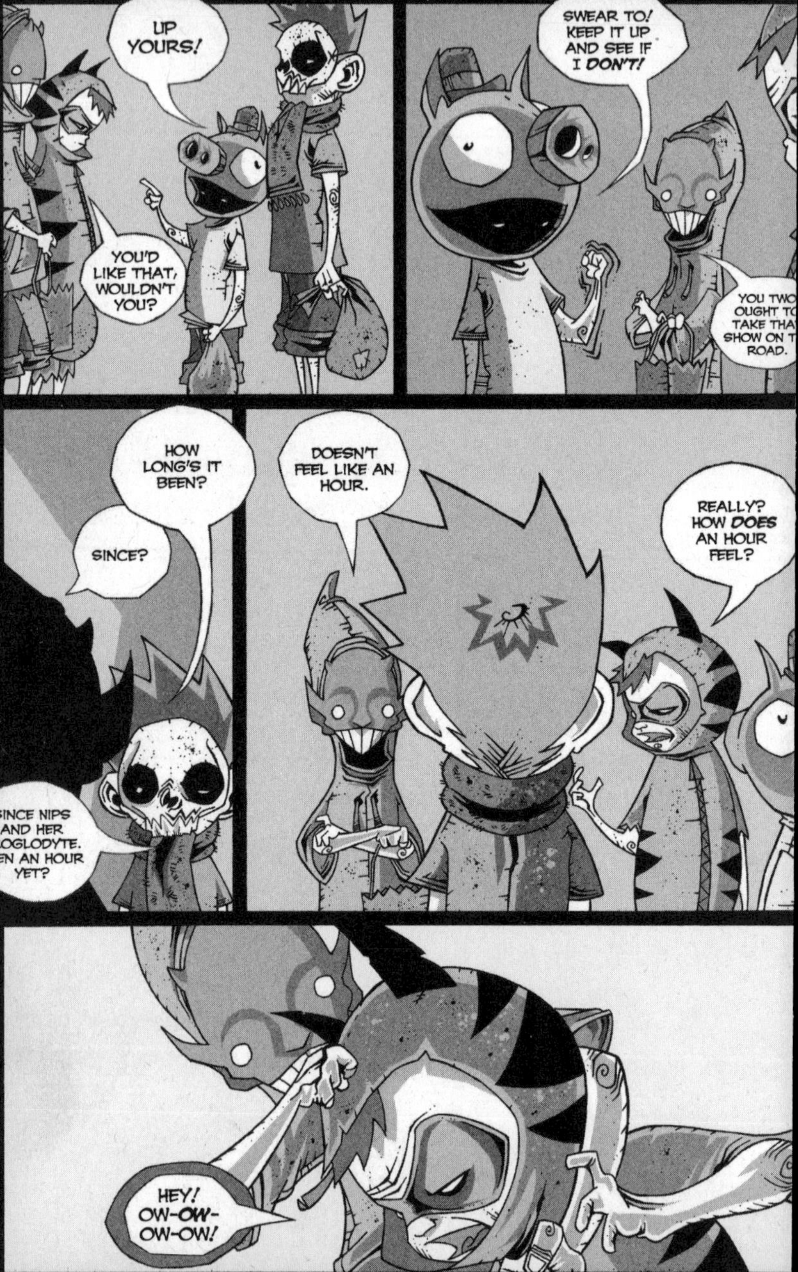
UP YOURS!
YOU'D LIKE THAT, WOULDN'T YOU?
SWEAR TO! KEEP IT UP AND SEE IF I *DON'T!*
YOU TWO OUGHT TO TAKE THA SHOW ON T ROAD.
HOW LONG'S IT BEEN?
SINCE?
SINCE NIPS AND HER TROGLODYTE. BEEN AN HOUR YET?
DOESN'T FEEL LIKE AN HOUR.
REALLY? HOW *DOES* AN HOUR FEEL?
HEY! OW-*OW*-OW-OW!

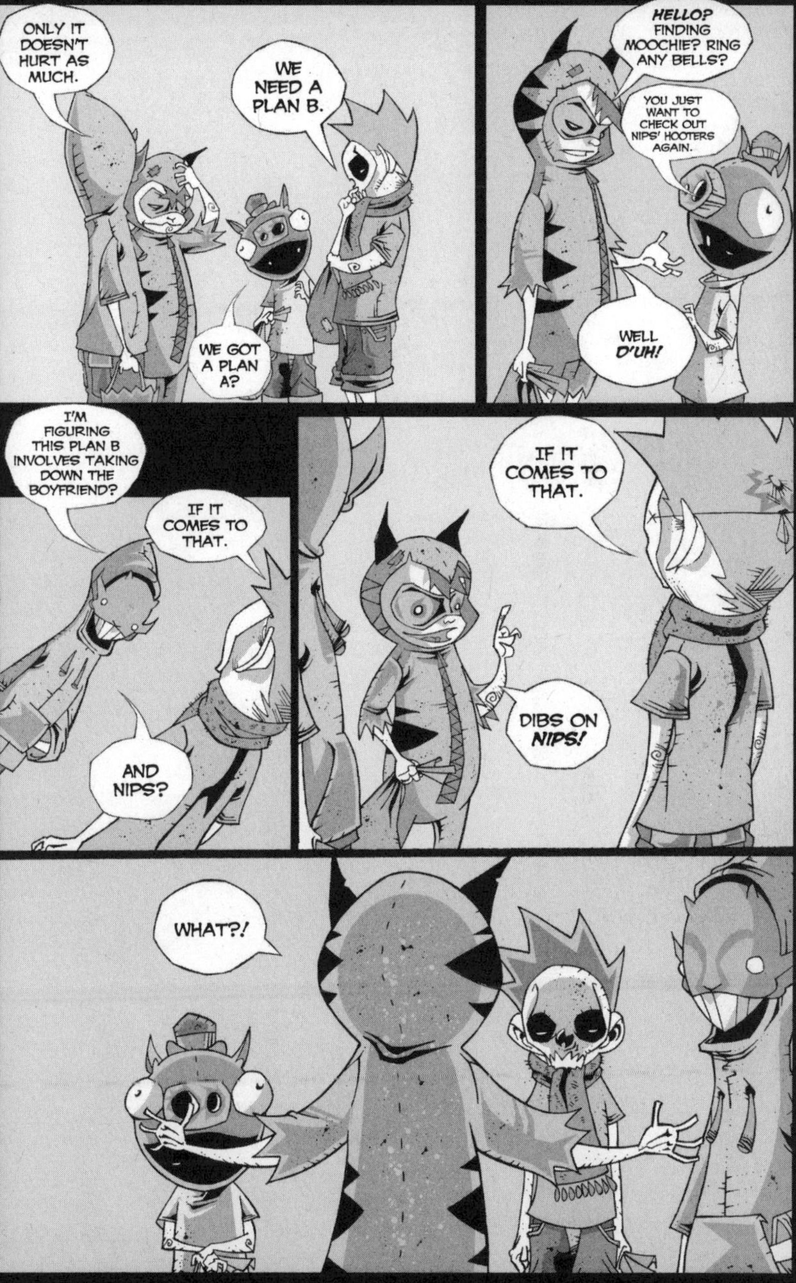
ONLY IT DOESN'T HURT AS MUCH.
WE NEED A PLAN B.
WE GOT A PLAN A?
HELLO? FINDING MOOCHIE? RING ANY BELLS?
YOU JUST WANT TO CHECK OUT NIPS' HOOTERS AGAIN.
WELL *D'UH!*
I'M FIGURING THIS PLAN B INVOLVES TAKING DOWN THE BOYFRIEND?
IF IT COMES TO THAT.
AND NIPS?
IF IT COMES TO THAT.
DIBS ON *NIPS!*
WHAT?!

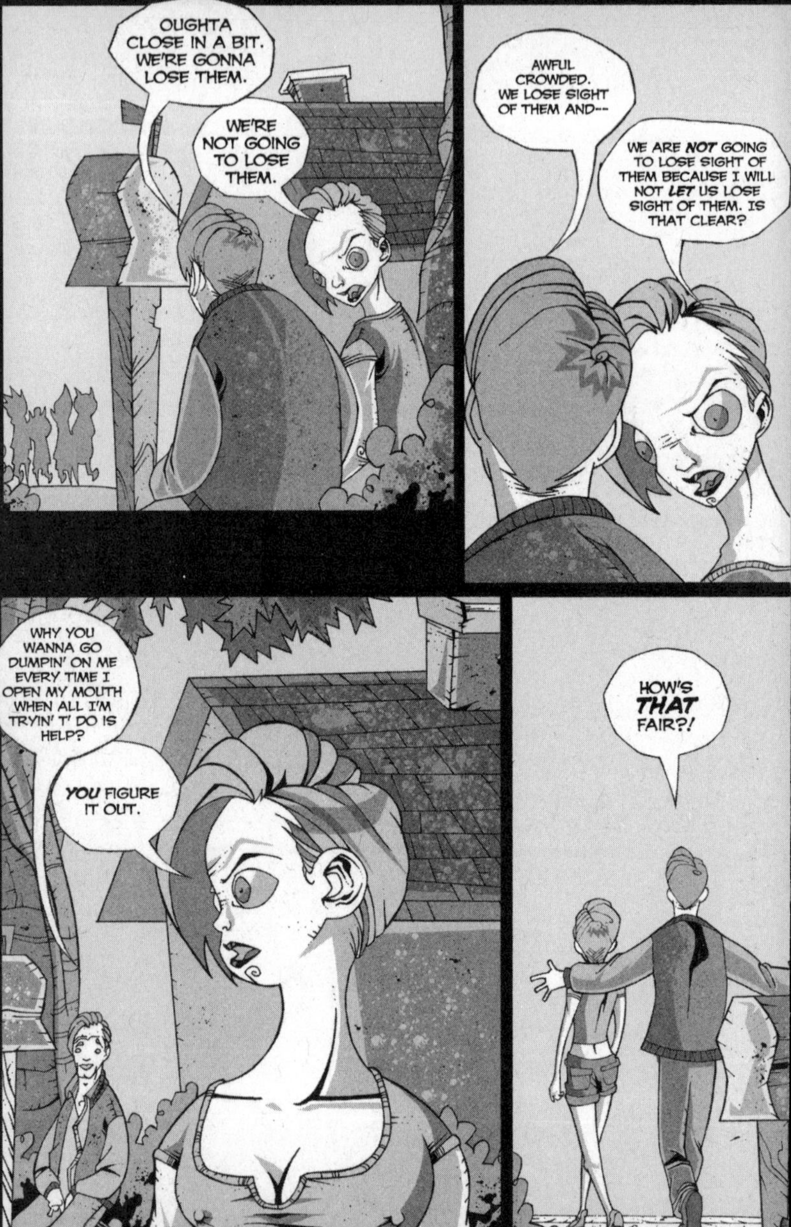
OUGHTA CLOSE IN A BIT. WE'RE GONNA LOSE THEM.
WE'RE NOT GOING TO LOSE THEM.
AWFUL CROWDED. WE LOSE SIGHT OF THEM AND--
WE ARE **NOT** GOING TO LOSE SIGHT OF THEM BECAUSE I WILL NOT **LET** US LOSE SIGHT OF THEM. IS THAT CLEAR?
WHY YOU WANNA GO DUMPIN' ON ME EVERY TIME I OPEN MY MOUTH WHEN ALL I'M TRYIN' T' DO IS HELP?
YOU FIGURE IT OUT.
HOW'S **THAT** FAIR?!

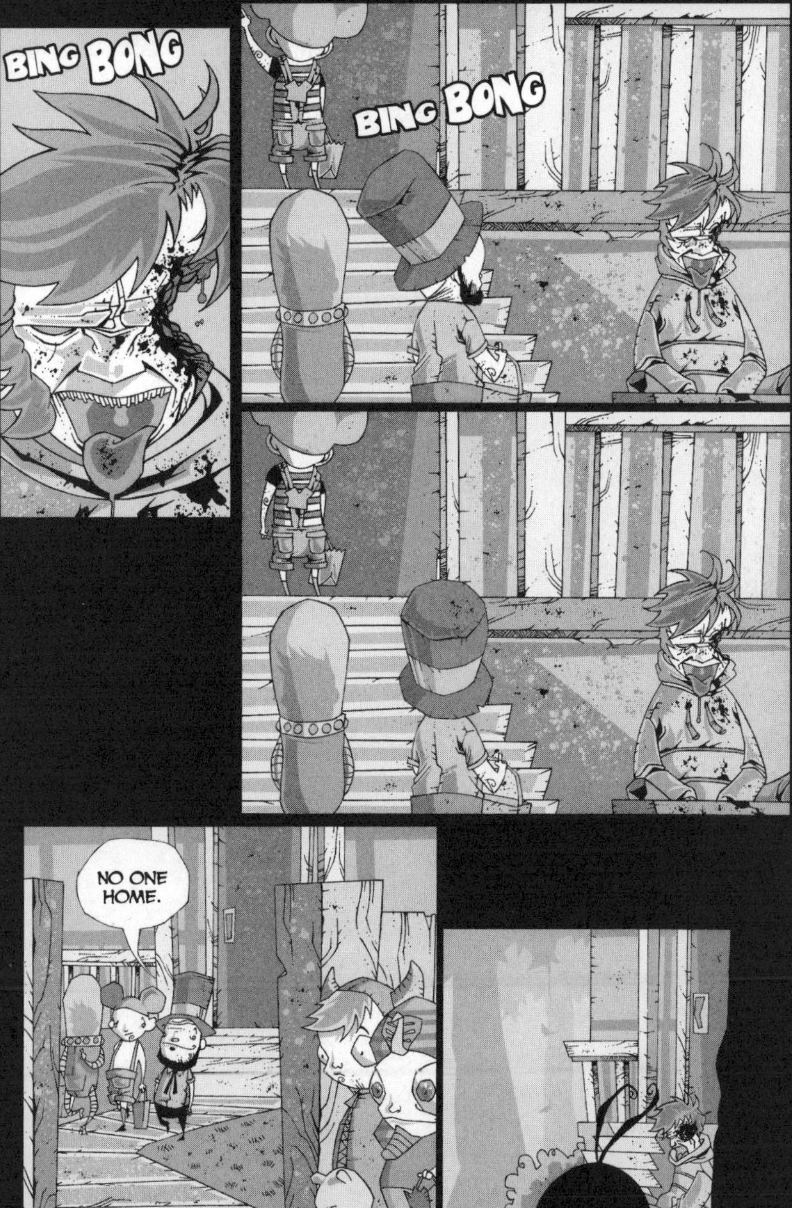
BING BONG
BING BONG
NO ONE HOME.

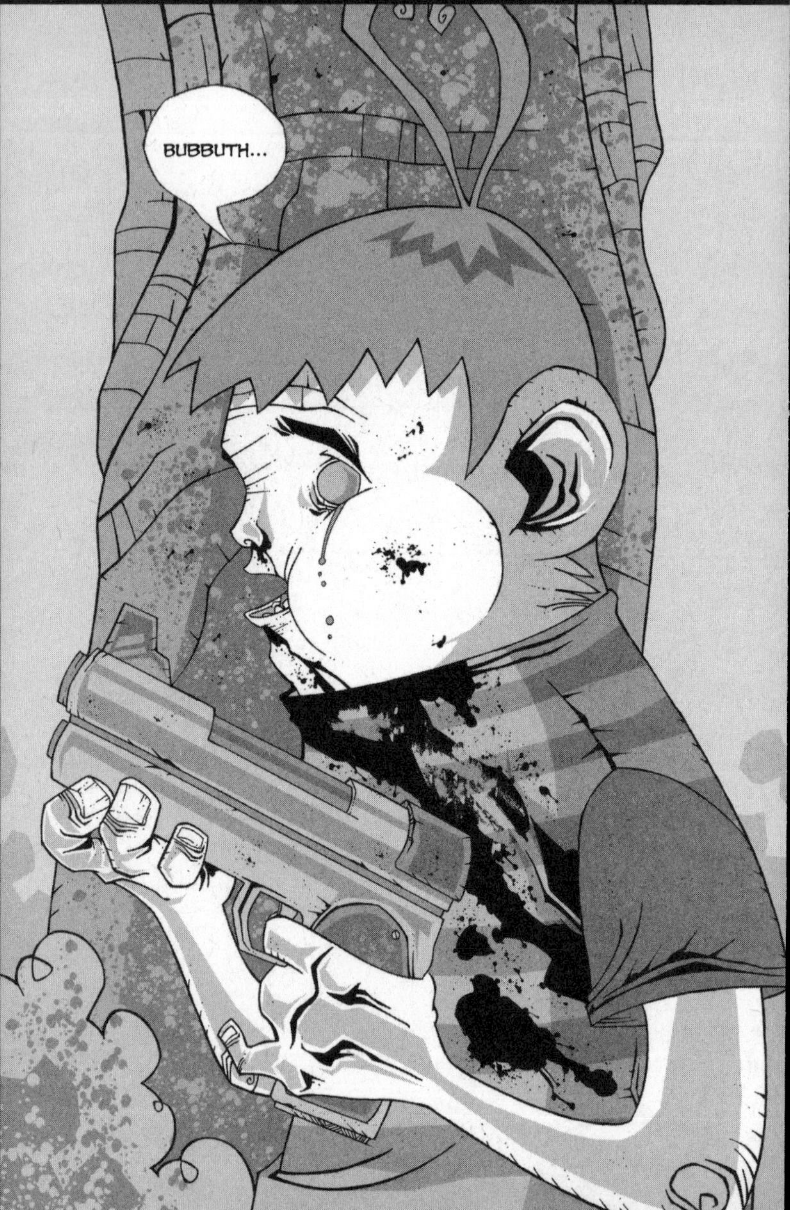
BUBBUTH...

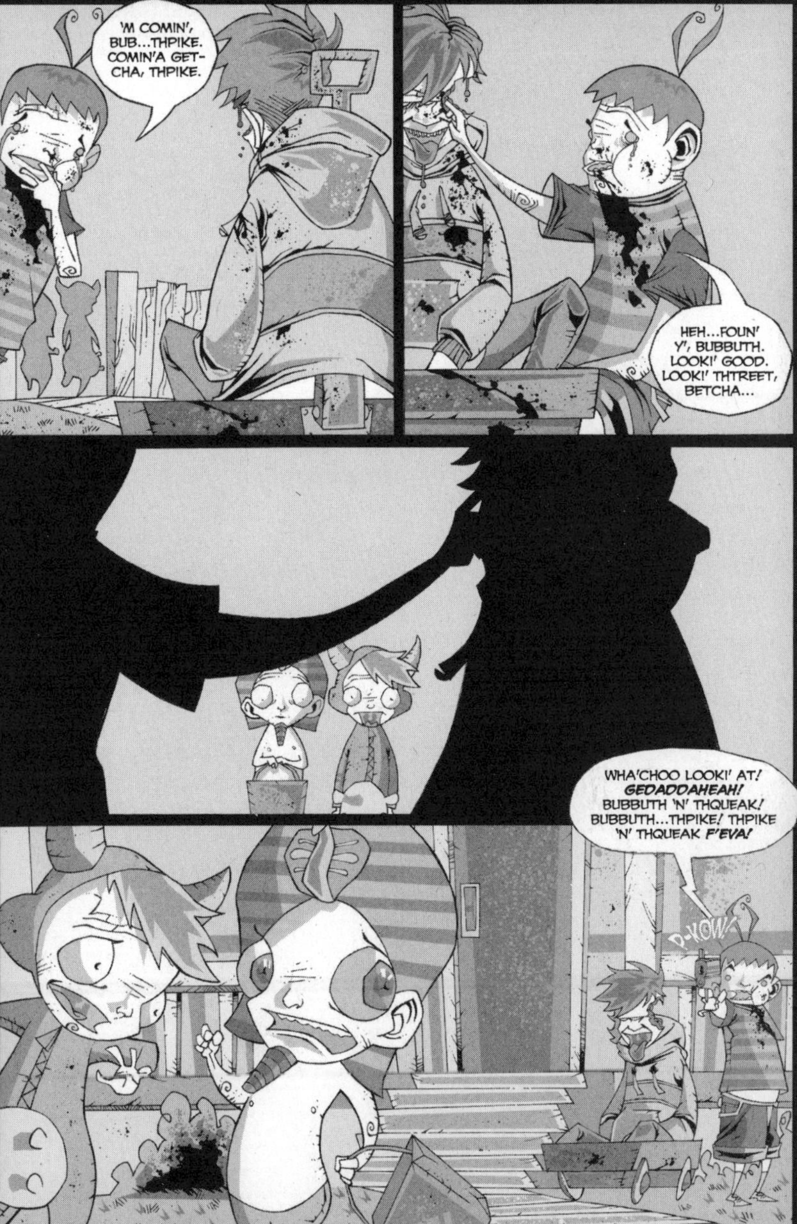
'M COMIN', BUB...THPIKE. COMIN'A GET-CHA, THPIKE.
HEH...FOUN' Y', BUBBUTH. LOOKI' GOOD. LOOKI' THTREET, BETCHA...
WHA'CHOO LOOKI' AT! *GEDADDAHEAH!* BUBBUTH 'N' THQUEAK! BUBBUTH...THPIKE! THPIKE 'N' THQUEAK *F'EVA!*
D-KOW!

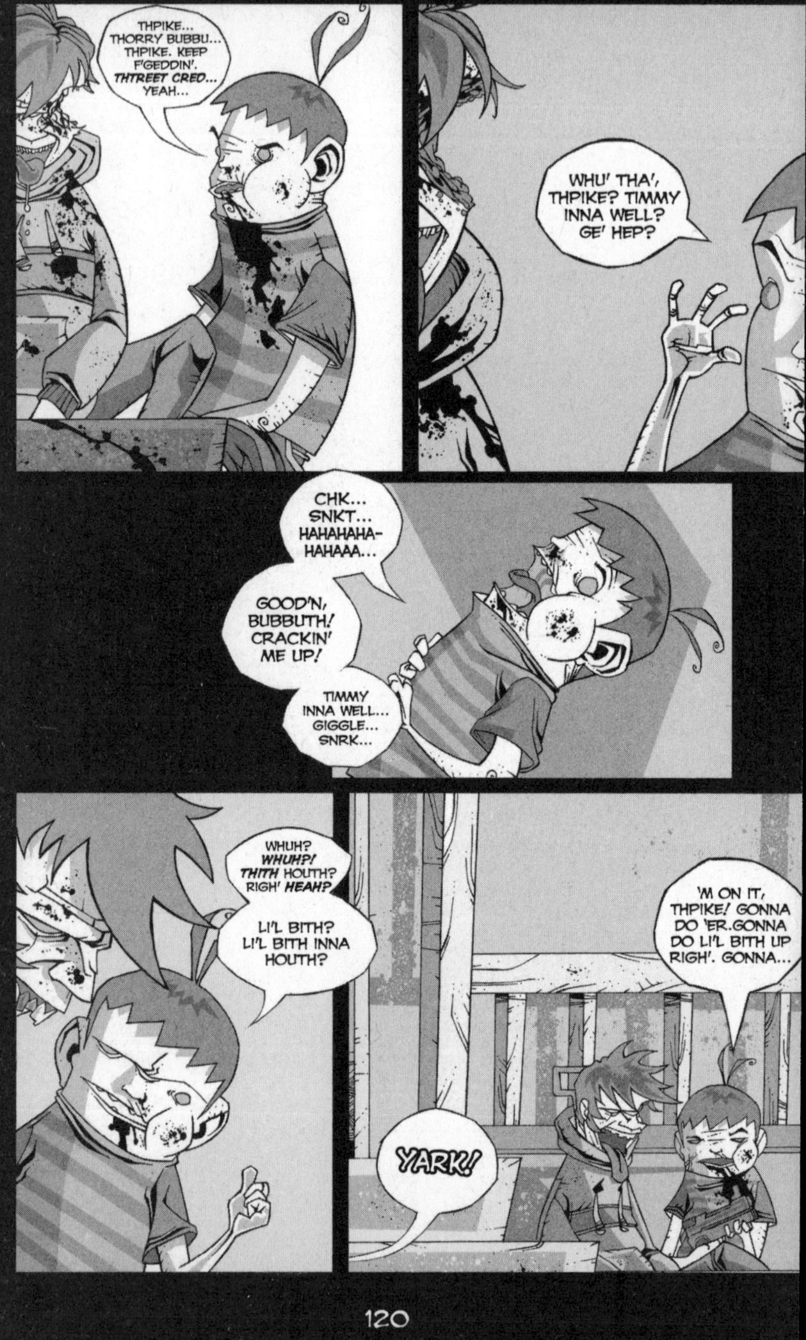
THPIKE... THORRY BUBBU... THPIKE. KEEP F'GEDDIN'. *THTREET CRED...* YEAH...
WHU' THA', THPIKE? TIMMY INNA WELL? GE' HEP?
CHK... SNKT... HAHAHAHA-HAHAAA...
GOOD'N, BUBBUTH! CRACKIN' ME UP!
TIMMY INNA WELL... GIGGLE... SNRK...
WHUH? *WHUH?!* *THITH* HOUTH? RIGH' *HEAH?*
LI'L BITH? LI'L BITH INNA HOUTH?
'M ON IT, THPIKE! GONNA DO 'ER.GONNA DO LI'L BITH UP RIGH'. GONNA...
YARK!

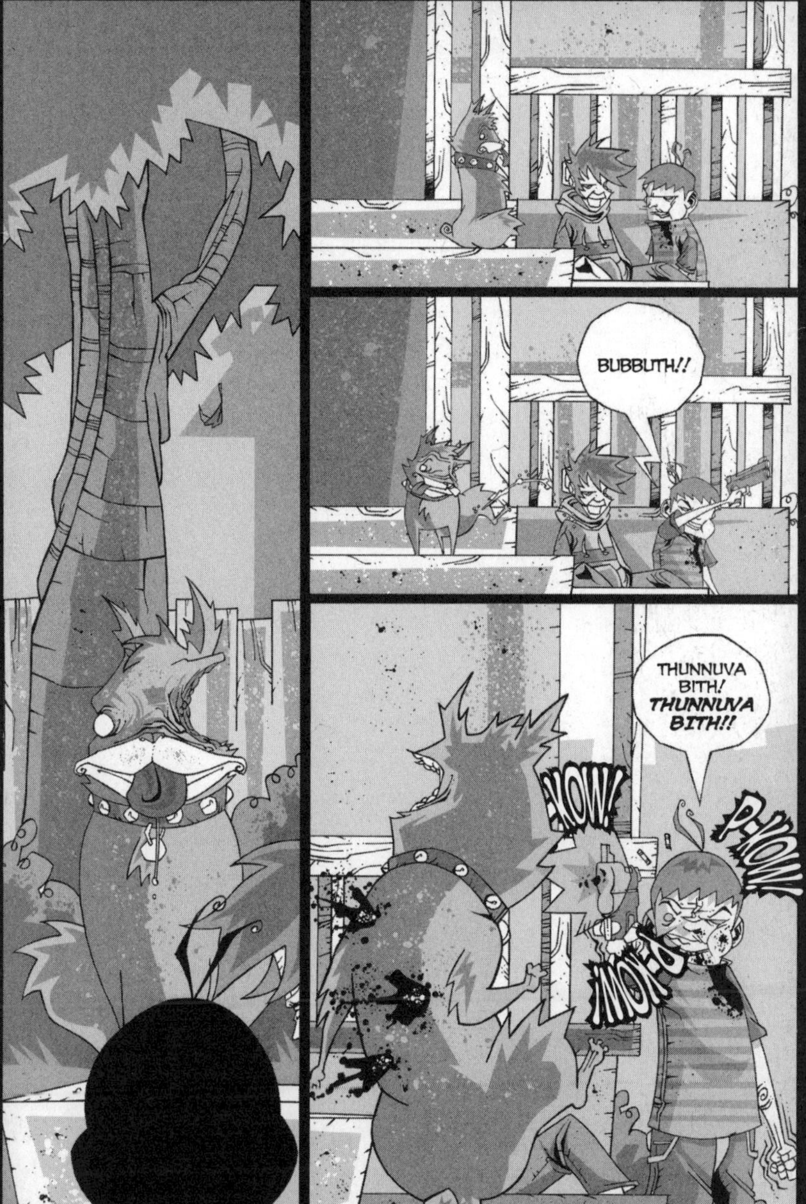
BUBBUTH!!
THUNNUVA BITH! THUNNUVA BITH!!
P-KOW!
P-KOW!
P-KOW!

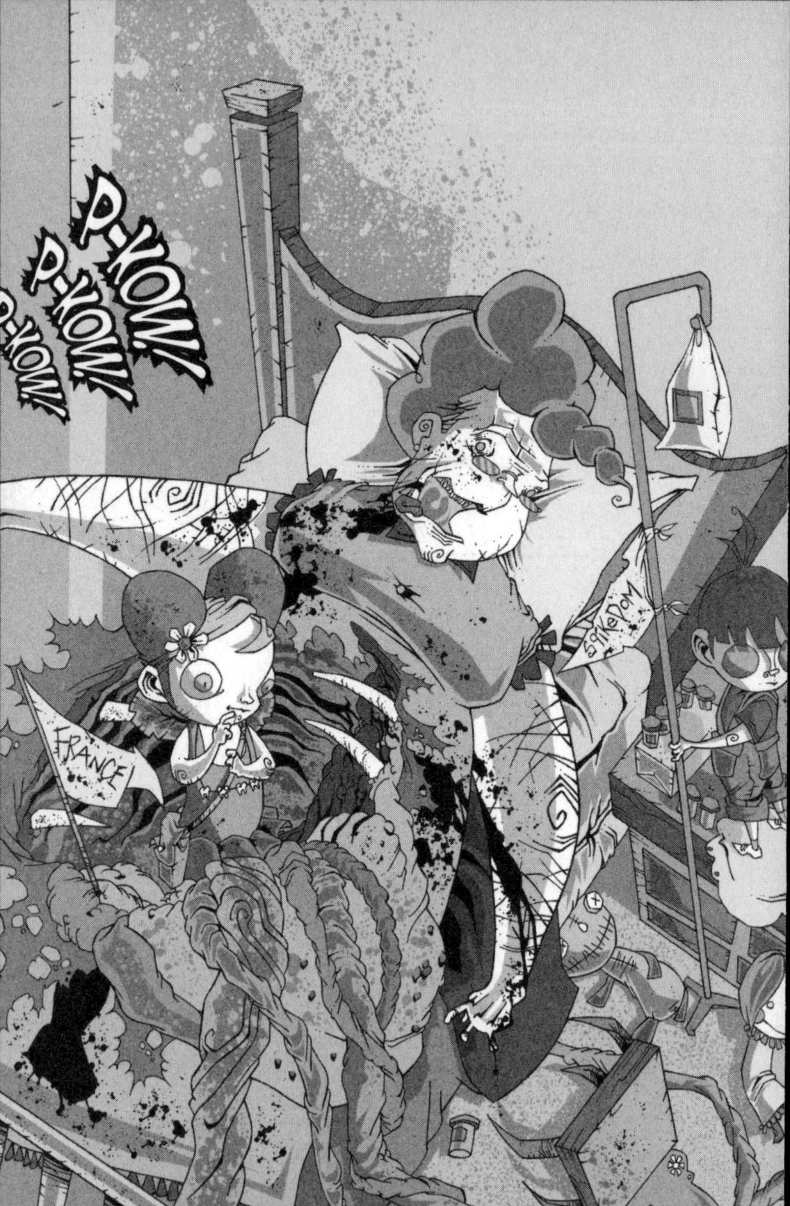
P-KOW!
P-KOW!
P-KOW!
FRANCE
SPIKEDOM

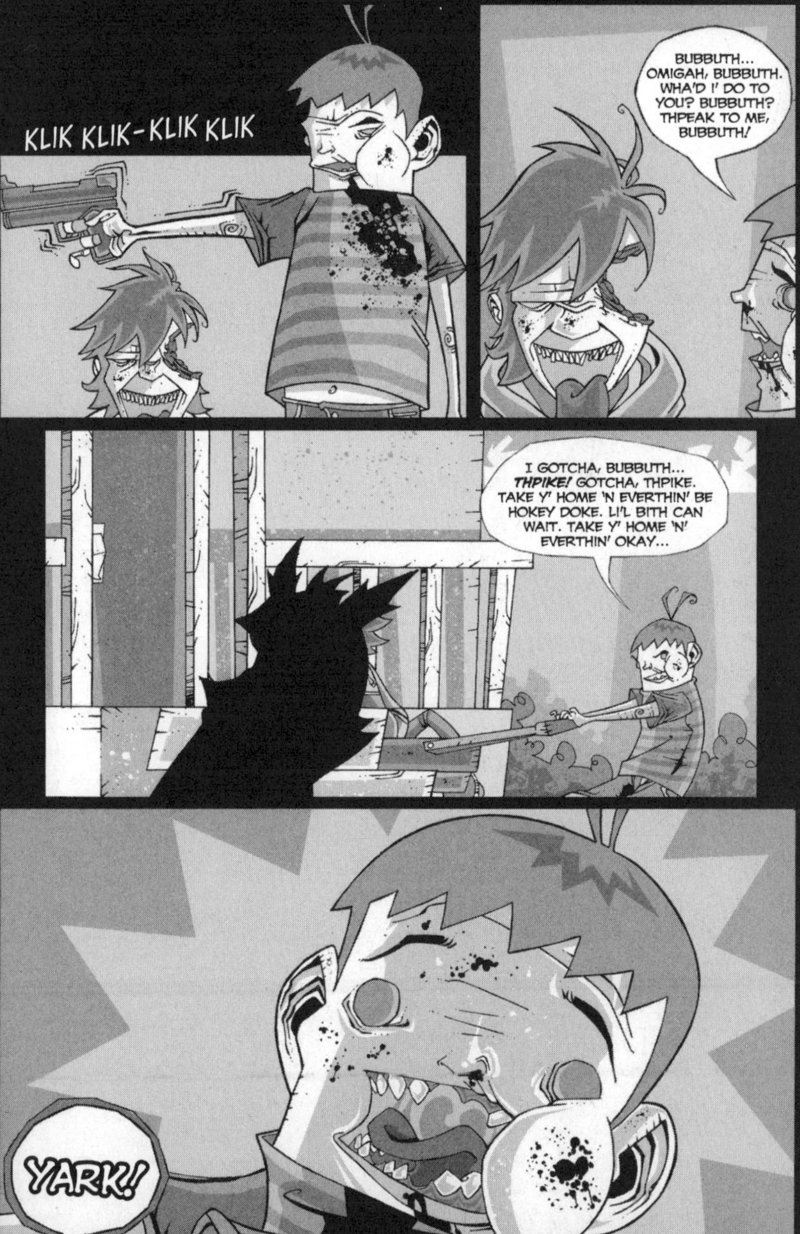
KLIK KLIK-KLIK KLIK
BUBBUTH... OMIGAH, BUBBUTH. WHA'D I' DO TO YOU? BUBBUTH? THPEAK TO ME, BUBBUTH!
I GOTCHA, BUBBUTH... *THPIKE!* GOTCHA, THPIKE. TAKE Y' HOME 'N EVERTHIN' BE HOKEY DOKE. LI'L BITH CAN WAIT. TAKE Y' HOME 'N' EVERTHIN' OKAY...
YARK!

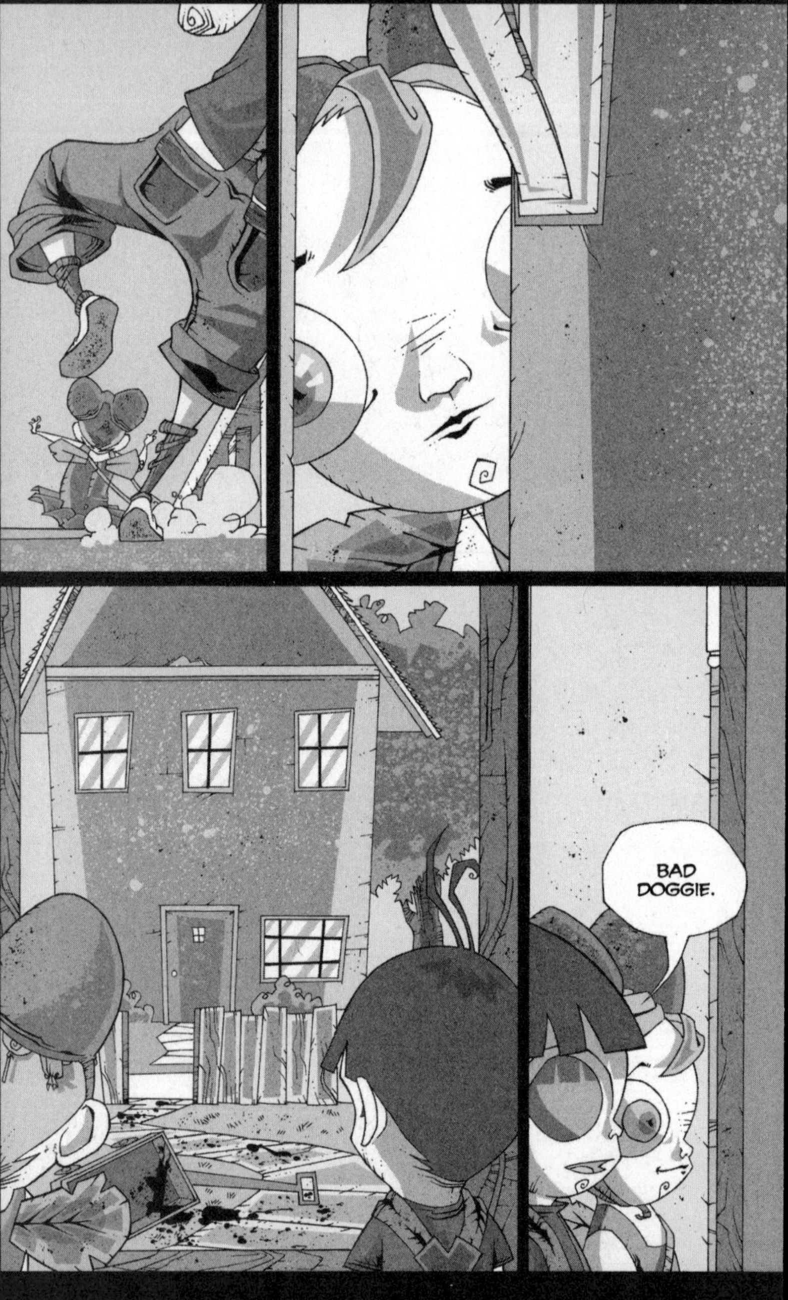
BAD DOGGIE.

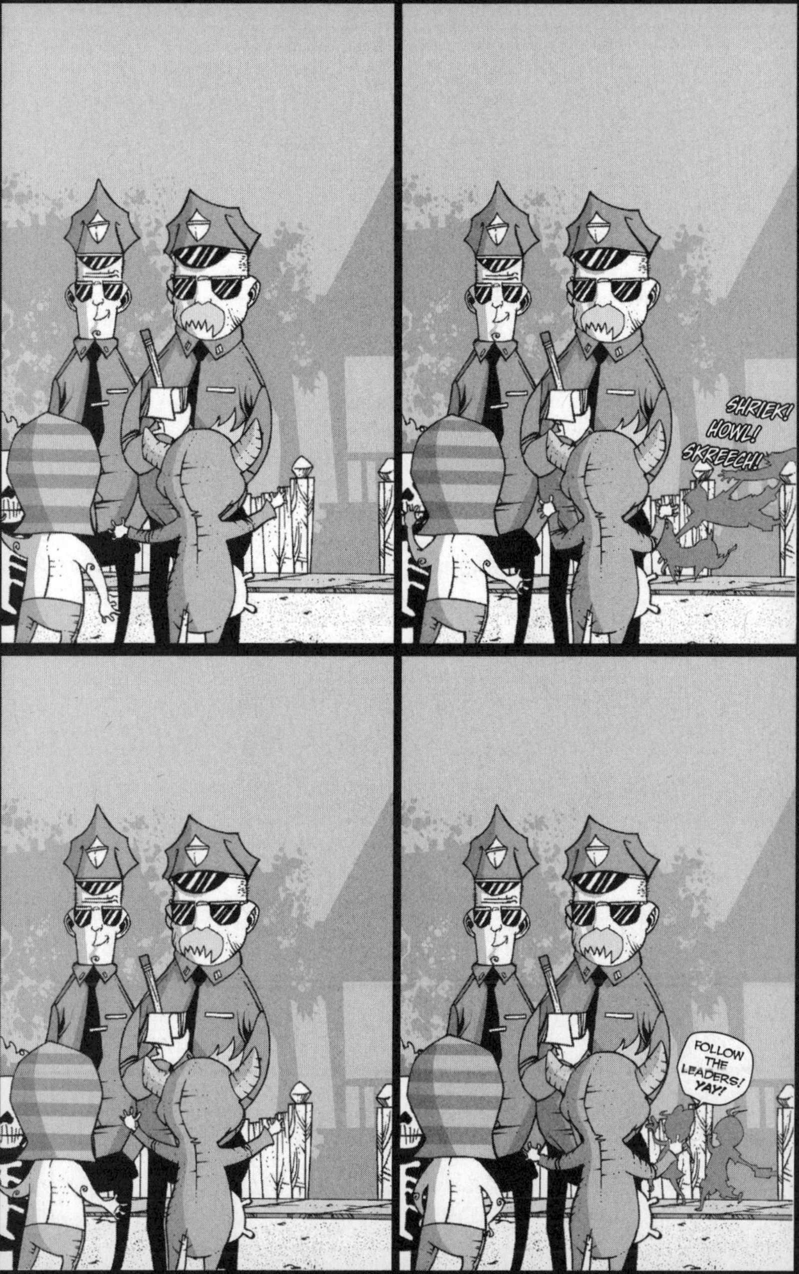
SHRIEK!
HOWL!
SKREECH!
FOLLOW THE LEADERS! YAY!

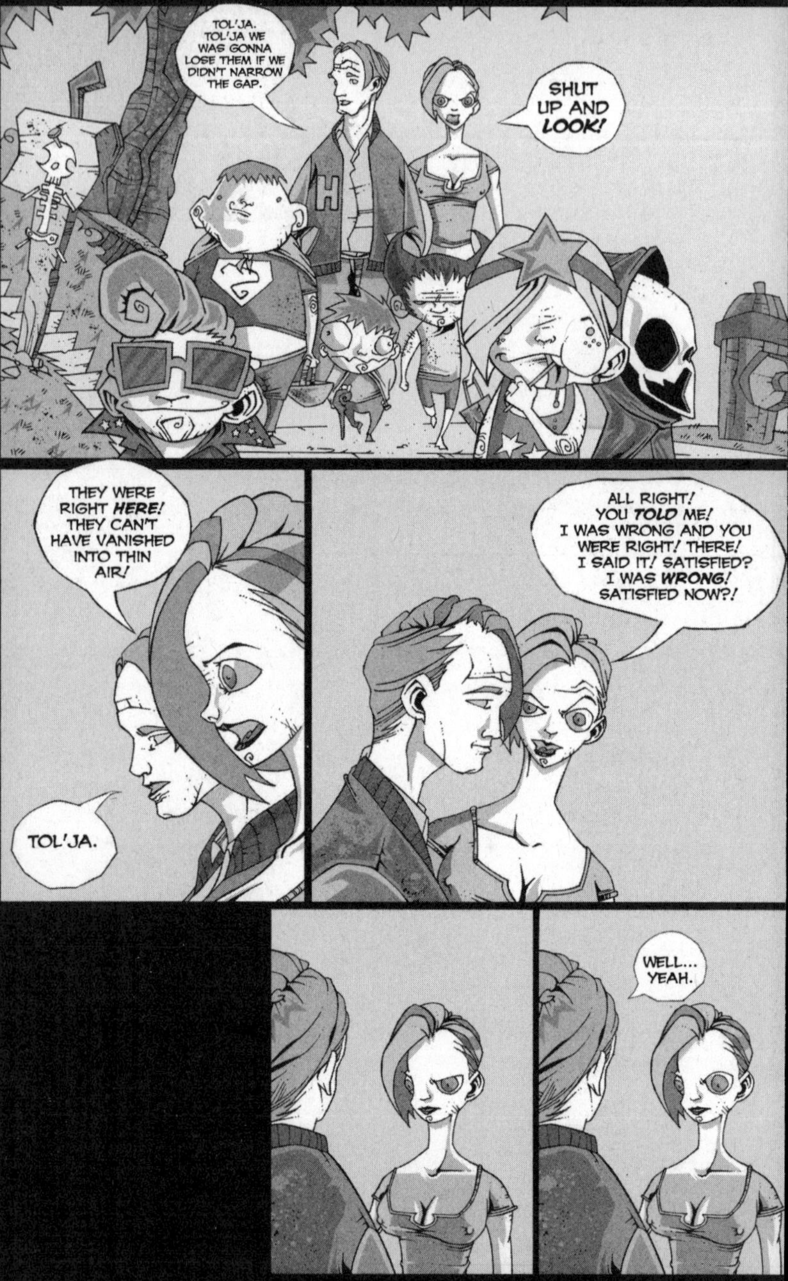
TOL'JA. TOL'JA WE WAS GONNA LOSE THEM IF WE DIDN'T NARROW THE GAP.
SHUT UP AND ***LOOK!***
THEY WERE RIGHT ***HERE!*** THEY CAN'T HAVE VANISHED INTO THIN AIR!
TOL'JA.
ALL RIGHT! YOU ***TOLD*** ME! I WAS WRONG AND YOU WERE RIGHT! THERE! I SAID IT! SATISFIED? I WAS ***WRONG!*** SATISFIED NOW?!
WELL... YEAH.

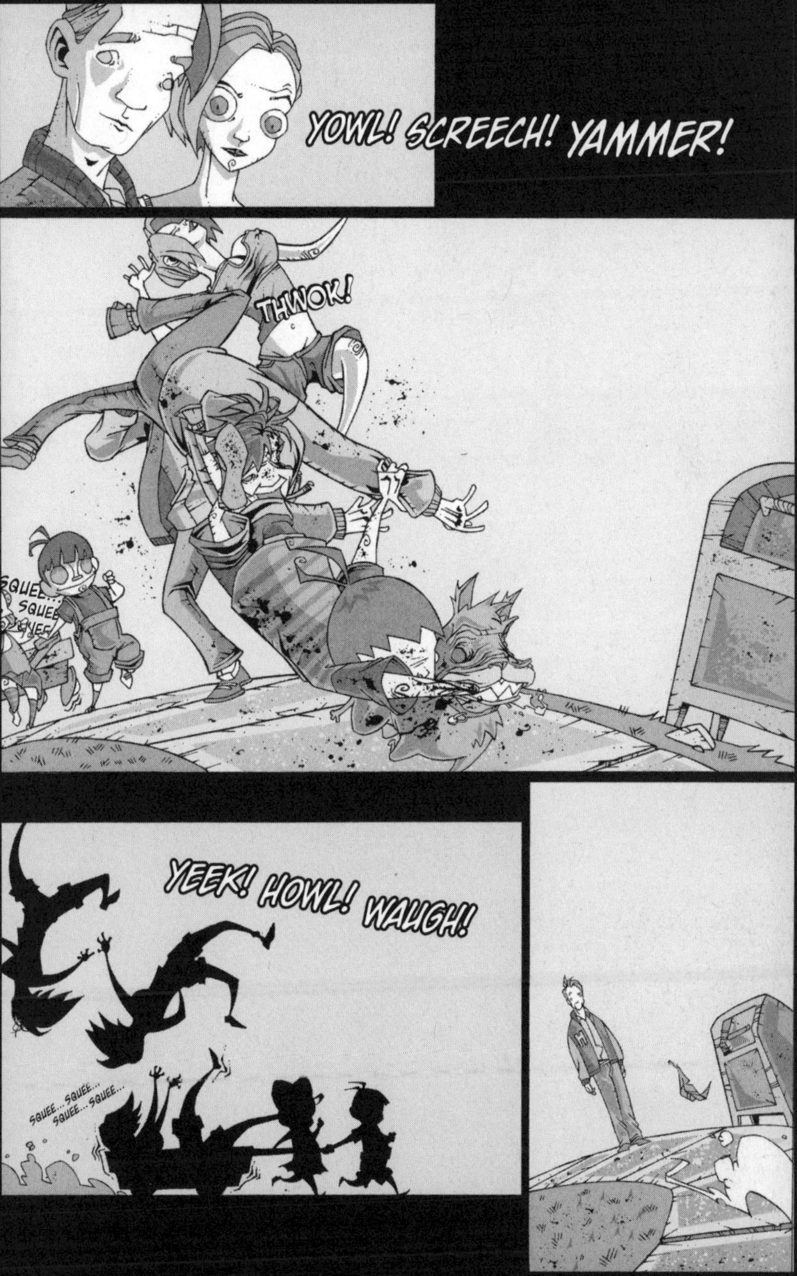
YOWL! SCREECH! YAMMER!
THWOK!
YEEK! HOWL! WAUGH!
SQUEE... SQUEE... SQUEE... SQUEE...

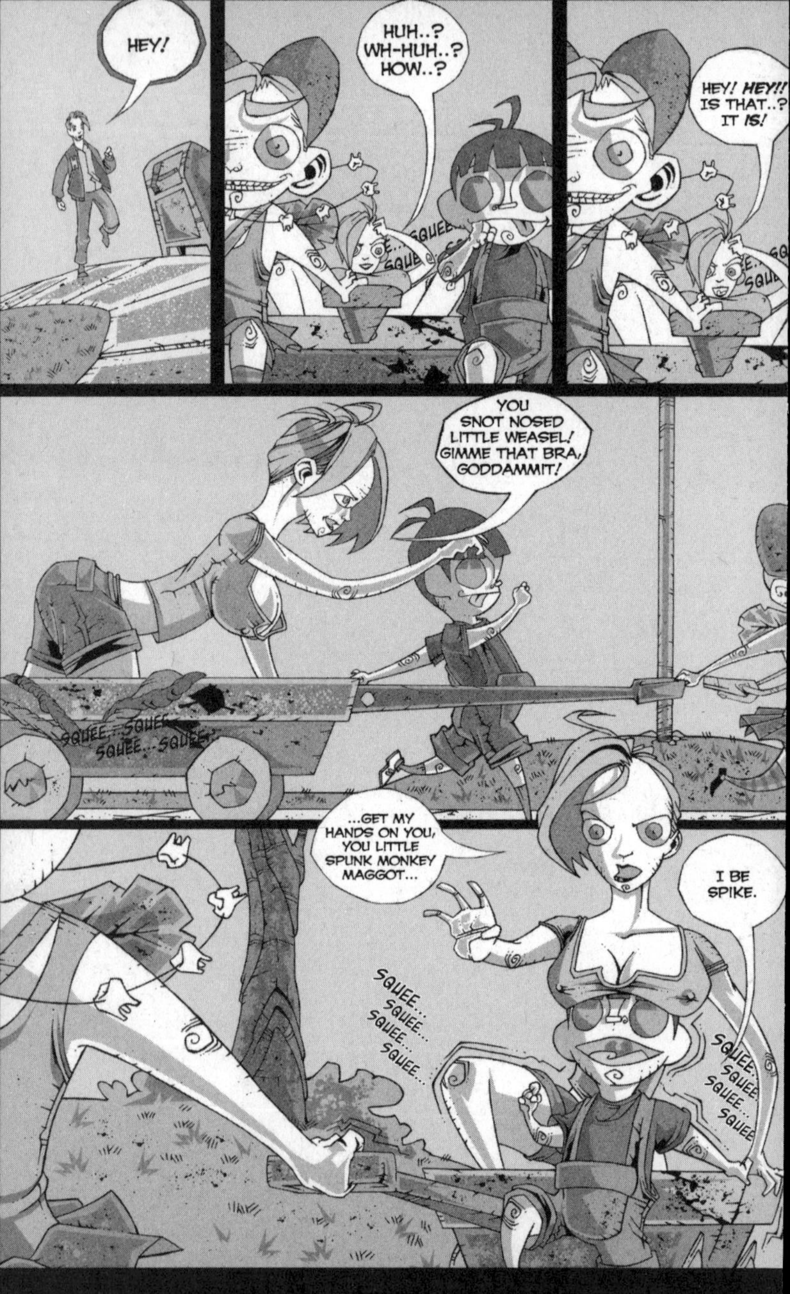
HEY!
HUH..? WH-HUH..? HOW..?
HEY! **HEY!!** IS THAT..? IT **IS!**
YOU SNOT NOSED LITTLE WEASEL! GIMME THAT BRA, GODDAMMIT!
SQUEE...SQUEE SQUEE...SQUEE
...GET MY HANDS ON YOU, YOU LITTLE SPUNK MONKEY MAGGOT...
I BE SPIKE.
SQUEE... SQUEE... SQUEE... SQUEE... SQUEE...
SQUEE SQUEE SQUEE... SQUEE... SQUEE

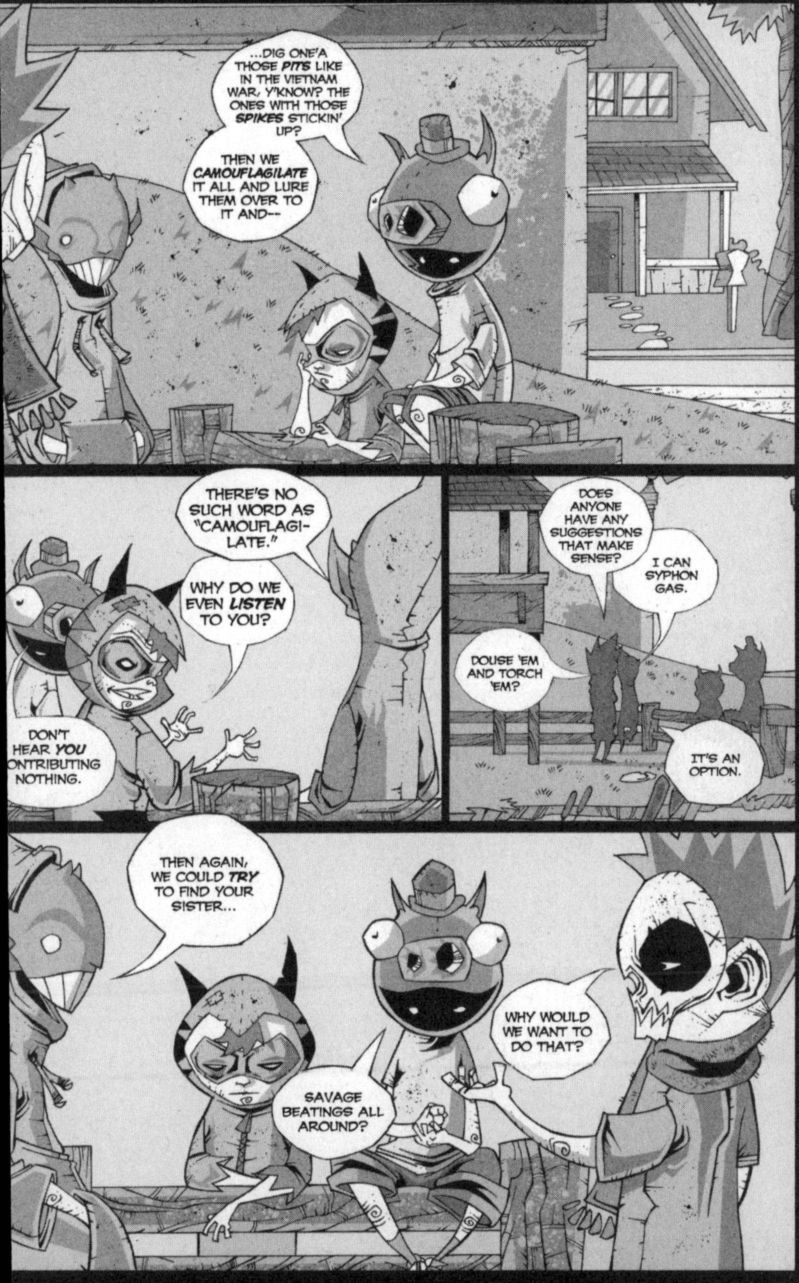
...DIG ONE'A THOSE *PITS* LIKE IN THE VIETNAM WAR, Y'KNOW? THE ONES WITH THOSE *SPIKES* STICKIN' UP?
THEN WE *CAMOUFLAGILATE* IT ALL AND LURE THEM OVER TO IT AND--
THERE'S NO SUCH WORD AS "CAMOUFLAGI-LATE."
WHY DO WE EVEN *LISTEN* TO YOU?
DON'T HEAR *YOU* ONTRIBUTING NOTHING.
DOES ANYONE HAVE ANY SUGGESTIONS THAT MAKE SENSE?
I CAN SYPHON GAS.
DOUSE 'EM AND TORCH 'EM?
IT'S AN OPTION.
THEN AGAIN, WE COULD *TRY* TO FIND YOUR SISTER...
WHY WOULD WE WANT TO DO THAT?
SAVAGE BEATINGS ALL AROUND?

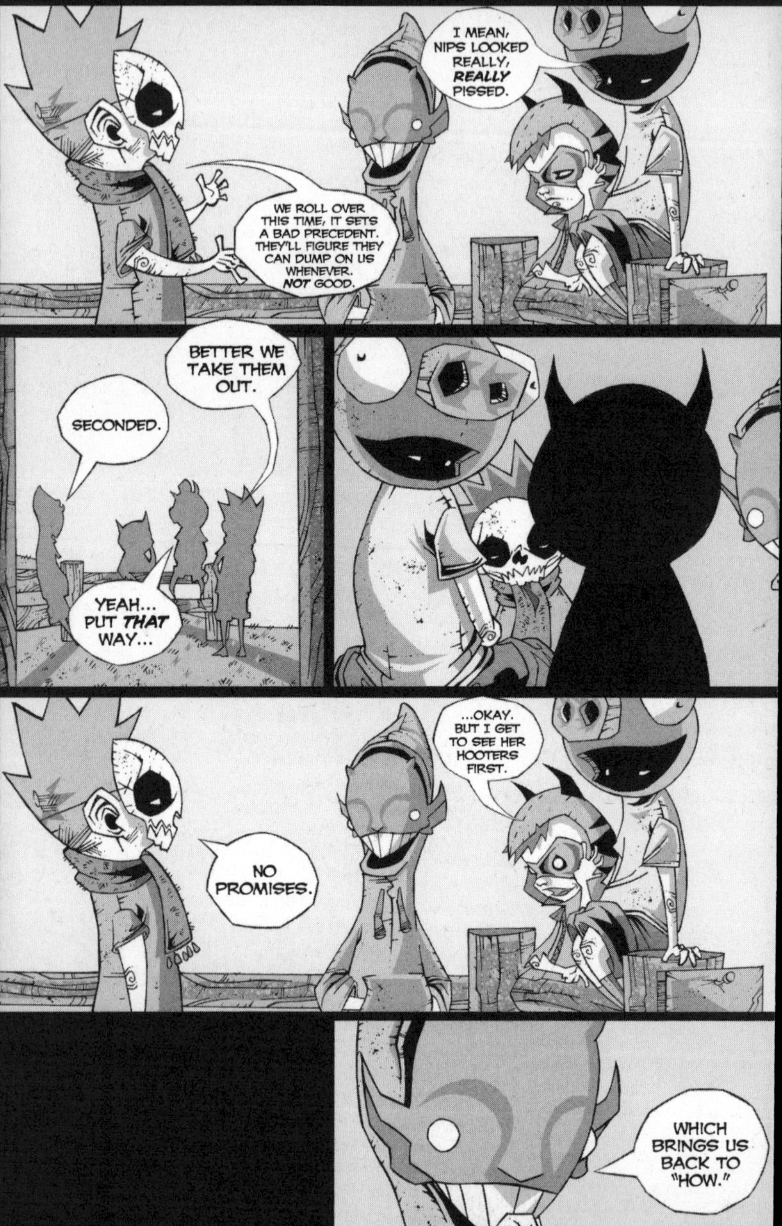
I MEAN, NIPS LOOKED REALLY, ***REALLY*** PISSED.
WE ROLL OVER THIS TIME, IT SETS A BAD PRECEDENT. THEY'LL FIGURE THEY CAN DUMP ON US WHENEVER. ***NOT*** GOOD.
BETTER WE TAKE THEM OUT.
SECONDED.
YEAH... PUT ***THAT*** WAY...
...OKAY. BUT I GET TO SEE HER HOOTERS FIRST.
NO PROMISES.
WHICH BRINGS US BACK TO "HOW."

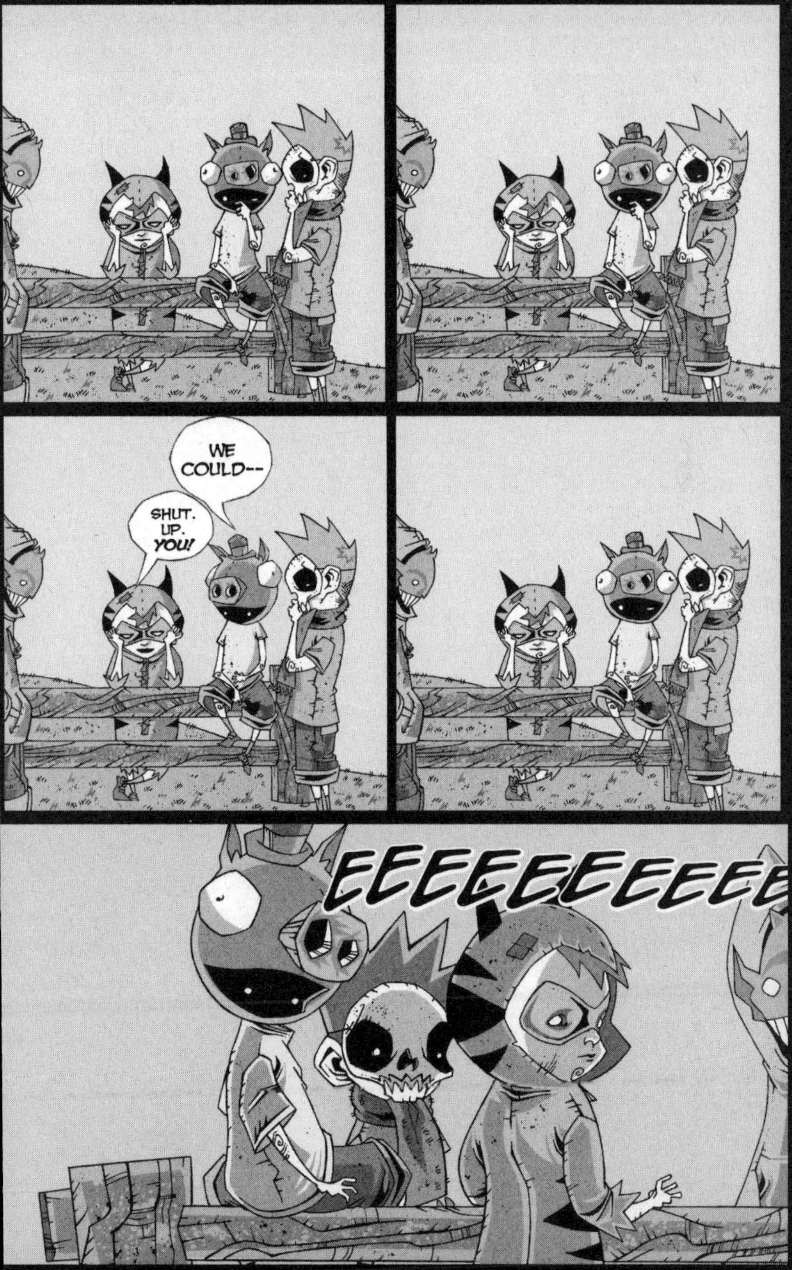
WE COULD--
SHUT. UP. YOU!
EEEEEEEEEEEE

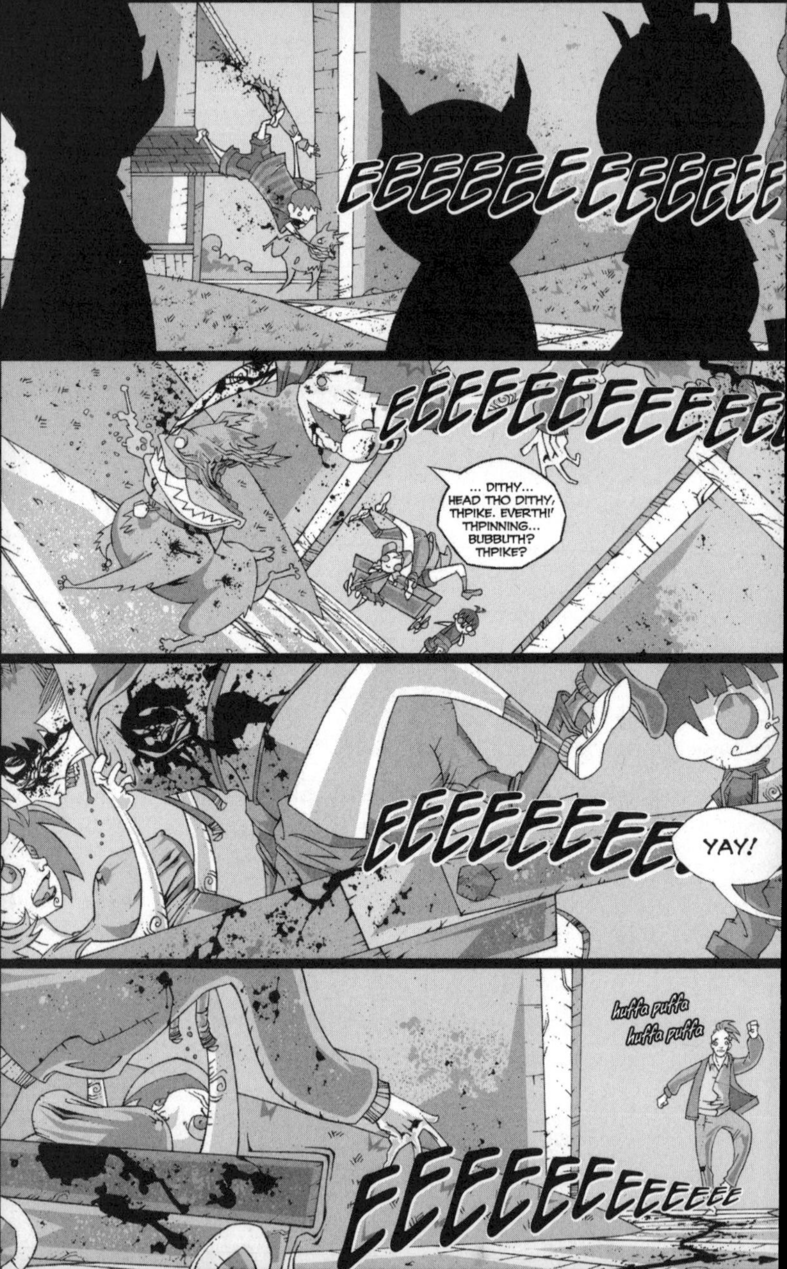
EEEEEEEEEEEEE
EEEEEEEEEEEE
... DITHY... HEAD THO DITHY, THPIKE. EVERTHI' THPINNING... BUBBUTH? THPIKE?
EEEEEEEEE
YAY!
huffa puffa huffa puffa
EEEEEEEEEEEEE

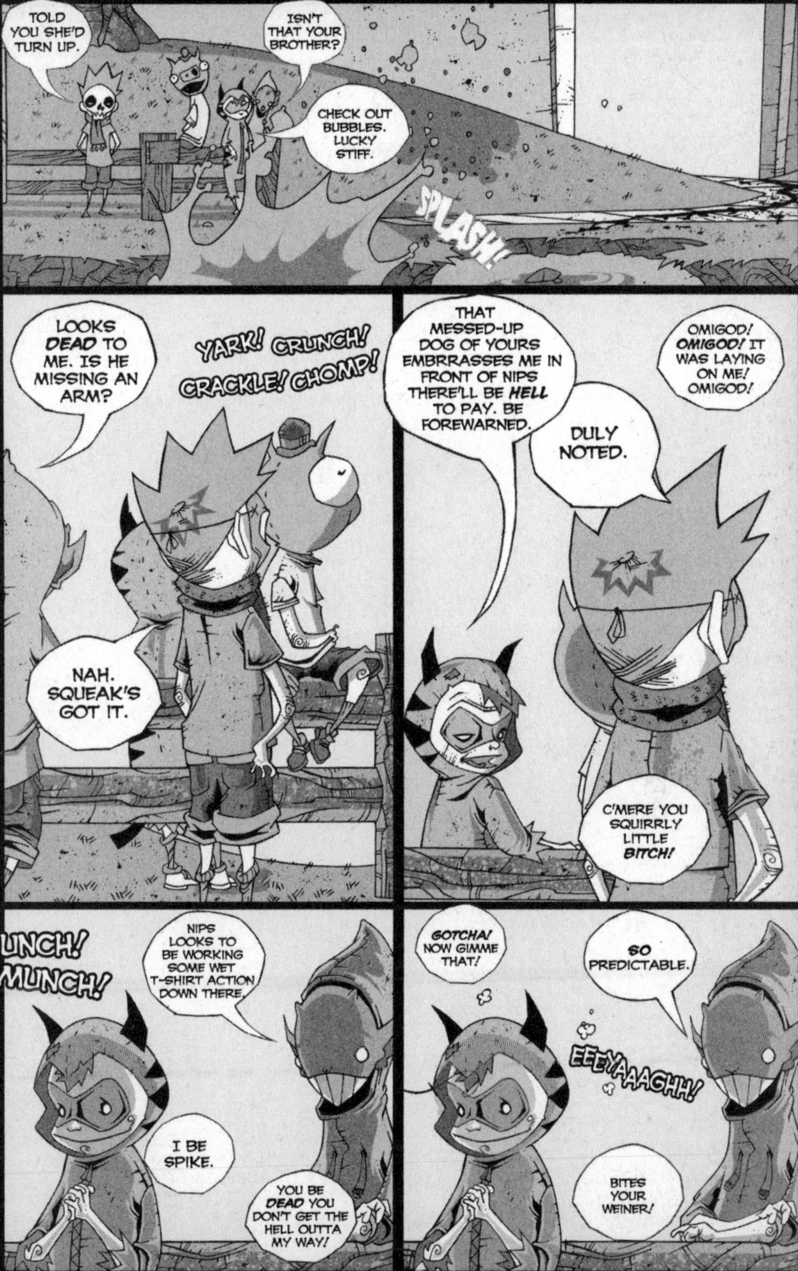
TOLD YOU SHE'D TURN UP.
ISN'T THAT YOUR BROTHER?
CHECK OUT BUBBLES. LUCKY STIFF.
SPLASH!
LOOKS *DEAD* TO ME. IS HE MISSING AN ARM?
YARK! CRUNCH!
CRACKLE! CHOMP!
NAH. SQUEAK'S GOT IT.
THAT MESSED-UP DOG OF YOURS EMBRRASSES ME IN FRONT OF NIPS THERE'LL BE *HELL* TO PAY. BE FOREWARNED.
DULY NOTED.
OMIGOD! *OMIGOD!* IT WAS LAYING ON ME! OMIGOD!
C'MERE YOU SQUIRRLY LITTLE *BITCH!*
RUNCH!
MUNCH!
NIPS LOOKS TO BE WORKING SOME WET T-SHIRT ACTION DOWN THERE.
I BE SPIKE.
YOU BE *DEAD* YOU DON'T GET THE HELL OUTTA MY WAY!
GOTCHA! NOW GIMME THAT!
SO PREDICTABLE.
EEEYAAAGHH!
BITES YOUR WEINER!

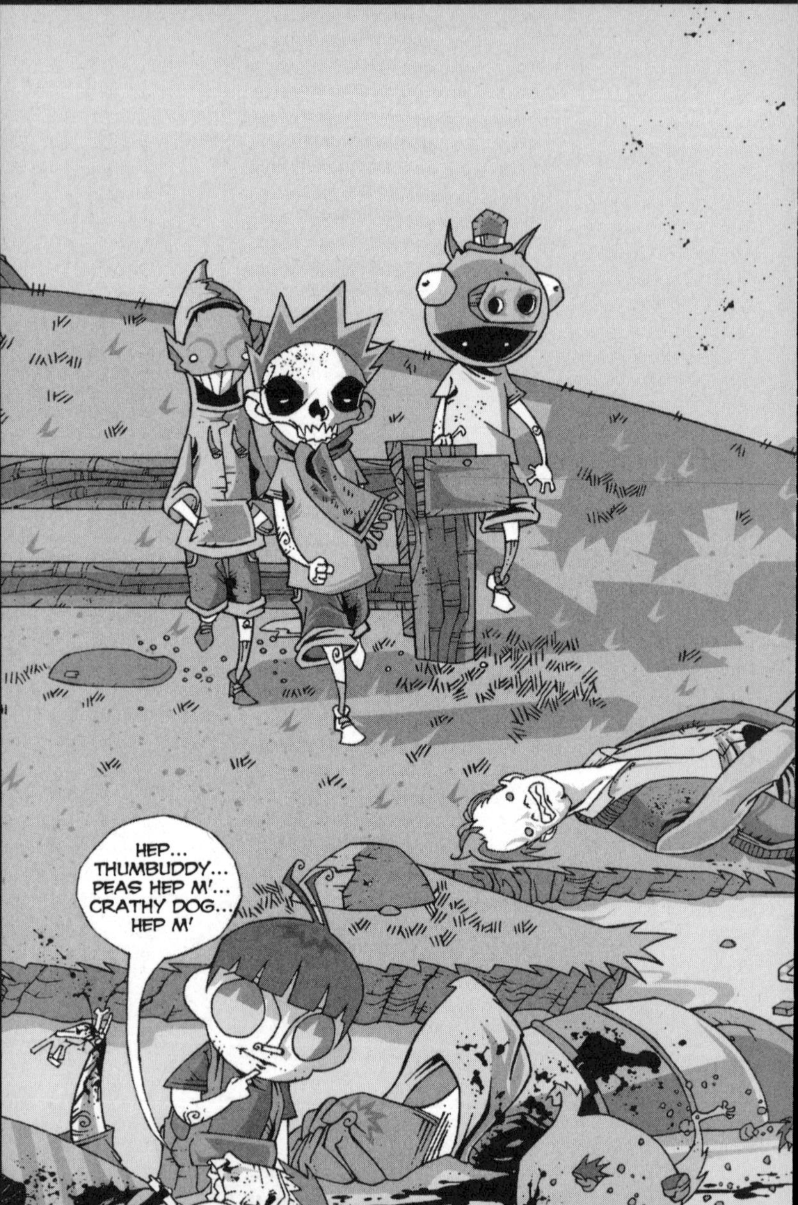
HEP... THUMBUDDY... PEAS HEP M'... CRATHY DOG... HEP M'

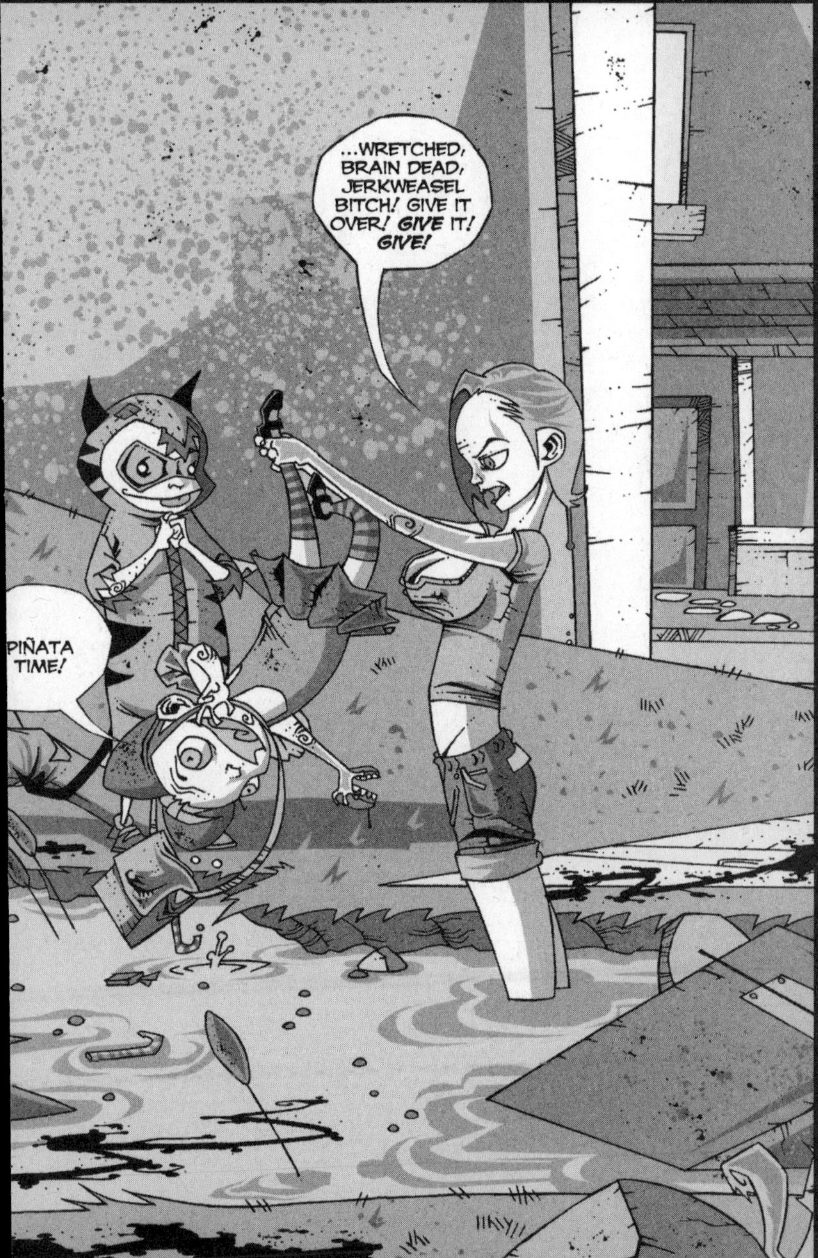
...WRETCHED, BRAIN DEAD, JERKWEASEL BITCH! GIVE IT OVER! GIVE IT! GIVE!
PIÑATA TIME!

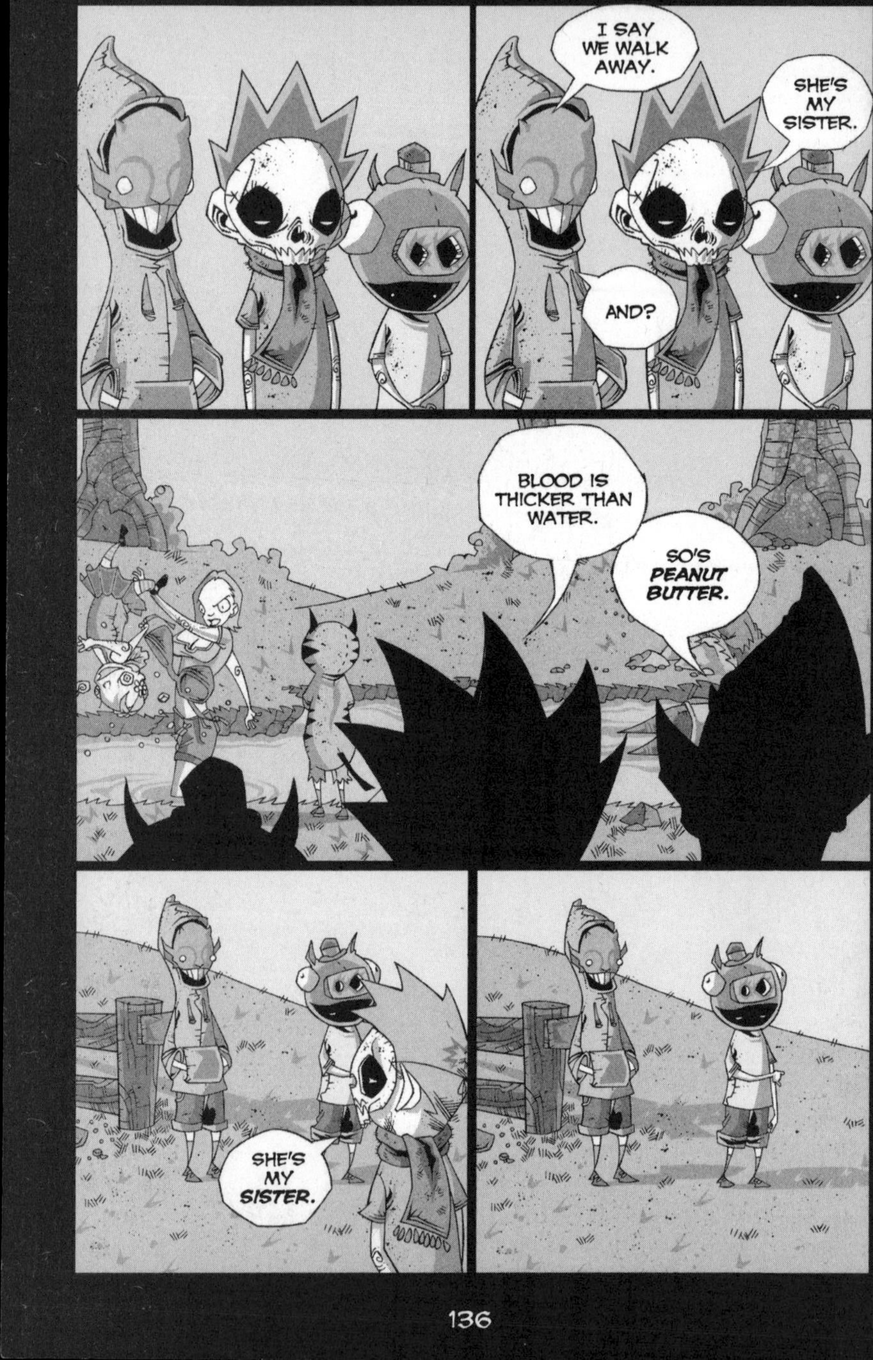
I SAY WE WALK AWAY.
SHE'S MY SISTER.
AND?
BLOOD IS THICKER THAN WATER.
SO'S *PEANUT BUTTER.*
SHE'S MY *SISTER.*

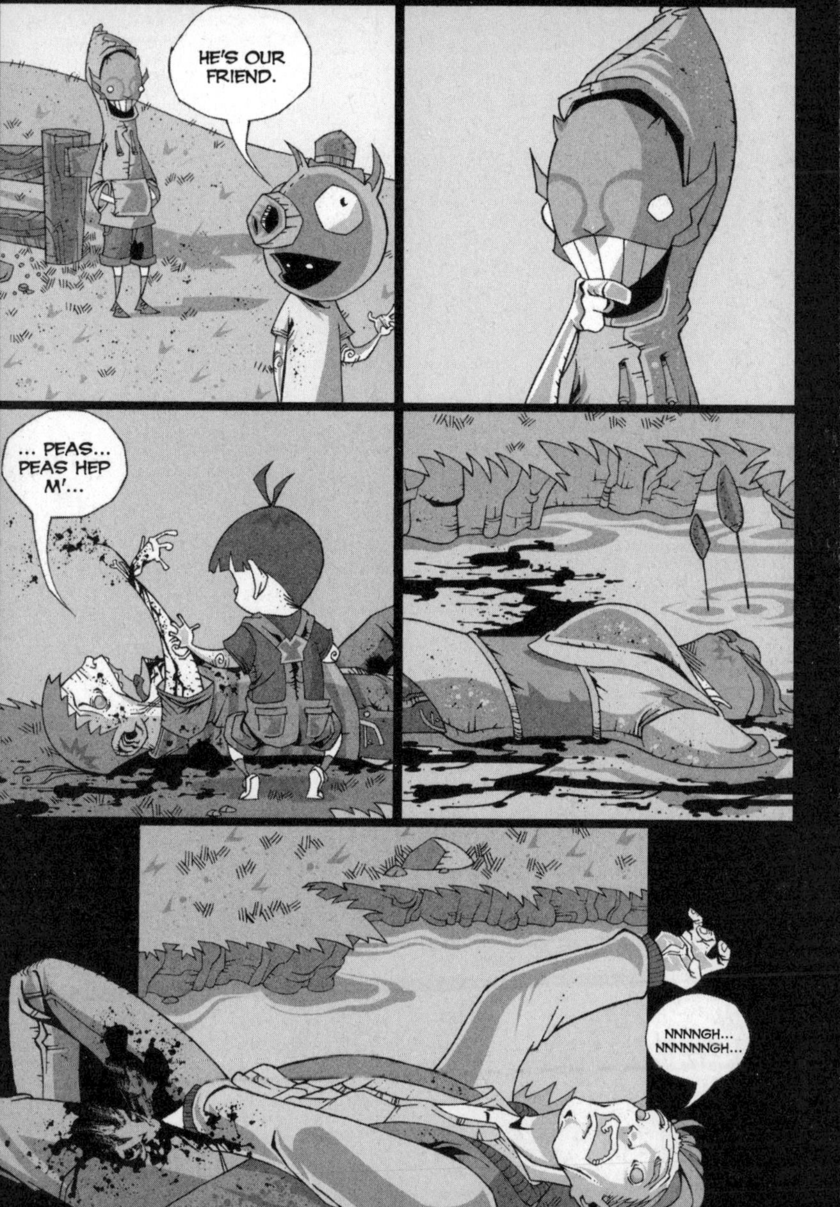
HE'S OUR FRIEND.
... PEAS... PEAS HEP M'...
NNNNGH... NNNNNNGH...

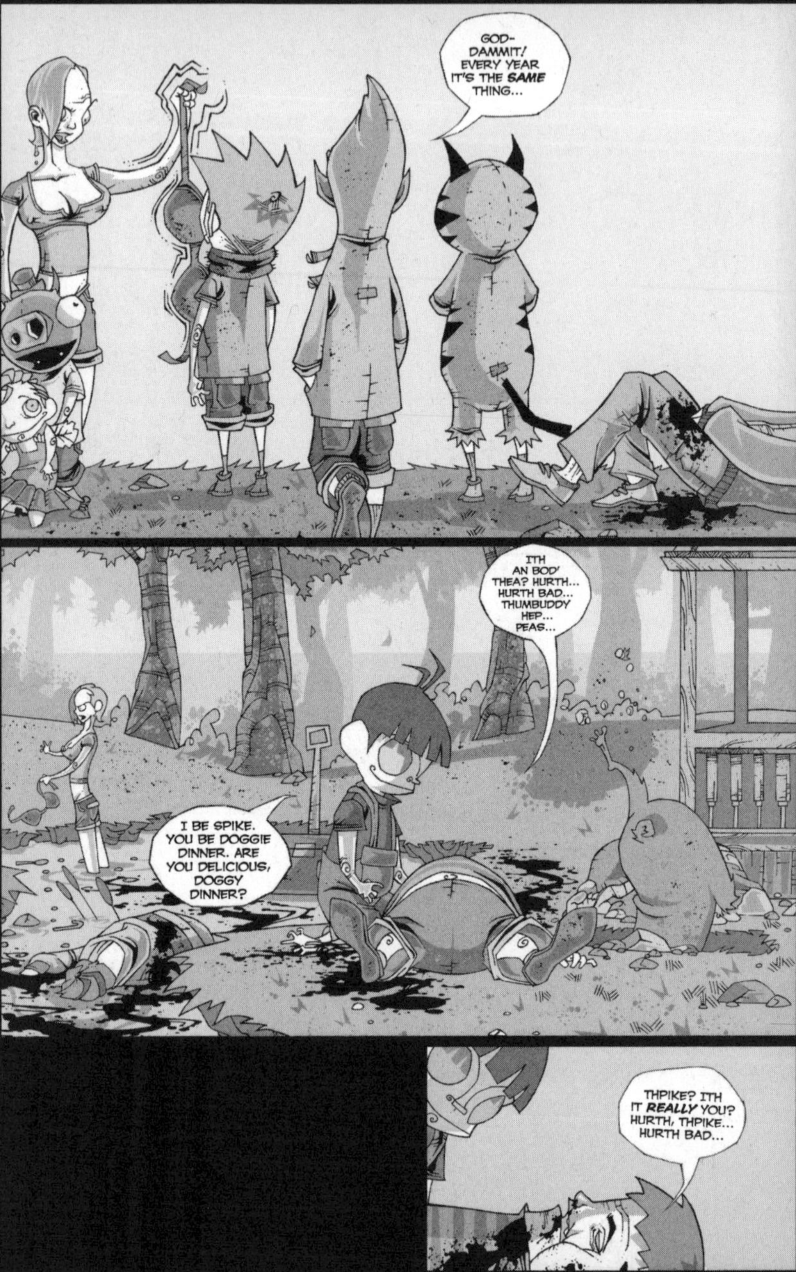
GOD-DAMMIT! EVERY YEAR IT'S THE **SAME** THING...
ITH AN BOD' THEA? HURTH... HURTH BAD... THUMBUDDY HEP... PEAS...
I BE SPIKE. YOU BE DOGGIE DINNER. ARE YOU DELICIOUS, DOGGY DINNER?
THPIKE? ITH IT **REALLY** YOU? HURTH, THPIKE... HURTH BAD...

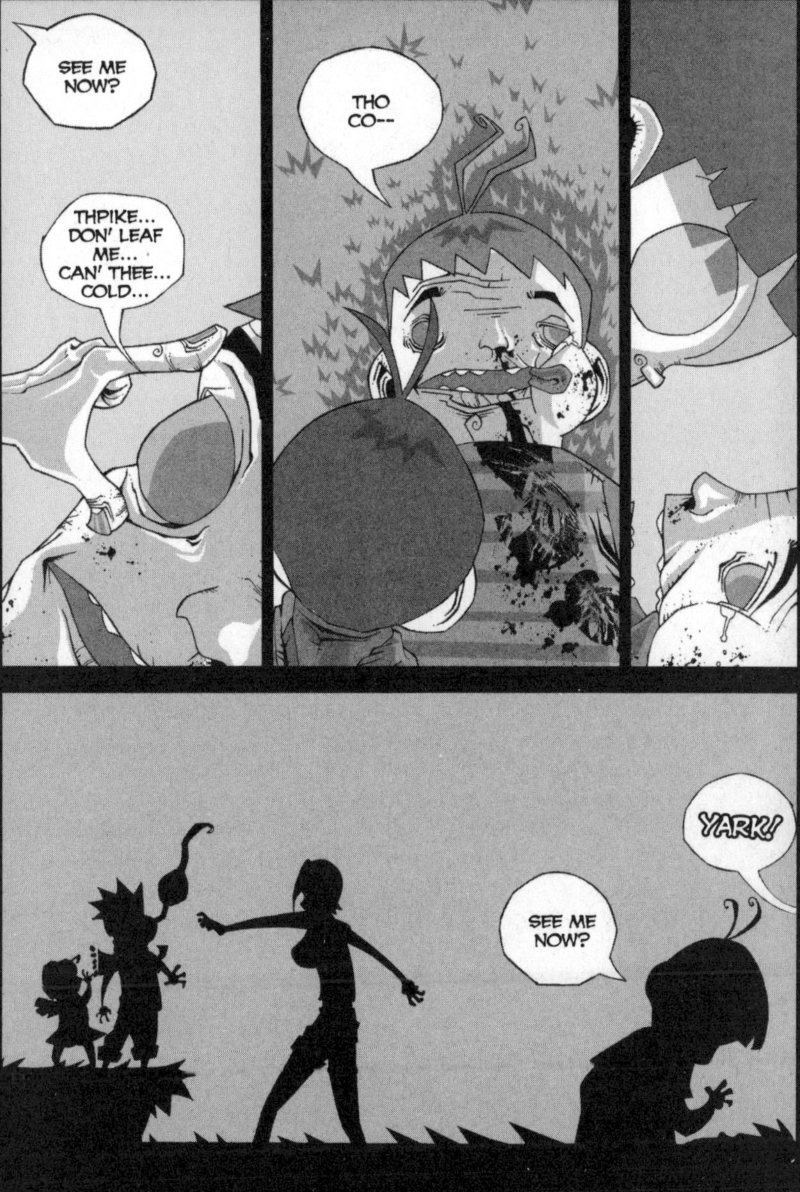
SEE ME NOW?
THPIKE... DON' LEAF ME... CAN' THEE... COLD...
THO CO--
SEE ME NOW?
YARK!

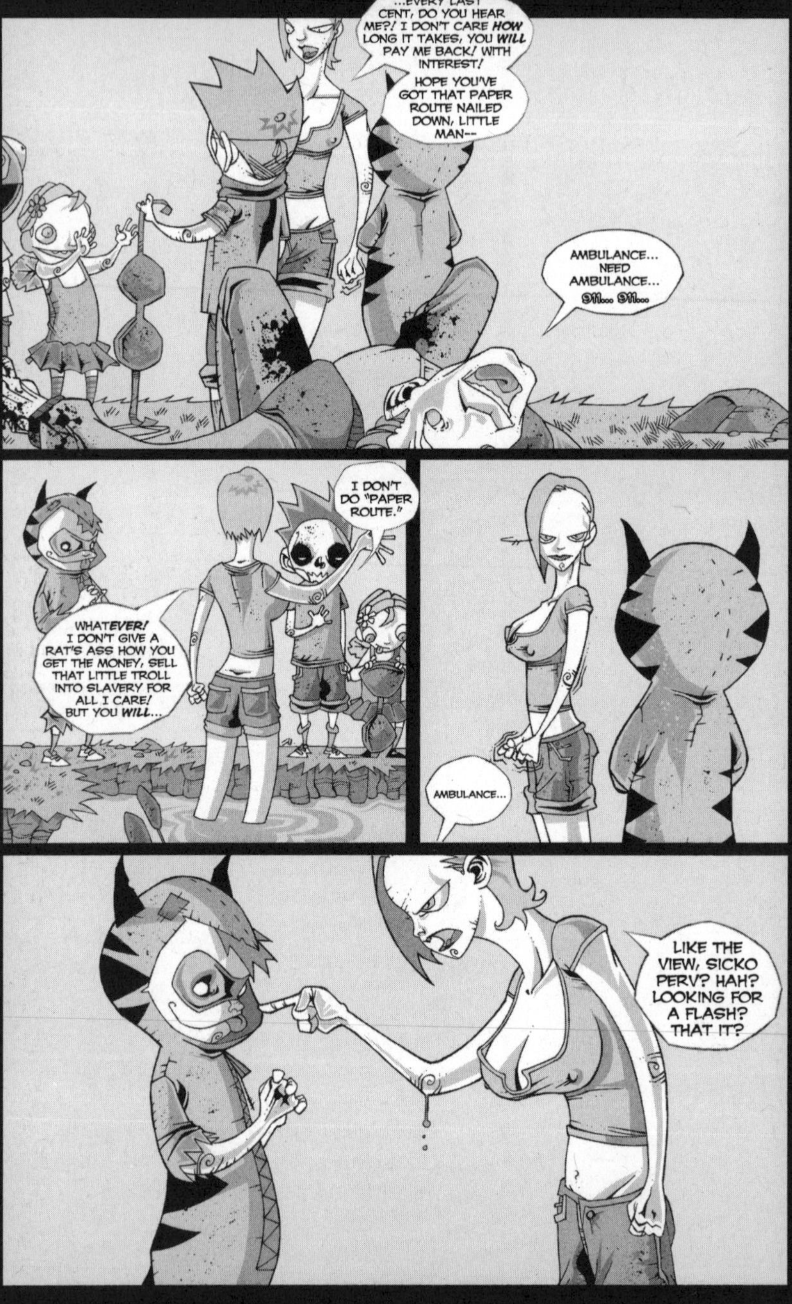
...EVERY LAST CENT, DO YOU HEAR ME?! I DON'T CARE HOW LONG IT TAKES, YOU WILL PAY ME BACK! WITH INTEREST!
HOPE YOU'VE GOT THAT PAPER ROUTE NAILED DOWN, LITTLE MAN--
AMBULANCE... NEED AMBULANCE... 911... 911...
I DON'T DO "PAPER ROUTE."
WHATEVER! I DON'T GIVE A RAT'S ASS HOW YOU GET THE MONEY, SELL THAT LITTLE TROLL INTO SLAVERY FOR ALL I CARE! BUT YOU WILL...
AMBULANCE...
LIKE THE VIEW, SICKO PERV? HAH? LOOKING FOR A FLASH? THAT IT?

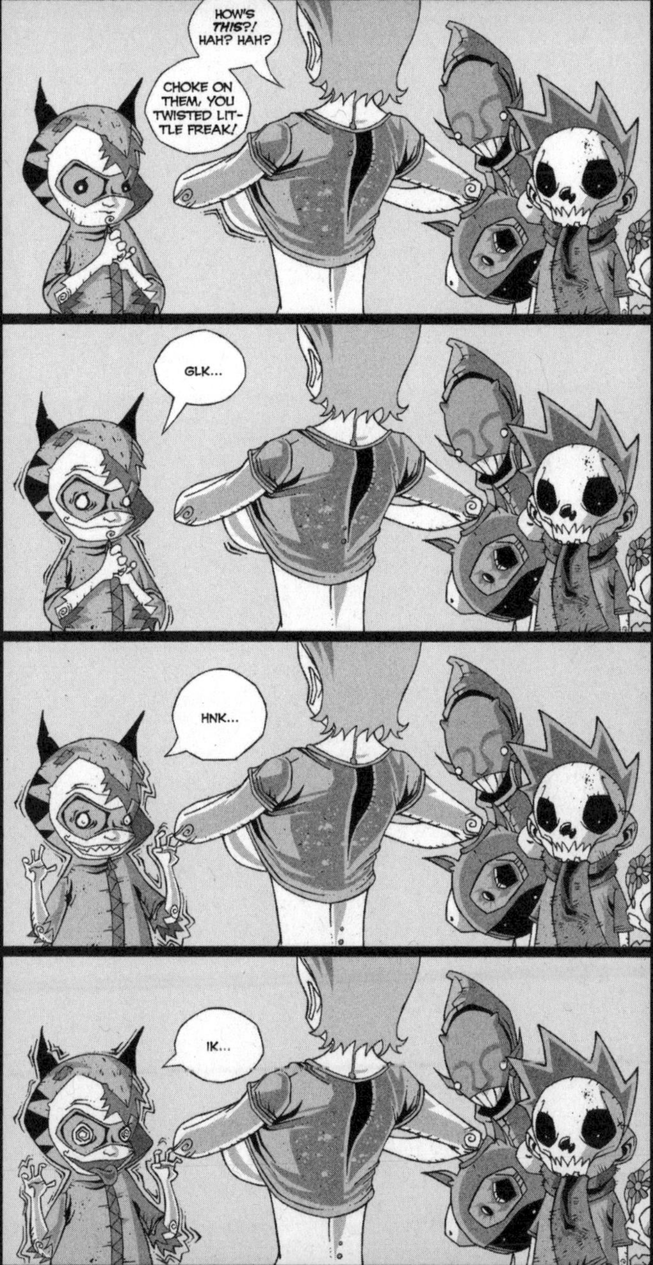
HOW'S *THIS*?! HAH? HAH?
CHOKE ON THEM, YOU TWISTED LIT-TLE FREAK!
GLK...
HNK...
IK...

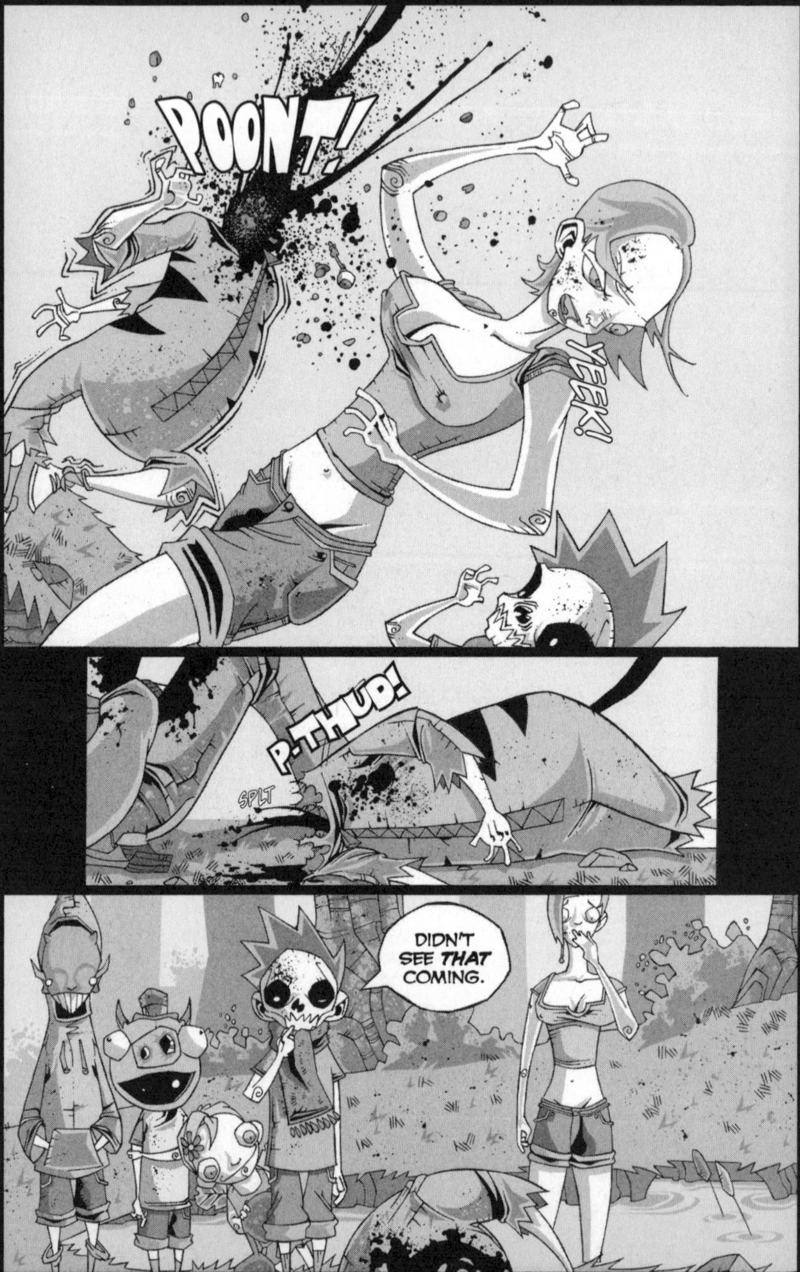
POONT!
YEEK!
P-THUD!
SPLT
DIDN'T SEE THAT COMING.

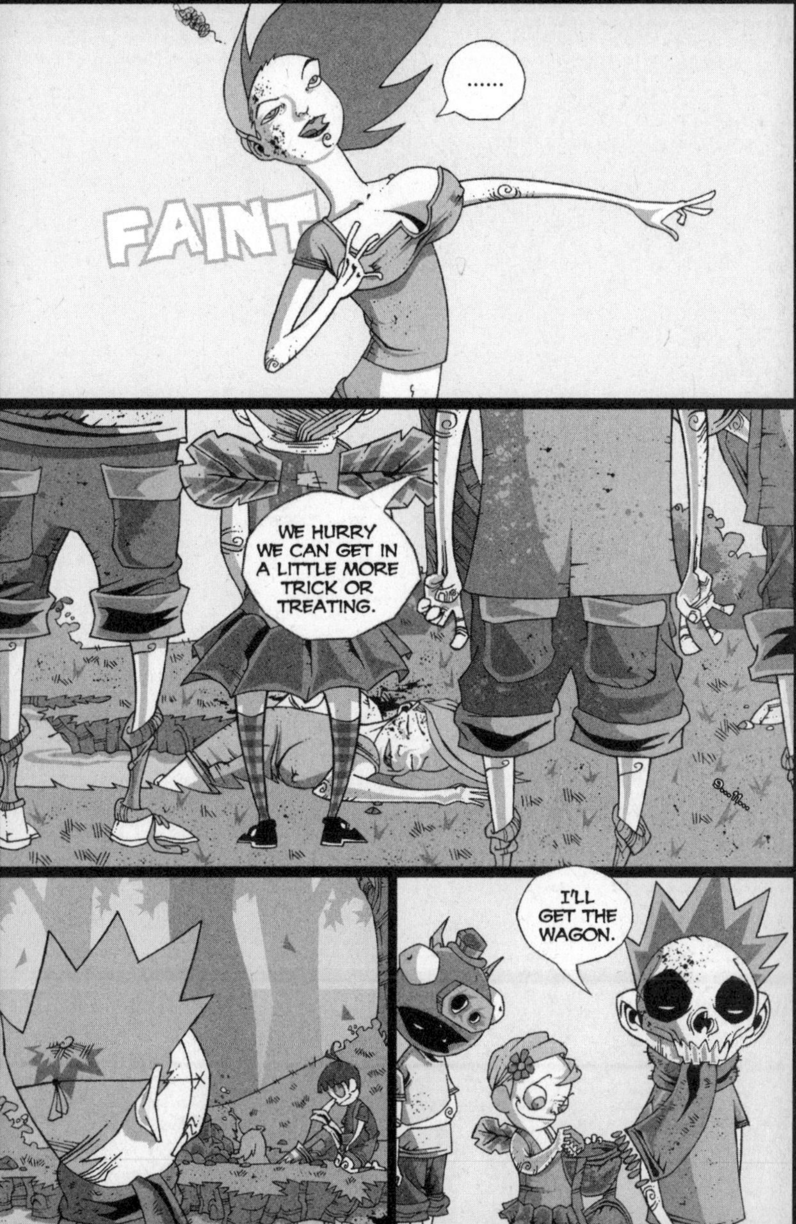
......
FAINT
WE HURRY WE CAN GET IN A LITTLE MORE TRICK OR TREATING.
I'LL GET THE WAGON.

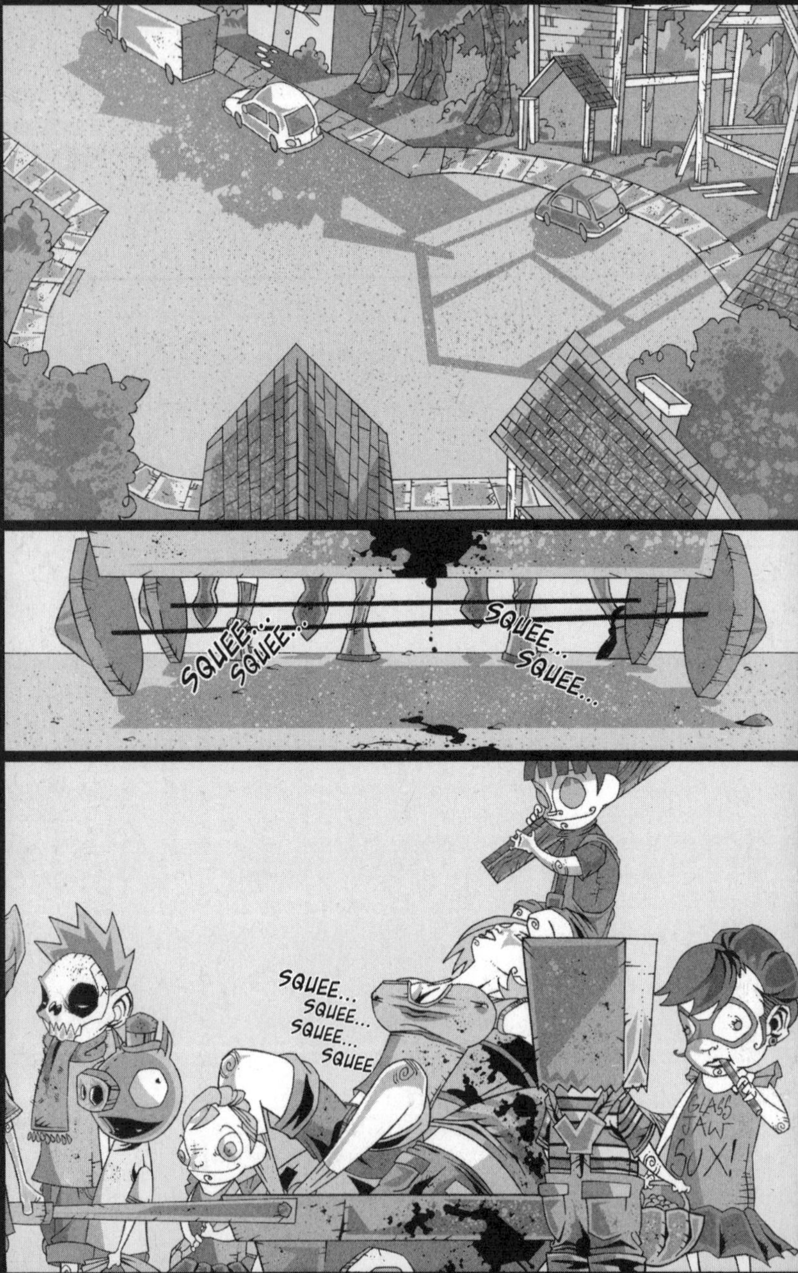
SQUEE... SQUEE...
SQUEE... SQUEE...
SQUEE... SQUEE... SQUEE... SQUEE
GLASS JAW SUX!

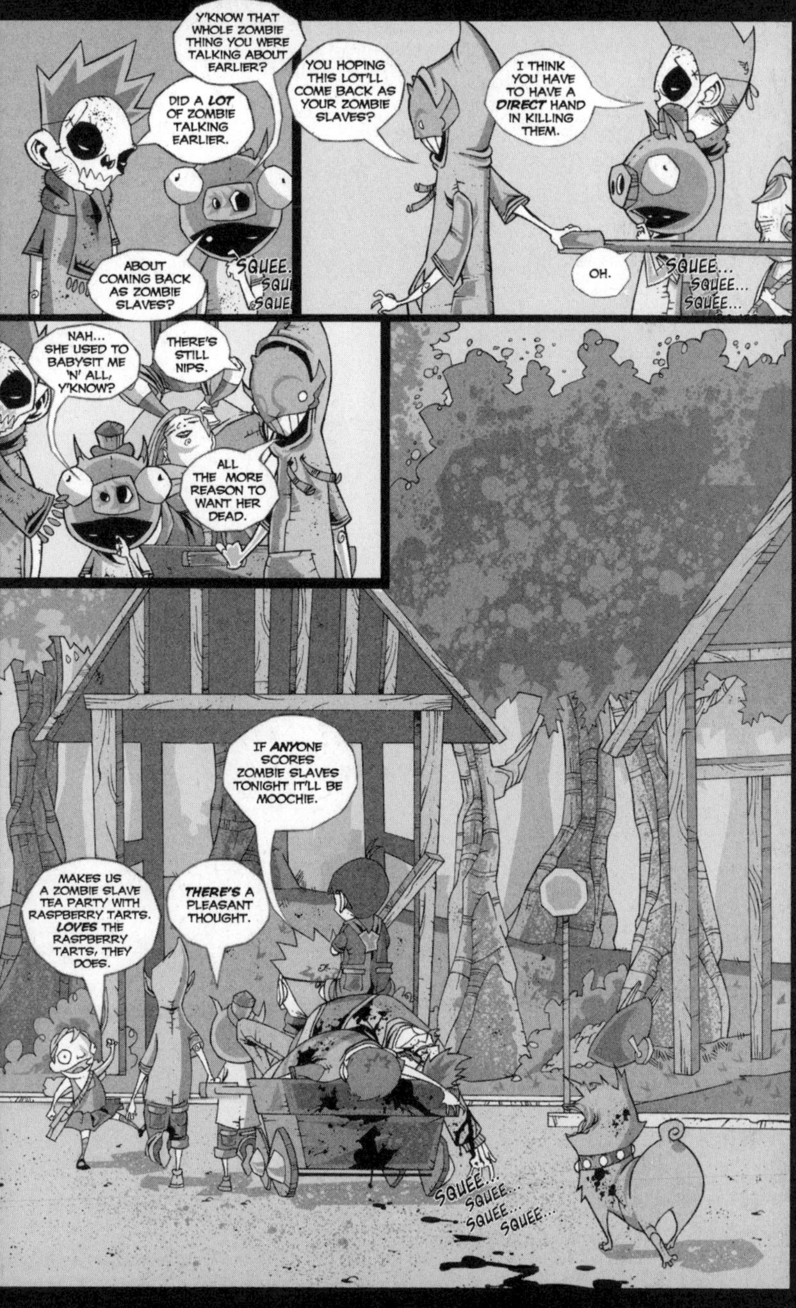
Y'KNOW THAT WHOLE ZOMBIE THING YOU WERE TALKING ABOUT EARLIER?
DID A LOT OF ZOMBIE TALKING EARLIER.
ABOUT COMING BACK AS ZOMBIE SLAVES?
SQUEE...
YOU HOPING THIS LOT'LL COME BACK AS YOUR ZOMBIE SLAVES?
I THINK YOU HAVE TO HAVE A DIRECT HAND IN KILLING THEM.
OH.
SQUEE... SQUEE... SQUEE...
NAH... SHE USED TO BABYSIT ME 'N' ALL, Y'KNOW?
THERE'S STILL NIPS.
ALL THE MORE REASON TO WANT HER DEAD.
IF ANYONE SCORES ZOMBIE SLAVES TONIGHT IT'LL BE MOOCHIE.
MAKES US A ZOMBIE SLAVE TEA PARTY WITH RASPBERRY TARTS. LOVES THE RASPBERRY TARTS, THEY DOES.
THERE'S A PLEASANT THOUGHT.
SQUEE... SQUEE... SQUEE... SQUEE...

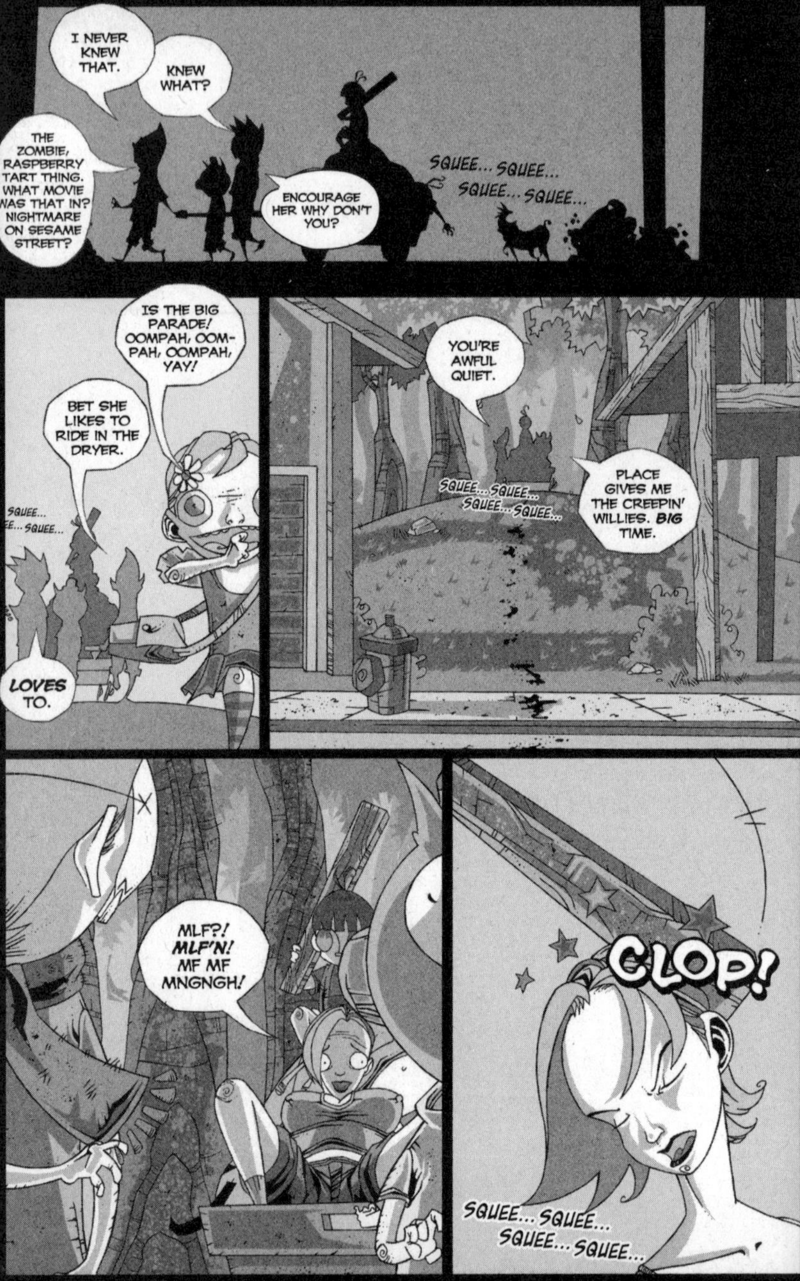
I NEVER KNEW THAT.
KNEW WHAT?
THE ZOMBIE, RASPBERRY TART THING. WHAT MOVIE WAS THAT IN? NIGHTMARE ON SESAME STREET?
ENCOURAGE HER WHY DON'T YOU?
SQUEE... SQUEE... SQUEE... SQUEE...
IS THE BIG PARADE! OOMPAH, OOM-PAH, OOMPAH, YAY!
BET SHE LIKES TO RIDE IN THE DRYER.
SQUEE...
LOVES TO.
YOU'RE AWFUL QUIET.
SQUEE... SQUEE... SQUEE... SQUEE...
PLACE GIVES ME THE CREEPIN' WILLIES. BIG TIME.
MLF?! MLF'N! MF MF MNGNGH!
CLOP!
SQUEE... SQUEE... SQUEE... SQUEE...

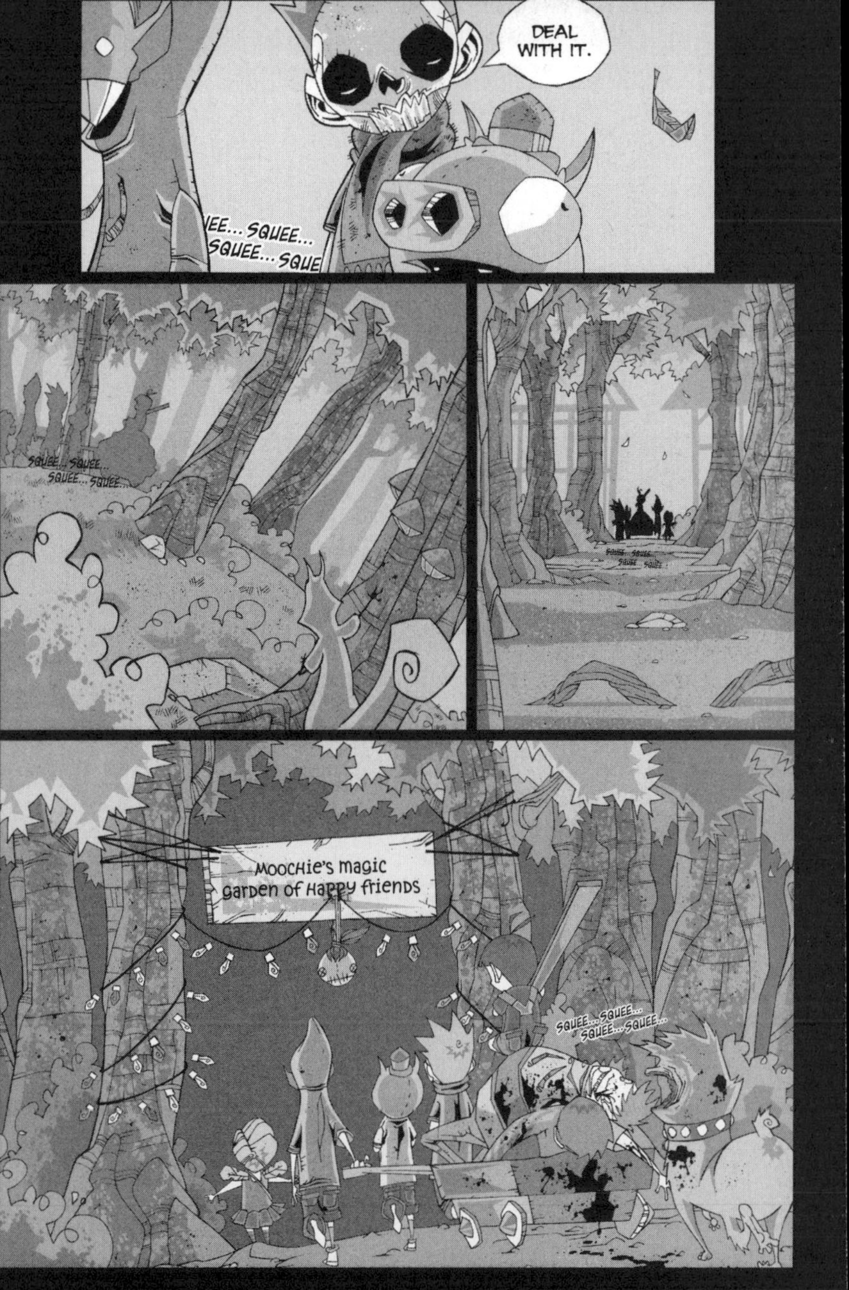
DEAL WITH IT.
EE... SQUEE... SQUEE... SQUE
SQUEE... SQUEE... SQUEE... SQUEE...
Moochie's magic garden of Happy friends
SQUEE... SQUEE... SQUEE... SQUEE...

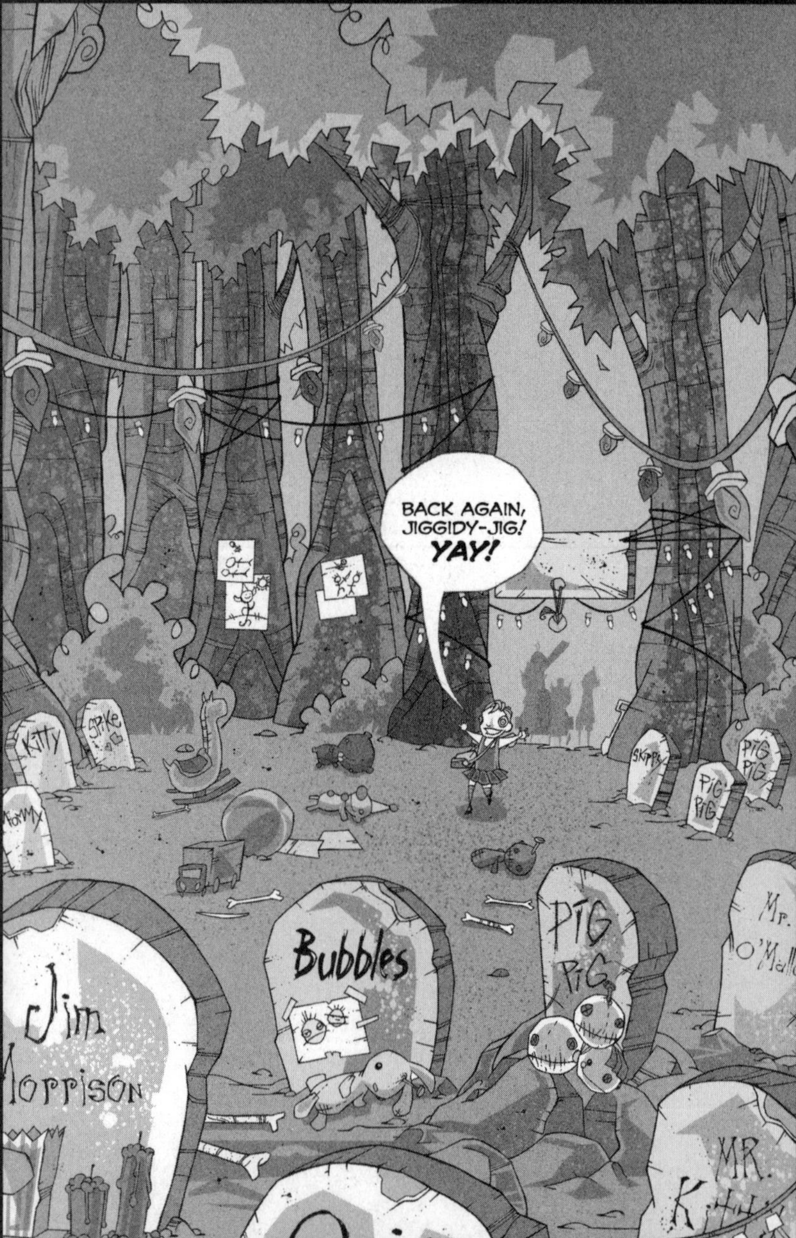
BACK AGAIN, JIGGIDY-JIG! YAY!
Kitty
Spike
Skippy
PIG PIG
PIG PIG
Bubbles
PIG PIG

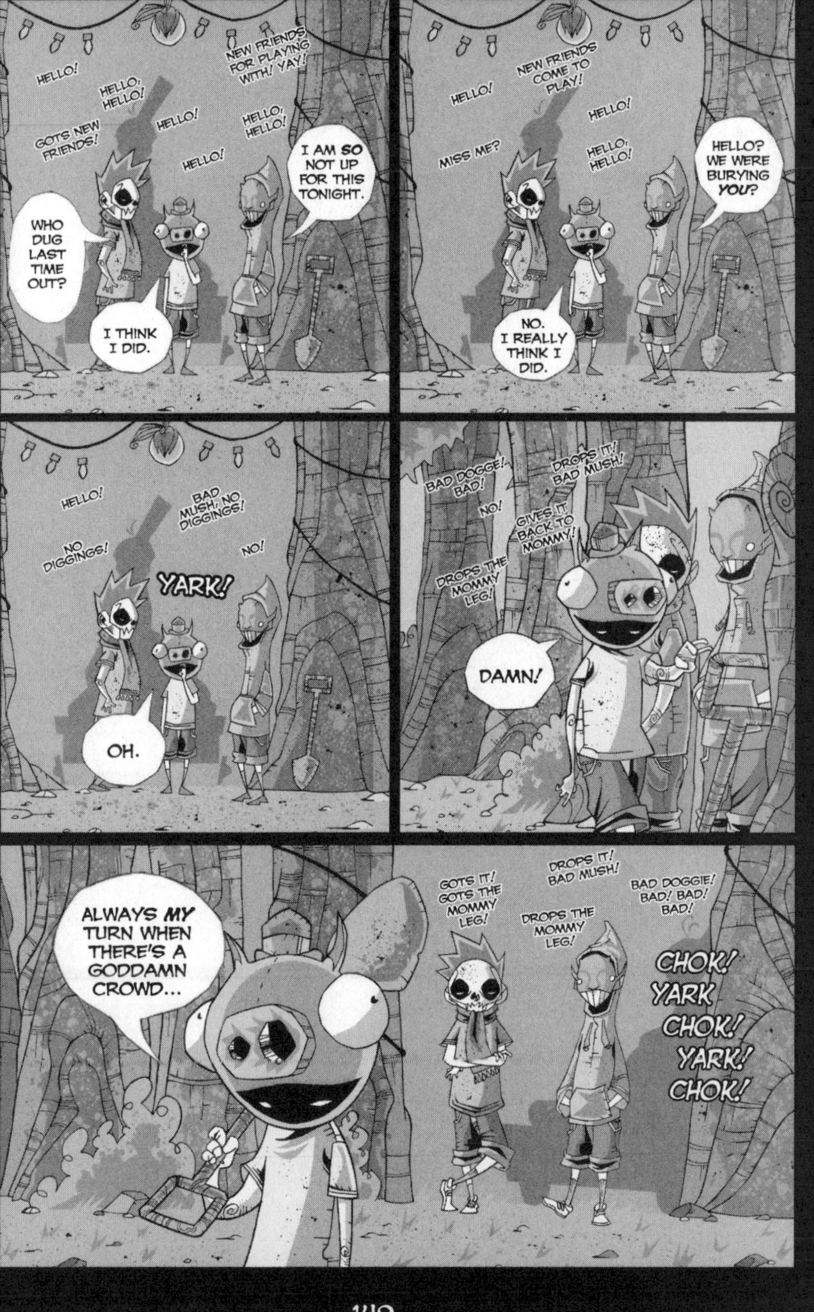
HELLO!
HELLO, HELLO!
NEW FRIENDS FOR PLAYING WITH! YAY!
GOTS NEW FRIENDS!
HELLO!
HELLO, HELLO!
HELLO!
I AM **SO** NOT UP FOR THIS TONIGHT.
WHO DUG LAST TIME OUT?
I THINK I DID.
HELLO!
NEW FRIENDS COME TO PLAY!
HELLO!
MISS ME?
HELLO, HELLO!
HELLO? WE WERE BURYING ***YOU***?
NO. I REALLY THINK I DID.
HELLO!
BAD MUSH, NO DIGGINGS!
NO DIGGINGS!
NO!
YARK!
OH.
BAD DOGGE! BAD!
DROPS IT! BAD MUSH!
NO!
GIVES IT BACK TO MOMMY!
DROPS THE MOMMY LEG!
DAMN!
ALWAYS ***MY*** TURN WHEN THERE'S A GODDAMN CROWD...
GOTS IT! GOTS THE MOMMY LEG!
DROPS IT! BAD MUSH!
DROPS THE MOMMY LEG!
BAD DOGGIE! BAD! BAD! BAD!
CHOK! YARK CHOK! YARK! CHOK!

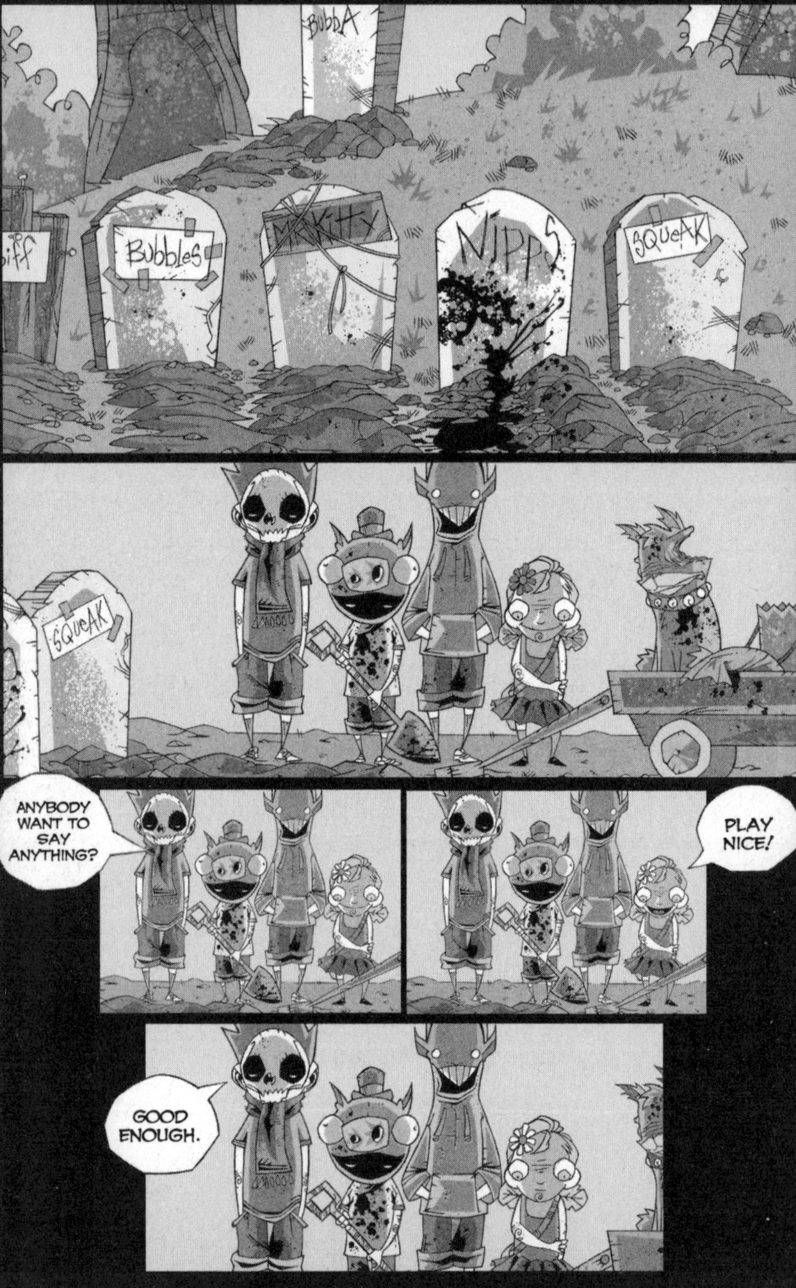
BubbA
Bubbles
MR Kitty
NIPPS
SQUEAK
SQUEAK
ANYBODY WANT TO SAY ANYTHING?
PLAY NICE!
GOOD ENOUGH.

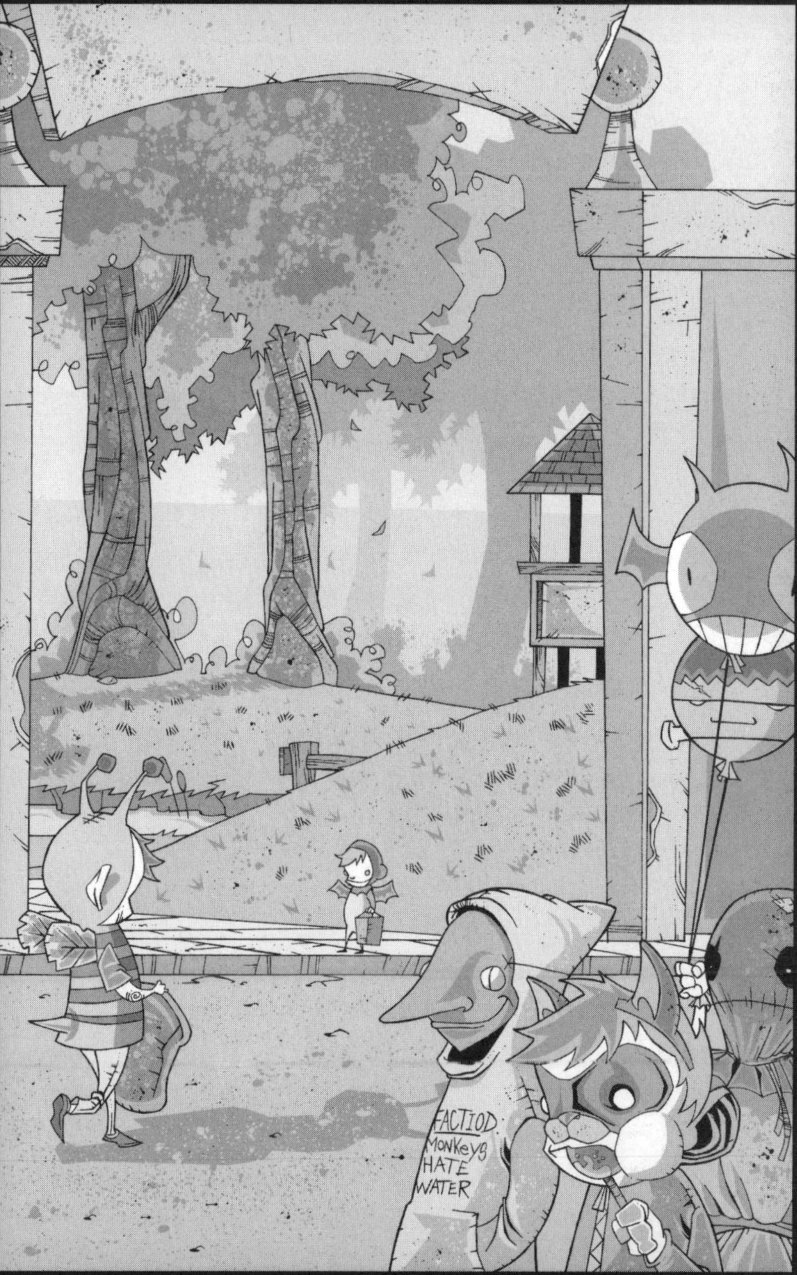
FACTIOD
MONKeyS
HATE
WATER

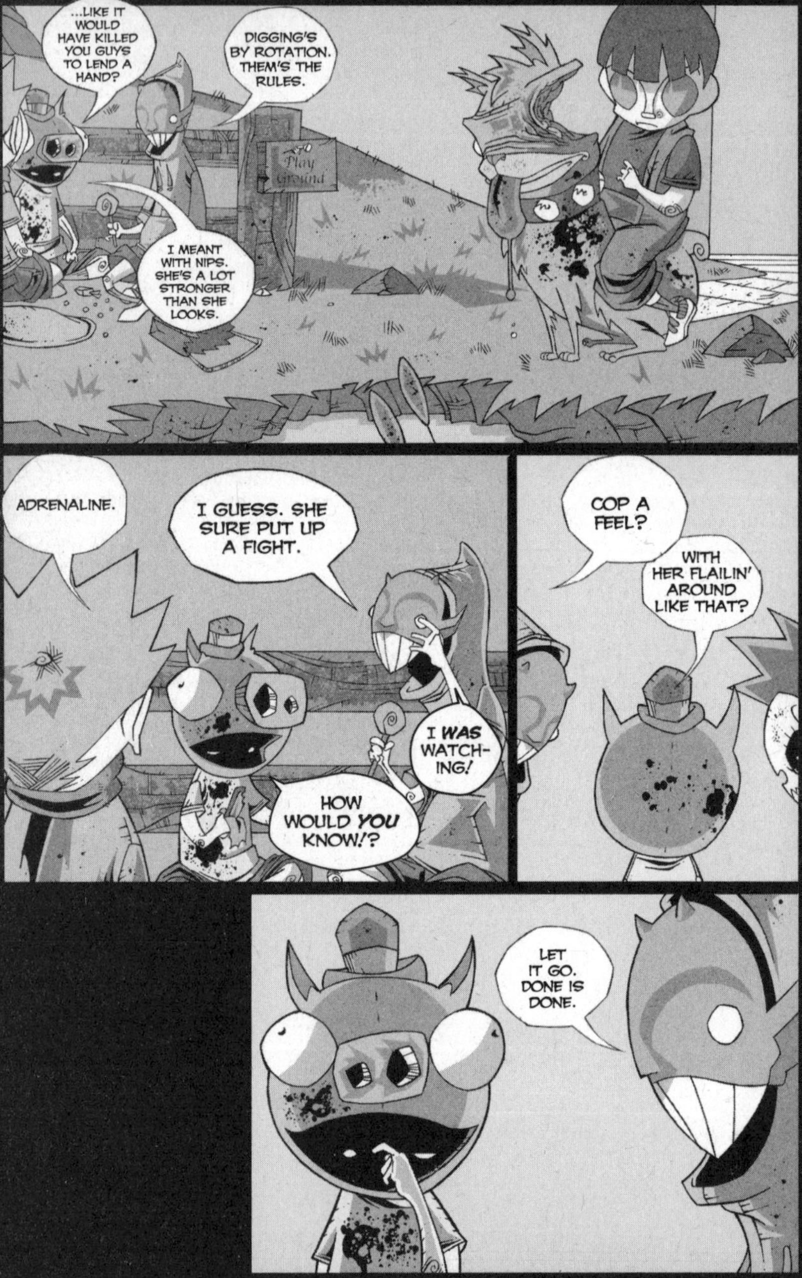
...LIKE IT WOULD HAVE KILLED YOU GUYS TO LEND A HAND?
DIGGING'S BY ROTATION. THEM'S THE RULES.
Play Ground
I MEANT WITH NIPS. SHE'S A LOT STRONGER THAN SHE LOOKS.
ADRENALINE.
I GUESS. SHE SURE PUT UP A FIGHT.
HOW WOULD *YOU* KNOW!?
I *WAS* WATCHING!
COP A FEEL?
WITH HER FLAILIN' AROUND LIKE THAT?
LET IT GO. DONE IS DONE.

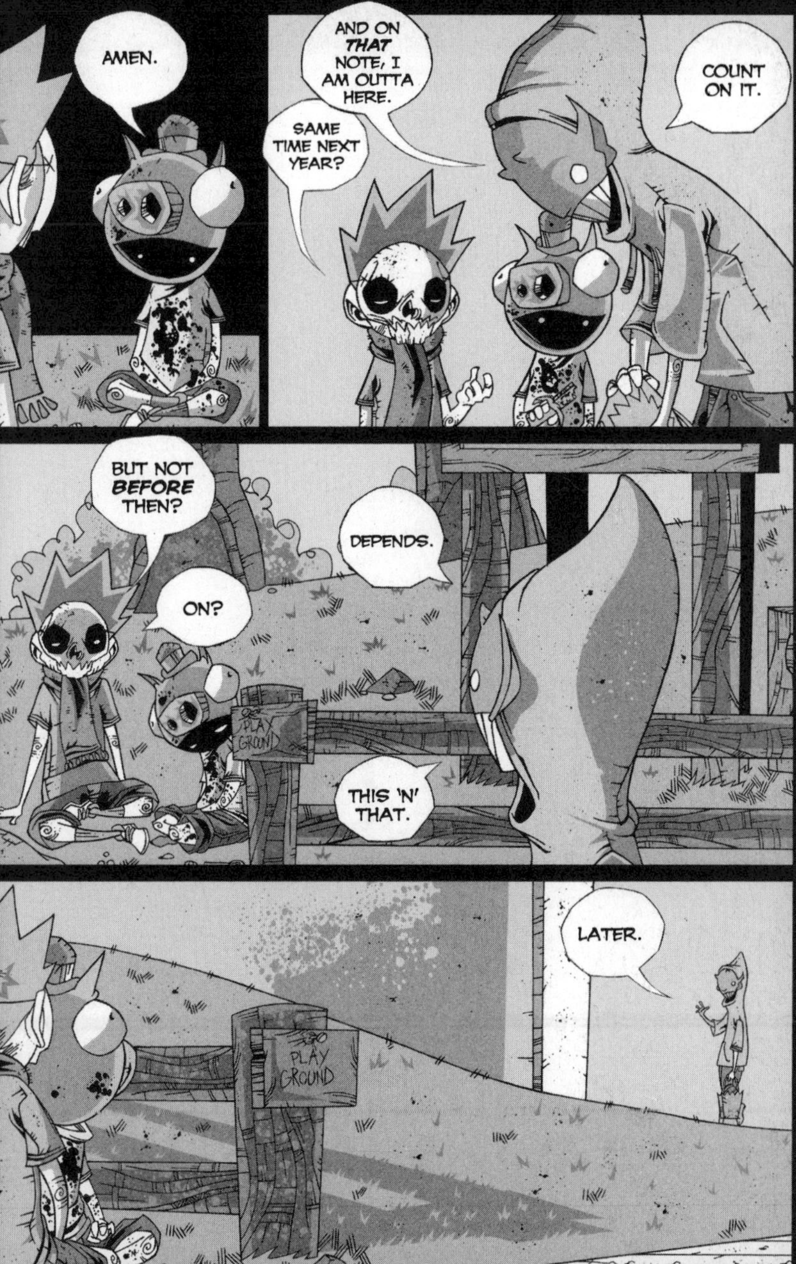
AMEN.
AND ON *THAT* NOTE, I AM OUTTA HERE.
SAME TIME NEXT YEAR?
COUNT ON IT.
BUT NOT *BEFORE* THEN?
DEPENDS.
ON?
PLAY GROUND
THIS 'N' THAT.
LATER.
PLAY GROUND

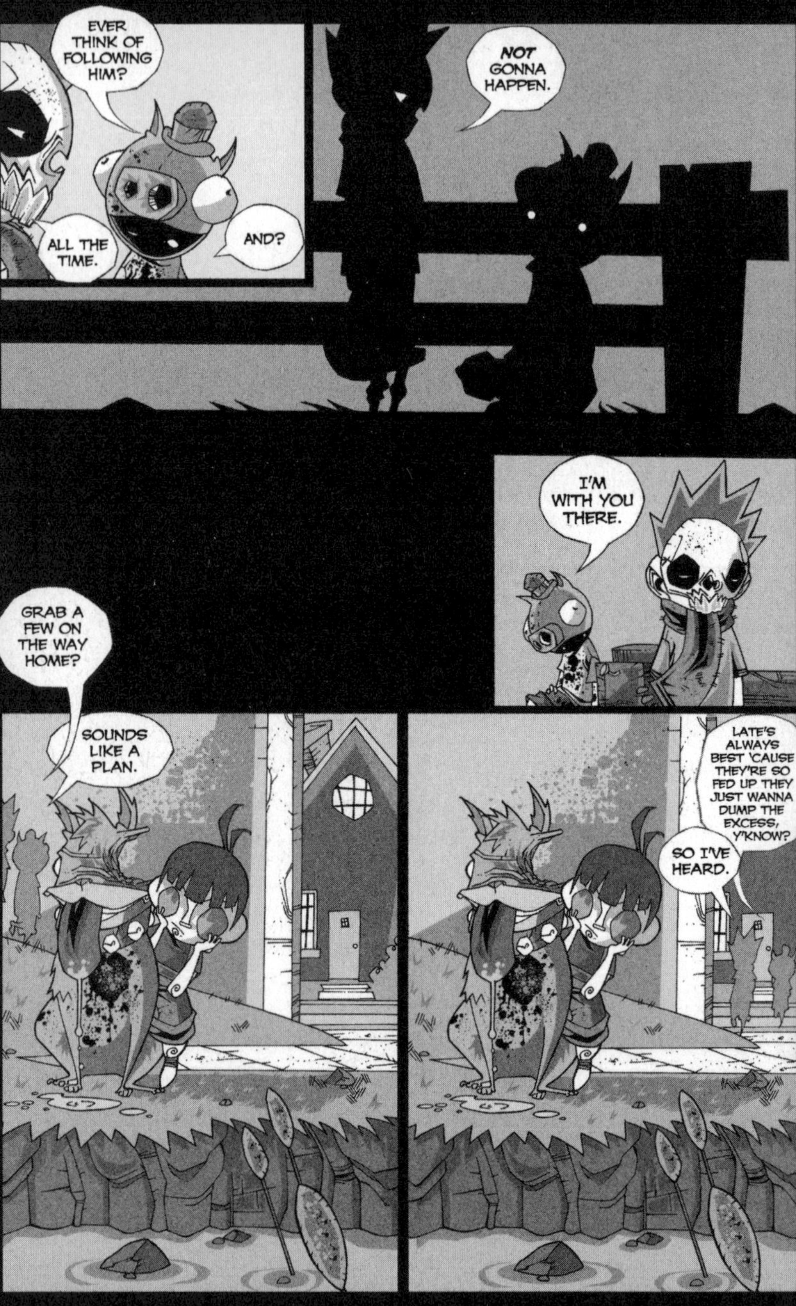
EVER THINK OF FOLLOWING HIM?
ALL THE TIME.
AND?
NOT GONNA HAPPEN.
I'M WITH YOU THERE.
GRAB A FEW ON THE WAY HOME?
SOUNDS LIKE A PLAN.
LATE'S ALWAYS BEST 'CAUSE THEY'RE SO FED UP THEY JUST WANNA DUMP THE EXCESS, Y'KNOW?
SO I'VE HEARD.

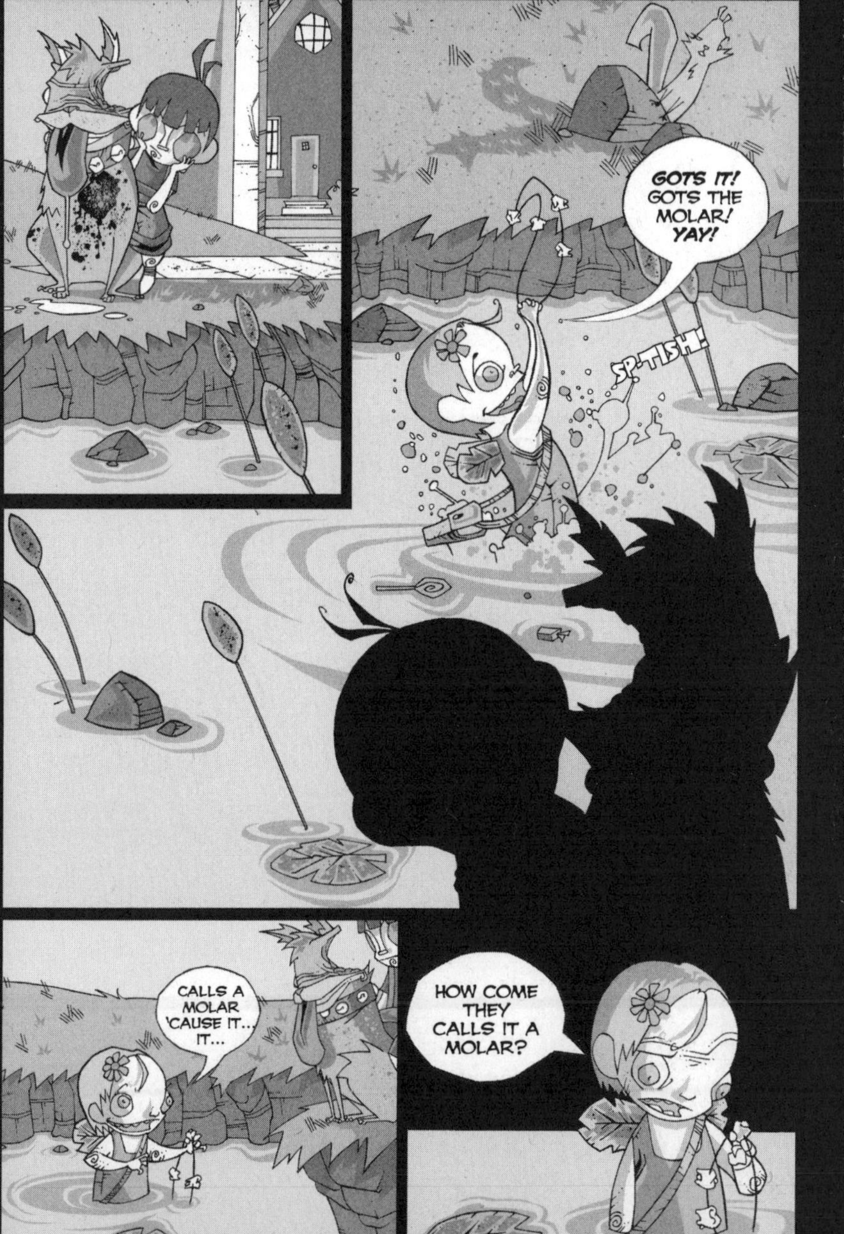
GOTS IT! GOTS THE MOLAR! YAY!
SP-TISH!
HOW COME THEY CALLS IT A MOLAR?
CALLS A MOLAR 'CAUSE IT... IT...

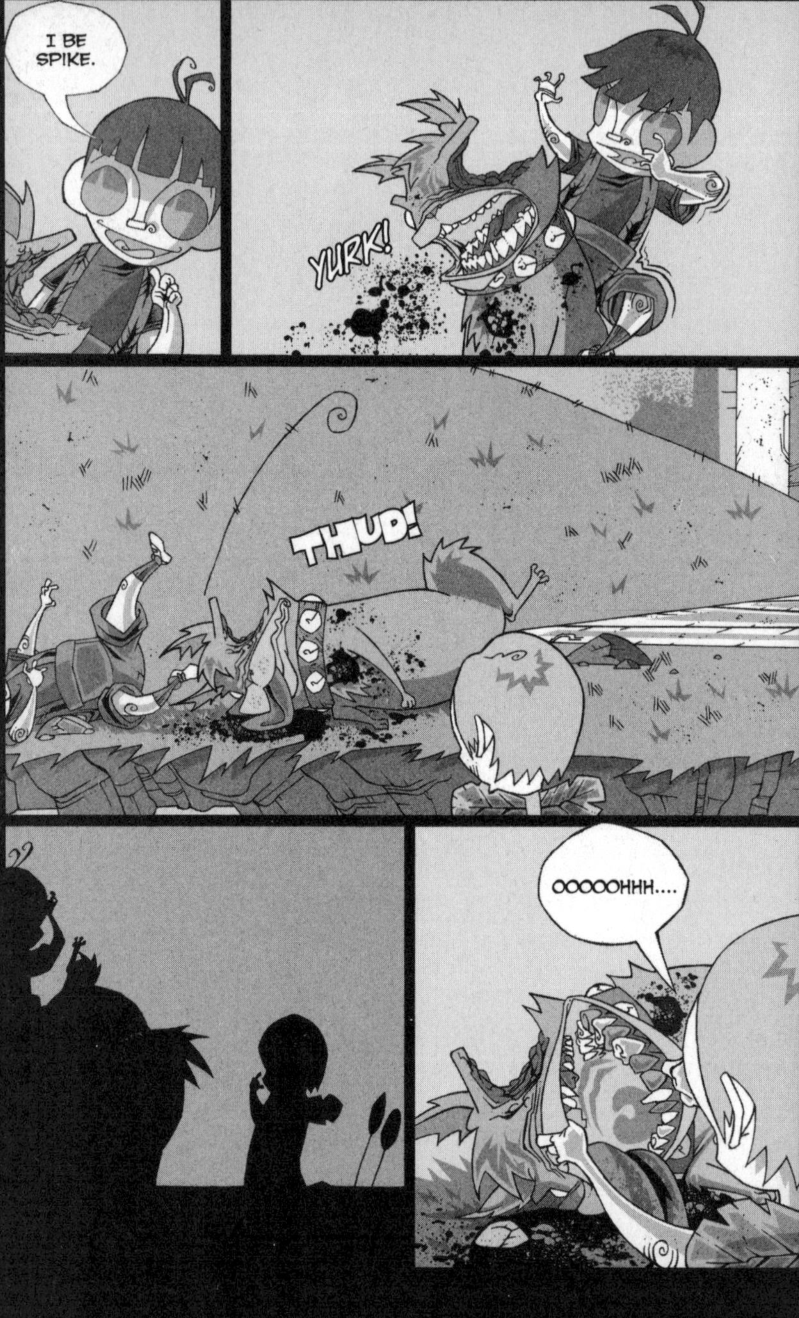
I BE SPIKE.
YURK!
THUD!
OOOOOHHH....

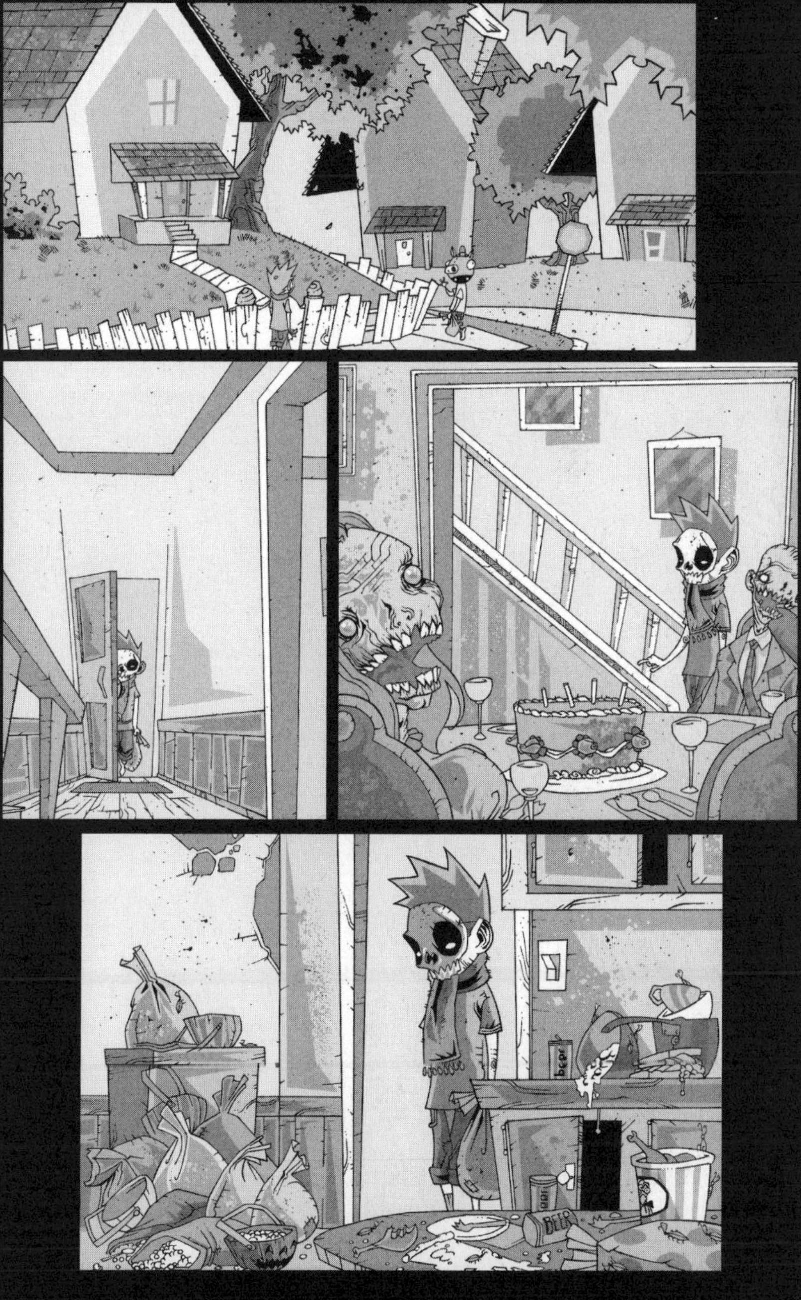
beer
BEER

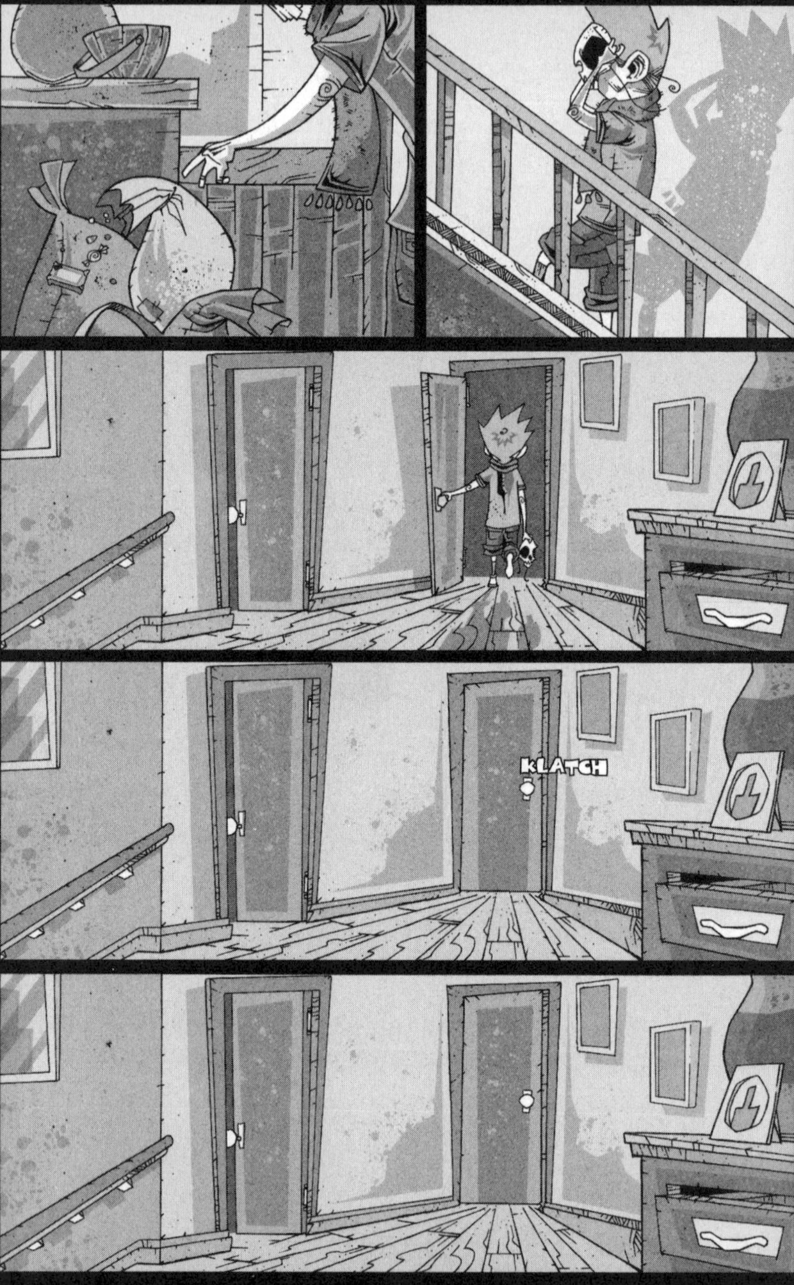
KLATCH

Molar n. A tooth with a broad crown for grinding food, located behind the bicuspids. [< Lat. *Molaris*, of a mill, grinding.]

NEXT TIME IN

I LUV HALLOWEEN™

THE TOWN IS UNDER FULL-BLOWN
ASSAULT BY THE *LIVING DEAD,*
BUT DOES THIS MAKE A BIT
OF DIFFERENCE TO FINCH AND
FRIENDS? *HELL NO!* THEY HAVE
ONE THING ON THEIR MINDS...
CANDY--AND THEY'LL GET IT
ANY WAY THEY CAN. AND KEEP
AN EYE OUT FOR THAT NEW KID,
HULLY GULLY--WHAT THE HELL'S
HIS PROBLEM ANYWAY?

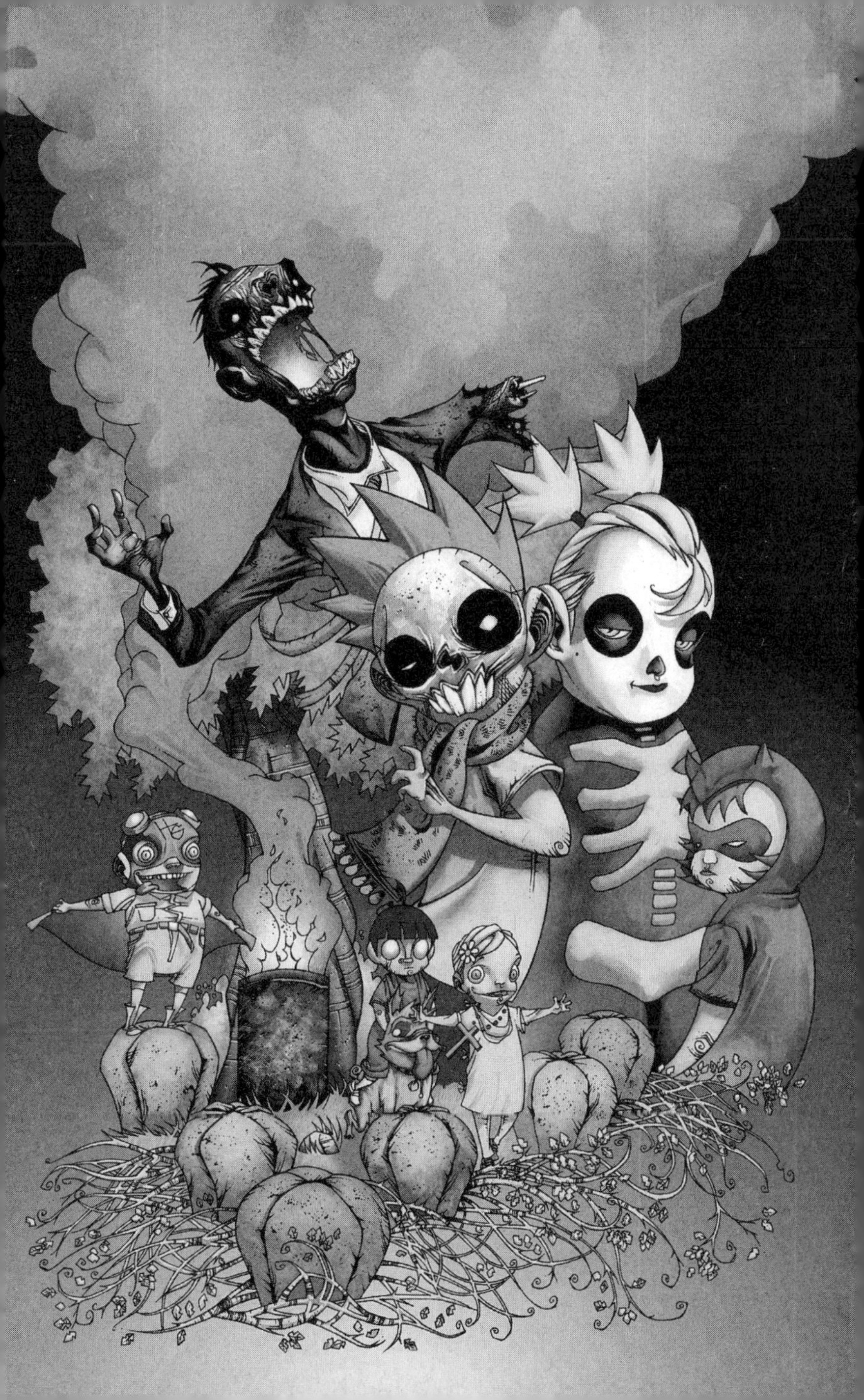

I Luv Halloween

SKETCHBOOK

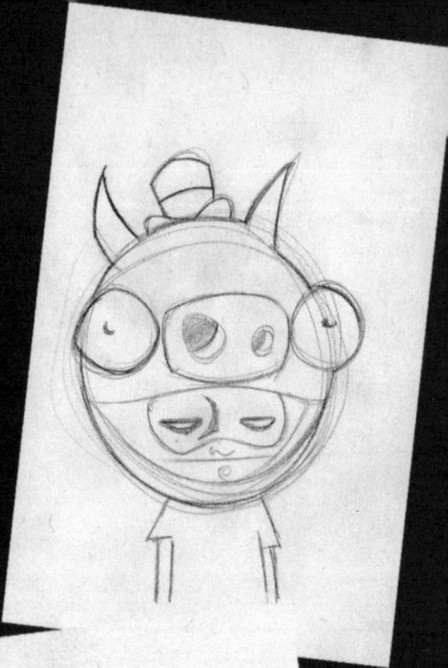

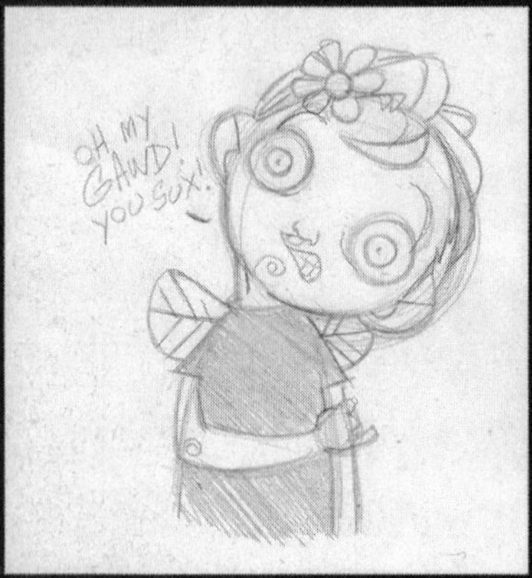
OH MY GAWD! YOU SUX!!

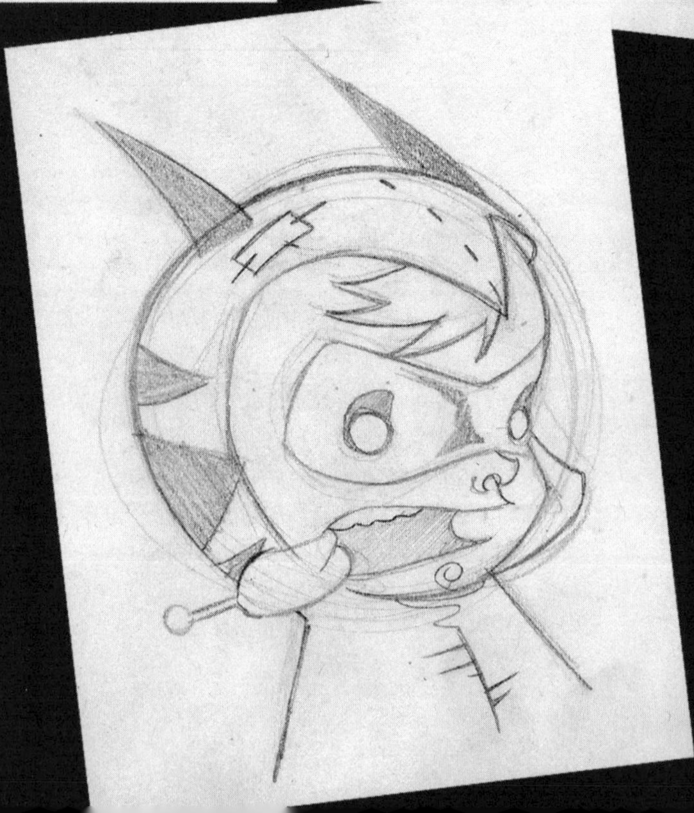

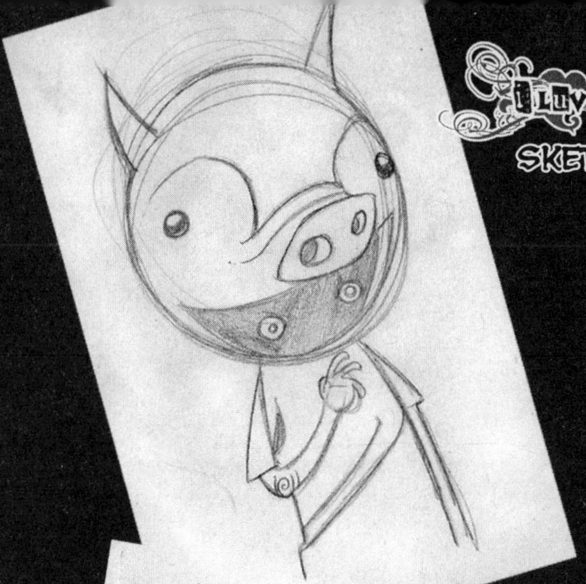

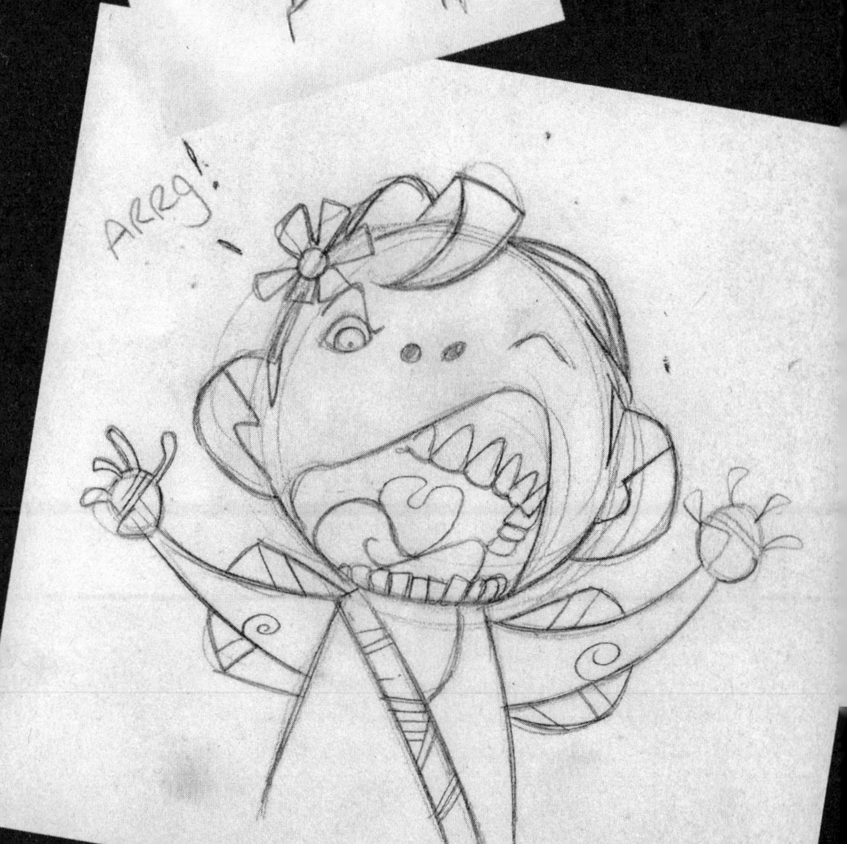
ARRG!

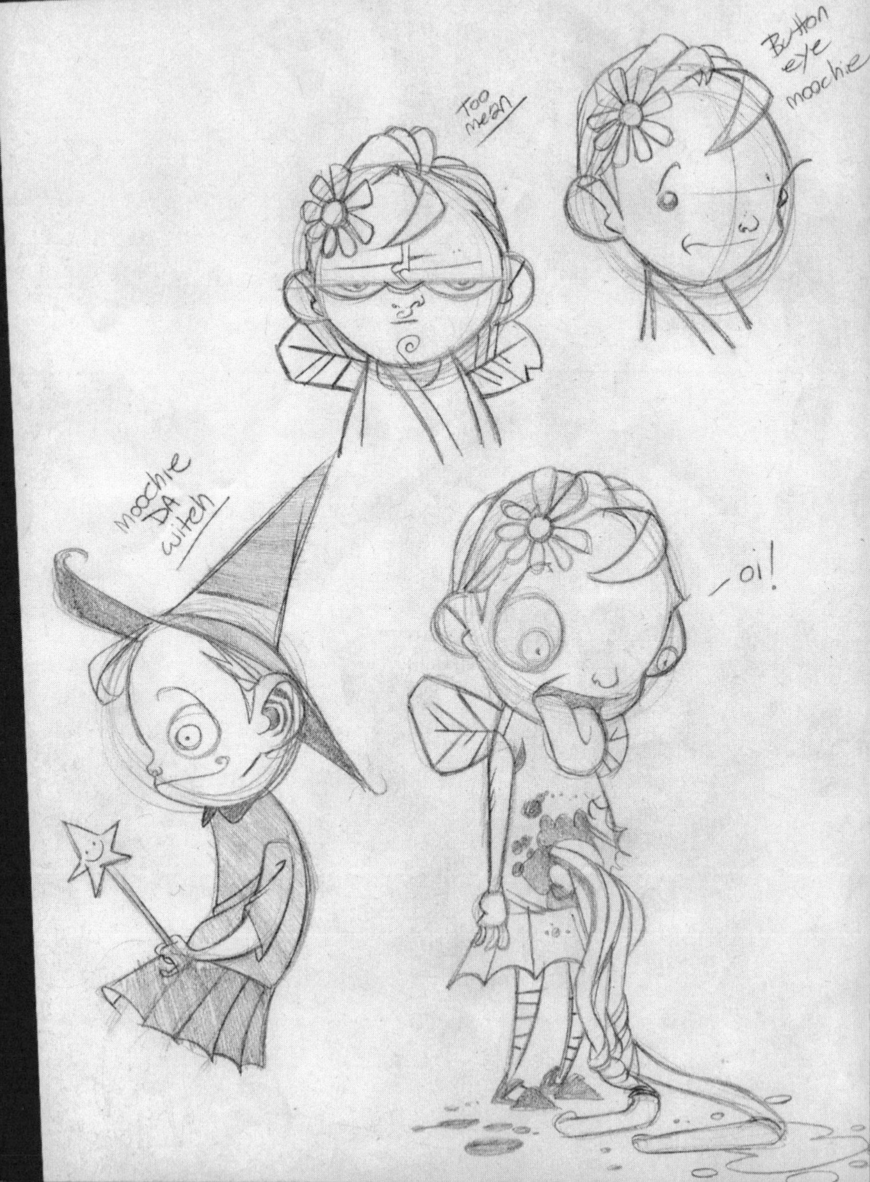
Too mean
Button eye moochie
moochie DA witch
-oi!

I LUV HALLOWEEN SKETCHBOOK

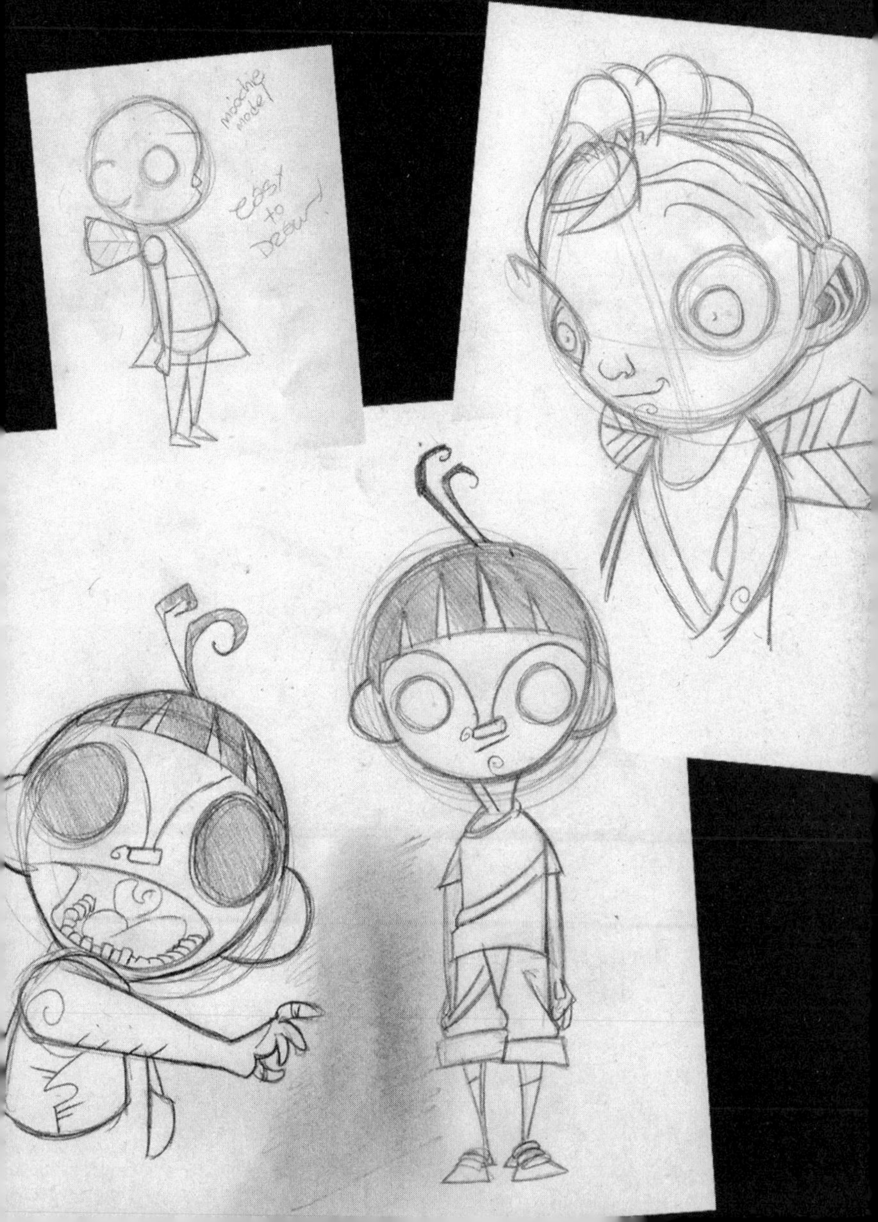
moodie model
easy to Draw

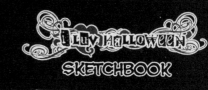

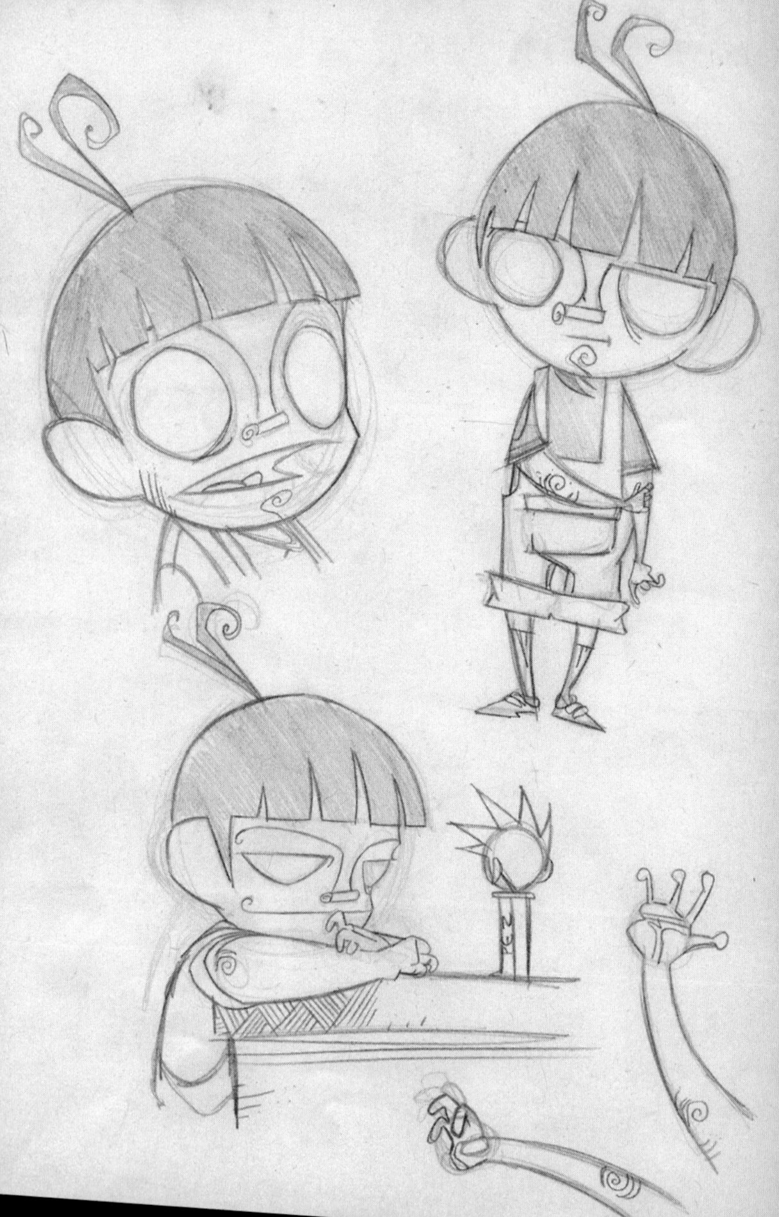

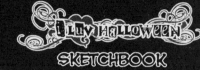

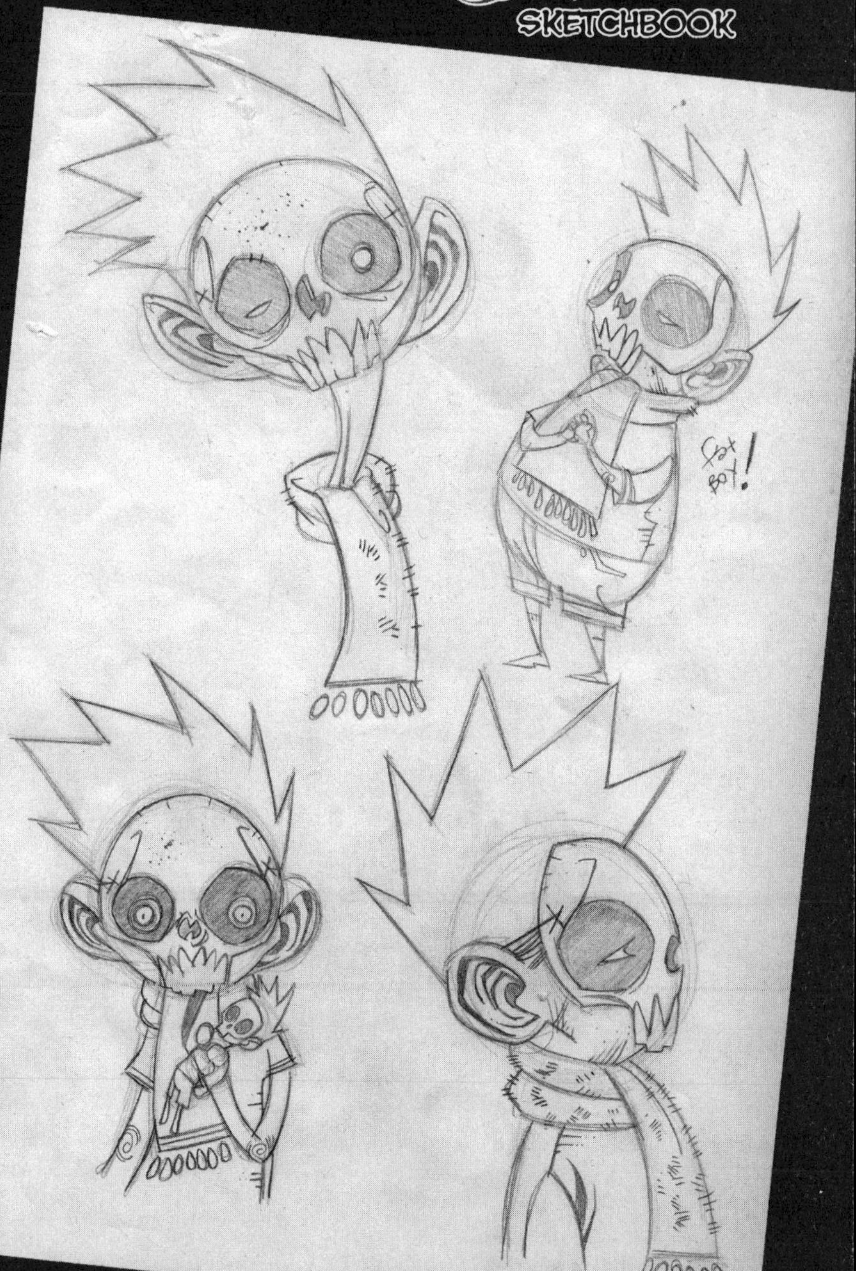
Fat boy!

I Luv Halloween
Sketchbook

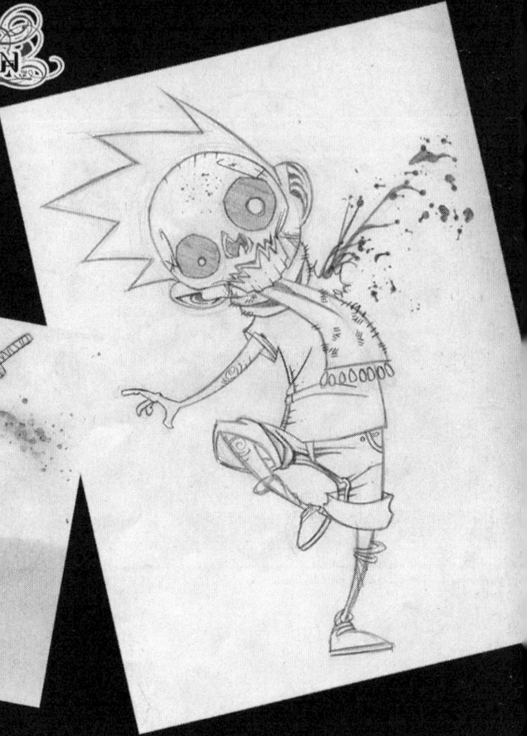

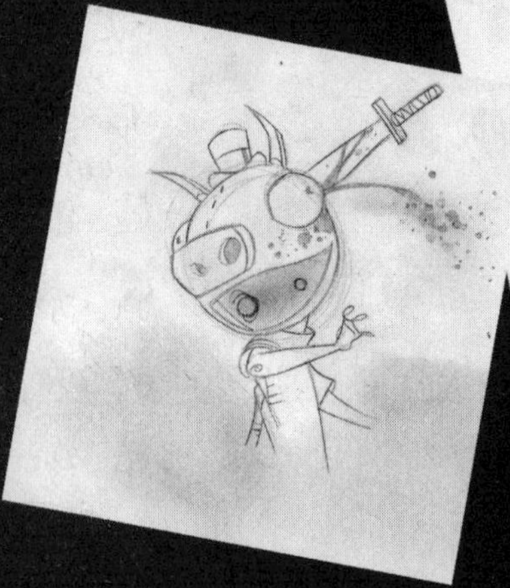

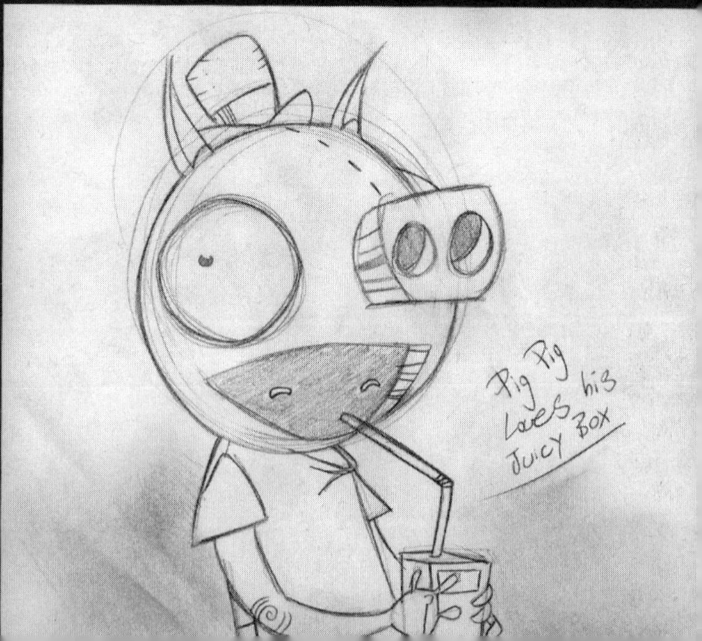
Pig Pig Loves his Juicy Box

I LUV HALLOWEEN
SKETCHBOOK

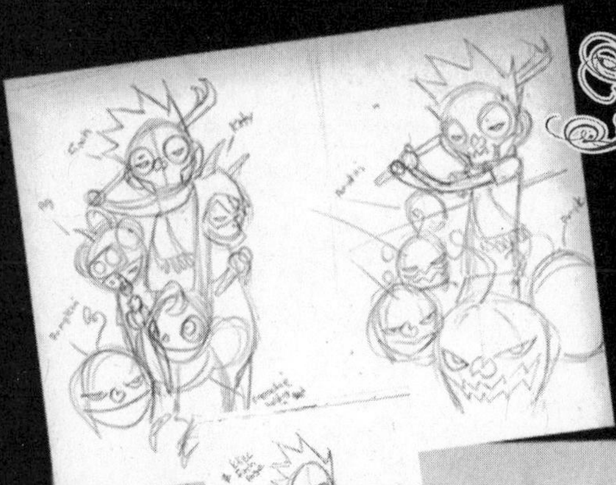

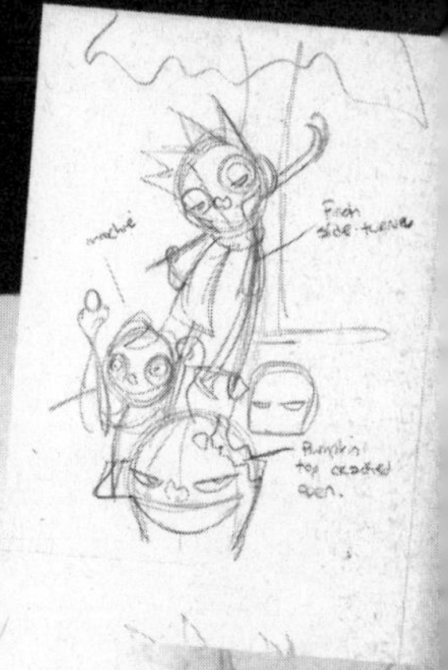
Pumpkin top cracked open.

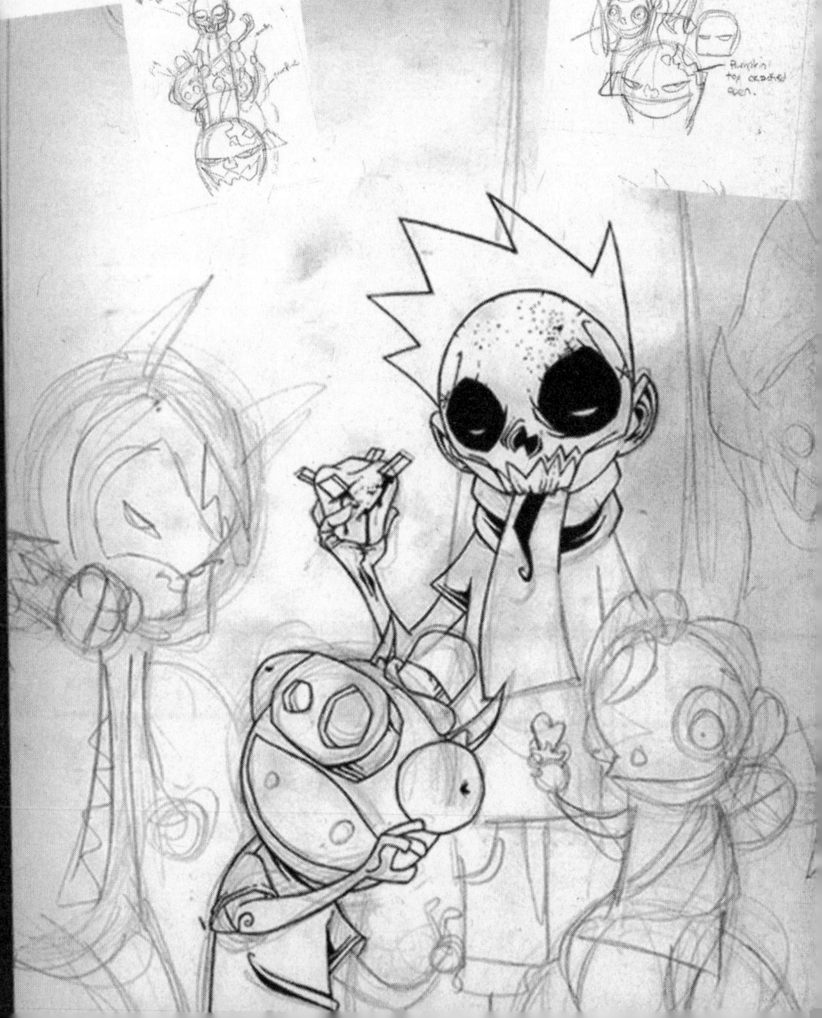

CREATOR BIOS

Benjamin
Roman

Keith Giffen is a veteran comic book writer and is probably best known for his critically acclaimed work on the titles Justice League and Legion of Super-Heroes. He currently does the English language adaptations of Battle Royale and Battle Vixens for Tokyopop.

Benjamin Roman was raised in Miami, where he worked and worked and worked on his portfolio, preparing it for con season. For 5 or 6 years, he went to San Diego and Chicago to try to get an editor, any editor, to look at it. After minimal success with one or two publishers, Roman had just about given up on trying to break into the industry, so he decided to move to Los Angeles. He got a job at a copy shop in Hollywood and assimilated into the strange and remarkable world that is L.A. One day a guy walked in and placed an order. After a brief conversation, Roman told the guy that he was an illustrator and proceeded to show him some art samples. After a few months went by, the guy returned to tell Benjamin Roman that he showed the samples to his editor and that his editor wanted to discuss publishing "I Luv Halloween" as a full-length series. The rest, as they say, is history. Go figure.

Keith Giffen

FOR NEARLY A MILLENNIUM, undead creatures have blended into a Europe heavy with religious dogma and intolerance. These beasts of the night allied themselves with factions of mortal men who aimed at shaking the foundations of the Catholic Church and freeing society from its strangling grip. But always were their true natures hidden, often even from even each other. The world was unable and unwilling to accept the existence of extra-mortal beings. *A Midnight Opera* is the story of two undead brothers, Ein and Leroux DeLaLune, divided in this epic struggle and forced to reconcile their differences in the modern day to stop an open assault on mankind by the dissatisfied elements among the rest of the undead.

Volume 1 focuses on Ein, who fled his brethren in the early 19th century, only to surface early in the 21st century as an underground goth metal sensation. But with his newfound fame comes the exposure that brings all the demons from his past. And the Ein who wanted simply to pursue a life of music and love will find that he may have no other choice but to forsake both and assume the weight of all salvation on his shoulders.

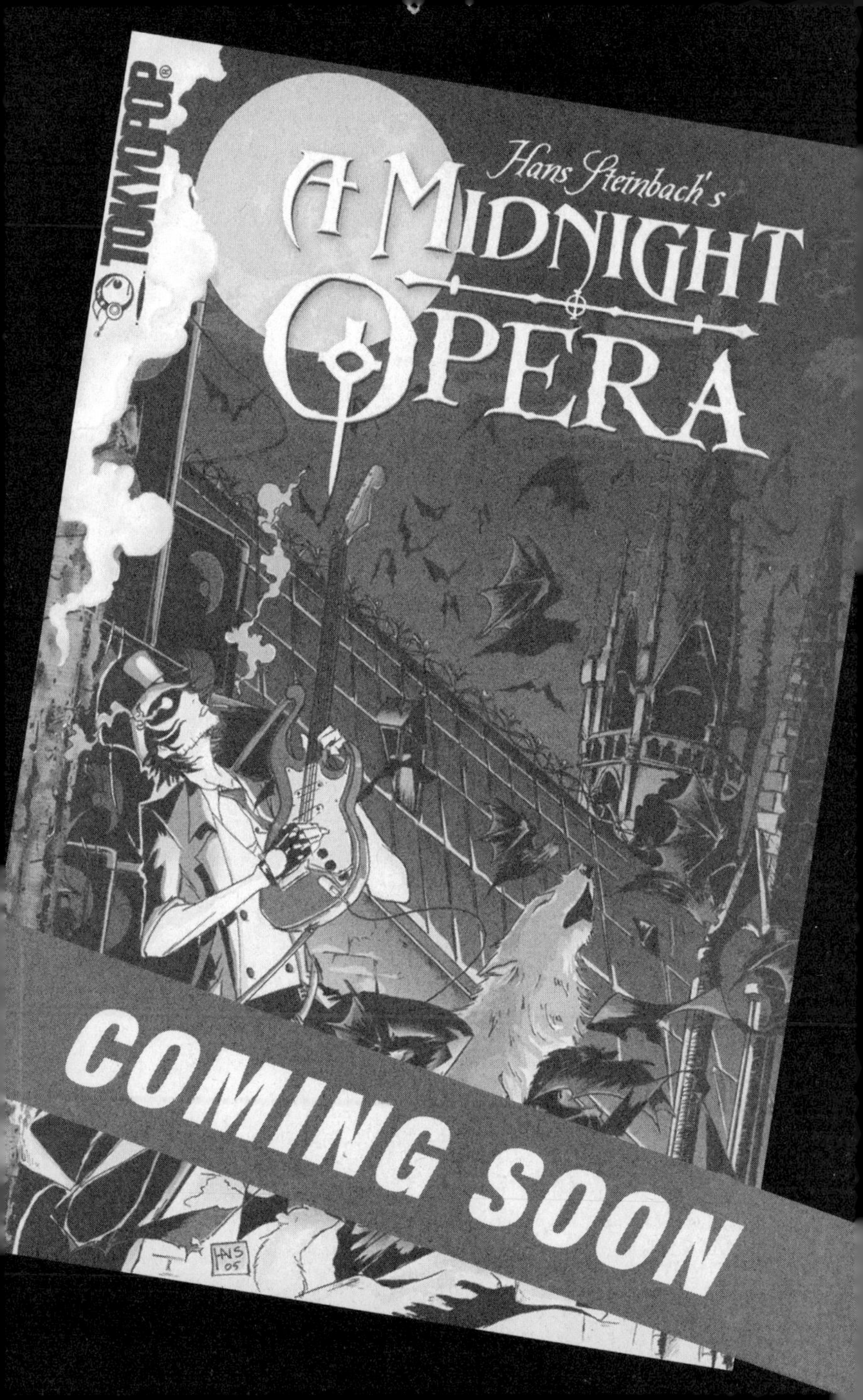
TOKYOPOP
Hans Steinbach's
A MIDNIGHT OPERA
HNS 05
COMING SOON

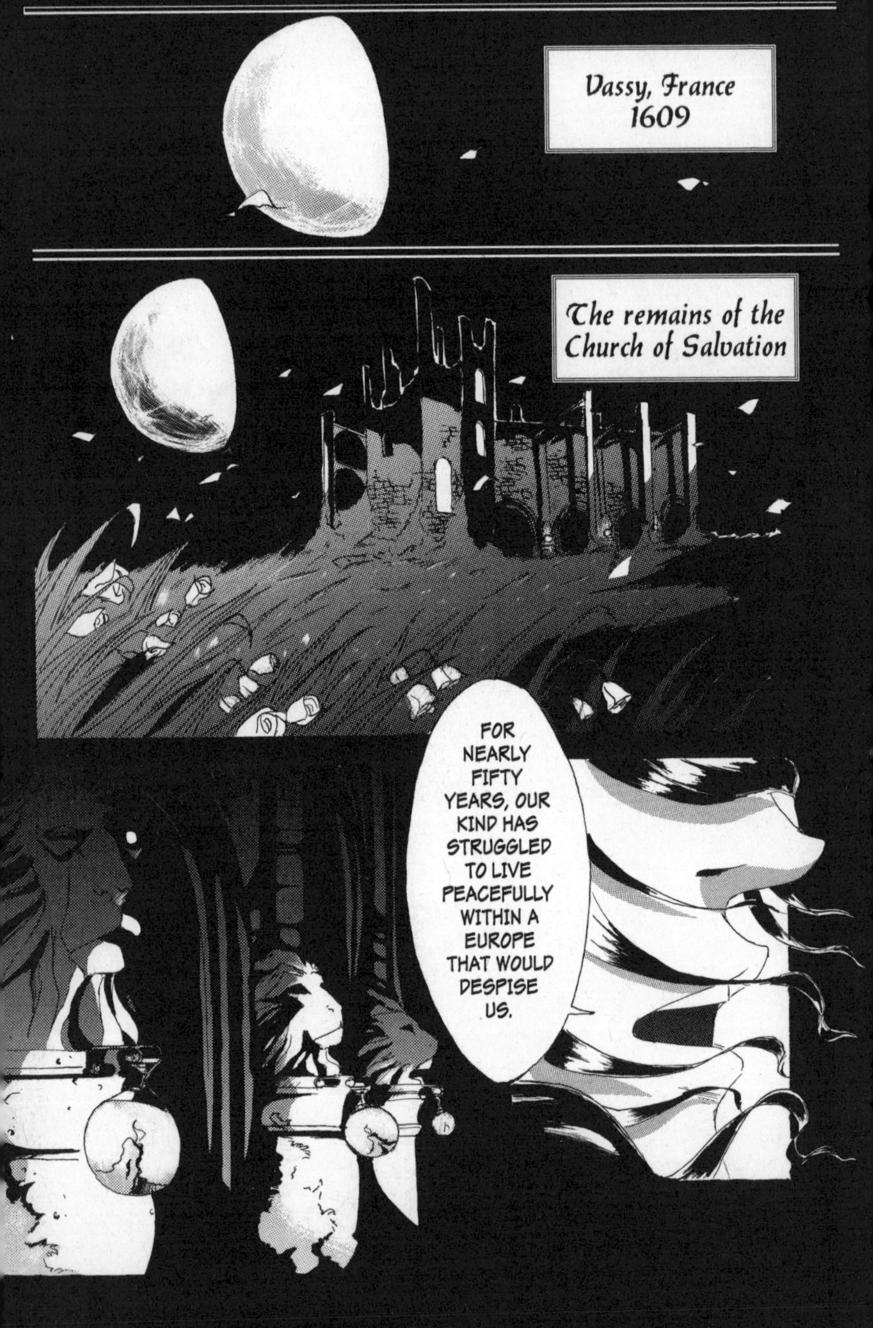
Vassy, France
1609
The remains of the Church of Salvation
FOR NEARLY FIFTY YEARS, OUR KIND HAS STRUGGLED TO LIVE PEACEFULLY WITHIN A EUROPE THAT WOULD DESPISE US.

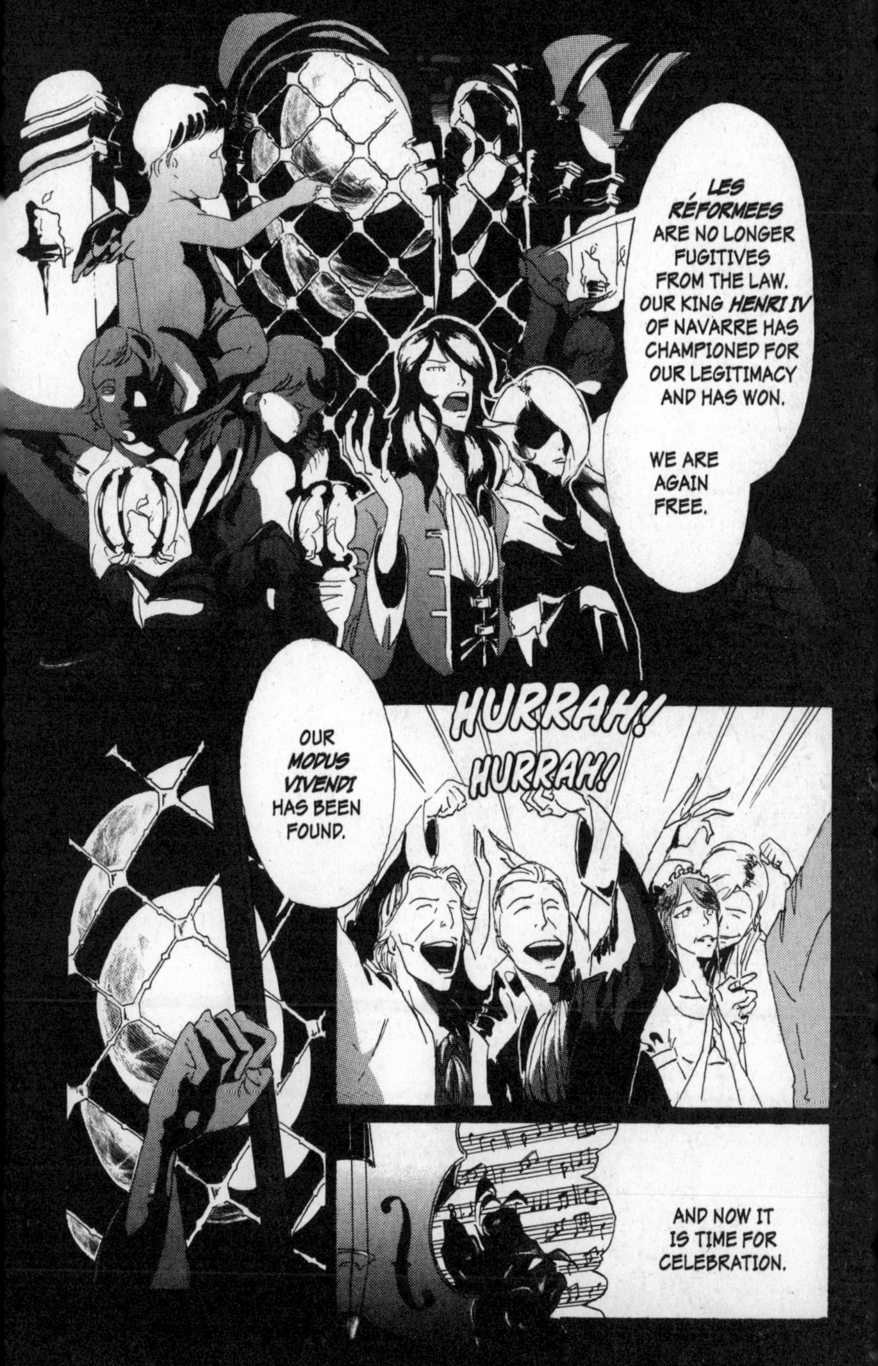
LES RÉFORMEES ARE NO LONGER FUGITIVES FROM THE LAW. OUR KING HENRI IV OF NAVARRE HAS CHAMPIONED FOR OUR LEGITIMACY AND HAS WON.
WE ARE AGAIN FREE.
HURRAH!
HURRAH!
OUR MODUS VIVENDI HAS BEEN FOUND.
AND NOW IT IS TIME FOR CELEBRATION.

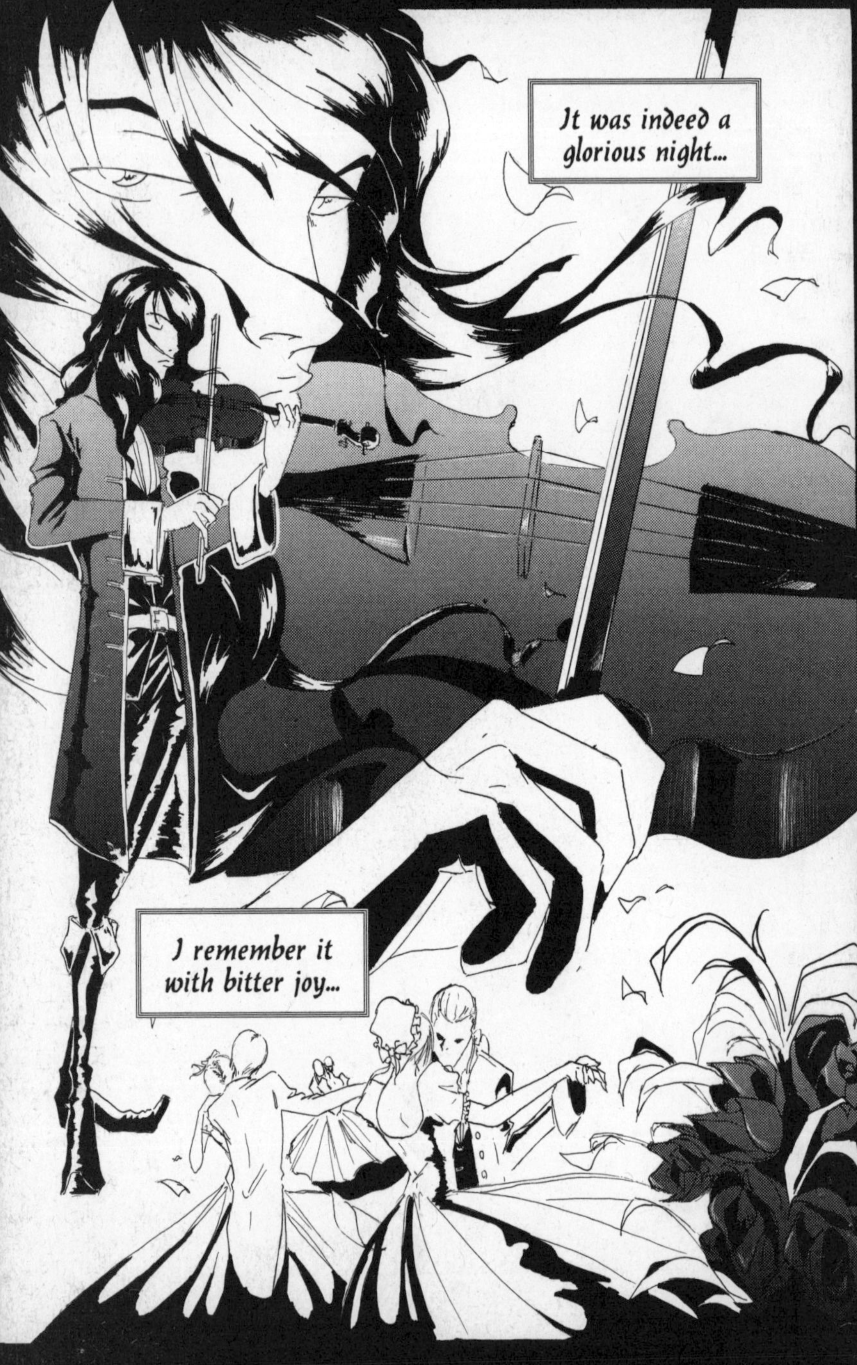
It was indeed a glorious night...
I remember it with bitter joy...

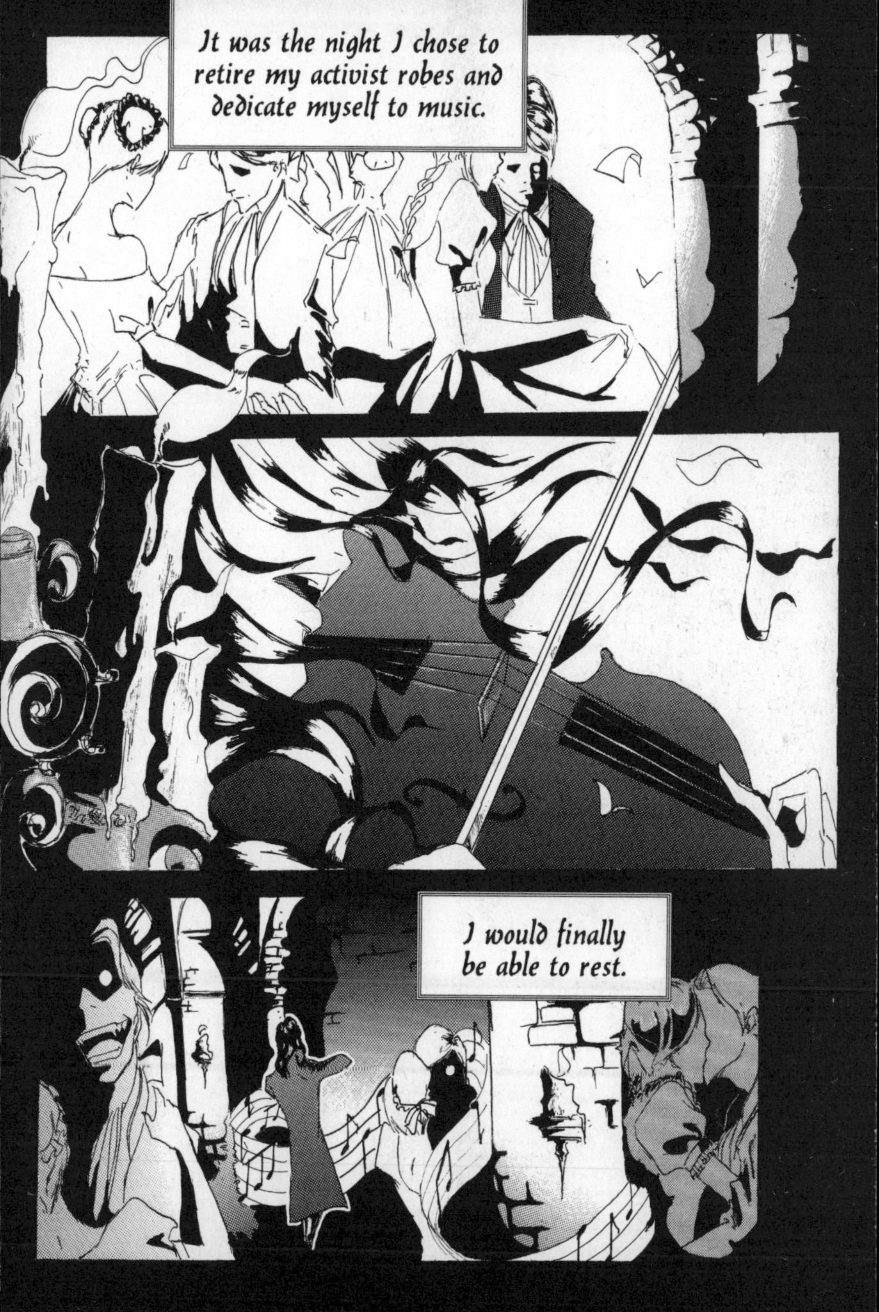
It was the night I chose to retire my activist robes and dedicate myself to music.
I would finally be able to rest.

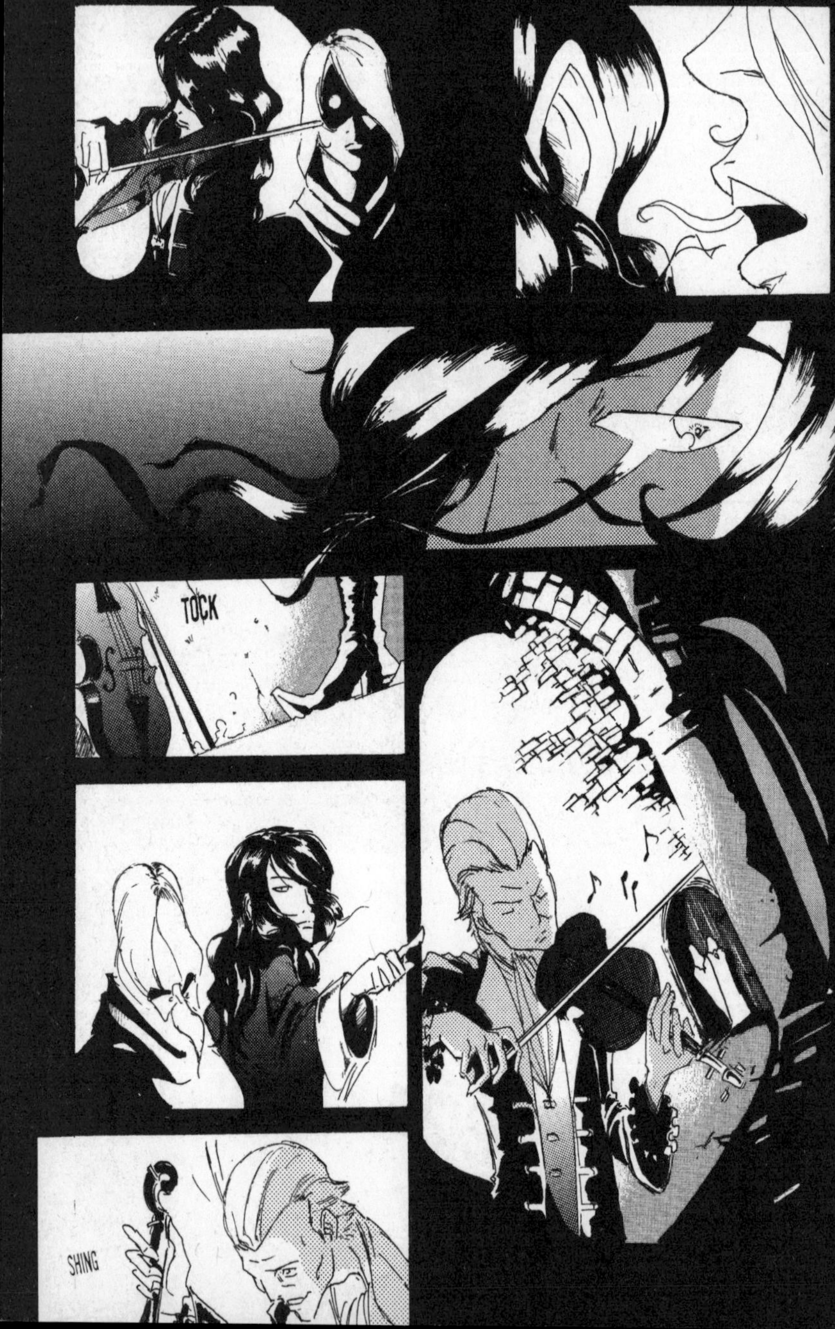
TOCK
!
SHING

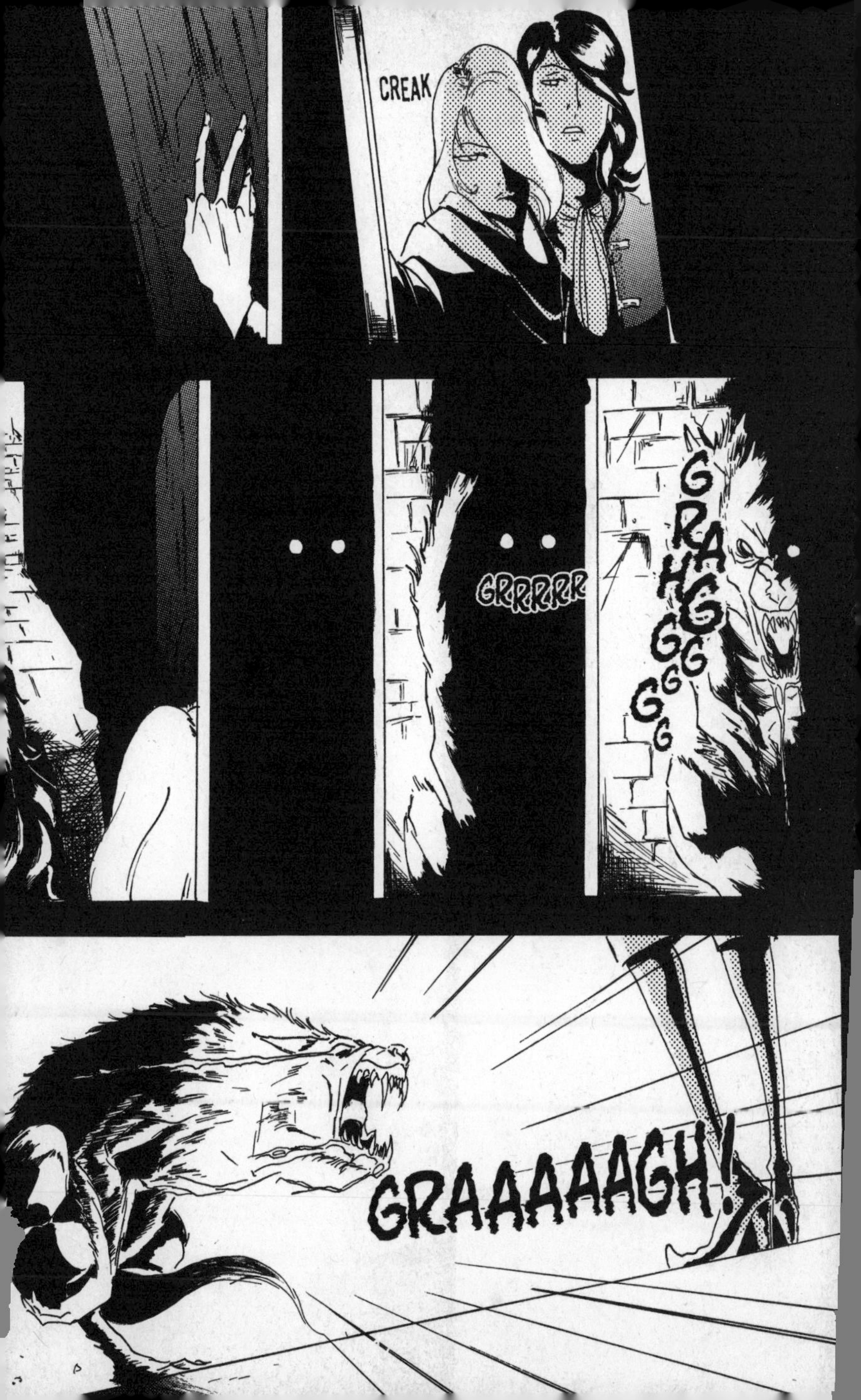
CREAK
GRAHGGGGGG
. . .
GRRRRR
. .
. .
GRAAAAAGH!

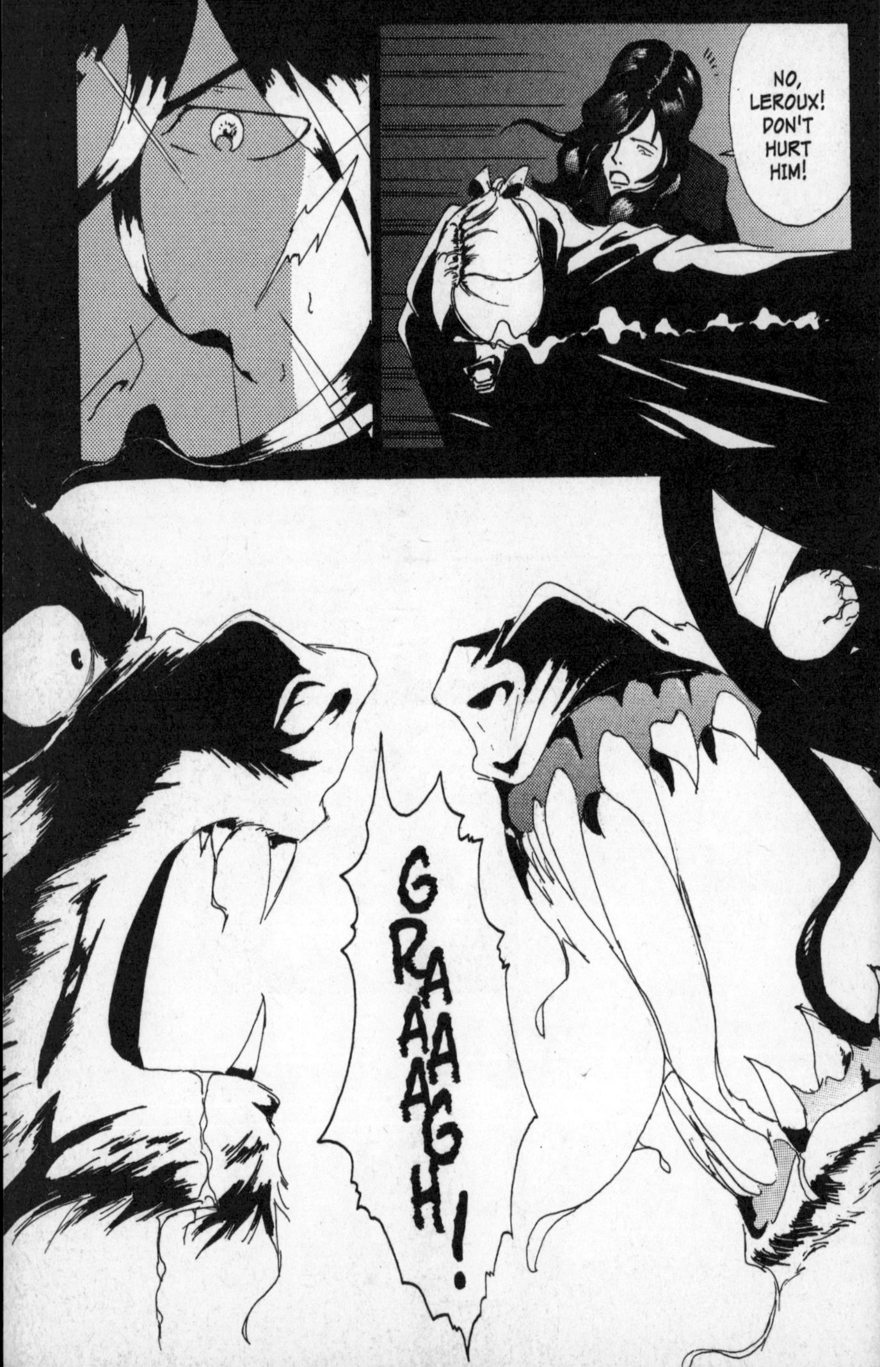
NO, LEROUX! DON'T HURT HIM!
GRAAAAGH!

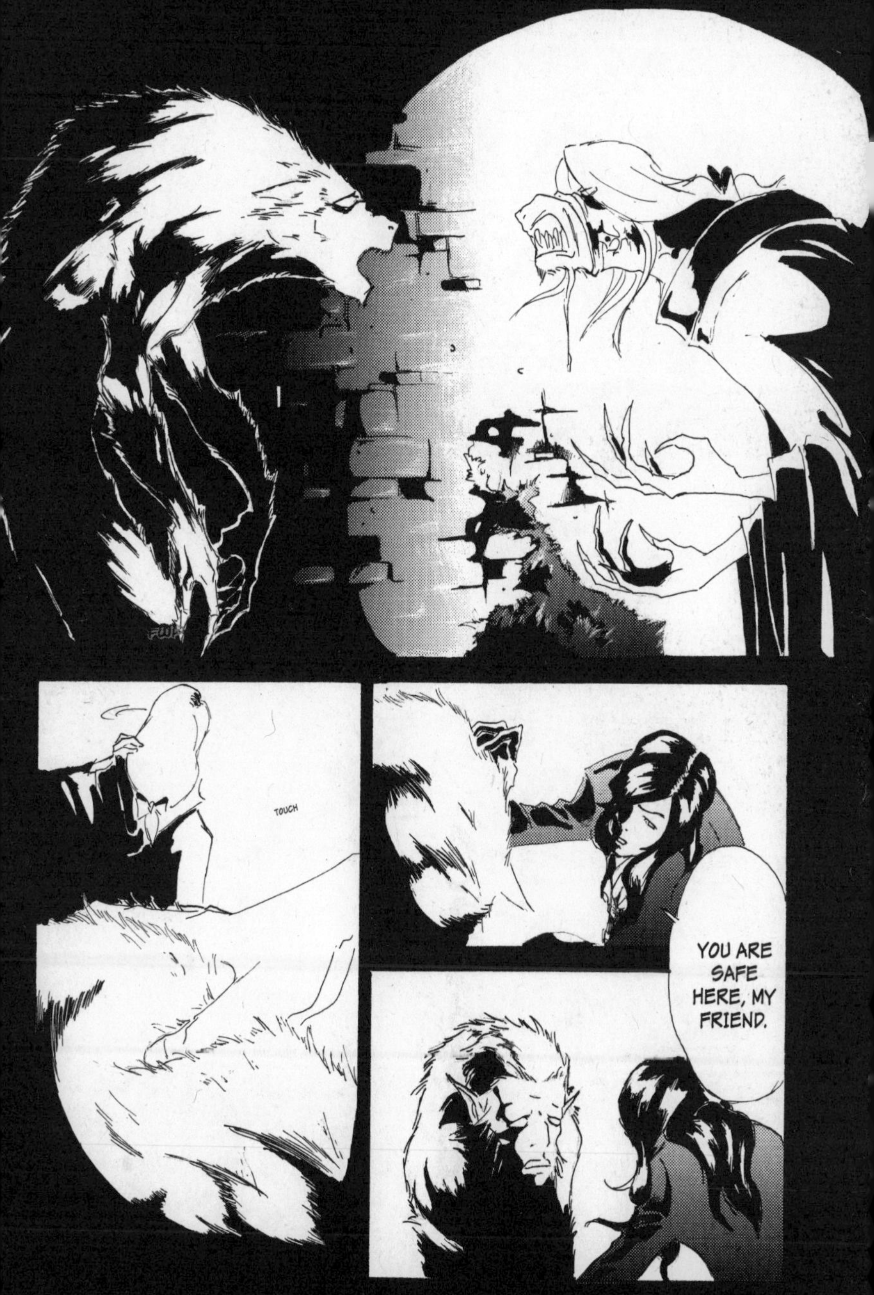
TOUCH
YOU ARE SAFE HERE, MY FRIEND.

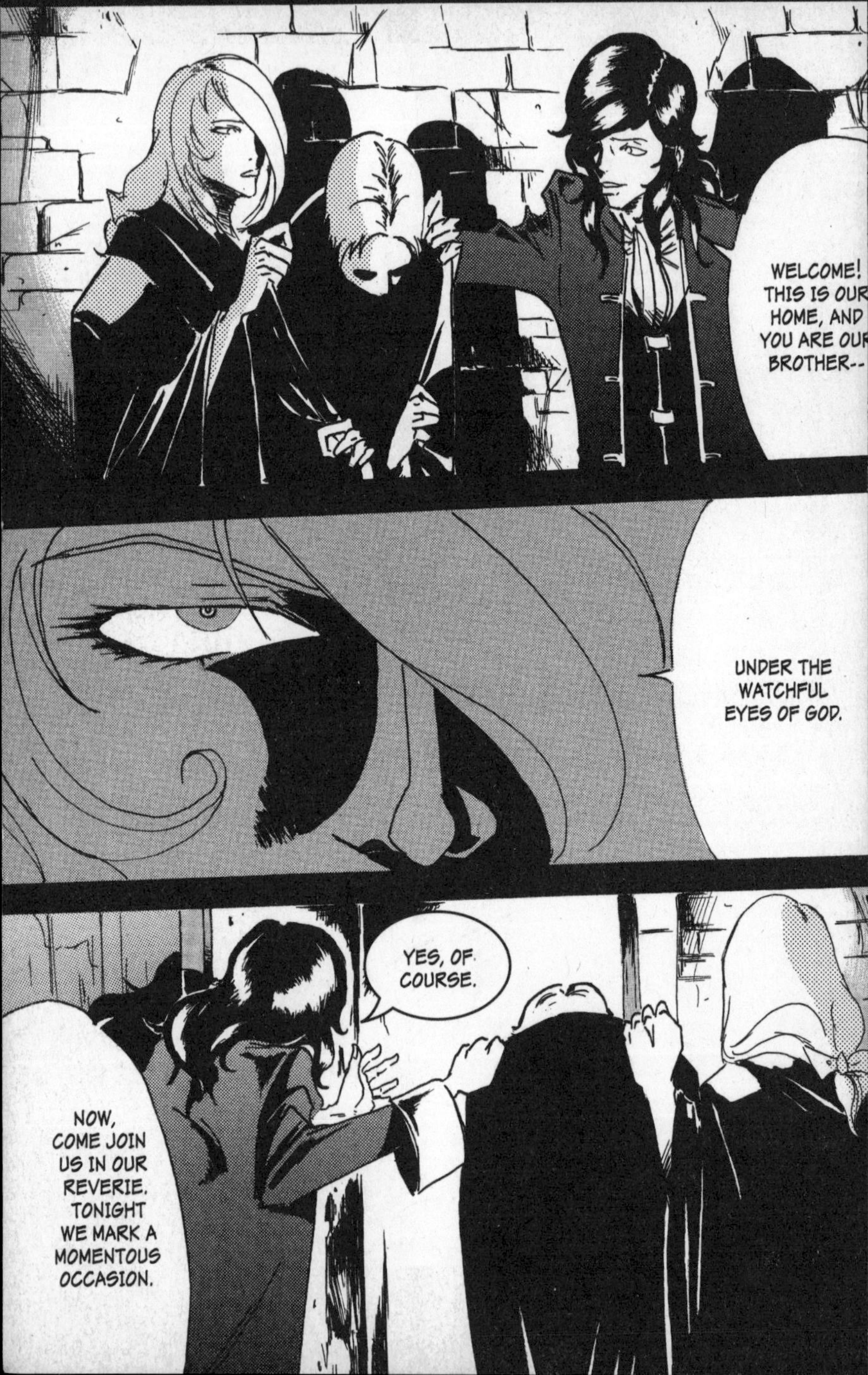
WELCOME! THIS IS OUR HOME, AND YOU ARE OUR BROTHER--
UNDER THE WATCHFUL EYES OF GOD.
YES, OF COURSE.
NOW, COME JOIN US IN OUR REVERIE. TONIGHT WE MARK A MOMENTOUS OCCASION.

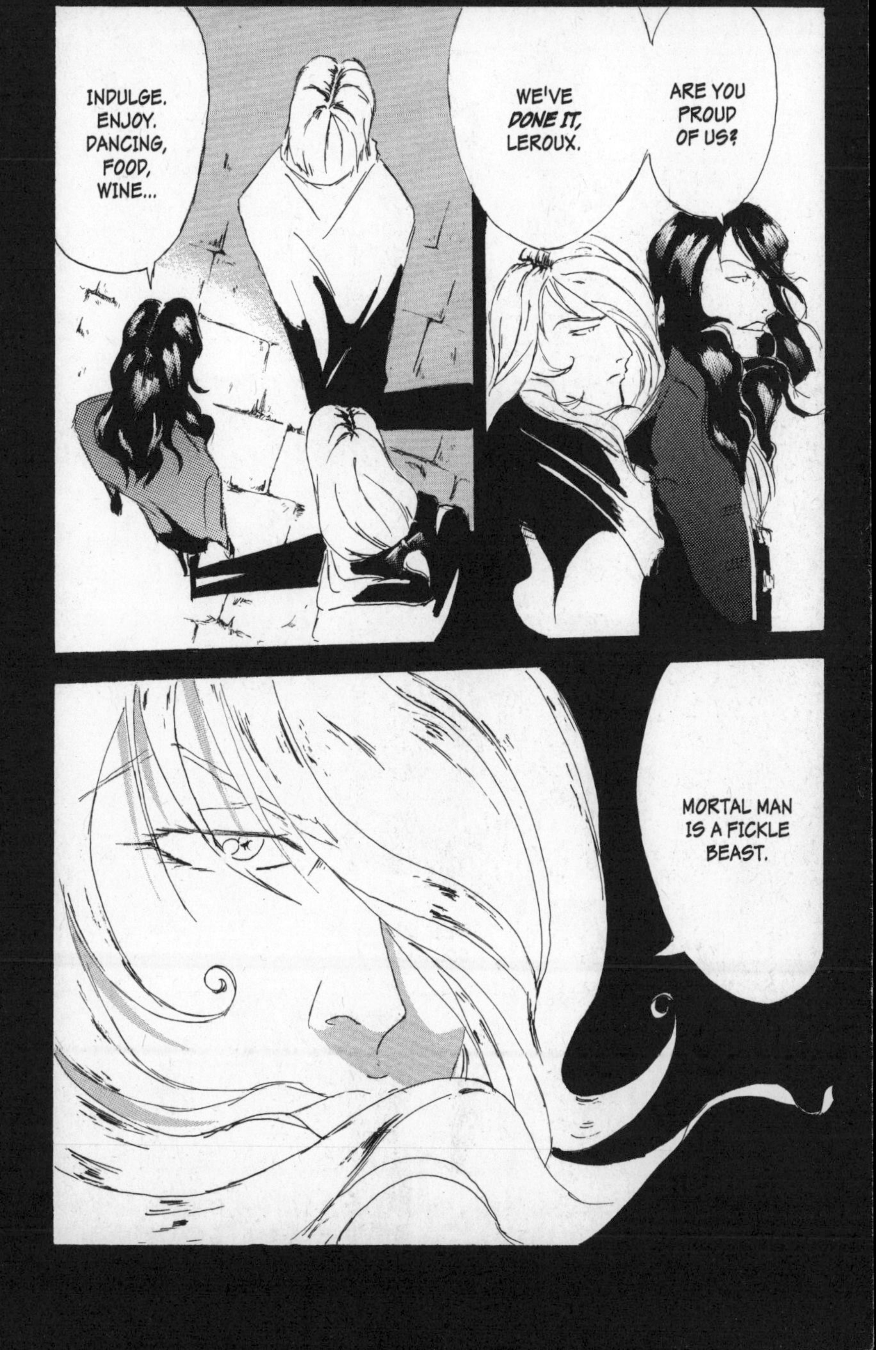
ARE YOU PROUD OF US?
WE'VE *DONE IT,* LEROUX.
INDULGE. ENJOY. DANCING, FOOD, WINE...
MORTAL MAN IS A FICKLE BEAST.

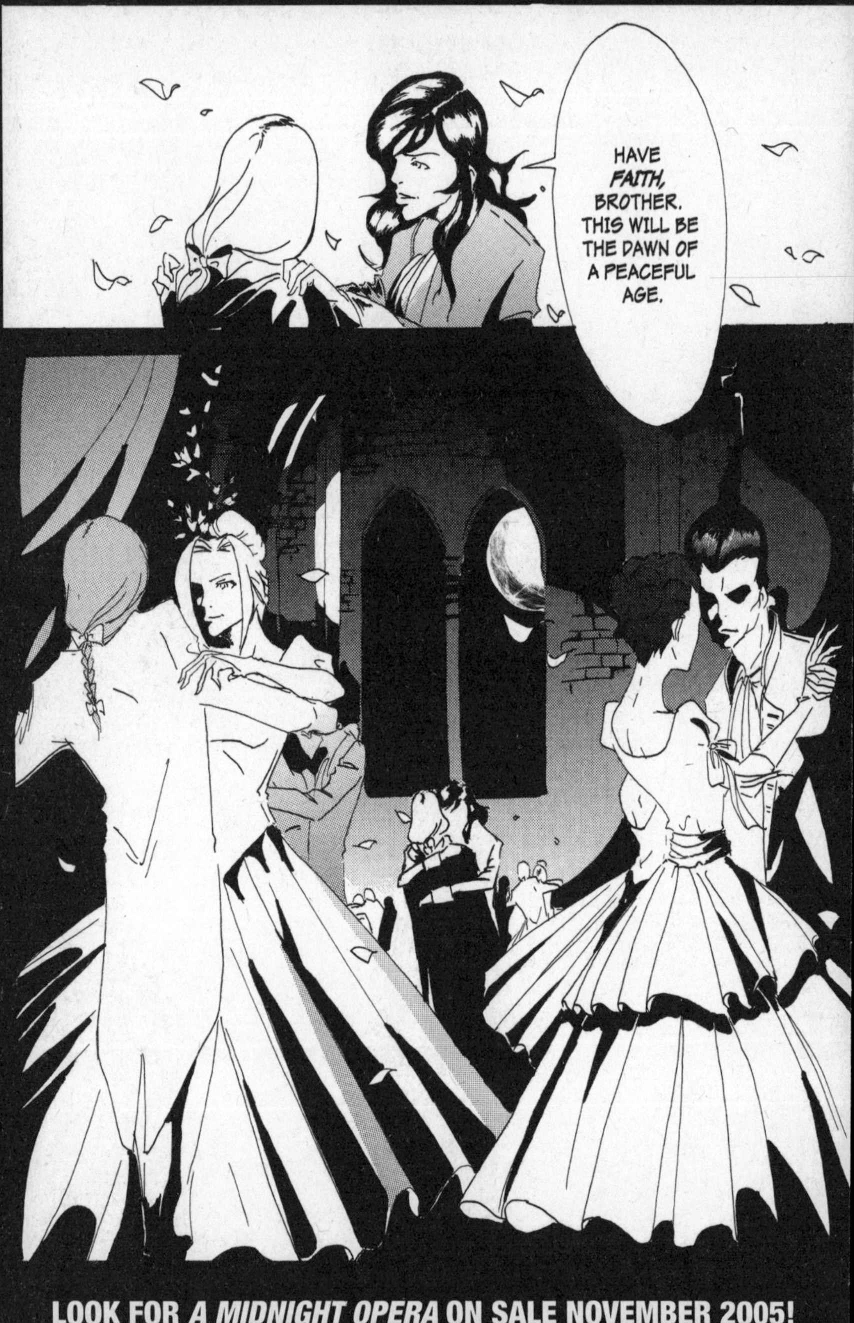
HAVE *FAITH,* BROTHER. THIS WILL BE THE DAWN OF A PEACEFUL AGE.

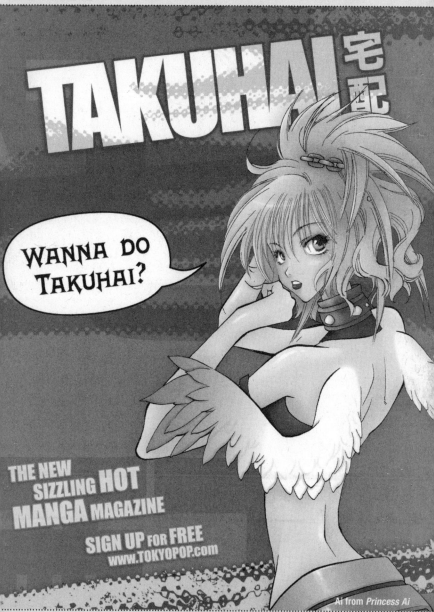

DRAMACON™

Sometimes even two's a crowd.

When Christie settles in the Artist Alley of her first-ever anime convention, she only sees it as an opportunity to promote the comic she has started with her boyfriend. But conventions are never what you expect, and soon a whirlwind of events sweeps Christie off her feet and changes her life. Who is the mysterious cosplayer that won't even take off his sunglasses indoors? What do you do when you fall in love with a guy who is going to be miles away from you in just a couple of days?

CREATED BY SVETLANA CHMAKOVA, CREATOR OF MANGA-STYLE ONLINE COMICS "CHASING RAINBOWS" AND "NIGHT SILVER"!

Preview the manga at:
www.TOKYOPOP.com/dramacon

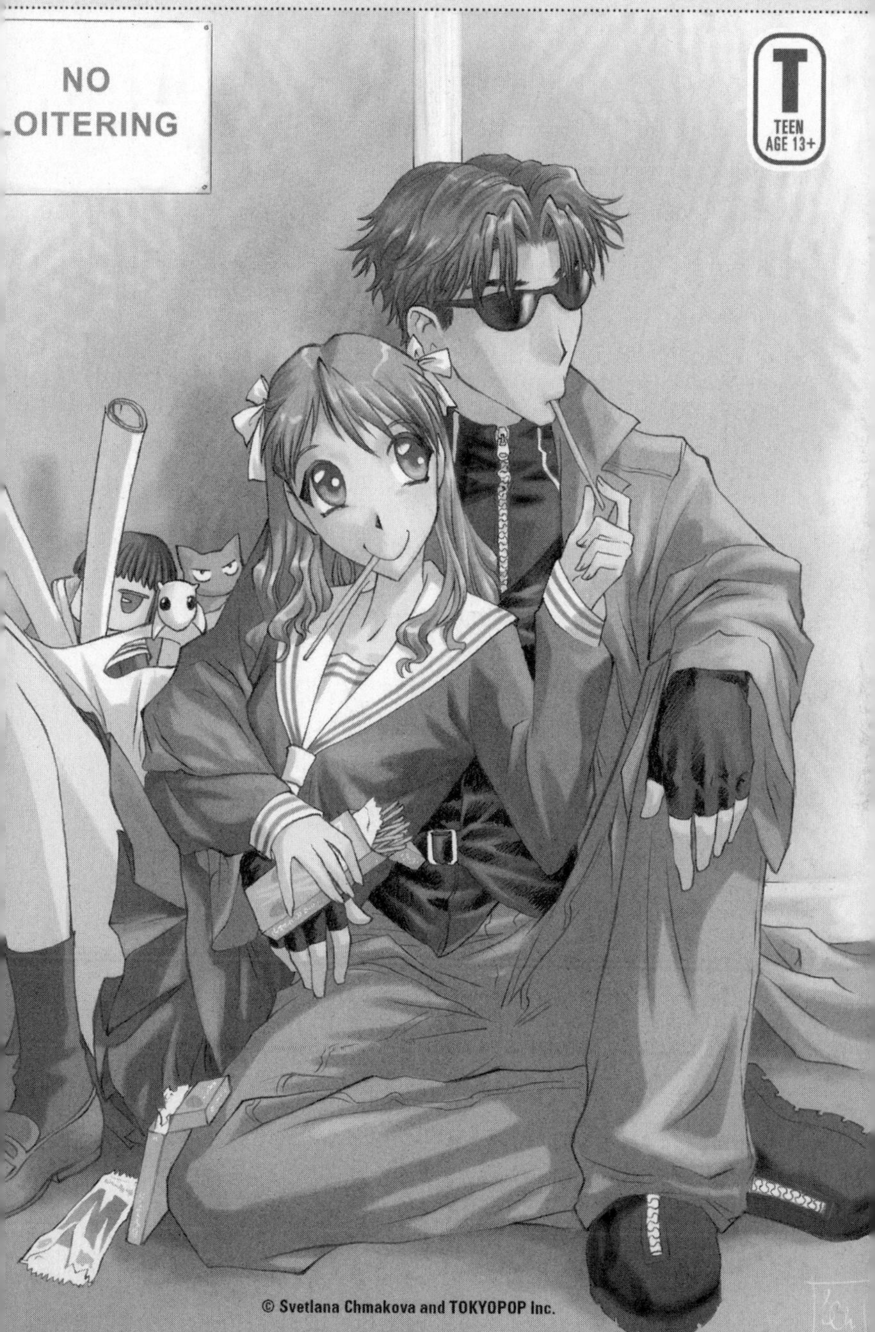
NO
LOITERING
T
TEEN
AGE 13+

SPOTLIGHT TOKYOPOP MANGA SUPPLEMENT

SAMURAI CHAMPLOO

BY MASARU GOTSUBO AND MANGLOBE

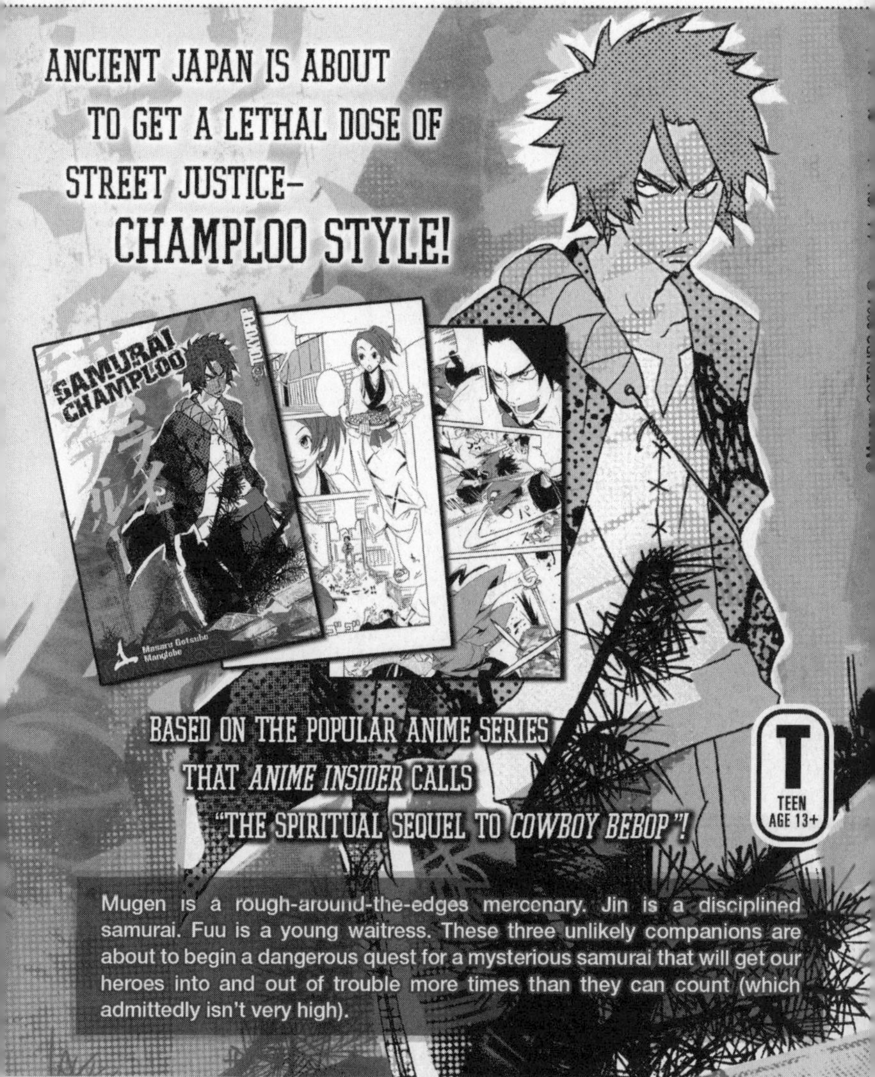
ANCIENT JAPAN IS ABOUT TO GET A LETHAL DOSE OF STREET JUSTICE—
CHAMPLOO STYLE!
SAMURAI CHAMPLOO
Masaru Gotsubo
Manglobe
TOKYOPOP
BASED ON THE POPULAR ANIME SERIES THAT *ANIME INSIDER* CALLS "THE SPIRITUAL SEQUEL TO *COWBOY BEBOP*"!
T
TEEN AGE 13+
Mugen is a rough-around-the-edges mercenary. Jin is a disciplined samurai. Fuu is a young waitress. These three unlikely companions are about to begin a dangerous quest for a mysterious samurai that will get our heroes into and out of trouble more times than they can count (which admittedly isn't very high).

FOR MORE INFORMATION VISIT: WWW.TOKYOPOP.COM

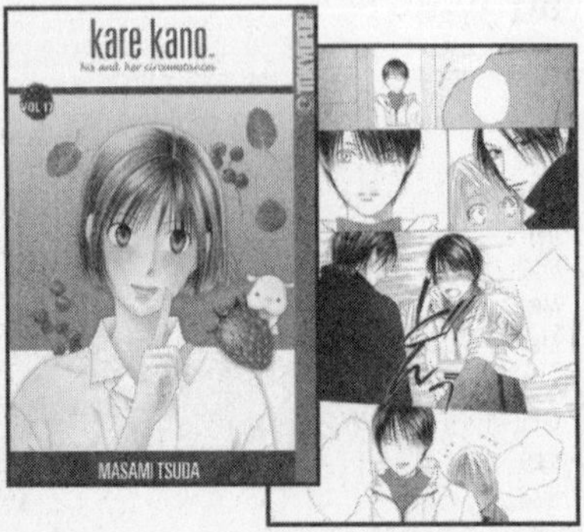
kare kano.
MASAMI TSUDA

BY MASAMI TSUDA

KARE KANO

Kare Kano has a fan following for a reason: believable, well-developed characters. Of course, the art is phenomenal, ranging from sugary sweet to lightning-bolt powerful. But above all, Masami Tsuda's refreshing concept—a high school king and queen decide once and for all to be honest with each other (and more importantly, themselves)—succeeds because Tsuda-sensei allows us to know her characters as well as she does. Far from being your typical high school shojo, *Kare Kano* delves deep into the psychology of what would normally just be protagonists, antagonists and supporting cast to create a satisfying journey that is far more than the sum of its parts.

~Carol Fox, Editor

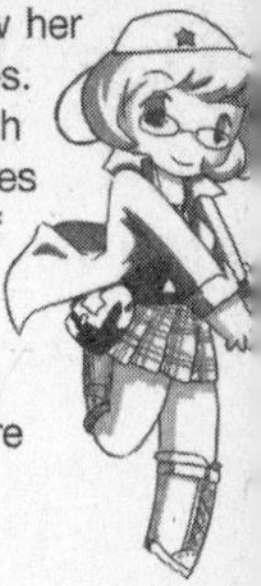

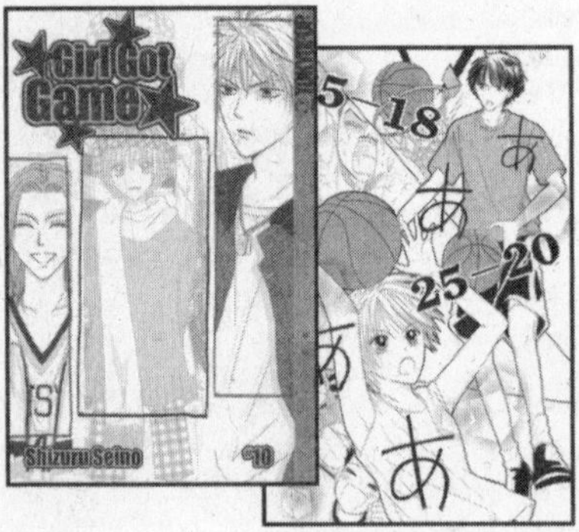
Girl Got Game
Shizuru Seino

BY SHIZURU SEINO

GIRL GOT GAME

There's a fair amount of cross-dressing shojo sports manga out there (no, really), but *Girl Got Game* really sets itself apart by having an unusually charming and very funny story. The art style is light and fun, and Kyo spazzing out always cracks me up. The author throws in a lot of great plot twists, and the great side characters help to make the story just that much more special. Sadly, we're coming up on the final volume, but I give this series credit for not letting the romance drag out unnecessarily or endlessly revisiting the same dilemmas. I'm really looking forward to seeing how the series wraps up!

~Lillian M. Diaz-Przybyl, Jr. Editor

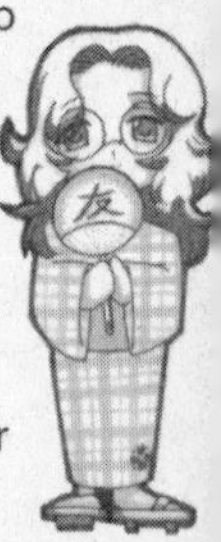